ut-icon" aria-label="Chat menu">

# *THE CLASSIC CUISINES*

# The Classic Cuisines

## MYRA WALDO

*Drawings by Ken Longtemps*

DODD, MEAD & COMPANY · NEW YORK

First published as a Dodd, Mead Quality Paperback in 1984

Copyright © 1971 by Myra Waldo
All rights reserved
No part of this book may be reproduced in any form
without permission in writing from the publisher.
Published by Dodd, Mead & Company, Inc.
79 Madison Avenue, New York, N.Y. 10016
Distributed in Canada by
McClelland and Stewart Limited, Toronto
Manufactured in the United States of America

Originally published under the title *Seven Wonders of the Cooking World*

Library of Congress Cataloging in Publication Data

Waldo, Myra.
  The classic cuisines.

  Includes index.
  1. Cookery, International. I. Title.
TX725.A1W277   1984     641.59     83-20819
ISBN 0-396-08352-8 (pbk.)

# CONTENTS

| | |
|---|---:|
| CHINA | 2 |
| THE ORIENT (other than China) | 56 |
| WHERE EAST MEETS WEST | 118 |
| MIDDLE EUROPE | 180 |
| ITALY | 242 |
| THE LATIN COUNTRIES | 294 |
| FRANCE | 350 |
| *Index* | 417 |

# THE CLASSIC CUISINES

*CHINA*

IN the vast land we call China, people speak different dialects, hundreds of them. In fact, there is almost no Chinese language as such. Some people may manage to make themselves understood by those living a few hundred miles away; others may find their regional dialects completely unintelligible. The same is not true of the written language, which has retained its integrity almost unchanged over many centuries.

The Chinese have a system of writing in which tens of thousands of arbitrary characters are used to convey one single meaning each. Thus, the written character for house, for example, is not used for any other purpose or meaning. No matter how difficult it may be for one person to carry on a conversation with another, the written language remains a bond among the people of China. A citizen of Peking may not understand the speech of a villager from a western province, but if one wrote a letter to the other, because the written language admits of no variations, it would be understood. Similarly, in Chinese cooking, there are regional variations, roughly equivalent to the language dialects, but beneath all the variations there is an unchanging and solid basis, much like the written language, which holds true for all Chinese cooking.

Running through the national cookery style are certain definite and basic principles. Very rarely are dishes prepared consisting of a single ingredient, as westerners would cook a steak, or serve a roast beef. The culinary style of China emphasizes combinations of different foods, so that a beef dish, for instance, will perhaps be combined with such other ingredients as noodles and vegetables, but almost never served alone.

This cookery style has developed, among other reasons, because China is an enormous nation, burdened with a teeming population, and since time began for this land, its people have lived on the bare edge of sufficiency, with hunger (indeed, famine) a constant consideration. Quite naturally, a cookery style has developed in which the largest portion, or base, of the dish consists of comparatively available, inexpensive ingredients such as noodles, rice and vegetables, flavored with a small amount of the scarce meat, poultry, or fish. Contrarily, the western cuisine generally emphasizes a single protein foodstuff, garnished with the lesser ingredients, such as potatoes, vegetables, and sauces.

The Chinese rarely, if given their choice and the means, eat a single preparation at lunch or dinner. Any family not living in poverty has several dishes, as many as six served at the same meal, although the total quantity of food consumed may not be great. Seldom is there anything that could be regarded as the main course of a meal, in the sense that westerners have appetizers, soups, and desserts but place their greatest emphasis upon main courses. The meal-in-one-dish or casserole, so popular in this country with housewives, would be regarded with astonishment in China.

Another underlying point of similarity, running through the entire Chinese cuisine, is the cutting of ingredients into small pieces, suitable for picking up with chopsticks. The ancient Chinese culture saw the introduction of the use of spoons for soup, but the fork has never found its way to the dinner table, nor indeed has the table knife. Thus, a large piece of beef could never be served in China, for there would be no way of cutting it, or picking it up with chopsticks. The cubes of food are cut with very sharp kitchen knives, for the Chinese place great emphasis upon the texture and attractive appearance of foods.

While cooking, foods are carefully seasoned, and therefore, the use of salt and pepper at the table by the diner is rarely necessary. Most Chinese cooks make good use of what's called the "stir-fry" method, a technique much like sautéeing, but one in which the foods are cooked very rapidly, stirred almost constantly. The entire cooking process is completed in short order; there is almost nothing in the way of elaborate sauces cooked for hours, a customary procedure in France.

As basic foodstuffs, most of the nation uses pork in preference to any other meat, although beef is quite popular. Veal is extremely rare, and there is little lamb consumed, except perhaps in Manchuria to the north, by nomadic people whose cuisine is somewhat rudimentary. Although Americans assume that rice is the staple food of the country, and that does hold true for most of China, wheat flour is much used in the northern portion of the nation. However, it is not eaten as a cooked cereal, as is rice, for wheat flour is made into noodles and pancakes.

Certain ingredients reappear continuously throughout all Chinese cookery styles—soy sauce, peanut oil, monosodium glutamate, garlic, onions, scallions, ginger root, rice, noodles, a wine resembling sherry, tea, and somewhat surprisingly, sugar. Soy sauce, a salty dark brown liquid obtained from soy beans, almost eliminates the need for salt in most recipes. Peanut oil is the standard cooking fat, although sesame oil is popular in Szechuan; it is important to bear in mind that butter or olive oil is totally unsuited to Chinese cookery. Monosodium glutamate is a white powder derived from vegetable sources, used to intensify the flavor of food. (It is, however, presently under investigation by the United States Government as a health hazard.) Certain western foods are almost never eaten in China. These include such dairy products as butter, milk, cream, and cheese, bread (although a Chinese type is used on rare occasions), and coffee. There are very few desserts in their culinary style, and sweet dishes are seldom encountered, being unimportant to the people. Chinese wines are merely passable by western standards, and the only completely satisfactory beverage with this cuisine—in addition to tea—is cold beer.

As is the case with the written language of China, these are the underlying, unchanging and integral fabric of the national cookery style. But, just as there are many local dialects, regional cooking styles create alterations and variations upon the basic theme. It may be that there are indeed hundreds of culinary dialects as there are language dialects, but scholars tend to divide China into five principal areas insofar as food is concerned, much as we, in a lesser way, divide the United States into New England, Southern, Pennsylvania Dutch and other culinary areas of our own country. These five parts of China are Canton, Shantung, Fukien, Honan, and Szechuan.

*Canton* (in the southeastern part of the country) is perhaps the best known all Chinese regional styles in the United States for a rather obvious reason. Most of the Chinese emigration, during the past century, was from the port city of Canton, not too far from Hong Kong, to America, where the newly arrived immigrants opened restaurants, cooking their own familiar Cantonese style. It featured the quickly prepared "stir-fry" dishes, the use of pork and seafood, and is generally bland to the taste. It has many dumpling and fried rice preparations, and those great and expensive delicacies of sharks' fins and birds' nests come from Canton.

Lying to the northeast is *Shantung*, which includes the city of Peking. Although certain restaurants describe themselves as serving Peking-style food, this is more precisely Shantung cooking, for Peking drew upon the entire province for its fare. The outstanding dish here is Peking Duck (rather difficult to prepare at home), spring (or egg) rolls, and the use of onions, garlic, and scallions. The seasoning is mild, and the food perhaps lighter than that of the other provinces.

Along the coast is *Fukien*, a little-known and comparatively unappreciated style of Chinese regional cooking, insofar as most Americans are concerned. It features pork and seafood, as in Canton, and the range of dishes is quite impressive. Most meals include soups of one sort or another, frequently several in the same repast. In addition, many dishes consist of preparations presented in a bowl with a considerable amount of liquid, making them similar to soups, although with far more solid ingredients.

*Honan* lies in the center of the nation, away from the seacoast. Therefore, fish dishes are typically made from river or other freshwater fish; surely the great favorite of this province is carp. Also popular are sweet-and-sour preparations, which Americans seem to enjoy. Unlike the three previous regions, where the food is mild and almost bland, Honan's is slightly spicy, often quite stimulating to the palate.

However, it is in *Szechuan*, in the west, that truly hot and spicy foods are found. This provincial cookery style, little known in the United States, is rich and somewhat oily, making liberal use of the red hot peppers which grow so profusely in this region. Almost everything appears in spicy form—fish, noodles, meat, or poultry.

These then, are the principal dialects, that is, regional styles of Chinese cookery, creating a fascinating and intricate series of patterns upon the basic cuisine of the nation, a country far too large and varied to have only one single cookery style.

SOME THOUGHTS ABOUT COOKING IN THE CHINESE MANNER

Western food, as served through Europe and the continents of the western hemisphere, is based on certain familiar, underlying, and oft-repeated techniques. Chinese food is quite different and requires a little explanation. Ingredients are prepared in advance, so that the actual cooking takes a rather short time. Once cooked, everything is served promptly, and cannot be held in the kitchen, for vegetables are ready to eat when still crisp, and Chinese food must not be overcooked. The beginner or novice in preparing Chinese dishes is urged to experiment with only one Chinese dish at a time; once learned, other dishes may be attempted.

All meats, poultry, and vegetables should be carefully sliced, or cut into cubes as described in the recipes. Vegetables are best sliced diagonally, because this exposes a greater area to the heat, permitting quicker cooking without loss of texture. Diced foods should be cut as neatly as possible; with experience, it is possible to make almost all of them a similar size, permitting even cooking. A diced food measuring one inch in size will take far longer to cook than a similar cube measuring only half an inch. Be sure to cook with peanut or vegetable oil; these recipes cannot be successfully made with butter or olive oil. Heat the oil until quite hot, and do not add any ingredients until it is well heated. Speed is essential in Chinese cookery, and the cook *must* remain with the pan until the food is ready to serve; stir the food almost constantly. When ready, serve without delay. Some people may find the vegetables somewhat undercooked by their standards, but this is deliberately done by the Chinese, for they enjoy the crisp crunch of barely cooked vegetables as a contrast to the other ingredients of the dish. Foods should be served hot, so your diners must be ready to eat when the dish is ready to serve. Do not overcook Chinese dishes or hold them past the specified cooking time.

*About the number of persons each recipe will serve:* The Chinese, as previously pointed out, believe in serving a fair number of different dishes at a meal. When a recipe specifies that it serves four, it is assumed that other dishes will be served. If this is not the case, as during the first cooking experiences with Chinese recipes, they will usually serve two people.

*Cooking ingredients:* Almost every town across the nation has a food shop that sells the ingredients typically used in Chinese cookery, such as soy sauce, bamboo shoots, spices, water chestnuts, and so forth. One thought: you can easily grow bean sprouts at home, if you wish, with little effort. Buy some mung peas, which are really small dried peas or beans, found in Chinese or Japanese food shops. Soak 1 cup of the dried peas in 6 cups of water overnight; drain well the following morning. Place the peas in a single layer on wet paper towels in a colander. Cover the top with a wet towel. Keep in a dark place at room temperature for 3 or 4 days, sprinkling twice daily with lukewarm water to thoroughly wet the peas and towel. Keep a container under the colander to catch the water which drains away. When the sprouts are developed, remove from the towels (they will stick a little, but pull off readily), and rinse under cold water. Then use as directed in the recipes. Assume that 1 cup of mung peas will produce about a pound of bean sprouts.

## SHRIMP TOAST

10 slices white sandwich bread, trimmed of crusts
1 pound shrimp, shelled and deveined
1 teaspoon minced ginger root
4 water chestnuts, minced
3 tablespoons minced onion
1 teaspoon dry sherry
1 teaspoon salt
2 teaspoons sesame oil
2 eggs, lightly beaten
2 tablespoons cornstarch
¼ cup sesame seeds
Vegetable oil for deep-frying
2 tablespoons chopped parsley

Press the bread slices down lightly with a rolling pin.

Chop the shrimp very fine. Add the ginger, water chestnuts, and onion and chop again until pasty. Mix in the sherry, salt, oil, eggs, and cornstarch. Mix thoroughly. Cut each slice of bread into 4 triangles and spread some shrimp mixture on each. Sprinkle the tops with the sesame seeds and press down lightly. Heat the oil to 375° and put the triangles into it, shrimp side down, until edges turn golden, then turn over and fry until bread is golden brown. Drain on paper towels. Sprinkle with parsley. Serve hot as an hors d'oeuvre.

Makes 40 triangles.

Sesame

## BARBECUED SPARERIBS

½ cup honey
½ cup soy sauce
1½ cups beef broth
3 tablespoons cider vinegar
2 tablespoons dry sherry
2 cloves garlic, minced
1 tablespoon sugar
1 teaspoon five-spice powder
2 racks spareribs (about 4 pounds), cracked horizontally

Combine the honey, soy sauce, beef broth, vinegar, sherry, garlic, sugar, and five-spice powder in a bowl. Add the spareribs and marinate at room temperature 2 hours, turning and basting frequently. Drain, reserving marinade. Arrange the ribs on a rack in a shallow roasting pan and roast in a 350° oven 1¼ hours; as fat accumulates, pour it off, and baste with the reserved marinade frequently. To serve, cut into individual ribs.
Serves 8–10.


## CHINESE BREAD

1 envelope yeast
½ teaspoon sugar
¼ cup warm water (about)
2 cups sifted flour
½ teaspoon salt
2 teaspoons sesame oil

Sprinkle the yeast and sugar into the water, Let stand 5 minutes, then mix until dissolved. Mix with the flour and salt until a dough is formed. If too dry, add a little more warm water. Knead until smooth and elastic. Place the dough in an oiled bowl and put the bowl in a pan of warm water. Cover and let rise 4 hours.

Divide the dough into 18 pieces. Roll out each piece into a thin circle and sprinkle each with a little of the sesame oil; then fold over into a half moon, pressing down lightly. Place a piece of parchment paper or aluminum foil under each, then arrange on a greased rack. Place the rack in a pan and add boiling water to just reach the rack. Cover the pan and cook over low heat 30 minutes.

## ENVELOPED CHICKEN

>2 whole chicken breasts
>3 tablespoons soy sauce
>1 tablespoon vegetable oil
>½ cup minced mushrooms
>3 water chestnuts, chopped
>¼ cup minced green onions
>1 tablespoon sesame seed oil
>2 teaspoons dry sherry
>¼ teaspoon ground ginger
>1 tablespoon oyster sauce
>Vegetable oil for deep frying

Cut the breast in half through the breast bone, then carefully remove the skin and bones. Cut each piece through the middle to make it thinner. Put each piece between two sheets of waxed paper and pound as thin as possible. Cut chicken into 2-inch-square pieces and sprinkle them with 2 tablespoons of the soy sauce. Let stand 10 minutes. Heat the vegetable oil in a skillet and sauté the mushrooms, water chestnuts, and green onions for 3 minutes. Stir in the sherry, ginger, sesame seed oil, and remaining soy sauce. Cool. Spread some of the mixture on one half of each chicken square, fold over, and pound edges together. Cut parchment paper, waxed paper, or aluminum foil into 4-inch squares and put one piece of chicken in the center of each. Fold like an envelope. Chill 2 hours.

Heat the oil to 370° and carefully slide the packages into the oil, a few at a time. Fry 5 minutes. Drain. Serve in the paper.

Makes about 10.

## SPRING ROLLS

### Pancake

2 cups sifted flour
2 eggs
2½ cups water
Vegetable oil for deep-fat frying
Cornstarch

Beat together the flour, eggs, and water until very smooth. Let stand 15 minutes.

Brush a hot 7-inch skillet with a little oil. Pour in 1 tablespoon batter, tilting the pan quickly to coat the bottom. Cook just until set. Turn out onto a napkin, cooked side down, and stack while preparing the balance of the pancakes. Place 2 tablespoons of the filling along one side of each pancake. Brush all the edges with a little cornstarch mixed with water. Fold opposite sides in and roll up, pressing the edges together with the cornstarch mixture. Fry in deep 370° oil until browned and crisp. Cut each roll into 3 pieces. Serve with mustard and *duk* sauce.

Makes about 24 rolls.

### Pork Filling

½ pound boneless pork
⅓ cup peanut or vegetable oil
¾ teaspoon salt
1 teaspoon cornstarch
1 tablespoon dry sherry
¼ cup thinly sliced green onions
½ cup julienne-cut water chestnuts
½ cup chopped mushrooms
½ cup bean sprouts
2 tablespoons soy sauce

Cut the pork in matchlike pieces. Heat half the oil in a wok or skillet; add the pork and stir fry until browned. Sprinkle with the salt, cornstarch, and sherry. Stir fry over low heat 3 minutes. Turn mixture into a bowl.

Heat the remaining oil in the pan; stir fry the green onions, water chestnuts, mushrooms, and bean sprouts 5 minutes, mix in the soy sauce. Add to the pork mixture, mix thoroughly and cool.

## SPICED CHICKEN WINGS

12 chicken wings
½ cup water
1 onion
¼ cup dry sherry
3 tablespoons soy sauce
1 tablespoon sugar
4 teaspoons salt
½ teaspoon pepper
1½ tablespoons cinnamon
1 teaspoon ground ginger

Remove any pinfeathers, wash and dry the wings. Cut off the wing tips, then cut each wing in half, where the bones join.

In a saucepan, combine the water, onion, sherry, soy sauce, and sugar. Add the wings, bring to a boil, cover, and cook over low heat 30 minutes or until tender. Turn the wings several times. Drain, dry, and cool.

Combine the salt, pepper, cinnamon, and ginger in a skillet. Heat, shaking the pan, then coat the wings with the mixture.

Serves 6–12.

## 14 CHINA

### BARBECUED PORK

>2 pork tenderloins (about 2 pounds)
>⅔ cup soy sauce
>¼ cup dry sherry
>2 cloves garlic, minced
>2 green onions, chopped
>3 thin slices ginger root
>3 tablespoons honey
>1 tablespoon sugar

If pork tenderloin is not available, buy a pork butt and cut it lengthwise into 2-inch-wide strips. A 6-rib boneless loin of pork, cut lengthwise into 2-inch-wide strips, may also be used.

Combine the soy sauce, sherry, garlic, green onions, and ginger root. Marinate the meat in the mixture for 3 hours. Drain. Place on a greased rack over a drip pan, with water on the bottom, and roast in a 375° oven 20 minutes. Brush the pork with a mixture of the honey and sugar. Reduce heat to 325° and roast 20 minutes longer, turning the meat once. Slice thin against the grain and serve hot or cold.

Serves 8–10.

### GARLIC SPARERIBS

>1 rack spareribs (about 2 pounds)
>6 cloves garlic
>1 slice ginger root
>½ teaspoon cinnamon
>½ teaspoon anise seed, crushed
>1½ teaspoons salt
>1½ teaspoons sugar
>½ cup soy sauce
>2 tablespoons dry sherry

Wash and dry the spareribs. Crush the garlic and ginger root, or put through a press. Mix with the cinnamon, anise, salt, sugar, soy sauce, and sherry. Brush over both sides of the spareribs and let stand 2 hours, basting frequently.

Place a rack in a shallow roasting pan. Add boiling water to reach the rack. Put the spareribs on the rack. Roast in a 400° oven 45 minutes, or until tender, turning the ribs once. Cut into individual ribs.

Serves 2–4.

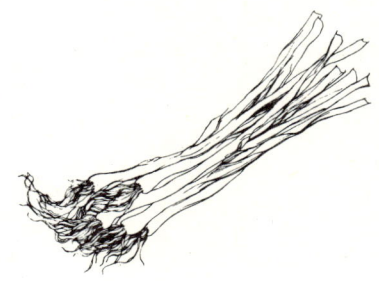

## ONION PANCAKES

¾ cup minced green onions
2 eggs
Milk
1½ cups flour
1 teaspoon salt
Dash cayenne pepper
¾ cup peanut or vegetable oil

If green onions aren't available, yellow onions may be used, but pour boiling water over them, then drain and dry. Use the green onions as they are.

Beat the eggs well, measure, and add enough milk to make 2 cups. Sift the flour, salt, and cayenne into a bowl; gradually add the milk-egg mixture, beating until smooth. Beat in ⅓ cup of the oil, then stir in the onions.

Heat 2 tablespoons oil in a skillet until it bubbles. Use a scant ladle of the batter, and pour it into the skillet, tilting the pan to spread the batter. Fry until browned on both sides, then drain on paper towels, and keep hot while preparing the balance. Serve as an appetizer or as an accompaniment to other dishes.

Makes about 12.

## CHINESE MUSTARD

1½ cups water
1 cup dry Chinese or English mustard

Bring the water to a rolling boil, then let cool to room temperature. You probably won't need all the water. Add the water to the mustard, spoon by spoon, stirring steadily, and add just enough to make the consistency a cross between mayonnaise and very heavy cream.

Makes about ⅔ cup.

## FRIED SHRIMP BALLS

1 pound raw shrimp, shelled, deveined, and minced
¼ pound fresh pork fat, chopped
3 water chestnuts, minced
2 tablespoons cornstarch
1 teaspoon salt
½ teaspoon minced ginger root
1 teaspoon dry sherry
1 egg white
Vegetable oil for deep-frying

Combine the shrimp, pork fat, water chestnuts, cornstarch, salt, ginger root, sherry, and unbeaten egg white. Chop together well and shape into 1-inch balls.

Heat deep oil to 300°. Drop in some balls, being careful not to crowd the pan. Fry 5 minutes. Drain. When all the balls are fried, heat the oil to 375°. Fry the balls again until golden brown. Drain on paper towels. Serve with heated salt and freshly ground black pepper as a dip.

Serves 4–6.

## SHRIMP IN BLACK BEAN SAUCE

2 tablespoons salted black beans
2 slices ginger root, minced
2 tablespoons dry sherry
1 teaspoon sugar
⅛ teaspoon freshly ground black pepper
1 tablespoon cornstarch
⅔ cup chicken broth
2 teaspoons soy sauce
3 tablespoons peanut or vegetable oil
1 clove garlic, crushed
1½ pounds raw shrimp, shelled, deveined, and washed

Wash the beans and soak in cold water 10 minutes. Drain, rinse with cold water, drain again, and crush lightly. In a cup, mix together the ginger, sherry, sugar, and pepper. In another cup, blend together the cornstarch, broth, and soy sauce.

Heat the oil in a wok or large skillet. Add the garlic, and stir fry a few seconds. Add the shrimp, and stir fry 2 minutes. Add the ginger mixture; stir fry 30 seconds. Add the black beans; stir fry 30 seconds. Stir in the broth mixture until thickened, then cook 2 minutes longer.

Serves 6–8.

## SHRIMP IN TOMATO SAUCE

1 pound raw shrimp, shelled and deveined
1 tablespoon dry sherry
2 tablespoons cornstarch
2¼ cups oil
½ cup sliced green onions
1 clove garlic, minced
2 teaspoons chopped ginger root
1⅓ teaspoons salt
1 teaspoon sugar
4 tablespoons ketchup
1 tablespoon soy sauce
½ cup water

Wash and dry the shrimp.

Toss shrimp with the sherry and 1 tablespoon cornstarch. Heat 2 cups oil in a wok or skillet; fry the shrimp in it until they turn pink. Remove the shrimp from the pan, and pour off the oil.

Heat the remaining oil in the pan; add the green onions, garlic, and ginger. Stir fry 1 minute. Blend together the salt, sugar, ketchup, soy sauce, water, and remaining cornstarch. Return the shrimp, and add the ketchup mixture. Cook over low heat, stirring steadily, until thickened.

Serves 4–6.


## FISH IN BROWN SAUCE

6 slices (about 3 pounds) fish, freshwater, if possible
⅓ cup cornstarch
½ cup oil
½ cup sliced green onions
1 clove garlic, minced
¾ cup sliced mushrooms
3 tablespoons dry sherry
¼ cup soy sauce
½ cup beef broth
1 teaspoon brown sugar
1 teaspoon five-spice powder

Wash and dry the fish. Dip lightly in the cornstarch. Heat the oil in a wok or skillet; brown the fish in it on both sides. Pour off all but 2 tablespoons oil. Add the green onions, garlic, and mushrooms; stir fry 1 minute. Add the sherry, soy sauce, broth, sugar, and five-spice powder. Bring to a boil, cover and cook over low heat 10 minutes, basting frequently.

Serves 6.

## SWEET AND PUNGENT SLICED FISH

6 slices white-meat fish
2 tablespoons dry sherry
2 tablespoons minced ginger root
5 tablespoons cornstarch
6 tablespoons soy sauce
2¼ cups vegetable oil
½ cup julienne-cut green peppers
½ pound snow peas
⅓ cup brown sugar
½ cup cider vinegar
½ teaspoon salt
¾ cup pineapple juice

Wash and dry the fish. Blend together the sherry, ginger, 4 tablespoons of the cornstarch, and 2 tablespoons of the soy sauce. Dip the fish in the mixture. Heat 2 cups of the oil until it bubbles. Fry the fish until crisp and brown on both sides. Drain, and keep hot.

Heat the remaining oil in a wok or skillet; stir fry the green peppers and snow peas 3 minutes. Stir in the sugar, vinegar, salt, and remaining soy sauce. Bring to a boil. Mix remaining cornstarch with the pineapple juice; add to the vegetables, stirring until thickened. Pour over the fish.

Serves 6.

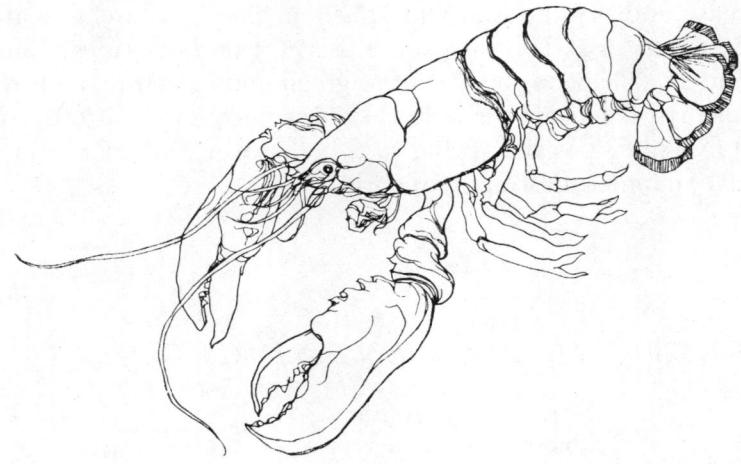

## STEAMED LOBSTER

2 1¼-pound live lobsters or 4 African lobster tails
4 tablespoons oil
¼ pound ground pork
3 eggs, beaten
¼ cup minced green onion
1 teaspoon salt
½ teaspoon freshly ground black pepper
2 tablespoons soy sauce
1 tablespoon dry sherry
½ teaspoon sugar

Have the live lobsters cut up in the shell into 2-inch pieces. Or cut the lobster tails crosswise into 2-inch pieces. Pour 2 tablespoons of the oil into a round, shallow baking dish large enough to hold the lobster in a single layer. Arrange the lobster in it. Mix together all the remaining ingredients, including the remaining oil, and spread over the lobsters.

Place the baking dish on a rack in a deep pan and add boiling water to barely reach the rack. Cover the pan, bring to a boil, and cook over low heat 35 minutes, adding boiling water from time to time to maintain the level.

Serves 4–6.

## LOBSTER AND ALMONDS

¼ pound shelled blanched almonds
2 1½-pound lobsters or 4 large African lobster tails
2 tablespoons minced ginger root
2 tablespoons dry sherry
½ cup chicken broth
½ teaspoon sugar
4 tablespoons oil
1 teaspoon salt
2 cloves garlic, minced
½ cup julienne-cut green peppers
1 cup bean sprouts
¼ pound mushrooms, sliced
½ pound snow peas
1 tablespoon cornstarch
2 tablespoons soy sauce
2 tablespoons water
Sesame oil

Spread the almonds in a shallow pan, and place in a 400° oven for 10 minutes, or until lightly browned, shaking the pan several times.

Wash the lobsters—if lobster tails are used, remove the meat from the shells, and cut in ½-inch slices. If lobsters are used, cut the lobsters in half lengthwise, and clean the bodies. Then chop, shell and all, into ½-inch sections.

Mix together the ginger, sherry, broth, and sugar.

Heat the oil in a wok or skillet; stir in the salt and garlic, then add the lobsters. Stir fry 2 minutes. Add the green peppers, bean sprouts, mushrooms, and snow peas; stir fry 2 minutes. Add the broth mixture, cover, bring to a boil quickly and cook 2 minutes.

Mix together the cornstarch, soy sauce, and water; stir into the pan until thickened. Turn into a heated serving dish, sprinkle with a little sesame oil, and garnish with the almonds.

Serves 4–6.

## STUFFED LOBSTER TAILS

1½ pounds African lobster tails
3 tablespoons salted black beans
1 teaspoon minced garlic
4 dried black mushrooms
½ cup water chestnuts
¼ cup sliced green onions
4 tablespoons oil
¾ pound boneless pork, ground
1 teaspoon salt
1 tablespoon cornstarch
2 tablespoons soy sauce
¾ cup beef broth

If possible, buy the smaller variety of lobster tails—6 to a pound. Wash the tails and remove the meat, reserving the shells.

Soak the black beans in cold water for 10 minutes, drain, rinse under cold water, and drain again. Mash the beans with the garlic. Soak the mushrooms in lukewarm water for 15 minutes and drain.

Finely chop the lobster meat, mushrooms, water chestnuts, and green onions.

Heat half the oil in a wok or skillet; stir fry the pork 3 minutes, or until no red remains, cool. Combine the pork with the lobster mixture and salt; mix thoroughly. Divide the mixture into as many balls as you have lobster shells. Slap each ball down several times onto a hard surface, then stuff the shells. Arrange, shell side down, in a baking dish. Put a rack in a large pan, and place the baking dish on it. Add boiling water to barely reach the rack. Cover tightly and cook 20 minutes, adding boiling water from time to time to maintain the level. Prepare the sauce meanwhile.

Blend together the cornstarch, soy sauce, and broth. Heat the remaining oil in a small skillet; add the mashed black beans, and stir fry for 30 seconds. Add the broth mixture, stirring constantly until thickened.

Arrange the lobster tails on a platter, and pour the sauce over them as evenly as possible.

Serves 6–8.

## STUFFED GREEN PEPPERS

        4 medium-sized green peppers
        ½ pound crabmeat
        6 hard-cooked eggs
        2 teaspoons soy sauce
        ½ teaspoon salt
        ½ teaspoon ground ginger
        ¼ cup chopped water chestnuts
        3 tablespoons minced green onions
        2 tablespoons sesame oil

    Wash the peppers and cut off the stems. Cut the peppers in half lengthwise, and scoop out the seeds and fibers.
    Pick over the crabmeat for any cartilage. Coarsely chop the eggs, and combine with the crabmeat, soy sauce, salt, ginger, water chestnuts, and green onions. Stuff the pepper halves with the mixture. Place a rack in a deep skillet and arrange the peppers on the rack. Add boiling water to barely reach the rack, cover, and cook over medium heat 20 minutes. Serve hot, sprinkled with the sesame oil.
    Serves 8.

## BROCCOLI WITH CRAB SAUCE

½ pound crabmeat
1 bunch broccoli
4 cups water
1½ teaspoons salt
1 teaspoon cornstarch
1 tablespoon soy sauce
½ cup chicken broth
⅛ teaspoon white pepper
1 egg white, stiffly beaten

Pick over the crabmeat and remove any cartilage. Wash the broccoli thoroughly and break into flowerets. Bring the water and salt to a boil in a saucepan; add the broccoli, and cook precisely 1 minute. Drain thoroughly, and place in a heated serving dish. Keep hot.

Mix the cornstarch with the soy sauce. Bring the broth and pepper to a boil in a saucepan; stir in the cornstarch mixture and cook over low heat until thickened. Add the crabmeat; cook 2 minutes. Remove from the heat and gradually fold in the egg white. Pour over the broccoli.

Serves 4–6.

## BASIC BROTH FOR USE IN COOKING CHINESE DISHES

5-pound fowl (stewing chicken) or 2 pounds lean pork
3 quarts water
2 teaspoons salt
1 cup diced onions
2 stalks celery and leaves
1 carrot, quartered
1 tablespoon dry sherry

Have the chicken quartered, or cut the pork in 1-inch cubes. Wash the chicken. Combine the chicken or pork with the water in a large kettle. Bring to a boil and skim the fat. Cover, and cook over low heat 1 hour. Add the salt and vegetables. Cook 30 minutes longer. Stir in the sherry. Strain the soup and skim the fat.

The chicken may be used in other recipes or eaten plain. The pork will be all cooked out but may be used in a spicy dish specifying cooked pork. If the broth is not to be used within a few days, pour it into a bottle, leaving a 2-inch space at the top, cover tightly, and freeze until needed.

Makes about 2½ quarts.

## CORN SOUP

½ pound raw pork
1 tablespoon cornstarch
½ teaspoon sugar
¼ teaspoon freshly ground black pepper
2 tablespoons soy sauce
2 tablespoons vegetable oil
1 clove garlic, minced
3 tablespoons minced onion
1 teaspoon minced ginger root
6 cups chicken broth
2 teaspoons salt
1½ cups fresh, frozen, or canned corn kernels
2 eggs, well beaten
2 green onions, thinly sliced

Carefully trim all fat from pork. Chop the pork and toss with the cornstarch, sugar, pepper, soy sauce, and 1 tablespoon oil. Heat the remaining oil in a saucepan and stir fry the garlic, onion, and ginger 1 minute. Add the broth and bring to a boil. Add the salt, corn, and pork mixture. Cover and cook over low heat 15 minutes. Combine the eggs and green onions and stir into the soup until set.

Serves 6–8.

## HOT-AND-SOUR SOUP

4 Chinese black mushrooms
1 cup water
¼ pound lean pork or 1 chicken breast
2 tablespoons vegetable oil
4 cups beef or chicken broth
2 tablespoons cornstarch
2 tablespoons dry sherry
2 tablespoons white vinegar
2 bean-curd cakes, cut in slivers (optional)
1 teaspoon salt
1 teaspoon soy sauce
⅛ teaspoon dried ground red peppers
1 egg, beaten
1 teaspoon sesame oil
1 green onion, thinly sliced

Wash the mushrooms, and soak in the water for 30 minutes. Drain and reserve the water; cut the mushrooms into matchlike strips. Cut the pork or chicken in very narrow strips. Heat the vegetable oil in a saucepan and stir fry the pork or chicken in it for 2 minutes. Add the broth, mushrooms, and mushroom water; bring to a boil and cook over low heat 10 minutes. Mix to a paste the cornstarch, sherry and vinegar; stir into the soup until thickened. Add the bean curd, salt, soy sauce and red pepper. Stir in the egg. Remove from the heat and sprinkle with sesame oil and green onion. Taste for seasoning; the soup should be a little tart and fairly spicy. Add more vinegar and red pepper if necessary.

Serves 4–6.

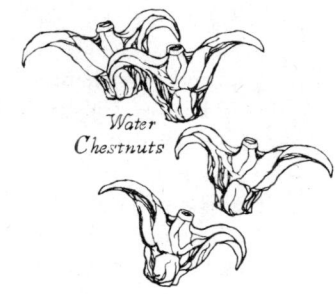

## SHARK'S FIN SOUP

½ pound dried skinless shark's fin
Water
2 cloves garlic
1 onion
4 dried black mushrooms
6 cups chicken broth
2 tablespoons dry sherry
1 cup flaked crabmeat
¼ cup minced water chestnuts
2 green onions, thinly sliced
Sesame oil (optional)

Buy the skinless shark's fin meat—it's dried, and must be soaked overnight in warm water to cover. (Ready to use shark's fin is available in some Chinese stores on order, but it's very expensive. Canned shark's fin is also available, but the flavor and texture are not so good. However, if you want to use it, omit the soaking and cooking process, and add the drained canned shark's fin to the chicken broth, following the instructions from that point.) Drain, rinse, and add fresh water to cover, and the garlic and onion. Bring to a boil, and cook over low heat 1 hour. Drain, and rinse again. Pull the shark's fin into strips.

Soak the mushrooms in lukewarm water for 30 minutes. Drain, and cut in narrow slices.

Bring the broth to a boil; add the shark's fin and mushrooms; cook over low heat 30 minutes. Add the sherry, crabmeat, and water chestnuts; cook 5 minutes. Taste for seasoning, adding salt if necessary. Turn into a bowl, or individual soup cups, and sprinkle with the green onions and a few drops of sesame oil.

Serves 6.

## SHRIMP-SPINACH SOUP

½ pound raw shrimp, shelled and deveined
2 egg whites, lightly beaten
1 teaspoon salt
½ teaspoon ground ginger
½ cup diced celery
1½ cups finely shredded cabbage
6 cups boiling chicken broth
4 tablespoons water
2 tablespoons cornstarch
½ cup raw chopped spinach
¼ cup thinly sliced green onions

Wash and dry the shrimp, then grind or chop very fine. Mix in the egg whites, ½ teaspoon salt, and the ginger.

Combine the celery, cabbage, broth, and remaining salt. Bring to a boil and cook over low heat 10 minutes. Mix the water with the cornstarch and stir into the boiling soup until thickened. Gradually add the shrimp mixture, stirring constantly to prevent lumps from forming. Cook 5 minutes. Mix in the spinach and green onions; cook 1 minute and serve.

Serves 6–8.

## CHICKEN VELVET SOUP

1 whole chicken breast
2 egg whites
1½ teaspoons salt
2 teaspoons dry sherry
1 8¾-ounce can cream-style corn
6 cups chicken broth
2 tablespoons minced Smithfield ham or canned deviled ham

Remove the skin, bones, and tendons of the chicken breast. Chop the chicken very fine. Beat the egg whites until they are frothy, and just before peaks form. Mix in the chicken, salt, and sherry. Beat the corn with an egg beater, until kernels are softened.

Bring the broth to a boil; add the corn. Bring to a boil again and cook 2 minutes. Stir in the chicken mixture, bring to a rolling boil, and serve.

Serves 6–8.


## WALNUT CHICKEN

2 whole chicken breasts
¼ cup soy sauce
3 tablespoons dry sherry
2 teaspoons sugar
1 teaspoon salt
3 tablespoons cornstarch
2 cups vegetable oil
2 cups blanched walnuts
1 cup cubed bamboo shoots
1 cup sliced green onions
½ cup diced water chestnuts
¼ cup chicken broth

Remove the skin and bones of the chicken.

Cut the chicken meat in small cubes; toss in a mixture of the soy sauce, sherry, sugar, salt, and cornstarch. Let stand 15 minutes.

Heat the oil in a wok or skillet; fry the walnuts in it until browned. Drain, reserving ⅓ cup oil. Heat 3 tablespoons of the oil in the pan; stir fry the bamboo shoots, green onions, and water chestnuts 3 minutes, stirring frequently. Remove from pan and pour off the oil.

Heat the remaining 3 tablespoons oil in the skillet; stir fry the chicken in it 3 minutes. Add the broth, cover, and cook over low heat 3 minutes. Return the vegetables and walnuts, and bring to a boil. Serve immediately.

Serves 4–6.

## CHICKEN WITH BROWN SAUCE

    2 whole chicken breasts
    4 Chinese dried mushrooms
    2 tablespoons cornstarch
    2 tablespoons dry sherry
    1 teaspoon salt
    2¼ cups vegetable oil
    2 bamboo shoots, cut in small cubes
    ¼ teaspoon dried ground red peppers
    4 tablespoons *chiang* (bottled Chinese brown sauce)

Remove the skin and bones of the chicken, and slice the chicken thin.

Soak the mushrooms in warm water 10 minutes. Drain, and cut in small dice. Toss the chicken with the cornstarch, sherry, and salt. Heat 2 cups of the oil in a wok or skillet until it bubbles. Fry the chicken in it until browned. Drain.

Heat the remaining oil in a wok or skillet and stir fry the mushrooms, bamboo shoots, and red peppers 2 minutes. Stir in the *chiang*. Add the chicken, and stir fry 1 minute. Serve hot.

Serves 4–6.

## FRIED PEKING CHICKEN

### CHICKEN

    3-pound frying chicken
    1 teaspoon salt
    ¼ teaspoon white pepper
    1 teaspoon sugar
    3 tablespoons soy sauce
    2 tablespoons dry sherry
    1 green onion, sliced
    2 slices ginger root, minced
    2 egg whites
    Cornstarch
    Vegetable oil for deep-frying

Have the chicken chopped up, bone and all, into 10 even-sized pieces. Wash and dry the chicken. Sprinkle with the salt, pepper, and sugar. In a bowl, mix together the soy sauce, sherry, green onion, and ginger. Add the chicken, and baste, to coat. Let stand 2 hours, turning the chicken several times. Drain, and put on paper towels for a few minutes.

Lightly beat the egg whites; dip the chicken into them, and then dip lightly in cornstarch.

Heat deep oil to 350°. Drop a few pieces of chicken at a time into the oil, and fry 5 minutes. Lift out the chicken with a slotted spoon or tongs, and place on paper towels. When all the chicken is fried, and cool, reheat the oil to 375°. Fry the chicken again, until golden brown, about 5 minutes. Drain again on paper towels. Serve with the sauce, if desired.

Serves 6–8.

### Sauce

2 tablespoons oil
2 green onions, minced
2 slices ginger root, minced
2 tablespoons soy sauce
¼ cup chicken broth
1 teaspoon dry sherry
1 tablespoon cornstarch
3 tablespoons water

Heat the oil in a small skillet; stir fry the green onion and ginger for 30 seconds. Mix in the soy sauce, broth, and sherry. Bring to a boil, and stir in the cornstarch, mixed to a paste with the water, until thickened and translucent. Pour over the chicken, or serve separately.

## LEMON CHICKEN

    2 whole chicken breasts
    2 eggs, beaten
    1 teaspoon salt
    ¼ teaspoon white pepper
    ⅔ cup cornstarch
    Vegetable oil for deep-frying
    1 cup chicken broth
    ¼ cup dry sherry
    1 tablespoon soy sauce
    2 teaspoons brown sugar
    ¼ cup lemon juice
    2 tablespoons water
    1 lemon, thinly sliced

Bone the chicken breasts, but leave the skin on. Wash, dry, and cut the chicken into 1-inch thick slices. Beat the eggs with the salt, pepper, and all but 1 tablespoon of the cornstarch. Dip the chicken pieces in the batter.

Heat deep oil to 365°. Fry the chicken in it until golden brown. Drain, and keep hot.

In a saucepan, combine the broth, sherry, soy sauce, brown sugar, and lemon juice. Bring to a boil, and stir in the reserved cornstarch mixed with the water. Cook, stirring steadily, until thickened. Add the chicken; cook 2 minutes. Turn into a heated serving dish, and garnish with the lemon slices.

Serves 4–6.

## BARBECUED CHICKEN

    5-pound roasting chicken
    2 teaspoons salt
    ¼ teaspoon freshly ground black pepper
    1 teaspoon sugar
    1 teaspoon five-spice powder
    2 cloves garlic, minced
    ¼ cup soy sauce
    2 tablespoons oil

Wash the whole chicken. Dry with paper towels. Rub inside and out with a mixture of salt, pepper, sugar, five-spice powder, and garlic. Place in a bowl, pour over the soy sauce and oil and let stand 1 hour. Drain, reserving any liquid. Place the chicken on a rack in a shallow roasting pan and pour in about 2 inches of water. Roast in a 425° oven 2 hours, or until tender and browned, basting with the reserved liquid and turning frequently. To serve, disjoint or chop into 2-inch wide pieces right through the bone.
Serves 4–6.

## LICHEE CHICKEN

    2 whole chicken breasts
    2 tablespoons cornstarch
    3 tablespoons soy sauce
    ½ teaspoon salt
    1 16-ounce can lichees
    6 tablespoons peanut or vegetable oil
    2 cups sliced onions
    1 cup sliced celery
    ¾ cup sliced water chestnuts

Remove the skin and bones of the chicken, and slice the meat thin. Toss in a mixture of the cornstarch, soy sauce, and salt. Drain the lichees, reserving ⅓ cup of the juice.

Heat 2 tablespoons oil in a wok or skillet; stir fry the onions 3 minutes. Remove the onions. Add 1 tablespoon oil to the pan; stir fry the celery and water chestnuts 3 minutes; remove from the pan and add to the onions. Heat the remaining oil in the pan; stir fry the chicken in it until browned and cooked through, about 5 minutes. Add the lichees and juice and return the vegetables. Cook, stirring frequently, until mixture boils, then cook 1 minute longer.
Serves 4–6.

## FRIED DUCK

> 5-pound duck
> 4 tablespoons dry sherry
> 4 teaspoons salt
> 1 teaspoon sugar
> ½ teaspoon dried ground red peppers
> 1 green onion, chopped
> 6 slices ginger root
> 6 star anise
> 5 tablespoons flour
> 2 eggs, lightly beaten
> Vegetable oil for deep-frying

Clean, wash, and dry the duck.

Rub the duck with the sherry and let stand 30 minutes, then rub with a mixture of the salt, sugar, and red peppers. Put the duck in a large bowl with the green onion, ginger root, and anise. Place the bowl on a rack in a large saucepan. Add enough boiling water to reach the rack, cover the saucepan and steam for 1½ hours, or until the duck is tender. Add more boiling water from time to time to maintain water level. Remove the duck, and dry.

Beat the flour into the eggs; coat the duck with mixture. Heat the oil to 365° and fry the duck until crisp and brown, about 15 minutes. Drain. Cut into small pieces through the bone. Serve hot with two dishes of condiments (for each person) for dipping—one dish containing 2 tablespoons ketchup, the other a combination of 2 teaspoons heated salt and 2 teaspoons coarsely cracked black pepper.

Serves 4–6.

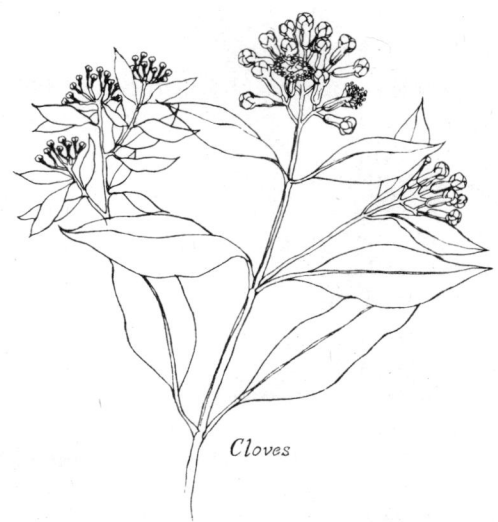
*Cloves*

## FRIED SPICED DUCK

>5-pound duck
>2 cups soy sauce
>1 cup sliced onion
>4 cloves garlic
>2 slices ginger root
>2 cloves
>1 teaspoon cinnamon
>2 anise seeds
>**Vegetable oil for deep-frying**

Wash and clean the duck. Combine in a deep pan with the soy sauce, onion, garlic, ginger root, cloves, cinnamon, and anise. Add enough water to cover. Bring to a boil, cover, and cook over low heat 1½ hours. Drain and cool. Dry the duck thoroughly, and refrigerate until cold.

Heat deep oil (being sure there will be enough to cover the duck) to 370°. Lower the duck into it, and fry until browned and crisp, about 10 minutes. Baste if necessary to cover all parts. Drain, and cut into small pieces through the bone.

Serves 10–12.

## PRESSED DUCK

Start the preparation of this recipe the day before it is to be eaten.

### Duck

5-pound duck
Boiling water
1 cup sliced onions
1 cup sliced celery
1 bay leaf
2 tablespoons soy sauce
2 teaspoons salt
¾ teaspoon freshly ground black pepper
1 tablespoon flour
1 tablespoon cornstarch
1 teaspoon sugar
1 egg, beaten

Wash the duck and remove as much fat as possible. Place the duck in a deep saucepan and cover with boiling water. Simmer over low heat 30 minutes; add the onion, celery, bay leaf, and soy sauce. Cook 1 hour longer, or until tender, turning the duck once or twice. Drain, reserving 1 cup of stock for the sauce. Cool, then carefully remove the skin of the duck, keeping the pieces of skin as large as possible.

Cut the meat of the duck in small pieces. Arrange the skin, skin-side down on the bottom of a square pan; sprinkle with 1 teaspoon salt, ¼ teaspoon pepper, and the flour. Toss the duck meat with the cornstarch, sugar, and remaining salt and pepper. Spread on the skin about ½ inch thick. Press down with a heavy pan or other weight for 30 minutes. Remove weight and brush top with the egg. Cover with foil or waxed paper and again weight it down. Refrigerate overnight. When ready to continue the preparation, cut the duck into 1-inch squares.

BATTER

1 egg
2 tablespoons water
¼ cup flour
½ teaspoon salt
Vegetable oil for deep-frying

Beat the egg and water; stir in the flour and salt until smooth. Dip the duck pieces in the mixture. Heat the oil to 375° and fry the squares in it until brown and crisp. Drain and keep hot.

SAUCE

1 cup reserved stock
1 tablespoon cornstarch
1 tablespoon soy sauce
1 tablespoon molasses
¼ cup minced green onion
¼ cup slivered toasted almonds

Mix the stock, cornstarch, soy sauce, and molasses together in a saucepan. Cook over medium heat, stirring constantly until thickened and clear. Pour the sauce into a serving dish, arrange the duck squares over it, and sprinkle with the green onion and almonds.
Serves 4–6.

## FRIED DUCK, SZECHUAN STYLE

Start the preparation the day before the duck is to be served, if possible.

> 5-pound duck
> ½ lemon
> 2 teaspoons five-spice powder
> 5 black peppercorns, crushed
> 3 teaspoons salt
> 2 tablespoons dry sherry
> 3 slices ginger root
> ¼ cup chopped green onions
> Flour
> 2 eggs, beaten
> Dry bread crumbs
> Vegetable oil for deep-frying

Wash the duck, and rub all over with the lemon. Let stand 20 minutes, then rinse in cold water, and dry with paper towels.

Mix together the five-spice powder, peppercorns, and half the salt and sherry. Rub this mixture into the skin. Into the cavity of the duck, put the ginger, green onions, and remaining salt and sherry. Wrap the duck with plastic wrap, or put it into a plastic bag, and refrigerate overnight, or for at least 4 hours.

When ready to cook, put the duck in a shallow pan, without a handle. Cover the pan completely with foil. Put a rack in a deep pot, or steamer, and place the pan containing the duck on the rack. Add enough boiling water to reach the rack. Cover the pot, and cook over medium heat for 1 hour, adding boiling water from time to time, to maintain the water level. Remove the duck, and dry it carefully with paper towels. Put the duck in the refrigerator until chilled.

Cut the duck into quarters, and dip in the flour, beaten eggs, and finally the bread crumbs. Heat deep oil to 375° and fry the duck quarters in it until golden brown. Drain, and with poultry scissors cut into small pieces. Serve hot.

Serves 6–8.

## PORK AND CLAMS

       1 pound lean boneless pork
       2 dozen small hard-shell clams
       2 tablespoons cornstarch
       ¼ cup soy sauce
       4 tablespoons oil
       ½ pound mushrooms, sliced
       1 8-ounce can tiny peas, drained
       2 green onions, thinly sliced

Cut the pork in very thin slices, against the grain. Wash the clams, scrubbing the shells with a brush, if sandy. Put the clams in a skillet, cover tightly, and place over medium heat until shells open, about 5 minutes. Discard any which stay tightly closed. Remove the clams from their shells. Measure and strain the clam liquid—there should be about ½ cup—and mix it with the cornstarch and soy sauce. Add the clams, and toss them to coat.

    Heat the oil in a wok or skillet; add the pork, and stir fry for 3 minutes. Add the mushrooms and peas; stir fry 3 minutes. Add the soy-clam mixture and green onions; stir fry 1 minute, or until sauce is thickened.

    Serves 6–8.

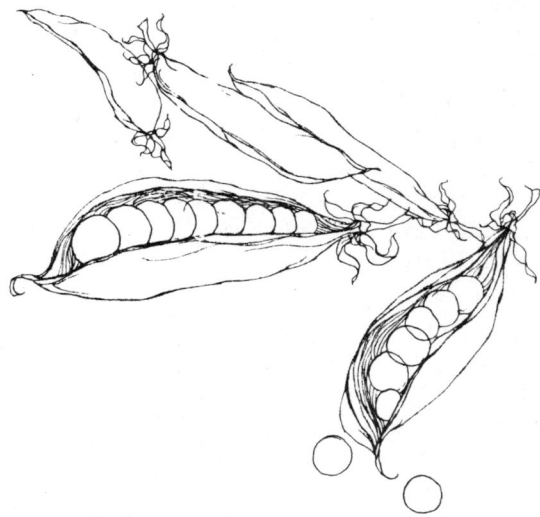

## MOO SHOO PORK

Moo Shoo Pork is customarily served with Peking Doilies, a type of thin pancake. But in Hong Kong and Taiwan, a very creditable substitute is being used more and more because the doilies are fairly difficult to prepare. It's actually steamed white bread, and to prepare it, trim ordinary white sandwich bread of its crusts, then with a sharp knife cut through the middle, to make it thinner. Or use the very thin melba or diet bread and trim the crusts. In either case, flatten the bread further by rolling gently with a rolling pin. Put the bread slices on a rack, in a pot, and add boiling water to barely reach the rack. Cover the pan, and steam gently for 10 minutes. The bread will then be moist and ready to roll up with the pork mixture.

### Pork Mixture

1 pound lean boneless pork
2 tablespoons soy sauce
1 teaspoon sugar
3 cloud ear mushrooms, or other dried mushrooms
1 cup bean sprouts
4 tablespoons oil
2 eggs, beaten
Dash cayenne pepper
2 slices ginger root, minced
1 teaspoon salt
¼ cup sliced green onions

Rinse and dry the pork. Cut in matchlike strips. Toss the pork with the soy sauce and sugar, and let stand 30 minutes. Soak the mushrooms in lukewarn water for 15 minutes. Drain and shred.

If canned bean sprouts are used, merely drain them. If you're using fresh bean sprouts, cover with water, bring to a boil, cook 30 seconds and drain.

Heat 2 tablespoons of the oil in a wok or large skillet; add the eggs and cayenne pepper, and scramble until set, but moist. Remove from the pan. If any egg adheres to the pan, wipe it with paper towels. Add the remaining oil to the pan, and heat it. Stir

the ginger root into the pan for 30 seconds, then add the pork. Stir fry for 4 minutes. Add the salt, green onions, mushrooms, and bean sprouts. Stir fry 1 minute, then cover and cook 2 minutes. Return the eggs just to heat. Heap in a heated serving dish. To eat, each person takes a piece of the bread, puts some of the pork mixture on it, rolls it up to cover the filling, and picks it up with the fingers.
Serves 6–8.

## SPARERIBS WITH BLACK BEAN SAUCE

1 rack spareribs (about 2 pounds)
1 teaspoon five-spice powder
2 tablespoons salted black beans
2 green onions, minced
2 cloves garlic, minced
3 tablespoons dry sherry
1 tablespoon cornstarch
1 tablespoon soy sauce
⅔ cup water
2 tablespoons oil
½ cup beef broth

Have the butcher cut the rack into individual ribs, and then chop each rib into 1-inch pieces, bone and all. You can do this with a cleaver at home, if you prefer, or don't have an accommodating butcher. Wash and dry the ribs. Toss with the five-spice powder.

Soak the beans in cold water for 15 minutes. Drain, rinse under cold water and drain again. Mash the beans to a paste with the green onions, garlic, and sherry. Mix together the cornstarch, soy sauce, water.

Heat the oil in a wok or heavy skillet; add the spareribs and stir fry for 10 minutes. Pour off the fat, and add the bean mixture. Stir fry over medium heat for 2 minutes. Add the broth, cover, and cook 4 minutes. Blend in the cornstarch mixture, and cook, stirring constantly, until thickened.
Serves 4–6.

## SWEET AND PUNGENT PORK

1½ pounds boneless pork
2 eggs
½ teaspoon salt
⅔ cup cornstarch
1¼ cups water
Vegetable oil for deep-frying
½ cup vinegar
¼ cup brown sugar
1 tablespoon molasses
1 8-ounce can pineapple wedges, drained
1 tomato, cut in 6 wedges

Cut the pork into 1-inch cubes. Beat the egg and salt; mix in ½ cup of the cornstarch and 3 tablespoons of the water until a smooth batter is formed. Dip the pork cubes in the mixture, coating the pieces on all sides. Heat deep oil to 365°. Fry the pork until browned on all sides. Don't crowd the pan. Drain on paper towels and keep hot.

Mix together the vinegar, brown sugar, molasses, and ¾ cup of the water in a saucepan. Bring to a boil. Mix the remaining cornstarch with the remaining water; stir into the sauce until thickened. Add the pineapple and tomato; cook over low heat 3 minutes. Mix in the pork and serve.

Serves 4–6.

## TWICE-COOKED PORK

2 pounds fresh bacon or other fatty pork
1 onion
3 cups water
2 tablespoons oil
2 cloves garlic
½ teaspoon salt
2 green peppers, seeded and diced
½ cup diced bamboo shoots
3 tablespoons minced ginger root
3 green onions, cut in 1-inch slices
2 tablespoons *hoisin* sauce
2 tablespoons dry sherry
1 teaspoon sugar
⅛ teaspoon hot pepper oil or cayenne pepper

If the unsmoked fresh bacon is not available, buy a streaky fat cut of boneless pork. Rinse the pork, and combine it in a saucepan with the onion and water. Bring to a boil, cover, and cook over low heat 1 hour. Drain and cool. Cut the pork in ¼-inch slices against the grain, and into strips about 1 by 2 inches.

Heat the oil in a wok or skillet; add the whole garlic cloves and salt. Stir fry until garlic browns, then discard. Add the pork strips and stir fry 5 minutes. Add the green peppers, bamboo shoots, and ginger; stir fry 3 minutes. Add the green onion, *hoisin* sauce, sherry, sugar, and pepper oil. Stir fry 2 minutes.

Serves 6–8.

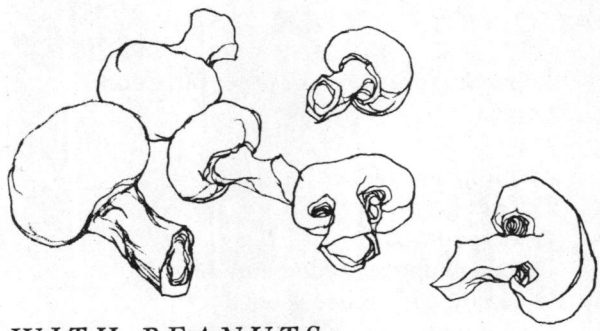

## PORK WITH PEANUTS

1 pound lean boneless pork
2 tablespoons dry sherry
2 tablespoons soy sauce
2 tablespoons cornstarch
¼ pound shelled untoasted peanuts
1 teaspoon salt
4 tablespoons peanut or vegetable oil
2 cloves garlic, minced
½ pound mushrooms, thinly sliced
2 green peppers, seeded and diced
2 tablespoons bottled Oyster sauce
Dash cayenne pepper or Tabasco
¾ cup chicken or beef broth
3 green onions, thinly sliced

Cut the pork in matchlike strips. Mix together the sherry, soy sauce, and cornstarch; toss in the pork, until coated.

Mix the peanuts with the salt. Heat half of the oil in a wok or skillet; add the peanuts, and toss them to coat with the oil, then continue stirring until delicately browned. Remove with a slotted spoon and drain on paper towels.

Add the remaining oil to the pan, and heat it. Stir in the garlic, then add the pork, and stir fry 3 minutes. Add the mushrooms and green pepper; stir fry 1 minute. Stir in the Oyster sauce and cayenne pepper for 1 minute, then add the broth. Cover, and cook over low heat 5 minutes. Turn into a heated serving dish and sprinkle with green onions.

Serves 4–6.

## BEEF WITH VEGETABLES

4 dried black mushrooms
1½ pounds sirloin steak
1 teaspoon sugar
3 tablespoons dry sherry
4 tablespoons soy sauce
4 tablespoons peanut or vegetable oil
1 clove garlic, minced
4 green peppers, seeded and cut in ¾-inch squares
½ cup sliced green onions
½ cup thinly sliced bamboo shoots
½ cup beef broth
2 teaspoons cornstarch
2 tablespoons water

Wash the mushrooms, cover with water, and let soak 15 minutes. Drain, and slice them. Cut the meat against the grain, in narrow slices. Mix together the sugar, sherry, and 3 tablespoons of the soy sauce. Add the beef, toss to coat, and let stand 30 minutes, mixing once or twice. Drain.

Heat half the oil in a wok or heavy skillet; add the garlic, peppers, green onions, and bamboo shoots; stir fry 3 minutes. Remove from the pan. Heat the remaining oil in the pan, add the beef, and stir fry until meat begins to brown. Return the vegetables. Add the broth; bring to a boil over high heat, cover, and cook over medium heat 3 minutes. Blend together the cornstarch, water, and remaining soy sauce, and stir into the pan until thickened. Garnish with fried rice noodles, if desired.

Serves 6–8.

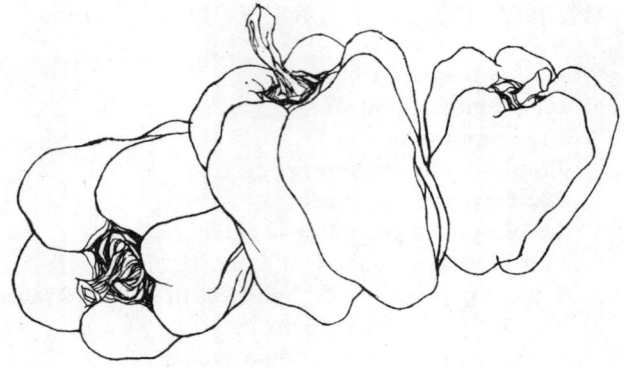

## BEEF AND PEPPERS

1 tablespoon cornstarch
¼ cup water
3 cloves garlic, minced
1 teaspoon five-spice powder
2 pounds sirloin or top round of beef, cut into thin strips
¾ cup peanut or vegetable oil
1½ cups chopped onions
2 green peppers, cut julienne
2 tomatoes, cut into small wedges
1 teaspoon sugar
1 teaspoon salt
¼ teaspoon freshly ground black pepper
1 cup chicken broth
4 tablespoons dry sherry

Mix the cornstarch and water to a paste and combine with the garlic, five-spice powder, and beef. Heat the oil in a wok or heavy skillet; add the meat mixture and stir fry over high heat 5 minutes. Remove meat. Reduce heat to medium and add onions, green peppers, and tomatoes. Stir fry for 2 minutes only—the vegetables should be crisp. Stir in the sugar, salt, pepper, broth, and sherry. Cook 3 minutes. Add meat and stir fry 2 minutes longer. Serve immediately with boiled rice.

Note: The specified cooking times should be followed exactly. Serves 6–8.

## FRIED WONTON

### Filling

¼ pound ground beef, pork, or chicken
1 green onion, minced
¼ teaspoon salt
⅛ teaspoon freshly ground black pepper
½ teaspoon soy sauce
½ teaspoon dry sherry
1 tablespoon broth or water
Dough for wrapping (below)
1 egg, beaten
Vegetable oil for deep-frying

Mix together the ground meat or chicken, the green onion, salt, pepper, soy sauce, sherry, and broth or water. Place 1 teaspoon of the mixture in the middle of each square. Moisten the edges of the squares with beaten egg and press the opposite corners together to form a triangle. Fry in hot (375°) oil until golden brown. Serve with *Duk* Sauce.

### Dough for Wrapping

2 cups sifted flour
1 teaspoon salt
⅔ cup lukewarm water
Cornstarch

Sift the flour and salt into a bowl and make a well in the center. Pour the water into the well. With a wooden spoon stir until the dough will form a ball. Place the ball on a floured board and knead until stiff. Cover the ball of dough with a damp cloth and let stand 30 minutes. Sprinkle the board with cornstarch and roll the dough into a long strip, 6 inches wide and less than ⅛ inch thick. Cut into 3-inch squares.

Makes about 36 wontons.

## SOFT NOODLES WITH PORK

1 pound boneless pork
½ pound fine noodles
¾ cup peanut or vegetable oil
4 dried black mushrooms
2 eggs, beaten
½ teaspoon salt
¼ cup soy sauce
4 teaspoons cornstarch
½ pound bean sprouts
1 cup thinly sliced green onions
2 bamboo shoots, cut in slivers
¼ pound fresh spinach, washed, drained, and shredded
¼ cup chicken or beef broth

Cut the pork in matchlike strips. Cook the noodles in boiling water 5 minutes, drain, and toss with 1 tablespoon of the oil, to prevent sticking. Spread on a plate to cool.

Soak the mushrooms in lukewarm water for 15 minutes. Drain, and cut in tiny dice.

Brush a heated skillet with a little of the oil, and pour in the eggs, tilting to spread them evenly. Cook until edges curl up, then turn out the egg pancake onto a plate. Shred fine, and reserve.

Heat half the remaining oil in a skillet; add the noodles, and stir fry until browned. Keep hot. Heat the remaining oil in a wok or skillet; add the pork, and stir fry 2 minutes. Mix together the salt, soy sauce, and cornstarch. Add to the pan, and stir fry until thickened. Add the bean sprouts, green onions, bamboo shoots, spinach, and broth. Stir fry 2 minutes. Heap the noodles on a heated flat serving dish, and pour the pork mixture over them.

Serves 4–6.

# NOODLE PANCAKES WITH CHICKEN LIVERS

### Pancake

6 cups water
1 teaspoon salt
½ pound fine noodles
⅓ cup peanut oil

Bring the water and salt to a rolling boil; add the noodles gradually, so that the water does not stop boiling. Boil 6 minutes, stirring several times. Drain immediately in a colander and rinse under cold water. Drain again, and spread on a plate. Mix with 1 tablespoon of the oil, and cool.

Heat the remaining oil in an 11-inch skillet; spread the noodles in it like a pancake and fry over medium heat until golden brown and crisp on the underside. Turn over, being careful not to break the pancake, and brown other side. (To facilitate turning, place a large plate over the pan and turn it over, plate side down. Then slide the pancake back into the pan, browned side up.) Keep hot.

### Chicken Livers

1 pound chicken livers
3 tablespoons oil
½ cup thinly sliced onions
¼ pound mushrooms, thinly sliced
½ cup chicken broth
2 tablespoons soy sauce
2 tablespoons dry sherry
1 tablespoon cornstarch

Wash the livers, cutting away any discolored spots. Cut each half of the liver in two pieces. Heat the oil in a wok or skillet; add the onions and mushrooms; stir fry 3 minutes. Add the livers, and stir fry until they lose their redness. Add the broth, bring to a boil over high heat, cover, and cook over medium heat 2 minutes. Blend together the soy sauce, sherry, and cornstarch. Stir into the pan until thickened. Pour over the pancake and serve.

Serves 4.

## RICE NOODLES

Rice noodles are made from rice flour, and look like thin, long white brittle threads. To prepare them as a garnish, break off the amount you want to serve and separate the threads. Heat deep oil to 350°, drop the noodles into it, and fry until puffed up, white and crisp. Under no circumstances let them brown. Remove with a slotted spoon, and drain on paper towels. They're ready to use as a garnish.

To use as a softer noodle, soak them in warm water for 10 minutes; drain, and cook in broth or boiling salted water for 10 minutes. Drain.

## FRIED RICE, YANGCHOW STYLE

1 pound boneless pork
½ cup soy sauce
2 teaspoons cornstarch
⅛ pound cooked smoked ham
3 slices ginger root
½ pound raw shrimp, shelled and deveined
1¼ teaspoons salt
½ teaspoon freshly ground black pepper
3 eggs
6 tablespoons lard or oil
1 carrot, grated coarsely
½ cup cooked or canned green peas
½ cup canned sliced mushrooms
¼ cup sliced green onions
4 cups cooked rice

Cut the pork in matchlike strips; add 4 tablespoons soy sauce and the cornstarch, and toss.

Cut the ham into tiny dice. Cut the ginger into slivers. Cut the shrimp in quarters and sprinkle with ¾ teaspoon of the salt and ¼ teaspoon of the pepper.

Beat the eggs. Heat 1 tablespoon of the lard in a 7-inch skillet.

Pour in half the eggs, turning the pan quickly to coat the bottom. Cook until underside browns, turn out and roll up. Cut into narrow strips. Repeat with remaining eggs and reserve.

Heat 2 tablespoons of the lard in the skillet; stir fry the ginger for a few seconds, then add the pork. Stir fry 5 minutes. Add the carrot, green peas, mushrooms, ham, and green onions; stir fry 2 minutes, stirring steadily. Add the shrimp, 2 tablespoons soy sauce, and remaining salt. Cook and stir for 3 minutes. Keep hot.

Heat the remaining lard in a large skillet; add the rice. Cook, stirring almost steadily, until very lightly browned, about 5 minutes. Mix in the remaining pepper and soy sauce, then the meat mixture, and half the egg strips. Fry for 1 minute, stirring steadily. Heap on a serving dish and sprinkle the remaining egg strips on top.

Serves 10–12.

## SZECHUAN PICKLES

2-pound head cabbage, Chinese if possible
1 white turnip, Chinese if possible
2 cucumbers
4 carrots
4 cups water
3 slices ginger root
10 black peppercorns
4 small dried red peppers
4 tablespoons coarse salt
2 tablespoons gin

Wash the cabbage, and remove the core. Shake, to drain, then cut into 2-inch cubes. Peel the turnip, and cut into 1-inch cubes. Peel the cucumbers, and slice 2 inches thick. Peel the carrots, cut in half crosswise, and then into quarters. Allow the vegetables to drain on paper towels for 1 hour.

Combine the water, ginger, peppercorns, red peppers, salt, and gin. Bring to a boil, cook 1 minute, then cool.

Arrange the vegetables in a layer in a jar or crock. Pour the spice mixture over them, cover tightly, and let stand at room temperature 3 days in warm weather, or 4 in cool weather. Taste to see if the vegetables are pickled, then refrigerate until needed.

Makes about 1½ pints.

CHINA 53

## EIGHT PRECIOUS PUDDING

>1½ cups glutinous rice
>½ teaspoon salt
>5 cups water
>2 tablespoons lard
>1½ cups sugar
>1 cup chopped candied fruits
>1 cup blanched almonds
>18 pitted dates
>½ cup seedless raisins
>1½ tablespoons cornstarch
>½ teaspoon almond extract

Wash the rice in cold water until water runs clear. Combine with the salt and 4 cups of the water in a saucepan. Bring to a boil; cover and cook over low heat 10 minutes. Mix in the lard and ½ cup of the sugar.

Arrange ¾ of the fruits and nuts on the bottom of a greased 2-quart baking dish. Carefully pour the undrained rice over them and arrange the remaining fruits and nuts on top. Tie a piece of parchment paper or aluminum foil over the top. Place the dish on a rack in a deep pot. Add boiling water to just reach the rack. Cover the pot and cook over medium heat 45 minutes. Add boiling water when needed to maintain level. While the pudding is cooking, prepare the sauce.

Mix the cornstarch with the remaining sugar and remaining water. Bring to a boil, stirring steadily, then cook over low heat 5 minutes. Stir in the almond extract; carefully unmold the pudding, and pour the sauce over it.

Serves 8–10.

## FRUIT WITH ALMOND JELLY

½ cup raw rice
1 cup blanched almonds
5 cups water
2 envelopes (tablespoons) gelatin
1 cup sugar
1 cup evaporated milk
2 teaspoons almond extract
1 17-ounce can fruit cocktail
1 can mandarin oranges

Soak the rice in cold water for 30 minutes. Drain. Combine the rice, almonds, and 1 cup of water in an electric blender, and blend until no pieces remain. Or grind the rice and almonds through the fine blade of a food chopper, adding the 1 cup of water as you grind. Pour the mixture into a muslin bag, or several layers of fine cheesecloth, and squeeze out all the liquid. There should be about 1 cup. Soften the gelatin in 1 cup of the remaining water.

Combine the sugar, milk, and remaining water in a saucepan; heat, but do not let boil, stirring until sugar dissolves. Stir in the gelatin until dissolved. Add the almond-rice water and cool. Stir in the almond extract. Pour into a large dish, about 12-by-12 inches, and chill until set. Cut into 1-inch diamond shapes.

Empty the fruit into a bowl, and chill. Add the almond jelly. Serve in Chinese soup cups or other small cups.
Serves 10–12.

## GLAZED FRUIT

2 firm apples
3 bananas
⅓ cup sifted cornstarch
3 egg whites
3 cups vegetable oil
1 cup sugar
¼ cup sesame seeds

Peel the apples and cut each into 8 wedges; remove the seeds. Peel the bananas and cut crosswise into 2-inch pieces. Mix together the cornstarch and unbeaten egg whites until smooth. Dip the fruits into the batter, coating them well. Heat the oil in a skillet until it boils. Fry the fruits in it until delicately browned. Drain. Pour off all but ¼ cup of the oil. Add the sugar; cook over low heat, stirring constantly until the sugar melts. Mix in the sesame seeds, then return the fruits. Baste and stir gently until the fruits are covered with the syrup. Turn the fruit and syrup into a flat, hot dish. Put a bowl of ice water on the table and give each person a fork and a plate. Each piece of fruit is dipped into the ice water, causing the fruit to glaze.

Serves 4–6.

# THE ORIENT
## *other than China*

JAPAN
KOREA
INDONESIA
THAILAND
MALAYSIA
INDIA
POLYNESIA

IN the culinary world that makes up the continent of Asia, the cuisine of China is comparable to the sun. Revolving about it in various orbits of greater and lesser importance are the satellite planets consisting of the other nations of the Orient. Using the same metaphor, the earth is merely a minor planet in another scheme of reference, the solar system. Nevertheless, the earth is quite important, and so, in Asia, some of the lesser cuisines constitute (as a group, although not singly) a wonder, gastronomically speaking.

It is difficult to imagine a foreign country concerning which more culinary misinformation has been repeated than that of Japan. Most Americans visualize a nation existing solely on such exotic foods as kelp, soybean curd, sea urchins, dried fish, pickled radishes, and so forth. There is, admittedly, a degree of truth in this belief, for all of these foods are actually eaten in Japan, but certainly not exclusively. (Many people think that the Chinese people delight in bird's nest soup and aged eggs every day of the week, whereas in fact they are expensive delicacies.) It is also true that the Japanese, as a nation, are extremely fond of raw fish, and this fact is often cited to prove the exotic quality of their cuisine. The American custom of eating raw clams and oysters, a similar taste, is typically disregarded.

The Japanese divide their cuisine into convenient categories. These include soups, including both *suimono* (clear soup) and *miso-shiru* (a type made with fermented malt); *nimono* (boiled food), a perfect example being a boiled chicken dish; *yakimono* (broiled food), typified by a national favorite, *kabayaki* (broiled eels); *agemono* (fried food), the best known being *tempura*, fried bits of fish and vegetables; *mushimono* (steamed food), which includes a wide range of steamed egg dishes; and *nabemono* (open frying-pan food), particularly *sukiyaki*, the sautéed dish of meat and vegetables flavored with soy sauce. Of all these varied and imaginative preparations, two particularly appeal to American and European palates; they are *tempura* and *sukiyaki*. In making *tempura*, the Japanese use torreya or gingelly oil, but our own vegetable fats and oils are quite satisfactory for the purpose. *Sukiyaki* has become enormously popular in America, and almost everyone, even the most timid, enjoys the slightly salty quality of the dish; it is made with soy sauce, which incidentally almost eliminates the need for table salt in this preparation, and indeed in most Japanese cookery. Another dish to American taste is *yakitori*, actually nothing more complicated than small bits of chicken (and parts) cooked on a skewer. The novel taste in the food comes from being prepared with *sake*, soy sauce, and ginger.

The everyday foods of the country include many routine and completely unexotic items, such as *gohan*, boiled rice, *udon*, wheat flour noodles, *soba*, buckwheat noodles, and *nimame*, boiled beans. Desserts are unimportant in the Japanese way of life, although some sweet preparations are occasionally made for holidays; but sweet foods rarely appear at the conclusion of a meal. Of course, tea (usually green) is the national beverage, but coffee has been making surprising inroads in recent years, particularly in the cities. In passing, the Japanese are to be complimented on their ability to make coffee, which is perhaps the best to be encountered on the vast continent of Asia. Needless to mention, and therefore redundantly being mentioned, is *sake*, the national drink. It is a clear white liquid, served warm in tiny cups, and has a moderate alcoholic content. *Sake* is usually described as a rice wine, but its method of preparation is more closely associated with the fermentation of beer. Probably because *sake* has a taste resembling sherry, it is commonly referred to as a rice wine.

In the same way that Korea lies between Japan and China, so does Korean food follow a rough compromise pattern. Of course, the repertoire of the Korean cook is far less ambitious and varied than that of his Chinese counterpart, where the range of preparations exceeds ten thousand, or even more. Contrastingly, the Japanese chef prepares bland food, whereas that of Korea is often spicy and sharp.

The single most interesting item in the Korean cuisine may well be *kim-chee*, the national pickle or relish, without which no meal is complete. The vegetable used varies according to what is available at the time of year, but regardless of what is used, *kim-chee* has a somewhat alarming, sharp (and sour) odor, although it tastes just fine. A classic dish of the country is *sin-sullo*, much like a New England boiled dinner, but with many delicious added ingredients. One fishes delicacies from a heated pot placed on the table over a small charcoal fire. The Koreans also like to broil thin slices of marinated meat at the table, a preparation called *bulgoogi*.

Far to the south is the nation of Indonesia, lying near the equator and consisting exclusively of islands. This comparatively new country includes two very famous old ones—Java and Bali. It also encompasses such less glamorous areas as Borneo, Sumatra, and the Celebes, but these are all quite unimportant gastronomically. Bali is one of the loveliest places on earth, but it is Java that concerns the gourmet, for its food is exceptionally interesting and includes a fairly wide range of worthwhile culinary items.

The heart and soul of this cuisine, as indeed of the cuisine of almost every other Asiatic country, is rice; but so interesting is the food of Java that it seems to have endless variations, much like the music of Mozart or Haydn, in which simple and basic themes are stated, and upon which countless imaginative themes are developed into full flower. Returning to rice, most people have heard of *rijsttafel*, that is, the Javanese rice table. Although the many dishes that go to make up this very original creation were Javanese, the Dutch (during their centuries of occupation and control) perfected this classic item into what amounted to a theatrical performance, at least at that time. In days gone by, the diner filled a large soup plate with an enormous portion of perfectly boiled rice, steaming, and vaguely salty to the palate. He then helped himself generously from a series of platters offered by waiters carefully arranged in line.

A typical *rijsttafel* then, and even now, might include thirty or forty different dishes, which is obviously beyond the capacity of an American housewife or amateur chef. However, many of the items served in the *rijsttafel* are not difficult to prepare, and well within the range of a home cook. These include *nasi goreng* (fried rice) and *bahmi goreng* (fried noodles); both are quite unique in taste and texture. Many of the *rijsttafel* dishes are very spicy, and it is customary to serve side dishes intended to cool the overheated taste buds, such as sliced cucumbers, bananas, and papayas. The only suitable drink to ease the torrid palate is ice cold beer. Just in passing, the somewhat outmoded American slang word for coffee is Java, which is still grown on the fertile island, and is remarkably good.

Southeast Asia, including Thailand and Malaysia, do not have extensive or truly great cuisines on their own, but they do feature a number of interesting preparations. Thus they contribute to this chapter. The food of southeastern Asia is basically built upon a solid foundation of rice, and as in Indonesia, the cuisine provides many clever and diverting variations. More often than not, it is rather spicy and hot to the taste, although not in every instance. Prepared desserts are relatively unimportant in this part of the world, but those that are served are novel. In the native cuisine, fresh fruits, grown in a tropical and humid countryside, are nothing less than superb.

In the south central part of the continent of Asia is the enigmatic nation of India, overflowing with an uncounted but obviously teeming population. Mere survival is a daily problem for millions. The people belong to many different religions and sects, including Buddhists, Parsis, Moslems, and Brahmins, all of which have their own very definite ideas, religious customs, and theories about what foods may, or may not, be eaten. Many of these ideas date back for tens of thousands of years, and show little signs of changing in the immediate future. For example, an extremist sect, the Jains, are not only strict vegetarians but do not eat any root vegetables, only consuming those which grow above the ground. One group eats beef but not pork; still another will not touch beef. However, India has a general cookery style, nonetheless, in which rice forms a basic part, plus the addition of various ingredients, employing different techniques. There is a general misconception about curried dishes, a favorite style of preparing food in this vast land, which requires some explanation.

In India the word curry, in general usage, means a group of spices, for there is no single spice called by that name. Curry varies from region to region, and in fact, from family to family, and includes such items as turmeric, coriander, cumin, pepper, and so forth. For convenience, some dealers in spices make up their own mixture, which they label as curry powder, and which is reasonably satisfactory, providing it's fresh. Curries may, but need not, be hot and burning, and there are many different categories of curried foods on the Indian culinary scene, some with considerable sauce, others quite dry, and so forth. To most non-Indians, the distinctions may appear to be quite minor. Beer is an excellent accompaniment to spicy foods of this sort. India has a general prohibition against the sale and consumption of alcoholic beverages. However, foreigners may sign a statement that they are addicted to the use of alcohol, and this permits them to purchase specified quantities of liquor; these addicts may also consume small quantities in specially enclosed Permit Rooms in their hotels, far from the sight of the local people, who might otherwise be tempted. Indians do not drink liquor or beer—instead, they will have *lassi*, a thin type of yogurt, or perhaps lemon squash.

Throughout India, clarified butter, called *ghee*, is the cooking fat preferred by the general public, assuming they can afford it. Its chief advantage is that it does not burn at comparatively high temperatures, as ordinary butter does. Because the solid particles making up a portion of ordinary butter have been removed in the heating process, the *ghee* will not readily turn an unpleasant dark shade, when used in cooking. Of course, *ghee* is not the exclusive cooking fat of the country, for mustard seed, coconut and sesame seed oils are used in other parts of the nation. The oils all have a delicate flavor, which does not mask the taste of the foods being cooked.

The islands that make up Polynesia are included in a triangle encompassing Hawaii, Tahiti, and New Zealand. Throughout this enormous area, with thousands of islands dotting the blue waters of the Pacific, the food is generally quite similar, that is, when authentic. Obviously, in an air-conditioned hotel in Honolulu, meals will be similar to those encountered in other luxury establishments catering to tourists. But the authentic food of this vast region has points of similarity, indeed repetition. On land, the coconut is used as a snack food and made into puddings; the meat is boiled, then strained, to create coconut cream, an all-purpose sauce. From the surrounding waters the Polynesians obtain fish, although surprisingly the fish are not nearly so plentiful and fishing not so reliable as one might think. Other staple foods are taro, yams, bananas, and breadfruit, which are tasty although tiresome. Only one meat is of importance in Polynesia, from the pig, the one domestic animal that manages to survive on tropical islands.

## COCONUT CREAM AND MILK southeast asia

Shake the coconut, to be sure it is full of liquid — which means it's fresh. Puncture two of the dark eyes with an ice pick or screwdriver. Drain all the liquid—it's delicious chilled, but this is not coconut milk.

Bake the coconut in a preheated 425° oven for 15 minutes. Put on a board, and immediately open by hitting sharply with a hammer. The shell will fall away from the meat. Cut into small pieces.

### Coconut Cream with Fresh Coconut

Put 2 cups prepared coconut (as above) in the bowl of an electric blender. Add 1 cup hot water and blend until a smooth purée is formed. Empty into a bowl and let stand 15 minutes, then put into a cheesecloth-lined sieve over a bowl. Press down with a spoon, to squeeze out all the liquid. If any liquid remains in the coconut, twist it firmly in the cheesecloth. You should have 1 to 1¼ cups coconut cream.

### Coconut Milk with Fresh Coconut

Use 2 cups hot water for 2 cups coconut, and proceed as directed. Makes 2 to 2½ cups. If you don't have a blender, grate the coconut by hand, and mix in the water.

### Coconut Cream with Packaged Coconut

Try to buy unsweetened packaged coconut — it can be found in health-food stores. If you can't get it, use Baker's Coconut, but rinse it under cold running water. For each cup of coconut, add 1 cup hot heavy cream in a blender. Blend until puréed, let stand 15 minutes, then squeeze in cheesecloth to extract the cream.

### Coconut Milk with Packaged Coconut

For each cup of coconut, use 2 cups hot milk, and proceed as directed.

If you don't have a blender, combine the coconut and cream or milk in a saucepan, and heat until just below the boiling point. Let stand 30 minutes before extracting the liquid.

## Ghee
## CLARIFIED BUTTER, INDIAN STYLE

INDIA

*Ghee* is used in many Indian dishes, so it's a good idea to learn how to make it. It can be kept in the refrigerator for two months, so prepare a quantity at a time. The difference between ordinary clarified butter and the Indian style is the long cooking, which gives the butter a slightly nutty flavor. Use an asbestos mat or flame tamer, if your range doesn't have a thermostatic control, because the butter will burn, if kept over more than 200° heat.

Use 1 pound of sweet (unsalted) butter, usually 4 sticks. If not in sticks, break the butter into 4 pieces. Put the butter in a heavy saucepan and place over moderate heat. Turn the butter with a spoon until melted, but be careful not to let it brown. When melted, bring the butter to a boil, which will bring the white foam to the top. Stir, and remove from the heat immediately. Return to the lowest possible heat (or use the alternative asbestos or flame tamer) and cook without stirring for 45 minutes. The milk deposits on the bottom of the pan will turn brown.

Line a sieve with several layers of moistened cheesecloth or a kitchen towel and pour the *ghee* through it into a bowl. If any solids come through, repeat the straining. Otherwise, pour it into a jar, cover tightly, and refrigerate until needed.

Makes about 1¼ cups *ghee*.

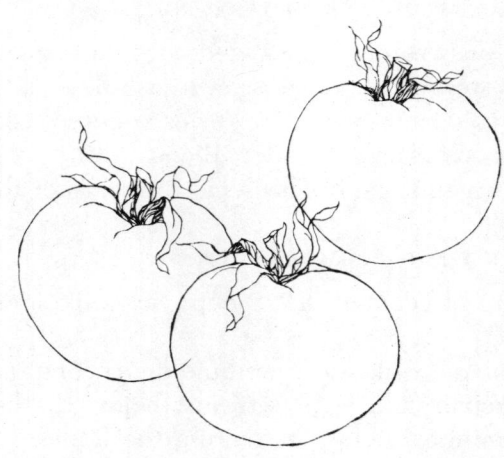

## Samosas
### MEAT STUFFED PASTRIES

INDIA

#### Filling

2 tablespoons butter
1 clove garlic, minced
½ cup minced onions
½ pound lean ground lamb
1 tomato, chopped
1 teaspoon salt
1 tablespoon Indian curry powder
⅛ teaspoon dried ground chili peppers
1 tablespoon finely chopped parsley

Melt the butter in a skillet; sauté the garlic and onions in it 5 minutes. Add the meat and cook over high heat until browned. Mix frequently. Add the tomato, salt, curry powder, chili peppers, and parsley. Cook over medium heat 5 minutes. Drain, if any liquid remains. Taste for seasoning and cool.

#### Pastry

1¾ cups flour
1 teaspoon salt
5 tablespoons melted butter
½ cup yogurt
Vegetable oil for deep-frying

Sift the flour and salt into a bowl; with the fingers, mix in the butter until mixture looks like coarse sand. Add the yogurt and knead gently until a dough is formed. Cover with a bowl and let stand 30 minutes.

Roll out the dough as thin as possible and cut into 3-inch circles. Place a heaping teaspoon of the filling on each and fold over into half-moons. Seal the edges with cold water. Heat deep oil to 375° and fry a few at a time until browned. Drain, and keep warm on a paper-towel-lined pan in a 200° oven while preparing the balance.

Makes about 30.

Note: Beef may be used in place of the lamb, if you prefer.

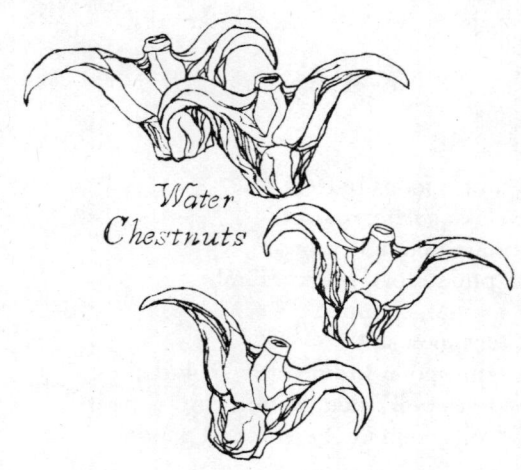

## Rumaki
### CHICKEN LIVER, WATER CHESTNUT AND BACON APPETIZER

JAPAN

>9 chicken livers
>18 water chestnuts
>6 green onions, cut into thirds, lengthwise
>8 slices bacon
>½ cup soy sauce
>½ teaspoon powdered ginger
>1 teaspoon ground cardamom seeds
>½ teaspoon ground cumin seeds

Cut the chicken livers in half and fold each piece over a water chestnut. Wrap a piece of green onion, then a strip of bacon around the liver, fastening each with a toothpick.

Marinate the *rumaki* in a mixture of the soy sauce and the spices for 1 hour. Drain and broil, turning frequently, until the bacon is browned and crisp. Replace toothpicks with cocktail picks or fresh toothpicks. Serve hot.

Makes 18 appetizers.

*Kani Sunomono*　　　　　　　　　　　　　　　　　　　　　JAPAN
## CRAB MEAT AND CUCUMBER

> ½ package *kombu* (seaweed), optional
> 3 tablespoons sesame seeds
> 2 cucumbers
> 3½ teaspoons salt
> ½ pound crab meat
> ¼ cup beef broth
> 2 tablespoons sugar
> 1 cup rice or white vinegar
> ½ teaspoon monosodium glutamate
> 2 tablespoons cornstarch
> ¼ cup water

Seaweed is available in oriental food shops. Wash the seaweed, cover with water, bring to a boil, and cook over low heat 2 hours or until seaweed is soft. Drain and cool.

Put the sesame seeds in a small skillet and place over low heat until browned. Wash the unpeeled cucumbers and slice thin. Sprinkle with 3 teaspoons salt and let stand 30 minutes. Rinse, drain, and squeeze dry. Pick over the crab meat, discarding any cartilage.

Combine the broth, sugar, vinegar, monosodium glutamate, and remaining salt in a saucepan. Bring to a boil, then stir in a paste of the cornstarch and water until thickened and clear. Cool, and stir in the sesame seeds.

Combine the crab meat, cucumbers, seaweed, and sauce. Chill. Serves 8.

## Yakitori
### SOY CHICKEN AND GIBLETS
JAPAN

½ pound chicken livers
½ pound chicken gizzards
2 whole chicken breasts
1 cup *mirin* (sweet *sake*) or medium sherry
1 cup soy sauce
1 cup chicken broth
2 tablespoons minced ginger root
3 tablespoons sugar
Freshly ground *Kona Sansho* (**Japanese pepper**) or black pepper

Wash the livers and gizzards and cut each in half. Remove the skin and bones of the chicken, and cut into 1-inch pieces.

In a saucepan mix together the wine, soy sauce, broth, ginger root, and sugar. Bring to a boil. Pour into a bowl and cool. Add the livers, gizzards, and chicken, and let stand 1 hour. Drain, reserving the marinade.

Using 16 small skewers, thread the ingredients on them alternately. Arrange on an oiled broiling pan, or place over charcoal. Broil 10 minutes, basting with the marinade, and turning several times to brown all sides. Sprinkle with the pepper, and serve accompanied by *Daikon* (pickled radish or turnip). (See recipe.)

Serves 4–8.

## Soto Ajam
### CHICKEN AND BEAN SPROUT SOUP
INDONESIA

5-pound chicken, disjointed
1 onion
2½ quarts water
1 tablespoon salt
2 teaspoons minced ginger root
3 tablespoons vegetable oil
1½ cups thinly sliced onions
2 cups bean sprouts
3 hard-cooked eggs, sliced
Sliced lime or lemon

Combine the chicken, onion, water, and salt in a saucepan. Bring to a boil, cover, and cook over low heat 1½ hours or until chicken is tender. Remove chicken; strain broth into a saucepan and add the ginger. Cut the chicken into thin strips, discarding the skin and bones.

Heat the oil in a skillet; sauté the onions until golden brown. Stir in the bean sprouts; cook over low heat 5 minutes. To serve, arrange the chicken, vegetables, and eggs in a bowl. Pour the soup into cups and place a slice of lime on top. Each person helps himself to the chicken, vegetables, and eggs.

Serves 8–10.

*Sukke Dhal*
LENTIL SOUP

INDIA

> 1½ cups lentils
> 8 cups water
> 3 tablespoons butter
> 1 cup chopped onions
> 1 clove garlic, minced
> 1½ teaspoons salt
> 2 teaspoons minced ginger
> 2 teaspoons ground coriander seeds
> ½ teaspoon turmeric
> 1 teaspoon ground cumin seeds
> 1 teaspoon lemon juice

Wash the lentils until the water runs clear. Combine in a saucepan with the water. Bring to a boil, cover loosely, and cook over low heat 1½ hours.

Melt the butter in a skillet; sauté the onions and garlic until browned. Add to the soup with the salt and spices. Cook 30 minutes, or until the lentils are tender. Purée the soup in an electric blender or force through a food mill. Stir in the lemon juice, taste for seasoning, and serve very hot.

Serves 6–8.

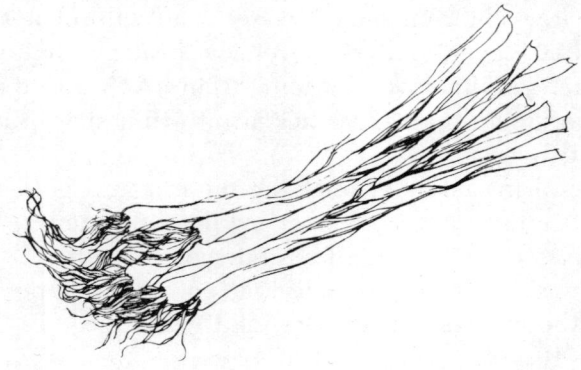

## *Miso-Taki*     JAPAN
## BEAN SOUP

    1½ cups cooked or canned lima beans or chick peas
    2 tablespoons vinegar
    2 tablespoons beer
    2 tablespoons soy sauce
    1 tablespoon peanut or vegetable oil
    ½ cup chopped onions
    6 cups beef broth
    ½ pound pork, cut julienne
    1 teaspoon salt
    ¼ teaspoon freshly ground pepper
    ½ pound medium egg noodles, cooked and drained
    2 tablespoons grated ginger root
    ½ cup diced cooked shrimp

Purée the beans in a blender or force through a sieve. Mix with the vinegar, beer, and soy sauce. Let stand 1 hour.

Heat the oil in a saucepan, add the onion, and cook 2 minutes. Stir in the bean mixture, broth, pork, salt, and pepper. Cook over low heat 15 minutes. Add the noodles, ginger root, and shrimp; cook 3 minutes.

Serves 4–6.

## THE ORIENT

*Umani*  JAPAN
### CHICKEN PATTY-VEGETABLE SOUP

> 2 pounds chicken necks and backs
> 3 quarts water
> 1½ tablespoons minced ginger root
> 4 green onions, sliced
> 2 dried mushrooms
> 1 whole raw chicken breast
> 2 tablespoons minced green onions
> 1 egg
> ½ teaspoon salt
> 2 teaspoons soy sauce
> ½ teaspoon sugar
> ½ teaspoon monosodium glutamate
> ½ cup fresh or thawed frozen green peas
> 2 bamboo shoots, cut into ½-inch cubes
> Narrow strips of lemon rind

Wash the chicken necks and backs and put in a saucepan with the water, ginger root, and sliced green onions. Bring to a boil and cook over medium heat 1½ hours. Strain into a clean saucepan.

Wash the mushrooms and soak in hot water 30 minutes. Drain and chop very fine. Discard the skin and bones of the chicken breast and chop the meat very fine. Mix the chicken meat with the mushrooms, minced green onions, egg, salt, soy sauce, sugar, and monosodium glutamate. Form the mixture into 8 flat patties. Put in a skillet with ½ cup of the soup stock. Cover and cook over low heat 15 minutes.

Bring the remaining soup to a boil; add the peas and bamboo shoots. Cook 5 minutes. Put the chicken patties into individual soup bowls, and pour the soup over them. Garnish with a lemon strip.
Serves 8.

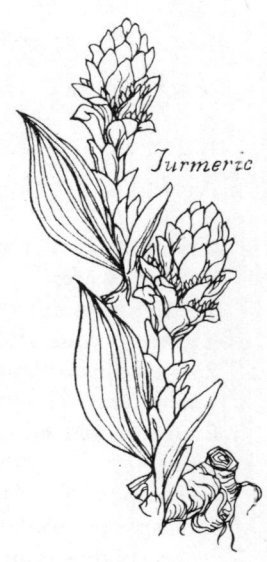

*Murghi Shoorva*
## CHICKEN MULLIGATUNNY

INDIA

    4-pound pullet, disjointed
    2 quarts water
    6 peppercorns
    1 tablespoon salt
    1 teaspoon turmeric
    2 teaspoons minced ginger root
    2 teaspoons ground coriander seeds
    2 teaspoons lemon juice
    1 tablespoon *ghee*
    ½ cup thinly sliced onions
    ¼ teaspoon dried ground chili peppers

Wash the chicken and combine in a saucepan with the water, peppercorns, and salt. Bring to a boil, cover loosely, and cook over low heat 1½ hours, or until tender. Remove the chicken and shred the meat, discarding the skin. Skim the fat from the soup, and return the shredded chicken.

Pound together to a paste the turmeric, ginger, coriander, and lemon juice. Melt the *ghee* in a skillet; sauté the onions and chili peppers over very low heat for 10 minutes without browning. Stir the spices into the onions and cook 5 minutes. Add to the soup and cook 10 minutes. Taste for seasoning.

Serves 6–8.

## Uwo Dango No Shiru
## FISH-BALL SOUP

JAPAN

    1 pound fillet of sole
    ½ pound shrimp, shelled and deveined
    3 green onions
    1 teaspoon salt
    ⅛ teaspoon pepper
    ½ teaspoon powdered ginger
    1 teaspoon cornstarch
    2 tablespoons oil
    { 7 cups water
      3-inch square *kombu* (dried kelp)
      1 cup *kotsuobushi* (dried bonito), chopped
          or
    { 3 cups beef broth
      3 cups clam juice
    1 teaspoon soy sauce
    2 teaspoons *sake* or dry sherry
    ½ pound spinach, shredded, or ½ package frozen, chopped, thawed

Pick out any bones of the sole, wash and dry it.

Grind together the sole, shrimp, and green onions; blend in the salt, pepper, ginger, cornstarch, and oil. Shape into walnut-sized balls.

Bring the water to a boil. Wash the *kombu* under cold running water, add it to the boiling water, bring it to a boil again, and remove. Flake the *kotsuobushi* and add it to the water, stirring steadily. Bring to a boil, and let stand 5 minutes, then strain through a cloth, or double layer of cheesecloth. If you don't want to make this broth, use the beef broth and clam juice. Add the soy sauce and sake to either broth, and bring it to a boil. Drop the fish balls into it. Cook over medium heat 10 minutes. Add the spinach, and cook 3 minutes longer.

Serves 6–8.

POLYNESIA

## FISH-SHRIMP CHOWDER

*Saffron*

2 pounds fillet of sole or sea bass
¼ cup vegetable oil
2 cloves garlic, minced
½ cup minced onions
1½ quarts water
2 cups bottled clam juice
2 teaspoons grated orange rind
1 bay leaf
½ teaspoon dried ground chili peppers
¼ teaspoon anise
¼ teaspoon saffron
1 pound raw shrimp, shelled, deveined, and cut in half
2 tablespoons cornstarch
2 tablespoons soy sauce
3 tablespoons dry sherry
1 16-ounce can crushed pineapple, drained

Remove the skin and bones of the fish and cut the fish into bite-size pieces. Heat the oil in a saucepan; sauté the garlic and onions 10 minutes. Add the water, clam juice, orange rind, bay leaf, chili peppers, anise, and saffron. Bring to a boil and cook 10 minutes. Add the fish; cook over medium heat 10 minutes. Add the shrimp, cover, and cook over low heat 5 minutes. Mix the cornstarch with the soy sauce and sherry until smooth, and stir into the soup until thickened. Add the pineapple and cook 5 minutes longer. Taste for seasoning, and discard the bay leaf. Serve with rice, if desired.

Serves 8–10.

*Telur Masak*  INDONESIA
## EGGS WITH SPICY SAUCE

    8 eggs
    ½ cup minced shallots or onions
    2 cloves garlic, minced
    ½ teaspoon dried ground chili peppers
    1 teaspoon shrimp or anchovy paste
    ½ teaspoon sugar
    1 teaspoon salt
    2 teaspoons grated lemon rind
    1 cup peanut or vegetable oil
    1 tablespoon soy sauce
    2 tablespoons lime or lemon juice
    1 cup Coconut Milk (see recipe)
    Cooked rice (optional)

With a pin, carefully puncture the pointed end of the eggs. Put the eggs in a saucepan of cold water, bring to a boil over low heat, then cook 15 minutes. Drain, cover with cold water, and when cool enough to handle, remove the shells. Dry the eggs.

Run in a blender, or pound or chop to a paste, the shallots, garlic, chili peppers, fish paste, sugar, salt, and lemon rind.

In a small deep saucepan, heat the oil until it boils; put 2 eggs in at a time, and fry them until browned. Drain, reserving a tablespoon of the oil.

Place the 2 tablespoons of the oil in a skillet; sauté the spice mixture 3 minutes, stirring frequently. Add the soy sauce, lime juice, and coconut milk; cook 5 minutes. Taste for seasoning.

The eggs may be served on a bed of rice, with the sauce poured over all, or you may merely serve the eggs with the sauce over them.

Serves 4.

## Briani Machchi
## MARINATED FISH AND RICE

INDIA

> 2 cups yogurt
> 1 cup finely chopped onions
> 2 cloves garlic, minced
> ⅛ teaspoon ground cloves
> 2 teaspoons turmeric
> 2 teaspoons salt
> ½ teaspoon ground cardamom
> 2 teaspoons ground coriander
> ½ teaspoon ground anise
> 4 fillets of sole
> ½ cup melted butter
> 3 cups half-cooked and drained rice
> 2 tomatoes, peeled and thinly sliced
> 1 tablespoon minced coriander leaves
>   (cilantro, Chinese parsley)

In a bowl, combine the yogurt, onions, garlic, and spices. Wash and dry the fish, and cut each fillet in half crosswise. Place in the yogurt mixture, and turn to coat. Cover, and let stand 1 hour. Remove the fish and reserve the marinade.

Heat 2 tablespoons of the butter in a casserole; lightly brown the drained fish in it. Add half the marinade and 2 tablespoons of the remaining butter. Cover with the rice. Arrange the sliced tomatoes over it and add the remaining marinade and melted butter. Cover tightly and bake in a 350° oven 30 minutes. Shake the casserole occasionally. Sprinkle with the coriander leaves.

Serves 4–6.

## Tali Machchi
### FRIED SPICED FISH

INDIA

> 6 fillets of sole
> 2 teaspoons salt
> ½ teaspoon dried ground chili peppers
> 2 teaspoons minced ginger root
> 2 cloves garlic, minced
> ½ teaspoon turmeric
> 2 teaspoons ground coriander seeds
> ½ teaspoon ground cumin seeds
> 2 tablespoons lemon juice
> 4 tablespoons *ghee*
> 2 tablespoons minced coriander leaves
>    (cilantro, Chinese parsley)

Wash and dry the fish. Cut each fillet into halves crosswise, and then into thirds, lengthwise. Put the fish in a bowl. Mix together the salt, spices, and lemon juice. Add to the fish, tossing well to coat the pieces. Cover and let stand 30 minutes.

Melt the *ghee* in a skillet; add the fish and cook, stirring frequently, for 10 minutes. Heap in a serving dish, and sprinkle with the coriander leaves.

Serves 6–8.

## Sambal Oedang
INDONESIA
### SHRIMP IN SPICED COCONUT SAUCE

> 2 pounds raw shrimp, shelled and deveined
> 1 cup chopped onions
> 3 cloves garlic, minced
> 2 teaspoons salt
> ¾ teaspoon dried ground chili peppers
> 2 tablespoons lemon juice
> 1 tablespoon grated lemon rind
> 2 teaspoons brown sugar
> 2 teaspoons minced ginger root
> ¼ cup vegetable oil
> 2 cups Coconut Milk (see recipe)

Wash the shrimp, and chop coarsely.

Pound or chop to a paste the onions, garlic, salt, chili peppers, lemon juice, rind, brown sugar, and ginger. Heat the oil in a skillet; sauté the mixture 3 minutes, stirring frequently. Add the shrimp; cook over low heat, stirring steadily for 3 minutes. Blend in the coconut milk. Cook over low heat 10 minutes. Taste for seasoning. Serve with *Bahmi Goreng* or *Nasi Goreng* (see recipes), or serve as a first course.

Serves 8, as a first course.


## Tempura
JAPAN
### BATTER-FRIED SEAFOOD AND VEGETABLES

Any combinations of raw foods may be used, but here are a few typical suggestions:

> 18 shrimp
> 2 fillets of flounder
> 6 scallops
> 1 lobster tail
> 1 small eggplant
> 1 green pepper
> 18 string beans

# THE ORIENT

Remove the shells from the shrimp, but leave the tail. Slit, and discard vein. Cut across underside to straighten shrimp. Cut flounder in 3-inch pieces. Cut scallops in slices. Remove meat of lobster and cut in bite-size pieces. Lightly peel the eggplant, then cut in quarters lengthwise, and then into ¼-inch slices. Cut green pepper into squares. Leave the string beans whole. Dry all the ingredients carefully, for no moisture should remain.

### TEMPURA BATTER

2½ cups sifted flour
¼ teaspoon baking soda
3 egg yolks
2 cups ice water
1 quart vegetable oil

Sift the flour 3 times. Beat the baking soda, egg yolks, and water together. Gradually add the flour, stirring lightly from the bottom with chopsticks or a wooden spoon. Don't overstir—flour should be visible on top, but the batter should be fairly thin; if necessary, add a little more water.

Heat the oil to 375°—a constant temperature is important for good tempura. Hold one shrimp at a time by the tail and dip in the batter; drop into the oil and fry until lightly browned. Don't fry more than 6 pieces of food at a time. Dip the other ingredients into batter on a spoon and gently drop into the oil. Serve the foods as soon as cooked, with the *tempura* sauce or coarse salt.

### TEMPURA SAUCE

¾ cup clam juice
¼ cup soy sauce
¼ cup *sake* (Japanese liquor) or dry sherry
½ teaspoon sugar
3 teaspoons sugar
3 tablespoons grated white radish
1 teaspoon powdered ginger

Mix together the clam juice, soy sauce, *sake*, and sugar. Divide among 6 small bowls. Just before serving place a little radish and ginger in each bowl.

Serves 6.

## Machchi Pilau
### CURRIED SHRIMP AND RICE

INDIA

> 2 cups long-grain rice
> ¼ pound (1 stick) butter
> ½ teaspoon saffron
> 4 cups boiling water
> 3 teaspoons salt
> 2 cups finely chopped onions
> ½ teaspoon freshly ground black pepper
> 1 cup yogurt
> 2 pounds raw shrimp, shelled and deveined
> 1 cup ground blanched almonds
> 2 teaspoons ground coriander seeds
> ½ teaspoon cinnamon

Put the rice in a colander and wash it under cold running water until the water runs clear. Drain well.

Melt half the butter in a heavy saucepan; add the rice, and cook, stirring frequently, until rice turns yellow. Dissolve the saffron in a little of the boiling water, and add to the rice with all the water, stirring with a fork. Stir in 2 teaspoons of the salt, cover, and cook over very low heat 25 minutes. Prepare the shrimp while the rice is cooking.

Toss together the onions, pepper, yogurt, shrimp, and remaining salt. Melt the remaining butter in a skillet; add the shrimp mixture and cook over high heat 2 minutes. Stir in the almonds and coriander. Cover and cook 3 minutes. Taste for seasoning.

Heap the rice in a heated serving dish, and pour the shrimp mixture over it. Sprinkle with the cinnamon.

Serves 6–8.

THE ORIENT 81

## FISH CROQUETTES IN COCONUT CREAM

POLYNESIA

¼ teaspoon dried ground chili peppers
2 large onions
2 pounds fillet of sole
3 cloves garlic, minced
1 teaspoon minced ginger root
2 tablespoons lemon juice
1 tablespoon cornstarch
2 teaspoons salt
1 cup vegetable oil
1 cup Coconut Cream (see recipe)

Soak the chili peppers in warm water for 5 minutes; drain. Grind or chop together until fine 1 onion, the fish, garlic, and ginger. Blend in the lemon juice, cornstarch, and salt. Shape into small croquettes. Slice the remaining onion.

Heat the oil in a skillet; sauté the sliced onion until browned. Remove onion with a slotted spoon and reserve. To the hot oil, add the croquettes in a single layer; fry until browned on both sides. Drain and keep hot. Pour off all but 1 tablespoon oil; blend the coconut cream into the pan. Bring to a boil and return the croquettes. Cook over low heat 10 minutes. Serve garnished with the browned onions.

Serves 6–8.

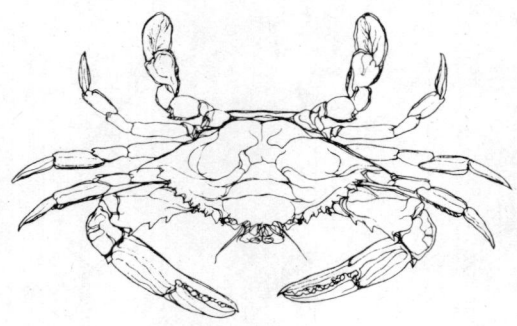

## *Kani Agemono*     JAPAN
## FRIED SOFT-SHELL CRABS

    6 soft-shell crabs
    Salt
    Flour
    3 eggs, beaten
    Fine dry bread crumbs
    Oil for deep-frying

Have the crabs cleaned; wash and dry them. Sprinkle the crabs with salt and let stand 10 minutes, then dip in the flour, in the eggs, and finally in the bread crumbs.

Use ⅔ sesame oil and ⅓ vegetable oil, if possible. If sesame oil is not available, use all peanut oil. Heat the oil to 360° and fry 2 crabs at a time until browned. Drain and serve with Tempura Sauce, as a dip.

### TEMPURA SAUCE

    ¾ cup *dashi* (fish-seaweed stock) or clam juice
    ¼ cup soy sauce
    ¼ cup rice wine or dry sherry
    3 tablespoons grated horseradish or white radish

*Dashi* is available in oriental food shops. If you can't get it, bottled clam juice is an adequate substitute. Combine the *dashi*, or clam juice, soy sauce, and wine. Bring to a boil and cool. Serve in small bowls with a little horseradish in the center of each.

Serves 8.

## Murghi Tandoori
INDIA
### SPICED MARINATED CHICKEN

Start the preparation of the chicken the day before you want to serve it. In India, the chicken is cooked in a special clay oven sunk in the ground, and heated from the bottom with charcoal or wood. A reasonably good method is to roast it on a spit or in a pan.

> 2 2-pound whole broilers
> 2 teaspoons salt
> ¼ cup lime or lemon juice
> 1 tablespoon minced garlic
> 2 tablespoons chopped ginger root
> 2 tablespoons ground coriander seed
> ¼ teaspoon cayenne pepper
> ½ teaspoon red food coloring
> 2 cups yogurt
> 3 tablespoons vegetable oil

Remove and discard the skin of the chickens. Prick the chickens all over and rub with the salt and lime juice. Let stand 30 minutes.

Combine the garlic, spices, food coloring, and ½ cup of the yogurt in an electric blender bowl and blend for a few seconds; then mix with all the yogurt. Or pound together the garlic and spices, then blend in the coloring and yogurt.

Make parallel shallow gashes on the chickens every inch or so, then brush the chickens inside and out with the yogurt mixture. Place in a bowl, cover, and refrigerate overnight.

When ready to cook, put the chickens on a spit or in a shallow roasting pan. Brush with the oil. If cooked on a spit, cook 1 hour, or until tender. If in the pan, roast in a preheated 450° oven 1 hour, or until tender, turning the chickens to brown all sides. Split or quarter the chickens, and serve with lime quarters and chopped onion.

Serves 4.

84    THE ORIENT

*Murghi Dal*                                                INDIA
CHICKEN AND CHICK-PEA CURRY

>3-pound fryer, disjointed
>1½ teaspoons salt
>6 tablespoons *ghee*
>2 tablespoons minced ginger root
>2 cups chopped onions
>2 cups cooked or canned chick-peas
>1 teaspoon ground cumin seed
>1 tablespoon ground coriander seed
>¾ teaspoon freshly ground black pepper
>1½ cups chicken broth

Wash and dry the chicken; rub with the salt. Melt the *ghee* in a deep skillet or casserole; brown the chicken, ginger, and onions in it. Add the chick-peas, cumin, coriander, and pepper; cover, and cook over low heat 10 minutes, shaking the pan frequently. Stir in half the broth; cover, and cook 20 minutes. Add the remaining broth and cook 15 minutes longer. The dish should have very little gravy. Taste for seasoning.
Serves 4.


*Saté Ajam*                                              INDONESIA
CHICKEN ON SKEWERS WITH
PEANUT SAUCE

>2 whole raw chicken breasts
>½ cup ground peanuts
>½ cup chopped onions
>2 cloves garlic, minced
>1½ teaspoons salt
>¼ cup lime or lemon juice

Remove the skin and bones of the chicken breasts. Cut the meat into about 1-inch squares. Run in an electric blender, or pound or chop to a paste the peanuts, onions, garlic, and salt. Mix in the lime juice. Toss the chicken pieces with the mixture and let stand 1 hour. Thread the chicken on 8 skewers. Arrange the skewers on an oiled broiling pan and broil 10 minutes, or until tender, turning the skewers frequently. Serve with the following sauce:

> 3 tablespoons vegetable oil
> 1½ cups thinly sliced onions
> 2 cloves garlic, minced
> ½ teaspoon dried ground chili peppers
> 1 cup blanched ground peanuts or ¾ cup peanut butter
> 1 teaspoon salt
> 2 tablespoons soy sauce
> 1 cup water
> 2 tablespoons lime or lemon juice

Heat 2 tablespoons oil in a skillet; sauté 1 cup of the onions until browned and crisp. Remove. Run in an electric blender, or pound or chop to a paste the garlic, chili peppers, peanuts, salt, and remaining onions. Heat the remaining oil in the skillet; cook the mixture in it 3 minutes, stirring frequently. Blend in the soy sauce, water, and lime juice. Cook over low heat 5 minutes. Taste for seasoning—it should be spicy. Pour into a bowl and sprinkle reserved onions on top. Serve as a sauce with the chicken skewers.
Serves 8.
Note: Beef or pork can be substituted. If pork is used, broil until no pink remains, about 15 minutes.

## Renden Santan
## COCONUT-GINGER CHICKEN

INDONESIA

½ cup grated coconut
2 tablespoons butter
1 teaspoon sugar
1 teaspoon salt
1 tablespoon ground coriander
1 teaspoon ground anise
2 cloves garlic, minced
2 tablespoons grated lemon rind
½ teaspoon saffron
2 tablespoons grated ginger root
½ teaspoon dried ground chili peppers
3 tablespoons lemon juice
2 tablespoons plum jam
2 cups coarsely chopped onions
3 whole chicken breasts
1½ cups Coconut Milk (see recipe)

If possible use fresh coconut. If dried coconut is used, and it is the sweetened type, rinse it under cold water, drain, and dry on paper towels. Melt the butter in a saucepan; add the coconut, and cook, stirring constantly, until brown. In a bowl, mix together the sugar, salt, coriander, anise, garlic, lemon rind, saffron, ginger, chili pepper, lemon juice, plum jam, and browned coconut. Add the onions.

Remove the skin and bone of the chicken, and cut the meat into small pieces. In a saucepan, put the chicken with the spice mixture and coconut milk. Cook over high heat, stirring to the boiling point. Reduce heat to low and cook 10 minutes, or until chicken is tender. Serve with boiled noodles or rice.

Serves 4–6.

## *Por Ajam*
## CHICKEN IN COCONUT CREAM

INDONESIA

    3 whole raw chicken breasts
    ¾ teaspoon dried ground chili peppers
    1½ teaspoons salt
    3 cloves garlic, minced
    ½ cup minced shallots or onions
    ½ teaspoon shrimp or anchovy paste
    5 tablespoons peanut or vegetable oil
    1½ cups diced fresh or canned pineapple
    2 tablespoons lime or lemon juice
    2 teaspoons grated lime or lemon rind
    2 cups Coconut Cream (see recipe)
    2 teaspoons soy sauce
    1 cup sliced green onions
    ½ cup dry-roasted peanuts

Remove the skin and bones of the chicken, and cut the meat into cubes. Run in a blender, or pound or chop to a paste the chili peppers, salt, garlic, shallots, and fish paste. Toss with the chicken cubes and let stand 1 hour.

Heat 3 tablespoons of the oil in a wok or large skillet; sauté the chicken and pineapple until lightly browned. Add the lime juice, rind, coconut cream, and soy sauce. Cook over low heat 20 minutes, or until chicken is tender. Taste for seasoning.

Heat the remaining oil in a skillet; sauté the green onions 3 minutes. Heap the chicken mixture in a heated serving dish, and sprinkle with the sautéed green onions and the peanuts.

Serves 6–8.

## Sin-Sullo
## KOREAN FIRE POT

KOREA

Advance preparation is required for this dish, with final assembly at the table. A fire pot is used, although a chafing dish or deep electric skillet are possibilities. (See Chabu-Chabu.)

### Egg Mixture

4 eggs
1 tablespoon water
¼ cup slivered smoked cooked ham
2 tablespoons sesame or vegetable oil

Beat together the eggs and water; mix in the ham. Heat a little of the oil in a 7-inch skillet and pour in enough of the egg mixture to thinly coat the bottom. Cook until delicately browned on both sides, then turn out, roll up, and cut into thin strips. Set them aside. Continue making the remaining egg mixture.

### Meat Balls

¾ pound ground beef
3 tablespoons soy sauce
2 tablespoons minced garlic
3 tablespoons minced green onions
3 tablespoons ground sesame seeds
¼ teaspoon freshly ground black pepper
5 tablespoons sesame or vegetable oil
¼ cup cornstarch
2 eggs, beaten

Mix together the meat, soy sauce, garlic, green onions, sesame seeds, pepper, and 2 tablespoons of the oil. Shape into ½-inch balls; roll in the cornstarch, then dip in the eggs. Heat the remaining oil in a skillet and fry the meat balls until brown, shaking the pan frequently. Drain and reserve.

### Pork Strips

¾ pound boneless pork
3 tablespoons cornstarch
½ teaspoon salt

⅛ teaspoon freshly ground black pepper
1 egg, beaten
3 tablespoons sesame or vegetable oil

Have the pork cut very thin, and pound it even thinner. Cut the pork into matchlike strips. Mix together the cornstarch, salt, and pepper; toss the meat in the mixture, then dip in the egg. Heat the oil in a skillet, and cook the pork in it until browned and cooked through, about 5 minutes. Drain and reserve.

### Beef

½ pound fillet of beef
2 tablespoons soy sauce
⅛ teaspoon freshly ground black pepper
2 teaspoons minced garlic
2 teaspoons ground sesame seeds
2 tablespoons minced green onions
1 tablespoon sesame or vegetable oil

Have the meat cut into paper thin slices, then into matchlike strips. Mix the remaining ingredients together, and marinate the meat in the mixture for 30 minutes.

### Vegetables

6 dried Chinese mushrooms
1 pound onions
10 bamboo shoots
2 bunches watercress
3 carrots
2 cups walnuts
4 cups beef broth

Wash the mushrooms, cover with water, and let soak 10 minutes. Drain and cut into slivers. Peel and thinly slice the onions. Cut the bamboo shoots into strips. Wash and remove the stems of the watercress. Cut the carrots into strips. Blanch the walnuts. Bring the broth to a boil.

To ASSEMBLE: Heat the selected utensil. Spread the marinated beef on the bottom of the dish, greasing it lightly. Make layers of the various ingredients (except the beef broth). When the ingredients begin to sizzle, quickly add the beef broth, and cook for 10 minutes from the time the broth is added. Supply each person with chopsticks or a long fork. Each person helps himself. Serves 6–8.

## *Chabu-Chabu*                     JAPAN
### STEAMED BEEF AND VEGETABLES

1½ pounds fillet of beef
12 green onions
12 mushroom caps
2 bunches watercress
½ pound fresh spinach
4 cups boiling beef broth
1 cup soy sauce
3 tablespoons vinegar
¼ teaspoon Tabasco
3 tablespoons grated ginger root
Salt
Freshly ground black pepper
½ pound *udon* (wheat noodles) or #2 spaghetti, cooked and drained

Chabu-Chabu must be cooked at the table, for each person cooks his own food. Use a fondue cooker, electric fryer, or a chafing dish. The traditional Japanese firepot is a pan with a funnel-like hole in the middle.

Have the beef cut paper thin, or if you do it yourself, freeze the meat for about 45 minutes to facilitate slicing. Arrange the meat in an overlapping design on a large platter. Wash and clean the green onions, and arrange them in a bunch on the platter. Trim, wash, and dry the mushrooms and watercress and arrange them on the platter. Wash the spinach, discarding the stems; drain and dry. Heap it in a bowl.

Put the boiling beef broth in the selected utensil, and turn heating unit on, to keep it boiling. Mix together the soy sauce, vinegar, Tabasco, and ginger root. Divide it among six small dishes. Arrange small dishes of salt and pepper. Put the noodles on a serving dish.

Provide each person with chopsticks, or long-handled fondue forks, and a plate. Each person picks up a piece of meat, and dips it into the broth, twirling it around until the meat turns light. It should not be cooked more than about 30 seconds, that is, if the meat is paper thin. The meat is then dipped into the sauce, or the salt and pepper, and eaten. The vegetables are cooked in the same manner. When all the meat and vegetables are eaten, the noodles are put in the broth, and then eaten, with or without the broth.

Serves 6.

## *Opar Daging*      INDONESIA
## STEAK IN COCONUT CREAM

> 2 pounds sirloin steak, cut ½ inch thick
> 1 teaspoon ground cumin
> ½ teaspoon dried ground chili peppers
> 1 teaspoon ground coriander
> 4 tablespoons peanut or vegetable oil
> 2 cloves garlic, minced
> 1½ cups chopped onions
> 1 teaspoon salt
> ½ cup Coconut Cream (see recipe)

Cut the steak into 1-inch by 2-inch strips. Toss with the cumin, chili peppers, and coriander. Heat half the oil in a skillet; brown the garlic and onions in it. Remove. Heat the remaining oil in the skillet; brown the steak in it. Return the onions. Add the salt and cream; cook over low heat 10 minutes.

Serves 4–6.

## SUKIYAKI — JAPAN

> 2 pounds fillet or sirloin steak
> Piece of beef fat
> ½ cup beef broth
> ¾ cup soy sauce
> ¼ cup sugar
> ¼ cup *sake* or dry sherry
> 2 cups thinly sliced onions
> 1 cup sliced celery
> 2 *Tofu* cakes (bean curd) cut into 1-inch cubes
> 1 cup sliced bamboo shoots
> ½ pound mushrooms, sliced thin
> 1 cup shredded spinach
> 4 green onions, cut into 2-inch pieces
> 1 8-ounce can *shiritaki* (noodle threads) heated and drained, or ½ pound vermicelli, cooked and drained
> Raw eggs (optional)

Have the fillet cut paper thin against the grain. If sirloin is used, cut paper thin, and then into 3-by-2-inch pieces. (If you do it yourself, partially freeze the meat to facilitate cutting.) Ask the butcher for a piece of beef fat—if he doesn't have it, use the fat trimmed from the meat. Combine the broth, soy sauce, sugar, and sherry in a bowl.

If you want to prepare the dish at the table, use an electric skillet or the skillet pan of a chafing dish set over a burner. Arrange each ingredient on a platter in rows in an attractive design. You may also prepare *sukiyaki* in a wok or skillet over the burners on your range. Heat the selected pan (electric skillet to 425°), and holding the beef fat with chopsticks or a fork, rub it over the bottom and sides until it melts slightly, and the fat in the pan bubbles.

Add the meat and brown on all sides. Add half the soy mixture to the meat. Push the meat to one side of the skillet. Add the onions and celery; cook over low heat for 3 minutes. Add the *tofu*, bamboo shoots, mushrooms, spinach, and remaining soy sauce mixture. Cook over low heat 3 minutes. Add the green onions and *shiritaki* and cook for 1 minute. Don't overcook.

In Japan, each person is given a small bowl with a raw egg in it. It is customary for him to beat the egg lightly, and dip the cooked sukiyaki into it before eating. It helps to cool the food and also adds a little different flavor. If you don't like it, it's not necessary.

Serves 4–6.

## Tariyaki
POLYNESIA
### SKEWERED STEAK, HAWAIIAN STYLE

2 pounds sirloin steak, cut ½ inch thick
1 16-ounce can pineapple chunks
1 cup soy sauce
⅓ cup dry sherry
1½ teaspoons minced ginger root
4 tablespoons brown sugar
2 teaspoons grated onion
1 clove garlic, minced
18 mushroom caps
1 tablespoon cornstarch

Cut the steak into 1-inch squares. Drain the pineapple and reserve 3 tablespoons of the juice. Mix together the soy sauce, sherry, ginger, brown sugar, onion, and garlic. Marinate the steak in the mixture for 3 hours at room temperature. Drain, reserving the marinade. Thread the steak, pineapple, and mushrooms on 6 skewers, starting and ending with the steak. Broil 4 minutes, or to desired degree of rareness, turning the skewers to brown all sides.

Mix together the cornstarch, marinade, and the reserved pineapple juice. Cook over low heat stirring steadily until thickened. Serve as a sauce with the skewered meat.

Serves 6.

## Bul-googi
KOREA
### BROILED MARINATED BEEF

    3 pounds fillet of beef
    ⅓ cup sesame or vegetable oil
    4 tablespoons sugar
    ½ cup sesame seeds
    ¾ cup soy sauce
    ½ teaspoon freshly ground black pepper
    ½ cup chopped green onions
    2 cloves garlic, minced
    2 tablespoons flour

Cut the meat in paper-thin slices. Mix with the oil and sugar. Let stand 10 minutes.

Put the sesame seeds in a skillet and cook, stirring frequently, until lightly browned. Add to the meat with the soy sauce, pepper, onions, garlic, and flour. Mix well and let marinate 30 minutes; mix a few times.

The meat can be broiled over a charcoal fire, in a very hot broiler, or sautéed in a little oil. Broil or sauté until browned on both sides and serve hot. Serve with spiced dill pickles.

Serves 8.


## Keema Korma
INDIA
### GROUND MEAT CURRY, BENGAL STYLE

    2 pounds ground beef
    2 cups yogurt
    2 teaspoons ground cumin seed
    ½ teaspoon ground cardamom
    ⅛ teaspoon ground cloves
    2 teaspoons ground coriander seed
    ¾ teaspoon freshly ground black pepper
    ½ teaspoon cinnamon
    1½ teaspoons salt
    2½ cups minced onions
    2 cloves garlic, minced
    4 tablespoons butter

Combine the meat, yogurt, spices, salt, onions, and garlic. Mix thoroughly and cover. Let stand in the refrigerator 3 hours.

Melt the butter in a heavy deep skillet. Add the meat mixture and stir well. Cover, and cook over very low heat 1 hour, stirring frequently. Taste for seasoning. Serve with rice.

Serves 6–8.

*Kaeng Phed*　　　　　　　　　　　　　　　　　　　THAILAND
SIAMESE MEAT CURRY

> ¾ teaspoon dried ground chili peppers
> ½ teaspoon freshly ground black pepper
> 1 teaspoon ground caraway seeds
> 1 teaspoon ground coriander
> 1 teaspoon salt
> ¼ cup finely shredded cabbage
> 2 tablespoons minced shallots or onions
> 2 cloves garlic, minced
> 2 teaspoons grated lemon rind
> ¼ teaspoon basil
> 3 pounds top sirloin, cut ¼ inch thick
> 4 cups Coconut Cream (see recipe)
> 2 teaspoons shrimp or anchovy paste

Pound or chop together the chili peppers, black pepper, caraway seeds, coriander, salt, cabbage, shallots, garlic, lemon rind, and basil. Cut the meat in 1-inch by 4-inch strips.

Bring half the coconut cream to a boil; add the meat, cover, and cook over low heat 20 minutes. Stir in the spice mixture, shrimp paste, and remaining coconut cream. Cook 15 minutes longer. Serve with rice or noodles.

Serves 8–10.

## Dondeng
### SPICED STEAK STRIPS

INDONESIA

3 pounds sirloin steak, cut ½ inch thick
2 cups chopped onions
4 cloves garlic, minced
⅓ cup coarsely chopped almonds
½ teaspoon dried ground chili peppers
2 tablespoons grated lemon rind
2 tablespoons minced ginger root
¼ pound (1 stick) butter
1 teaspoon sugar
2 teaspoons salt
4 tablespoons lemon juice
3 tablespoons plum jam
2 cups boiling water
4 cups cooked rice

Cut the steak into strips 2 inches long and 1 inch wide.

Mix together the onions, garlic, almonds, chili peppers, lemon rind, and ginger. Roll the steak strips lightly in the mixture.

Melt the butter in a skillet and cook the strips over high heat 5 minutes, stirring constantly. Mix together the sugar, salt, lemon juice, plum jam, and water and add to the meat. Cook over low heat 15 minutes, or until meat is tender, stirring occasionally. Taste for seasoning. Heap the rice in a heated serving dish, and pour the steak and gravy over it.

Serves 6–8.

## Raan
INDIA
### MARINATED LEG OF LAMB

Begin the preparation of the lamb 48 hours before you want to serve it.

> 5-pound leg of lamb
> ¼ cup lemon juice
> 4 large cloves garlic, peeled and sliced
> 1 tablespoon salt
> ½ teaspoon freshly ground black pepper
> 1 teaspoon cumin seeds
> 1 teaspoon coriander seeds
> 4 cloves
> 1 teaspoon turmeric
> ½ teaspoon dried ground chili peppers
> 1 cup yogurt
> ¾ cup blanched almonds
> ½ cup currants or seedless raisins
> 2 tablespoons dark brown sugar
> 1 cup boiling water

Have the fell removed from the lamb. Cut deep slits all over the lamb, about 1 inch apart.

In a blender bowl, combine the lemon juice, garlic, salt, and spices. Blend until all the spices are pulverized. Rub the mixture over the lamb, pressing it into the slits. Put the lamb in a roasting pan or casserole.

In the blender bowl, combine the yogurt, almonds, and raisins. Blend until smooth, then spread over the leg of lamb. Sprinkle with brown sugar, cover tightly, and refrigerate for 48 hours.

When ready to cook, pour the boiling water into the pan. Bring to a boil over direct high heat, then cover tightly and bake in a preheated 350° oven 2 hours, or until the lamb is tender.

Let the lamb stand uncovered at room temperature until cool. Carve the lamb, and serve with the sauce.

Serves 6–8.

## Saté Kambing
## MARINATED LAMB CUBES

INDONESIA

3 pounds boneless lamb, cut into ½-inch cubes
1 cup cider vinegar
½ cup minced onions
2 cloves garlic, minced
2 teaspoons salt
½ teaspoon dried ground chili peppers
2 teaspoons ground coriander
1 teaspoon ground cumin
½ teaspoon turmeric
1 teaspoon powdered ginger
4 tablespoons peanut or vegetable oil
½ cup water

Marinate the lamb in the vinegar for 30 minutes. Drain. Run in a blender, or pound or chop to a paste, the onions, garlic, salt, chili peppers, coriander, cumin, turmeric and ginger; roll the lamb in the mixture. Let stand 30 minutes.

Heat the oil in a deep, heavy skillet or Dutch oven; brown the lamb in it. Stir in the water; cover, and cook over low heat 45 minutes or until tender. Watch carefully and add a little boiling water if necessary to prevent burning.

Serves 6–8.

## Pulao Yakhni
## LAMB AND RICE CURRY

INDIA

### Meat

2 pounds boneless lamb
2½ teaspoons salt
2 teaspoons cinnamon
¼ teaspoon ground cloves
2 teaspoons minced fresh green chilies or ½ teaspoon dried, ground chili peppers
1 tablespoon minced ginger root
2 cloves garlic, minced
4 cups water

Wash the lamb, cut up into small pieces, and combine with all the remaining ingredients in a saucepan. Bring to a boil and cook over low heat 1½ hours. Remove the meat and strain the broth. Reserve the meat and broth.

RICE

2 cups long-grain rice
4 tablespoons *ghee*
2 large onions, peeled and sliced
2 teaspoons cumin seeds
¼ teaspoon ground cloves
½ teaspoon ground cardamom
1 teaspoon cinnamon
½ teaspoon powdered bay leaf
1 teaspoon turmeric
2 teaspoons chili powder

Wash the rice, cover with warm water, and let soak 30 minutes. Drain and dry.

Melt the *ghee* in a deep skillet. Sauté the onions in it until golden brown. Remove the onions and reserve. Add the meat to the pan, and brown it; remove. Put the spices in the skillet; cook 2 minutes, stirring constantly. Add the rice; cook until lightly browned, stirring frequently. Add the reserved broth. Bring to a boil and cook over low heat 10 minutes. Add the reserved meat. Mix, cover, and cook 10 minutes longer, or until the liquid is absorbed. Taste for seasoning. Garnish with the fried onions.

Serves 8.

*Cloves*

*Dhansak*  INDIA
## LAMB CURRY WITH LENTILS

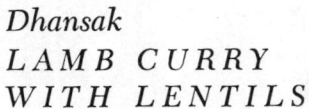

2 cups lentils
2 cups chopped onions
2 cloves garlic, minced
2 teaspoons cumin seeds
2 teaspoons coriander seeds
10 black peppercorns
3 cloves
½ teaspoon cardamom seeds
½ teaspoon dried ground chili peppers
½ teaspoon cinnamon
1½ teaspoons salt
½ cup yogurt
2 pounds lamb, cut in 1-inch cubes
¼ pound (1 stick) butter
2 cups chopped tomatoes
1½ cups boiling water

Wash the lentils thoroughly; cover with water, bring to a boil, cook 30 minutes and drain.

Run in an electric blender, or pound together the onions, garlic, spices, and salt; gradually blend in the yogurt. Add the lamb, tossing until well coated. Let stand 1 hour.

Melt the butter in a casserole or Dutch oven; add the undrained meat. Cook over low heat 15 minutes, stirring frequently. Stir in the lentils, tomatoes, and boiling water. Cover, and cook over low heat 45 minutes, or until meat and lentils are tender and dry. Watch carefully and add a little more water if necessary. Taste for seasoning.

Serves 6–8.

## Roghan Josh
## CURRIED LAMB

INDIA

3 pounds boneless lamb
2½ teaspoons salt
½ teaspoon dried ground chili peppers
2 teaspoons ground coriander seeds
2 teaspoons minced ginger root
1 teaspoon ground cumin seed
1 cup yogurt
6 tablespoons *ghee*
1 cup chopped onions
¼ teaspoon saffron
1 cup boiling water
2 tablespoons minced coriander leaves

Buy leg or shoulder of lamb, and have it cut 1 inch thick, then into 1-inch squares. Put the lamb in a bowl, and sprinkle it with the salt and chili peppers. Toss to coat. Mix together the coriander, ginger, cumin, and yogurt. Pour the mixture over the lamb, and toss well. Cover the bowl tightly and let stand at room temperature for 1 hour. (If you prefer, the lamb may be marinated overnight in the refrigerator.)

Drain the lamb, reserving the marinade. In a deep 12-inch skillet, or Dutch oven, melt the *ghee*. Add the onions and lamb. Cook over high heat, stirring almost constantly for 5 minutes. Add the marinade and bring to a boil, stirring constantly. Cover tightly, and cook over low heat for 45 minutes. Mix the saffron with ¼ cup of the boiling water and add to the lamb, mixing well. Recover and cook 15 minutes. Mix in half the remaining water, recover, and cook 15 minutes. Add the remaining water, and cook 15 minutes. Taste for seasoning.

Heap the lamb on a heated serving dish and sprinkle with the coriander leaves.

Serves 6–8.

*Aush Bhogar*  INDIA
## LAMB CURRY WITH DUMPLINGS

2½ cups chopped onions
3 cloves garlic, minced
1 teaspoon ground cumin
1 tablespoon ground coriander
1½ teaspoons turmeric
1 tablespoon minced ginger root
½ teaspoon dried ground chili peppers
2½ teaspoons salt
2 cups water
2 pounds boneless lamb, cut into 1-inch cubes
4 tablespoons butter
2 egg yolks
2 tablespoons melted butter
⅓ cup cracker meal
2 egg whites, stiffly beaten

Run in a blender or chop to a paste the onions, garlic, cumin, coriander, turmeric, ginger, chili peppers, 2 teaspoons of the salt, and ¼ cup of the water. Toss with the meat. Let stand 30 minutes. Melt the 4 tablespoons butter in a casserole or Dutch oven; cook the meat in it, stirring frequently until browned. Add the remaining water; cover and cook over low heat 45 minutes.

Beat together the egg yolks, melted butter, and remaining salt; stir in the cracker meal. Let stand 10 minutes. Fold in the egg whites. Chill 10 minutes and shape into walnut-size balls. Arrange around the top of the meat; cover, and cook over low heat 25 minutes.

Serves 4–6.

## Sagh Mhas
### LAMB-SPINACH CURRY

INDIA

> 2 pounds boneless lamb
> 1 pound spinach, or 1 package frozen chopped spinach, thawed
> 2 large onions
> 4 tablespoons *ghee*
> 2 teaspoons ground coriander seeds
> 1 teaspoon turmeric
> ¾ teaspoon powdered ginger
> ½ teaspoon crushed dried chili peppers
> 2½ teaspoons salt
> 1 tablespoon mustard seed
> ¼ cup yogurt
> **Boiling water**

Cut the lamb into 1½-inch cubes. If fresh spinach is used, wash it thoroughly, drain and shred it. If frozen, squeeze all of the water out of the thawed spinach, and spread on paper towels until needed. Peel and thinly slice the onions.

Melt the *ghee* in a casserole or Dutch oven; add the onions, and cook until lightly browned. Add the lamb, coriander, turmeric, ginger, and chili peppers. Mix well, and cook over medium heat 10 minutes, turning the meat frequently. Mix in the spinach, salt, mustard seed, and yogurt. Cover, and cook over low heat 45 minutes, adding a little boiling water from time to time, as the liquid is absorbed. The finished dish should have no gravy, so if any liquid is left when the lamb is tender, remove the cover, and cook over high heat, turning the mixture almost constantly with a fork, until fairly dry. Taste for seasoning.

Serves 4–6.

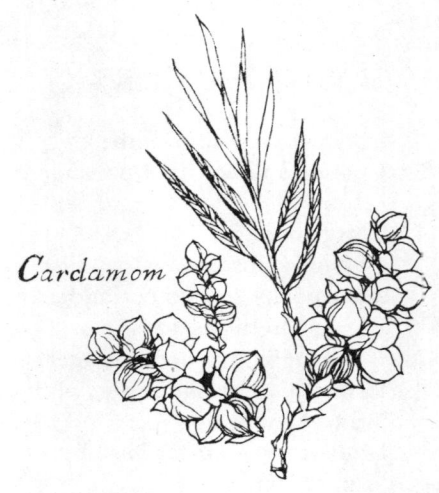
Cardamom

*Malai Korma*   INDIA
## LAMB AND ALMOND CURRY

½ teaspoon powdered ginger
2 teaspoons turmeric
½ teaspoon cinnamon
1 teaspoon ground cumin
¼ teaspoon ground cardamom
2 pounds lean lamb, cut in ½-inch cubes
5 tablespoons butter
2½ cups chopped onions
1 bay leaf
1 cup yogurt
1½ teaspoons salt
¾ cup finely ground blanched almonds
½ cup heavy cream

Combine the ginger, turmeric, cinnamon, cumin, cardamom, and lamb, tossing together until coated. Let stand 1 hour. Melt 3 tablespoons butter in a casserole or Dutch oven; sauté the onions 10 minutes. Remove. Melt the remaining butter in the casserole; lightly brown the meat in it. Return the onions and add the bay leaf, yogurt, and salt. Cover, and cook over low heat 45 minutes or until tender. Blend in the almonds mixed with the cream; cook 10 minutes. Taste for seasoning.

Serves 4–6.

## Bahmi Goreng
INDONESIA
### NOODLES, CHICKEN, AND SHRIMP

2 whole chicken breasts
⅓ cup soy sauce
1 pound vermicelli or fine egg noodles
2 eggs, beaten
¾ cup peanut or vegetable oil
1½ cups thinly sliced onions
2 cloves garlic, minced
1 teaspoon ground cardamom seeds
2 teaspoons minced ginger root
3 cups shredded Chinese or green cabbage
1 cup bean sprouts
1½ cups diced cooked shrimp
¼ cup chopped green onions
½ teaspoon freshly ground black pepper

Remove the skin and bones of the chicken and cut the meat into matchlike strips. Put it in a bowl, add all but 1 tablespoon soy sauce, and refrigerate, tossing the chicken occasionally while preparing the noodles.

Cook the noodles in boiling salted water until almost tender. Drain, and spread on a flat surface to cool, then chill for 2 hours. Make an omelet of the eggs. Roll up and slice fine.

Heat 2 tablespoons of the oil in a skillet or chafing dish; sauté the chicken for 5 minutes. Remove and keep warm. Heat 2 tablespoons oil in the same skillet; sauté the onions, garlic, cardamom, and ginger for 3 minutes. Remove and keep warm. Heat 2 tablespoons oil in the same skillet; sauté the cabbage and bean sprouts 3 minutes. Add the shrimp and sauté 2 minutes. Return all the sautéed ingredients and add the green onions, pepper, and remaining soy sauce. Cook 2 minutes.

In a separate skillet, heat the remaining oil; turn the noodles into it and fry until browned, stirring frequently. Add to the chicken mixture and sprinkle with the sliced omelet.

Serves 4–6.

## Nasi Goreng
### FRIED RICE

INDONESIA

Cook the rice the day before you want to serve it, if possible. If you can't, chill the rice for as long as possible.

> 2 cups raw long-grain rice
> 3½ cups chicken broth
> 1½ teaspoons salt
> ⅓ cup peanut oil
> 3 cloves garlic, minced
> 2 cups chopped onions
> 1 tablespoon minced ginger root
> 1½ cups chopped cooked shrimp
> 2 cups julienne-cut cooked chicken
> 1 cup cubed smoked ham
> 2 teaspoons ground coriander
> 1½ teaspoons ground cumin seed
> ½ teaspoon dried ground chili peppers
> ¼ teaspoon mace
> 4 tablespoons peanut butter
> 1 cup cooked or canned crab meat

Wash the rice in several changes of water until water runs clear. Combine in a deep saucepan with the chicken broth and salt; bring to a boil, cover, and cook over low heat 20 minutes. If any liquid remains, cook over high heat until rice is dry. Spread out in a flat pan and chill overnight, or for at least 2 hours. Heat the oil in a wok or large skillet; sauté the garlic and onions 10 minutes. Mix in the rice, and cook until browned, stirring frequently. Add the ginger, shrimp, chicken, ham, coriander, cumin seed, chili peppers, mace, and peanut butter. Mix well and cook over low heat 5 minutes, stirring frequently, but carefully. Add the crab meat, and cook 5 minutes longer. Serve with side dishes of any sambal and sliced, chilled cucumber, chutney, finely chopped peanuts, and sliced banana.

Serves 6–8.

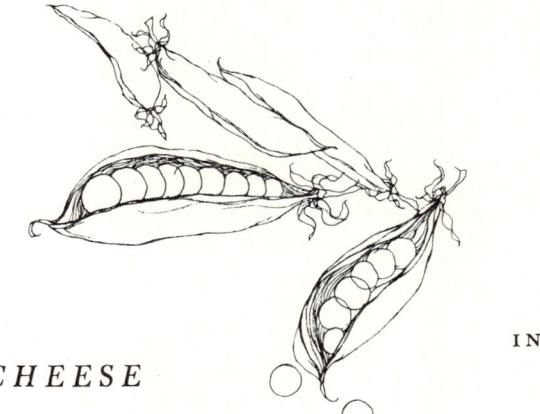

*Mattar Panir*
PEAS AND CHEESE

INDIA

    1 pound farmer cheese
    2 tablespoons vegetable oil
    6 tablespoons butter
    1½ cups chopped onions
    2 cloves garlic, minced
    ½ teaspoon dried ground chili peppers
    1½ teaspoons ground coriander
    ¾ teaspoon turmeric
    2 teaspoons minced ginger root
    1½ cups peeled, chopped tomatoes
    1½ pounds peas, shelled, or 1 package frozen, thawed
    ¾ cup water
    1 teaspoon salt
    Minced coriander leaves (cilantro, Chinese parsley)

Cut the cheese into ½-inch cubes. Heat the oil in a skillet until it boils, and brown the cheese in it over high heat. Remove with a slotted spoon and reserve.

Melt the butter in a large skillet; sauté the onions and garlic until browned. Stir in the chili peppers, coriander, turmeric, and ginger; sauté 2 minutes, stirring almost constantly. Add the tomatoes, water, and salt. Bring to a boil, cover, and cook over low heat 15 minutes. Add the peas; re-cover and cook fresh peas 10 minutes, frozen, 5 minutes. Add the reserved cheese and cook 10 minutes longer. Taste for seasoning. Turn into a bowl, and sprinkle with the coriander leaves.

Serves 4–6.

## Sabzi Bhindi
### BATTER-FRIED OKRA

INDIA

> 1 pound okra or 2 packages frozen, thawed
> ½ teaspoon ground cardamom
> ⅛ teaspoon powdered cloves
> 1 teaspoon crushed cumin seeds
> 1 teaspoon cinnamon
> ½ cup flour
> ⅛ teaspoon salt
> 1 egg, beaten
> Water
> Vegetable oil for deep-frying

If fresh okra is used, wash and scrape gently. Dry thoroughly and make a small slit lengthwise in each. If frozen okra is used, pat dry thoroughly, and slit.

In a small skillet, put the cardamom, cloves, cumin, and cinnamon. Cook over high heat 2 minutes, stirring constantly. Put a little of the spice mixture in each slit of the okra.

Mix together the flour, salt, and egg, and enough water to make a fairly thick batter. Dip the okra in the batter. Heat the oil to 370° and fry the okra until golden brown. Drain and serve hot. Serves 8.

## Dal
### FRIED LENTILS

INDIA

> 2 cups lentils, preferably red
> 4 tablespoons *ghee*
> 1 cup chopped onions
> 2 cloves garlic, minced
> ¼ teaspoon dried ground chili peppers
> 2 teaspoons ground cumin seed
> 1 teaspoon turmeric
> 1½ teaspoons salt
> ½ cup chopped coriander leaves (cilantro, Chinese parsley)
> 1 large onion, thinly sliced and fried

Wash the lentils, cover with water and let soak 1 hour. Bring to a boil and cook 45 minutes. Drain thoroughly, and dry.

Melt the *ghee* in a skillet; add the onions, garlic, chili peppers, cumin, turmeric, lentils, and salt. Cook over low heat, stirring frequently, for 20 minutes. Watch carefully to prevent burning. Taste for seasoning. Serve sprinkled with coriander and fried onion rings.

Serves 8.


*Raita*     INDIA
## CUCUMBERS AND TOMATOES IN YOGURT

>3 cucumbers
>1 tablespoon salt
>3 tablespoons minced onions
>2 tomatoes
>3 cups yogurt
>½ teaspoon pepper
>2 tablespoons minced coriander leaves (cilantro, Chinese parsley)
>2 teaspoons cumin seeds

Pare the cucumbers lightly, and cut in half lengthwise. Scoop out the seeds, then slice thin. In a bowl, combine the cucumbers, salt, and onion. Mix well, and let stand for 10 minutes. Drain very well.

Cut the tomatoes into small cubes, and combine with the cucumbers, yogurt, pepper, and coriander. Mix well, cover, and chill for 2 hours.

Put the cumin seeds in a dry skillet. Keep over medium heat for 1 minute, stirring constantly, then crush to a powder.

Put the *Raita* in small bowls, and sprinkle the tops with the cumin.

Serves 6–8.

Note: In India, *Raita* is served as a salad, but on a hot day, it could be a first course.

## COCONUT RICE

MALAYSIA

> 2 cups raw long-grain rice
> 2 tablespoons sesame oil or peanut oil
> 2 cups coarsely chopped onions
> 2 teaspoons salt
> 4 cups Coconut Milk (see recipe)

Wash the rice under cold running water, until water runs clear.

Heat the oil in a deep saucepan, sauté the onions 10 minutes. Add the rice and cook over high heat until a dark yellow, stirring constantly. Stir in the salt and coconut milk. Cover and cook over low heat 20 minutes or until rice is tender, stirring rice up from the bottom of the pan several times. When all the liquid is absorbed, the rice is ready. It should not be completely dry.

Serves 6–8.

## *Seroendeng*
## COCONUT SAMBAL

INDONESIA

> 3 cups flaked coconut
> 1 cup chopped onions
> 3 cloves garlic, minced
> 1 teaspoon salt
> ½ teaspoon ground cumin
> 1 teaspoon ground coriander
> 1 tablespoon minced ginger root
> 2 teaspoons grated lemon rind
> 1 tablespoon peanut or vegetable oil
> ¼ cup heavy cream
> ½ cup blanched toasted peanuts

Try to buy the unsweetened coconut, usually sold in health-food stores. If the sweetened variety is used, rinse it under cold water, drain well, and dry with paper towels.

Run in a blender or pound or chop to a paste the onions, garlic, salt, cumin, coriander, ginger, and lemon rind. Heat the oil in a skillet; sauté the coconut and spice mixture until delicately browned, stirring almost constantly. Blend in the cream; cook over low heat until dry. Cool and mix with the peanuts. Serve as an accompaniment to curries.

Makes about 3 cups.

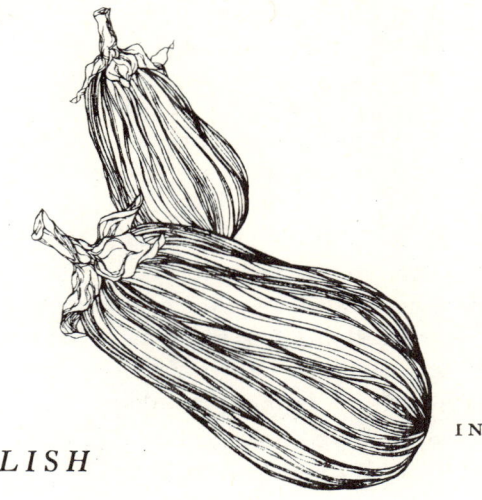

*Brinjal Boortha*
EGGPLANT RELISH

INDIA

    2-pound eggplant
    2 tablespoons vegetable oil
    ½ cup finely chopped onions
    ¼ cup finely chopped green peppers
    ¼ cup unsweetened coconut
    1½ teaspoons salt
    1 teaspoon ground cumin seeds
    1 teaspoon ground coriander seeds
    ¼ teaspoon dried ground chili peppers
    3 tablespoons heavy cream
    2 tablespoons lemon juice

Bake the eggplant in a 350° oven for 1 hour. Cool, peel, and dice. Heat the oil in a skillet, sauté the onions and green peppers in it for 5 minutes. Add the eggplant and coconut and cook 5 minutes longer, stirring frequently.

Chop together the eggplant mixture, salt, cumin, coriander, and chili peppers. Blend in the cream and lemon juice and continue chopping until very fine. Taste for seasoning and chill.

Makes about 3 cups.

Note: Brinjals are served just as you would any relish.

## Kim-Chee
KOREA
### PICKLED SALTED VEGETABLES

> 6 pounds celery (Chinese) cabbage or green cabbage
> 3 tablespoons coarse salt
> 2 cups sliced green onions
> 4 cloves garlic, minced
> 1 tablespoon ginger root, minced
> ¾ teaspoon dried ground chili peppers

Shred the cabbage 1 inch wide. Mix with half the salt and let stand 30 minutes. Wash and drain. Mix together the green onions, garlic, ginger, chili peppers, cabbage, and remaining salt. Pack into a sterilized crock or glass jar. Add enough cold water to cover the vegetables. Cover the containers and set aside in a cool place for 5 days. Taste to see if the vegetables are pickled sufficiently—if not, let stand 2 more days. Chill and serve as a relish. (This recipe is for a type of winter *kim-chee*. In the summer, cucumbers are used instead of cabbage. Buy 6 pounds of small, very firm cucumbers. Wash and scrub them with a brush. Cut each cucumber into thirds, crosswise, then continue preparing the *kim-chee*, as directed in the recipe above.)

## Daikon
JAPAN
### RADISH OR TURNIP PICKLES

> 2 pounds *daikon* (Japanese white radish) or
>   white turnips
> 1 cup water
> ¼ cup rice wine vinegar or white vinegar
> 1 cup sugar
> ¼ cup coarse salt

Wash the *daikon* or turnips, peel, and cut in paper-thin slices. Pack the slices into a jar. Combine and bring to a boil the water, vinegar, sugar, and salt. Cool, then pour over the vegetable. Cover and let pickle in the refrigerator 3 days before serving.
Serve as you would any pickles.

## Gado-Gado
### SPICED VEGETABLE SALAD

INDONESIA

4 cups shredded cabbage
½ cup flaked coconut
2 tablespoons peanut or vegetable oil
¼ cup finely chopped onions
2 cloves garlic, minced
½ cup peanut butter
1 teaspoon sugar
1 teaspoon salt
¼ teaspoon dried ground chili peppers
2 teaspoons grated lemon rind
¾ cup light cream
¾ cup water
2 tomatoes, diced
2 cucumbers, sliced
2 hard-cooked eggs, coarsely chopped

Cover the cabbage with water, bring to a boil, cook 2 minutes, then drain. Rinse the coconut under cold water, drain, and dry.

Heat the oil in a skillet; sauté the onions and garlic 3 minutes. Stir in the coconut, peanut butter, sugar, salt, chili peppers, lemon rind, and very gradually the cream, mixed with the water. Cook over low heat 5 minutes, stirring frequently. Cool.

In a bowl, toss together the cabbage, tomatoes, and cucumbers. Pour the dressing over it, mix lightly, and chill 1 hour before serving, sprinkled with the eggs.

Serves 6–8.

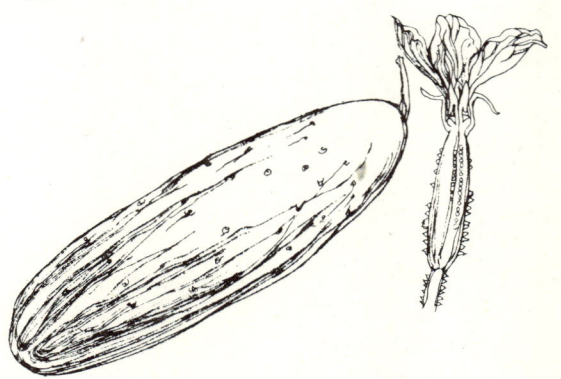

## Chatni
### FRUIT CHUTNEY
INDIA

      1 cup malt or cider vinegar
      1¼ cups dark brown sugar
      1 tablespoon dark molasses
      1½ teaspoons salt
      ¼ teaspoon dried ground chili peppers
      1 teaspoon cinnamon
      1 teaspoon ground cumin seed
      ½ teaspoon freshly ground black pepper
      ½ teaspoon ground cloves
      ½ teaspoon ground coriander
      2 teaspoons powdered ginger
      2 cloves garlic, minced
      1 pound apples, diced
      ½ pound prunes, diced
      ½ pound dried apricots or peaches, diced
      ½ cup grated coconut

Combine all the ingredients in a saucepan. Bring to a boil and cook over low heat 1 hour or until soft and brown, stirring frequently. Cool. Pour into a jar, cover, and refrigerate. The chutney will keep fresh about one month.

Makes about 1 pint.

## Poori
### DEEP-FRIED BREAD
INDIA

      1½ cups whole wheat flour
      1½ cups all-purpose flour
      ⅛ teaspoon salt
      4 tablespoons butter
      ¾ cup lukewarm water (about)
      Vegetable oil for deep-frying

Sift together the two flours and the salt. With the fingers, blend in the butter until the mixture looks like cornmeal. Add just enough of the water to make a firm dough. Knead vigorously for a few minutes until dough is smooth and elastic. Cover with a damp cloth and let stand 30 minutes. Knead again. Break off about 2 tablespoons of the dough at a time, and press each down gently, until flat, and about a 2-inch circle. Then roll into about a 5-inch circle.

Heat the oil in a deep skillet to 350° and drop one circle at a time into it. Immediately turn them over and press down with a spatula. (They begin to puff unevenly at once.) Fry until golden brown and puffed. Drain on paper towels and serve hot.

Makes about 16.

*Variation:* Chapatis

Prepare and shape the dough as for *Pooris*. Heat an ungreased griddle or heavy skillet until a drop of water bounces on it immediately. Put a circle of dough on it, and shaking the pan constantly, cook for 1 minute. Turn over and cook until lightly browned. Keep warm while preparing the balance.

## COCONUT CREAM CUSTARD PUDDING

MALAYSIA

> 2 tablespoons butter
> ¾ cup sugar
> 4 tablespoons sifted flour
> ¼ teaspoon cinnamon
> 6 egg yolks
> 1½ cups Coconut Cream (see recipe)
> 6 egg whites, beaten stiff

Cream the butter; gradually beat in the sugar. Mix in the flour and cinnamon. Add 1 egg yolk at a time, beating after each addition until light and fluffy. Gradually mix in the coconut cream. Fold in the egg whites. Divide among 8 buttered custard cups. Set in a shallow pan of hot water. Bake in a preheated 350° oven 45 minutes or until set. Chill.

Serves 8.

*Sevian*  
VERMICELLI DESSERT

INDIA

    1 cup water  
    4 tablespoons honey  
    2 tablespoons sugar  
    1¾ cups vermicelli (very thin noodles)  
    6 tablespoons butter  
    ¼ cup pine nuts or slivered blanched almonds  
    ¼ teaspoon nutmeg  
    ¼ teaspoon cinnamon

Combine the water, honey and sugar in a saucepan; bring to a boil stirring constantly, then cook over high heat 4 minutes. Break the vermicelli into small pieces. Melt the butter in a skillet; add the vermicelli and cook, stirring almost steadily, until browned. Mix in the nuts. Add the syrup, mixing well. Cook until syrup is absorbed. Mix in the nutmeg and cinnamon. Serve hot.

Serves 4–6.

## Kluay Khaek
### BATTER-FRIED BANANAS

THAILAND

1 cup rice flour or cornstarch
⅛ teaspoon salt
½ cup Coconut Milk (see recipe)
1 tablespoon oil
2 egg yolks
2 egg whites, beaten stiff
½ cup flaked coconut
5 firm bananas, peeled and cut in 2-inch lengths
Vegetable oil for deep-frying

Sift the flour or cornstarch and salt into a bowl; beat in the coconut milk, oil, and egg yolks until smooth. Fold in the egg whites and coconut. Dip the bananas into the batter.

Heat the oil to 380°. Fry a few pieces at a time until delicately browned. Drain and serve hot.

Serves 6–8.

# *WHERE EAST MEETS WEST*

RUSSIA

ROUMANIA

GREECE

TURKEY

IRAN

ISRAEL

MAPS are a fascinating source of entertainment for people who are geographically minded. It is entertaining to study the bright colors and wonder at the fact that no matter how strange the shapes and forms of the countries may be, only three different colors are required, although they may be contiguous to each other at many points. Maps, always regarded as utterly truthful, are as deceitful as the suggestion of spring on an unseasonably warm day in February. They promise much, but deliver little. By their very nature maps lie, because they attempt to represent rounded areas, taken from the globe that is the world, on flat surfaces.

In considering the area simultaneously joining and separating Europe and Asia, the mind must reel at the boundary changes that have occurred over the past score of centuries. Although events seemingly moved with the lethargy of a three-toed sloth, drastic and shattering events took place regularly during the many long, and ultimately eventful, years. Gone forever are such nations as Lycia, Cilicia, Mesopotamia, Armenia, and Cappadocia, those historic lands of the Bible. But still others have survived the violence of the past two thousand years, although with somewhat different forms, boundaries, and governments.

In matters culinary it seems clear that (as Rudyard Kipling wrote) East is East and West is West. The food of Europe differs resolutely and steadfastly from that of Asia, certainly in most respects, although some slight points of similarity can be noted. Disregarding politics and matters mundane for the sake of the discussion, there are many nations, extending from north to south, that act as a sort of culinary buffer between the two continents. These countries are Russia, Roumania, Greece, Turkey, Iran, and Israel. (Bulgaria is omitted here because it lacks a complete, national cuisine, even though there are some interesting preparations. Israel is included for reasons to be discussed subsequently. On the other hand, the Arabic nations are excluded because their cuisine is quite limited in range, and they do not act in the capacity of a culinary buffer, as do the others selected.) Thus Russia, Roumania, Greece, Turkey, Iran, and Israel, although otherwise differing widely, act in union to separate the wonderful worlds of cooking which exist in Europe and Asia. In so doing, they show certain unique influences and original cuisines at the point where East Meets West.

To begin with the north, Russia has made a goodly number of culinary contributions to our gastronomy. The first point to consider is what's called Russian Service, that it, the passing of platters of food from which each person helps himself. In direct contrast is the French Service, in which portions of food are placed upon individual plates; in general the French Service is used in restaurants and the Russian style is typical of most homes.

The Russians, or in any event their Czarist predecessors, were excessively fond of appetizers or snack foods, called *zakuska*. Indeed, the arguments rage as to whether French *hors d'oeuvre* or *zakuska* came first; at this stage, all of the various theories advanced seem apocryphal. Of all the appetizers, the Russians love caviar beyond measure, but it is now expensive and scarce, most of it being shipped to dollar countries, where the currency is firm. However, if caviar is not to be had, most Russians are almost as happy with herring, and there is nothing wrong with salted salmon or smoked sturgeon. Those choices go marvelously well with vodka, the national strong drink of the Soviet. Vodka, almost always drunk straight, with no chaser, and very cold, is available in the customary style, of which Stolichnaya is the best brand. It is also made with lemon, onion, red pepper, garlic, and other flavorings, and sometimes fortified with brandy. If you like red vodka, there's *riabinovka*, but if you prefer yellow, you can find it steeped in herb grass and sold as *zubrovka*.

As to soups, of course everyone knows *borscht*. Many people with Russian ancestry are inclined to view with suspicion any type of *borscht* other than that which their mother prepared for them in their childhood. The fact is that there are dozens, perhaps more, of different types of *borscht*, all authentic. Most people know the familiar beet borscht, but it may equally be made with cabbage, meat, fish, or other ingredients. Regular soups include those made with caraway seeds, kidneys, barley, potatoes, and vegetables. There is a fine cold soup made with sour milk. With many soups, particularly *borscht*, a small meat-filled pastry may be served.

The main courses include *cotletki pojarski*, perhaps best described as a sort of minced chicken cutlet; also there is chicken *à la Kiev*, in which chicken is wrapped around a fair quantity of butter. This last must be cut into with care, to prevent splattering. A *coulebiac* (also appearing as *koulebiaka*) is a meat or fish pie which can be superb, if prepared with a delicate hand. As to beef Stroganoff, the discussion rages—is it really Russian, or a French creation? After all, how Russian is Russian dressing, something completely unknown in the Soviet Union. In passing, it should be noted that the Russians are fond of acid tastes, including sour cream, sour milk, and especially *kefir*, a unique beverage somewhat resembling buttermilk in consistency. As an all-purpose cereal, number one in popularity is *kasha* (buckwheat groats). The Russians like whole-grained breads, mostly dark and heavy of texture, which are really quite delicious when spread with a thick layer of bright yellow butter.

The desserts are weak and limited in scope. There are several fairly good fruit desserts, which taste like (but better than) our own gelatine desserts. Pancakes are the best bet, but some passable cake and pastry is made, although not otherwise unique in taste. But the Russians, to a man, are devoted to ice cream, which they adore beyond all reason. It is not unusual to see people eating what can only be called an Eskimo Pie, outdoors, with the temperature below zero, munching happily on their tiny portion, which costs the equivalent of a dollar in American money. And as snow flurries by in large flakes and the wind whistles ominously, they shiver and smile happily with their dessert of desserts.

Tea is the national drink. Anyone who has tasted coffee in the Soviet will know the reason for that obvious choice. By a custom which is now disappearing in the cities, water is boiled in a samovar, and the tea traditionally made in a pot, and not in the samovar as most people assume.

To the south, Roumania is a compact and rather pleasant country, with a totally different personality from the giant bear that walks like a man, Russia. The caviar here is called *icre*, and it is made from carp or pike roe, rather than from sturgeon. It is an excellent appetizer, customarily consumed with a surprisingly large glass of *tzuica*, a kind of clear plum brandy, which is deceptively smooth to the taste.

Roumania's national dishes are interesting, and too little known. There is *ghivetch*, which is a vegetable stew. Every possible vegetable available in the marketplace (certainly not less than a dozen different varieties for the one dish) is used, and the fresher the better. Yesterday's vegetables are past their prime, in the opinion of many Roumanians about to make a *ghivetch*. It is made with plenty of olive oil, and cooked in a casserole. On a cold day few things are better to eat. Of course, if the mood strikes the cook, meat or fish may be added to the vegetables.

Then there is *musaca*, another national dish but one which is somewhat difficult to describe. It is a casserole made with ground or chopped meat, to which vegetables (such as peppers, tomatoes, eggplant, and so forth) are added. The eggplant, that oddly shaped vegetable, is the object of a national cult in Roumania, where it is regarded as an all-purpose food. It is eaten chopped, as an appetizer; it is baked and fried as a vegetable; it is stuffed with meat or rice as a luncheon dish; and made into a main course, as a *tocana,* a stew.

The country has all the soups found in Europe, including potato, bean, and other vegetable soups. But the Roumanian national soup is the *ciorba,* a sourish soup made with a wide variety of ingredients. The slightly acid taste is usually obtained by using fermented wheat bran. Other sour sources are lemon juice, sorrel, unripe grapes, and sauerkraut juice. *Ciorbas* can be made with beef, veal, rabbit, lamb, vegetables, and so forth.

The single most popular dish of the national cuisine is *mamaliga,* which is cornmeal cooked until quite firm, and it usually takes the place of potatoes. It is good with *brinza* cheese, or with butter, or made into dumplings, or fried crisp, or consumed with sauerkraut.

The Roumanians have a particularly sweet tooth, and love jams, jellies, and preserves of all sorts. The cherry confections are good, but the most unique sweet preserves are those made with rose petals. A specialty is *gogosi,* a sort of doughnut, usually served with a sweet sauce. Pancakes and strudels are also excellent.

The Ottoman Empire, based in present-day Turkey, came into existence during the middle of the fifteenth century and controlled that region we know now as Greece. As a result, for centuries Greece remained under Turkish domination in almost all respects. Small wonder then, that the two nations have an interlocking cuisine—partly European, partly Asiatic. Where the cuisine begins or ends is lost in the mists of antiquity and folklore. The Greeks proclaim proudly that certain dishes are theirs and theirs alone, and the Turks reply that they were originally Anatolian, and therefore by inheritance uniquely Turkish.

But there are differences. The best Greek appetizer is *taramasalata,* often called Greek caviar, made from mullet or carp roe. Also good is *spanakopita,* a flavorsome appetizer made with spinach and pastry into a type of pie, but cut into squares. Of course, a drink wouldn't be worthwhile (the Greeks think) without olives, sometimes green, but more likely, the wrinkled, astringent black type.

As to soups, *avgolemono* is outstanding; it is made with chicken and lemon and is very good indeed. The other Greek soups are not unusual, although the various fish soups are just fine. Fish is important to the Greek people, and they often prepare them with olive oil, tomatoes, onions, and garlic. They are always served with plenty of lemon halves, perhaps as many as a dozen. Most Greeks think life would be unbearable without lemons to flavor food. In fact, the favorite sauce of the country is made with lemons.

Lamb is the meat of Greece; it is roasted, or cut into chunks, skewered and broiled, or overcooked with vegetables until too soft, or cooked with rice, and so on. A national dish is *moussaka*, consisting of eggplant and lamb. Of course beef is eaten, but not nearly so much as lamb. A good beef preparation is the *stiffado*, a beef and onion stew. Also notable is the *pastichio*, a ground meat and macaroni affair. Chicken is important and often flavored with oregano, a favorite spice.

*Feta* cheese, white and sharp to the taste, is particularly good when crumbled into a green salad. The other important cheese is *kasseri*, made from goat milk and often served hot as an appetizer.

*Ouzo* is the Greek national drink, with an anise flavor. Wines are fairly good, but not great. Many wines are available as *retsina*, which contains resin, but they are definitely an acquired taste.

Turkish food is similar to, but far from identical with, that of various Middle Eastern countries lying to its south. Culinarily speaking, the country cooks with an aluminum pot on a European stove, and another copper utensil cooking with charcoal in Asia. This compares with its geographical situation, for Turkey is partly in Europe, although most of it lies in Asia.

The *mezeler*, or appetizers, are tasty, and typically consist of beans in a spicy oil dressing, chopped vegetables (typically eggplant) in still more oil, caviar, slices of garlicky or smoked sausage, and always stuffed mussels. *Pastirma*, spiced beef, is popular and its name shows a kinship or affinity with the more familiar pastrami of our own delicatessens. Vine leaves, another standby, are commonly stuffed with rice, meat, and so forth.

The soups are good and hearty. Some are made with yogurt and flavored with dill; best of all are the fish soups and chowders. As to meat, this being a Muslim country, pork is almost never encountered. Instead, lamb is the favorite, and beef and chicken are reasonably important. Duck is rare, veal appears only on occasion. Chunks of meat on a skewer, *kebabs*, are known all over the world. Even better is *döner kebab*, a turning arrangement of lamb, held vertically before a charcoal fire; it is too elaborate for homes, and is generally found only in restaurants. Meat is often served with yogurt, and although the combination may sound strange, the taste is just fine.

Rice forms the basis of the Turkish cuisine, an example of the fashion in which the Asiatic influence has made itself felt on a partly European nation. The rice may be plain, or more elaborate with seedless raisins or currants, whole or pieces of nuts, and colored by saffron. The flavor may be enhanced with spices—cumin, coriander, turmeric, and fennel are usual. Frequently garlic is laid on with a heavy hand. Vegetables are often stuffed, particularly those which form a natural container, such as eggplant, peppers, and vine leaves.

As to desserts, the most distinctive is *baklava*, very thin layers of pastry, baked with nuts and butter and covered with a sweet syrup. Often, this may be enhanced with a dollop of *kaymak*, milk boiled down to a semi-solid concentrate, and tasting like solidified sweet cream. Other pastry desserts are interesting but overly sweet, and often bear such names as Women's Dimples, Lady's Navel, Glad Eyes, Sweetheart's Lips, and so forth. Turkish candies are good, and the best known confection is *lokum*, which we call Turkish Delight.

Although Iran lies completely within Asia, this nation retains one foot within the culinary boundaries of the Middle East, flirts briefly with the food of India and Pakistan, and yet has an original cooking style. In keeping with the general area, lamb is the preferred meat. An outstanding preparation is *chelow kebab*, skewered pieces of lamb served on a generous portion of rice. A great novelty is *shirini polo*, an orange-flavored chicken pilaf; true, it's a trifle sweet, but quite delicious. Also noteworthy is *fesenjan*, duck cooked with walnuts. In Iran, this dish is prepared with fresh pomegranate juice, not easily obtainable in America, but a substitute is suggested in the recipe. As in the Middle East, a great many stuffed vegetable preparations are served. All in all, the cuisine of this fabled land, once called Persia, is quite original, and bridges (at least in part) the culinary gap between East and West.

Israel is unusual on many counts. Most countries have developed gradually, and have existed for centuries (or more) during which traditional foods came into daily use. Although Israel had a nucleus of native-born population, the *sabras*, it has become a homeland for thousands upon countless thousands of dispossessed people from Europe. These exiles, or immigrants if you prefer, mostly had a cold weather background in central Europe—Germany, Austria, Poland, Czechoslovakia, Hungary, and Russia. And yet the land of Israel is semitropical in climate, with excessive midsummer heat. The foods of Europe, suitable to cold weather, are generally inappropriate for the geographical position of the new nation with its ancient history extending for many thousands of years.

As a result, there has been a cultural compromise in the culinary sense. From their Arabic neighbors (certainly not their friends), the Israelis have wisely adopted many foods suitable to the climate. For example, the new nation finds itself eating and liking foods never (or rarely) eaten in the *schtetls*, the small Jewish villages of Europe. Notable is the increased dependence upon fresh vegetables (never a strong point in the Jewish cuisine), green salads, fresh fruits of the tropics, and cooling iced drinks and sherbets.

The traditional and heavy foods of European Jews, sometimes called Jewish-style cooking, includes such favorites as *chulent*, *gefilte* fish, *blintzes, kugel, borscht*, and so forth, and they're all adaptations of preparations found in various European countries. These are still well liked in Israel, but the young people are gradually turning to lighter items better suited to the hot climate.

Of all the nations lying across the north to south line that divides Europe from Asia, Israel typifies the perfect example of the point where East meets West, culinarily speaking.

## Taramasalata
### GREEK CAVIAR

GREECE

6 slices white bread, trimmed
1 cup milk
4 ounces *tarama* (salted fish roe)
¼ cup lemon juice
¾ cup sesame, safflower, vegetable, or olive oil
¼ cup grated onion

An electric mixer should be used for making the *taramasalata* as long beating is necessary. A blender may be used, but the electric mixer is better.

Soak the bread in the milk for 5 minutes. Drain, and squeeze dry. Put the bread in a bowl, and beat until a smooth paste is formed. Add the tarama, a tablespoon at a time, beating until smooth after each addition. Beat in the lemon juice, then 1 tablespoon of the oil at a time, beating well after each addition. After half the oil has been used up, the remainder should be added in a slow, steady stream. Continue beating until fluffy and pale pink. Beat in the onion. Chill, and when ready to serve, form into a mound on a flat plate, or heap in a bowl. Serve with Arabic bread or thinly sliced French bread.

Makes about 2 cups.

Note: Sesame seed or safflower oil gives the *tarama* a delicate flavor. Olive oil alone is too heavy, so if you use it, mix it with vegetable oil, half and half.

Safflower

## Baba Ghannouj
### EGGPLANT SPREAD

MIDDLE EAST

1 1¼-pound eggplant
4 tablespoons *Taratoor* (sesame sauce, see recipe)
2 cloves garlic, put through a press or minced
¼ cup lemon juice
1¼ teaspoons salt
¼ cup minced onions
3 tablespoons minced parsley
1 tablespoon sesame or olive oil

Wash and dry the eggplant. Place it on a baking sheet, and prick it in several places. Broil as close to the source of heat as possible for about 40 minutes, turning it to brown all sides.

Let stand until cool enough to handle, and peel it. Chop the eggplant until very smooth and almost a paste. Beat in the *taratoor*, garlic, lemon juice, and salt.

Heap on a flat dish, or put in a bowl, and sprinkle the top with the onions, parsley, and oil. Serve with Arabic bread or thinly sliced French bread.

Makes about 2 cups.

## Hummus
### CHICK-PEA APPETIZER

MIDDLE EAST

1½ cups dried chick-peas
2 teaspoons salt
1 cup *Taratoor* (sesame sauce, see recipe)
⅓ cup lemon juice
¼ cup minced onions
2 cloves garlic, minced
¼ cup minced parsley

Wash the chick-peas, cover with water, and bring to a boil. Cook 1 minute, remove from the heat, and let soak 1 hour. Drain, and with the fingers, rub off the skins. Put the chick-peas in a saucepan, cover with water, bring to a boil, and cook over low heat 1½ hours, adding the salt after 1 hour. Drain. Purée the chick-peas in an electric blender, or force through a food mill.

Cool, and mix in the *taratoor*, lemon juice, onions, and garlic. Mound on a serving dish and sprinkle with the parsley. Serve with Arabic bread, or thinly sliced French bread.

Makes about 3 cups.

## *Buerek*     MIDDLE EAST
### FLAKY CHEESE APPETIZER PASTRIES

16 *phyllo* leaves or 4 packages strudel leaves
½ pound Feta cheese
½ pound cream cheese
3 eggs
¾ cup melted butter
½ cup minced dill or parsley

*Phyllo* leaves are available in Middle East food shops, and strudel leaves are generally found in the frozen-food section of markets.

Mash the cheeses smooth, then beat in the eggs and 1 tablespoon of the melted butter. Mix in the dill or parsley.

Carefully lift up one pastry leaf and place it on a damp towel. (Keep the remaining leaves covered with another damp towel to keep them from drying out.) Cut the leaf in half crosswise, which will result in two pieces, each about 8 by 11 inches. Fold each piece into thirds lengthwise and brush the top layer with some of the butter. Place a heaping teaspoon of the filling on one corner of the long side and fold over into a triangle, continuing to fold from one side to another until the end is reached. Place on a well-buttered baking sheet and cover with plastic wrap while preparing the remaining pastries. When all are made, brush the tops with melted butter and bake in a preheated 350° oven 20 minutes, or until the tops are golden. Serve warm.

Makes 32.

## Piroshki
## LIVER PASTRIES

RUSSIA

### Pastry

2 cups sifted flour
½ teaspoon salt
½ teaspoon baking powder
¾ cup shortening
1 egg yolk
4 tablespoons ice water

Sift the flour, baking powder, and salt into a bowl. Cut in the shortening. Beat the egg yolk and water together and toss with the flour mixture until a ball of dough is formed. Chill 30 minutes.

### Filling

6 tablespoons butter
½ cup minced onions
½ pound chicken livers
2 tablespoons minced parsley
1½ teaspoons salt
¼ teaspoon freshly ground black pepper

Melt half the butter in a skillet; sauté the onions 5 minutes. Remove the onions, and set aside. Melt the remaining butter in the skillet and cook the livers in it 5 minutes. Chop together the onions, livers, parsley, salt and pepper. Cool.

Roll out the dough on a lightly floured surface ⅛ inch thick; cut into 3-inch circles. Place a tablespoon of filling on each round of dough. Fold over into a half-moon shape and press the edges together with a little water. Arrange on a greased baking sheet. Bake in a preheated 400° oven 15 minutes or until browned.

Makes about 24 pastries.

Serve hot with soups, as an hors d'oeuvre, or as an accompaniment to meats.

## *Midea Yemista*
### STUFFED MUSSELS

GREECE

    3 dozen mussels
    1 cup dry white wine
    ¼ cup water
    ¾ teaspoon salt
    ¼ cup olive oil
    ¾ cup chopped onions
    ½ cup raw rice
    ½ teaspoon freshly ground black pepper
    ¼ teaspoon ground allspice
    ¼ teaspoon cinnamon
    ¼ cup currants
    ¼ cup pine nuts or slivered almonds
    3 tablespoons minced parsley

Wash and scrub the mussels under cold running water. With a scissors, cut off the beards of the mussels. Rinse, and place the mussels in a deep skillet. Add the wine, water, and salt. Bring to a boil, cover tightly, and cook over medium heat 5 minutes, or until the shells open. If some are not open at this point, discard them. Let stand until cool enough to handle, then remove the mussels from the shells. Save 36 of the more shapely shells. Strain the pan juices.

Heat the oil in a skillet; sauté the onions 5 minutes; stir in the rice until coated with the oil. Add the pan juices; cover, and cook over low heat 15 minutes. Mix in the pepper, allspice, cinnamon, currants, nuts, and parsley. Taste for seasoning, and cook 5 minutes longer. Cool.

Put a mussel in each shell, and cover with the rice mixture. Chill.

Serves 6–8 as a first course, or arrange on a tray, and serve as an hors d'oeuvre.

## Tabbouleh
MIDDLE EAST
### WHEAT AND TOMATO APPETIZER SALAD

>½ cup fine *bulgour* (crushed wheat)
>1½ cups chopped tomatoes
>¾ cup minced green onion
>1 cup chopped parsley
>1½ teaspoons salt
>2 tablespoons fresh mint or ½ teaspoon, dried
>⅓ cup sesame or olive oil
>⅓ cup lemon juice

Put the *bulgour* in a large bowl, and cover it with lukewarm water. Rub the wheat several times, picking it up in handfuls and rubbing between the palms. Let soak for 10 minutes, then drain thoroughly. Spread it out on a towel, and dry it.

In a bowl, combine the wheat, tomatoes, onions, parsley, and salt. Mix thoroughly but gently. If fresh mint is used, mince it; if dried mint is used, soak it in warm water for 5 minutes, drain and crumble it.

Just before serving, combine the oil, lemon juice, and mint, and pour it over the salad. Serve from the bowl, or divide into individual portions in a mound shape.

Serves 6.


## Soupa Avgolemono
GREECE
### LEMON SOUP

>½ cup rice
>6 cups chicken broth
>2 egg yolks
>2 tablespoons lemon juice

Wash the rice in warm water and let soak 15 minutes; drain.

Bring the broth to a boil; add the rice and cook over low heat 15 minutes. Beat the egg yolks and lemon juice in a bowl. Gradually add about 1 cup of the hot broth, stirring constantly, to prevent curdling. Return to the balance of the broth, stirring constantly. Taste for seasoning, but do not allow to boil. Serve with a slice of lemon in each plate.

Serves 6–8.


*Balik Çorbasi*                                         TURKEY
*FISH CHOWDER*

        4-pound whole fish (sea bass, snapper, mackerel)
        2½ quarts water
        2 whole onions
        3 carrots
        2 stalks celery and leaves
        2 bay leaves
        1 tablespoon salt
        ¾ teaspoon freshly ground black pepper
        ¾ teaspoon thyme
        3 tablespoons butter
        2 cups chopped onions
        2 cloves garlic, minced
        3 tablespoons grated coconut
        2 tablespoons minced dill or parsley

Have the fish filleted, but ask for the head, skin, and bones. The more fish trimmings, the better the chowder will be; if possible, request some extra heads. Wash the fish and trimmings thoroughly. Cut the fish into 2-inch pieces, and refrigerate until needed.

In a large saucepan, combine the trimmings, water, onions, carrots, celery, bay leaves, salt, pepper, and thyme. Bring to a boil and cook over medium heat 1 hour. Strain, pressing through all the liquid.

Melt the butter in a saucepan; sauté the onions and garlic 5 minutes. Add the fish stock and cook over low heat 15 minutes. Add the fish and coconut; cook over low heat 35 minutes. Taste for seasoning and serve sprinkled with the dill or parsley.

Serves 6–8.

## Yoğurt Çorbasi
## YOGURT SOUP

MIDDLE EAST

¼ cup raw rice
6 cups beef broth
2 tablespoons flour
½ cup cold water
3 egg yolks
1 cup yogurt
1 teaspoon diced mint leaves, crushed

Crush the rice with a rolling pin. Bring the broth to a boil and add the rice; cook over low heat 15 minutes. While the broth is cooking, mix the flour with the water in a small pan. Beat the egg yolks with the yogurt; gradually stir in a half cup of the broth. Stir this into the flour mixture, and cook over low heat, stirring steadily until it boils. Stir into the broth, and taste for seasoning. Serve sprinkled with mint.

Serves 6–8.

## Ashe Reshte
## NOODLE-MEATBALL SOUP

MIDDLE EAST

3 cups beef broth
4 cups water
½ cup lentils
½ pound ground beef
¼ cup grated onion
½ teaspoon cinnamon
½ teaspoon freshly ground black pepper
2 teaspoons salt
1 cup fine noodles
½ cup minced parsley
1 teaspoon dried mint

Combine the broth and water in a large saucepan. Bring to a boil and add the lentils. Cook 30 minutes. Prepare the meatballs meanwhile.

Mix together the beef, onion, ¼ teaspoon of the cinnamon, ¼ teaspoon of the pepper, and ½ teaspoon of the salt. Shape into walnut-sized balls and add to the lentils with the noodles, parsley, and remaining salt. Cook over low heat 35 minutes.

Rub the mint to a powder with the hands, and add to the soup with the remaining cinnamon and pepper.

Serves 6.

## *Jajik*
## CUCUMBER SOUP

MIDDLE EAST

>4 cucumbers
>1½ teaspoons salt
>2 cloves garlic, minced
>2 tablespoons lemon juice
>6 cups yogurt
>1 tablespoon finely chopped dill
>¼ cup sesame or olive oil
>2 teaspoons chopped mint

Peel the cucumbers, cut in quarters lengthwise, scoop out the seeds, then slice thin. Sprinkle with the salt and let stand 15 minutes. Drain well. Stir together the garlic, lemon juice, yogurt, and dill. Mix with the cucumbers. Pour the oil over the top and sprinkle with the mint. Serve at room temperature.

Serves 6–8.

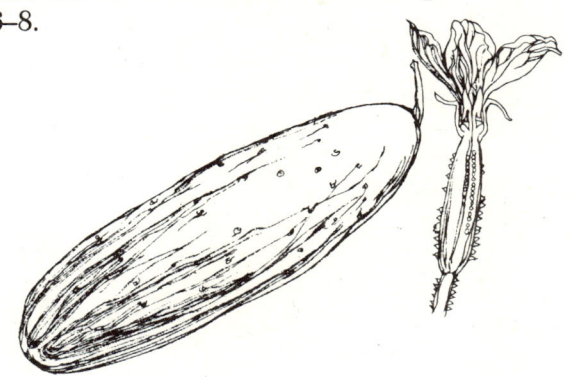

## Uskumru Dolmasi
## DATE-STUFFED FISH

TURKEY

>    3 1-pound mackerel
>    Salt
>    ¾ cup cooked rice
>    1 cup ground almonds
>    ½ pound pitted dates
>    4 tablespoons melted butter
>    ¾ teaspoon freshly ground black pepper
>    ¼ cup sesame or vegetable oil
>    1 cup chopped onions
>    6 slices lemon
>    6 slices tomato
>    1 cup water

Have the fish split and boned, and heads removed or not, as you prefer. Wash the fish, cover with water and add ¼ cup salt. Let stand 15 minutes. Drain, rinse and pat dry with paper towels.

Mix together the rice, almonds, dates, melted butter, and ¼ teaspoon of the pepper. Divide the mixture evenly into three parts, and stuff the fish. Fasten the openings with skewers, toothpicks, or sew with thread.

Use a baking pan large enough to hold the fish in a single layer. Brush with a little of the oil. Sprinkle the onions on the bottom. Arrange the fish over the onions and sprinkle with the remaining pepper. Arrange 2 slices of lemon and 2 slices of tomato on each fish, and pour the remaining oil on top. Pour the water around the fish. Bake on the middle level of a preheated 450° oven 30 minutes. Move the pan to the top level and bake 15 minutes longer. Remove the fastenings from the fish and serve.

Serves 3–6.

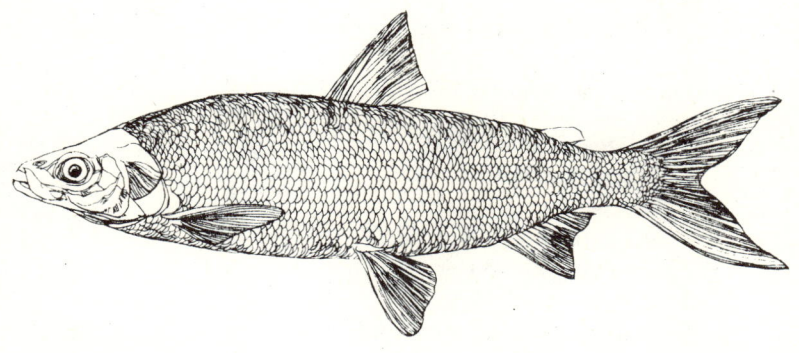

*Ghivetch*                                                                                   ROUMANIA
*FISH AND VEGETABLE CASSEROLE*

1 cup olive oil
2 cups diced potatoes
2 packages frozen mixed vegetables, thawed
1½ cups shredded cabbage
1 green pepper, cut julienne
2 cups diced eggplant
1 cup onions, chopped
2 cloves garlic, minced
2 tomatoes, chopped
½ pound okra, sliced
⅛ teaspoon thyme
1 bay leaf
4 teaspoons salt
1 teaspoon freshly ground black pepper
6 slices (3 pounds) freshwater fish
2 tablespoons butter

Heat the oil in a casserole until it bubbles. Add the potatoes, mixed vegetables, cabbage, green pepper, eggplant, onions, garlic, tomatoes, okra, thyme, bay leaf, 2 teaspoons salt, and ½ teaspoon pepper. Mix lightly. Bake in a 350° oven 30 minutes. Season the fish with the remaining salt and pepper and arrange over the vegetables. Dot with the butter. Bake 45 minutes longer. Discard bay leaf before serving.

Serves 6.

## BAKED SWEET AND SOUR FISH        ISRAEL

¼ cup vegetable oil
2 cups sliced onions
6 slices pike, whitefish, or mackerel
2 teaspoons salt
½ teaspoon pepper
1½ cups diced tomatoes
2 lemons, sliced thin
½ cup water
3 tablespoons cider vinegar
2 tablespoons sugar
1 bay leaf

Heat the oil in a deep skillet with ovenproof handle. Brown the onions in it. Arrange the fish over the onions and sprinkle with the salt and pepper. Add the tomatoes, lemon slices, water, vinegar, sugar, and bay leaf. Cover, and bake in a 325° oven 40 minutes, removing the cover for the last 5 minutes. Discard the bay leaf. Serve hot or cold.

Serves 6.


## *Tchakhokhbili*         RUSSIA
## CHICKEN STEW

2 3-pound frying chickens, disjointed
4 tablespoons butter
1 cup chopped onions
2 teaspoons salt
¾ teaspoon freshly ground black pepper
¼ cup Vodka
1 tablespoon cider vinegar
1 tablespoon tomato paste
¼ cup beef broth
4 firm tomatoes, peeled and quartered
Lemon slices
Minced dill or parsley

Wash and dry the chicken pieces. In a Dutch oven or heavy skillet, melt the butter; brown the chicken pieces in it. Add the onions, salt, and pepper; mix well and cook 5 minutes. Add the vodka, vinegar, tomato paste, and broth. Bring to a boil, cover, and cook over low heat 45 minutes. Add the tomatoes, and cook 10 minutes longer. Arrange the chicken on a heated serving dish, and put a slice of lemon on each piece. Sprinkle with the dill or parsley.

Serves 4–6.

## *Cotletki Pojarski*      RUSSIA
### CHICKEN CUTLETS

> 3 whole raw chicken breasts
> 4 slices homemade-style white bread
> ½ cup light cream
> 1½ teaspoons salt
> ½ teaspoon white pepper
> Dash nutmeg
> ¼ pound (1 stick) butter, melted (about)
> 2 eggs, beaten
> ¾ cup freshly made bread crumbs

Remove the skin and bones of the chicken, and put the meat through the fine blade of a food chopper. Trim the crusts from the bread, then soak the bread in the cream. Mash smooth, and mix with the chicken. Add the salt, pepper, nutmeg, and 2 tablespoons of the butter. Chop until very fine. Shape the mixture into 6 large cutlets. Dip in the eggs, and then in the bread crumbs, coating them evenly. Chill 1 hour.

Heat 4 tablespoons of the butter in a skillet. Arrange the cutlets in it, and fry over low heat until browned on both sides, about 20 minutes. Add more butter, if necessary. Serve with Hollandaise Sauce (see recipe) mixed with 1 cup sliced Sautéed Mushrooms (see recipe).

Serves 6.

## Shirini Polo
### ORANGE-FLAVORED CHICKEN PILAF

IRAN

**Orange Mixture**

- 2 cups julienne-cut carrots
- 1 cup water
- 6 tablespoons butter
- ½ cup candied orange peel
- 1 cup blanched slivered almonds

Cook the carrots with the water over high heat until the water evaporates. Melt half the butter in a skillet; sauté the carrots in it for 10 minutes. Add the orange peel and cook over very low heat for 5 minutes, stirring frequently. In a separate small skillet, melt the remaining butter and lightly brown the almonds in it.

**Rice**

- 2 cups long-grain rice
- Water
- Salt
- 4 tablespoons butter, melted

Wash the rice very well and combine it in a bowl with water to cover and 3 tablespoons salt. Let soak 2 hours and drain.

In a 3-quart saucepan, bring 6 cups water to a boil; very gradually add the rice. Stir, then cook over high heat for 12 minutes. Drain; stir in the melted butter. Keep warm.

**Chicken**

- 4 tablespoons sesame or vegetable oil
- 3 whole chicken breasts, cut in half
- 2 teaspoons salt
- ¼ teaspoon freshly ground black pepper
- ¾ cup water
- 1 teaspoon saffron
- 1 tablespoon boiling water
- 2 tablespoons melted butter

Heat the oil in a skillet; brown the chicken in it. Sprinkle with the salt and pepper, and add the water. Cover and cook over low heat 30 minutes, or until the chicken is tender. Discard the bones of the chicken.

In a buttered 3-quart casserole, spread half the rice. Over it put half the orange mixture, half the almonds, then half the chicken. Cover with half the remaining rice, the the remaining orange mixture, almonds and chicken. Cover with the remaining rice. Cover the casserole. Put in a 350° oven for 10 minutes. Dissolve the saffron in the boiling water and pour over the rice with the butter. Cut through several times with a spoon and serve.

Serves 6.

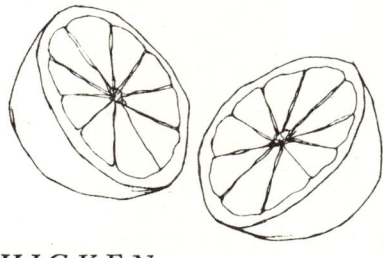

*Kates Riganati*
OREGANO CHICKEN

GREECE

    2 4-pound roasting chickens
    ½ cup olive oil
    4 tablespoons lemon juice
    3 teaspoons salt
    ¼ pound butter
    2 cups canned tomatoes
    2 teaspoons oregano
    1 teaspoon freshly ground black pepper

Rub the chickens, inside and out, with a mixture of the oil, lemon juice, and 2 teaspoons of the salt. Arrange in a roasting pan and roast in a 375° oven for 1 hour.

Melt the butter in a saucepan. Add the tomatoes, oregano, pepper, and the remaining salt and cook over medium heat 5 minutes, stirring occasionally. Pour over the chickens, reduce heat to 350° and roast 1 hour more, or until tender, basting frequently.

Serves 6–8.

## Kotopita
### CHICKEN PIE

GREECE

For the pastry, you can buy *phyllo* or *strudel* leaves in specialty food shops. These prepared leaves are completely authentic. Three other possibilities: frozen patty shells (thawed, rolled out, and used as a top-and-bottom crust), or pie pastry mix, or your favorite pie pastry recipe.

#### SAUCE

4 tablespoons butter
5 tablespoons flour
2 cups milk
1½ teaspoons salt
½ teaspoon freshly ground black pepper
¾ cup Parmesan cheese
4 eggs, beaten

Melt the butter in a saucepan. Blend in the flour. Remove the pan from the heat, and beat in the milk until smooth. Return to medium heat, add the salt and pepper, and cook, stirring steadily, to the boiling point. Then cook 5 minutes longer. Mix in the grated cheese, and let cool 5 minutes. Then beat in the eggs.

#### FILLING

3 tablespoons vegetable oil
1 cup chopped onions
1 clove garlic, minced
3 cups shredded cooked chicken or turkey
1 teaspoon salt
½ teaspoon freshly ground black pepper
½ cup dry vermouth or white wine
½ teaspoon nutmeg
¼ cup minced parsley

Heat the oil in a skillet; sauté the onions until browned. Add the garlic, chicken, salt and pepper. Cook, stirring frequently, until chicken browns. Add the vermouth; cook over high heat 3 min-

# WHERE EAST MEETS WEST 143

utes. Add the nutmeg and parsley, and combine with the previously prepared sauce. Mix well, and taste for seasoning; the mixture should be fairly well seasoned.

To prepare the pie, use a 9-inch-deep pie plate. If you're using the *phyllo* or strudel leaves, place 4 layers on the bottom of the pie plate, brushing each layer with melted butter. Turn the filling into the lined pie plate, and cover with 4 more layers, again brushing each layer with melted butter. Seal the edges well.

If you're using the rolled-out patty shells or pie pastry, merely line the pie plate with it, fill the shell, and cover with the top layer. Seal the edges well, and prick the top.

Bake in a preheated 425° oven 10 minutes; then reduce the heat to 350°, and bake 15 minutes longer or until golden brown. To serve, cut in wedges.

Serves 6–8.

Nutmeg

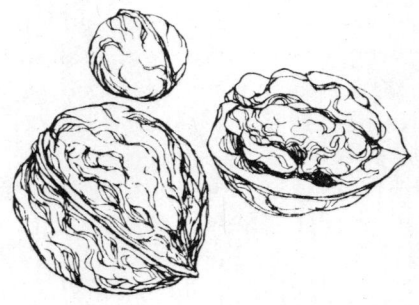

## Çerkes Tavûgu
### CIRCASSIAN CHICKEN

TURKEY

    4-pound chicken, split in half
    1 quart water
    1 onion
    2 cloves garlic
    2 teaspoons salt
    2 cups shelled walnuts
    2 slices white bread, trimmed
    1 teaspoon paprika
    Dash cayenne pepper

Wash the chicken. Bring the water to a boil; add the onion, garlic, salt, and chicken. Cover loosely, and cook over low heat 1 hour, or until the chicken is tender. Remove the chicken, and cook the broth until reduced to 2 cups. Strain.

Pulverize the nuts in an electric blender, or put through a mouli grater twice. The nuts must be very fine, almost like a powder. Soak the bread in a little broth, and add to the blender. Or mash it very smooth, then add to the nuts. Using the blender, or an electric mixer, very gradually add the broth, to the nut mixture, then the paprika and cayenne and beat until mixture looks like a heavy mayonnaise. Taste for seasoning.

Discard the skin and bones of the chicken and cut the meat into strips, about 1½ inches long and ¼ inch wide. Mix half the sauce with the chicken to coat the pieces. Heap the chicken in a mound on a serving dish, and cover with the remaining sauce. Sprinkle with additional paprika if you wish, and chill.

Serves 6–8 as a first course.

## *Fesenjan*
## DUCK WITH WALNUTS

IRAN

       4–5-pound duck
       3 teaspoons salt
       ¾ teaspoon freshly ground black pepper
       ¾ pound shelled walnuts
       2 tablespoons sesame or vegetable oil
       1 cup chopped onions
       3 cups water
       3 tablespoons lemon juice
       2 tablespoons sugar
       ¼ cup raspberry jelly

Wash the duck, and remove as much fat as possible. Dry the duck inside and out with paper towels, then rub it with 2 teaspoons of the salt and ½ teaspoon of the pepper. Place the duck on a rack in a shallow roasting pan, and roast in a 450° oven 1 hour, turning it to brown all sides. Cut the duck into serving-sized pieces.

While the duck is roasting, pulverize the walnuts in an electric blender, or put through a mouli grater or other nut grinder. Heat the oil in a casserole and sauté the onions 10 minutes, stirring frequently. Mix in the walnuts, water, and remaining salt and pepper. Bring to a boil and cook over low heat 20 minutes. Add the duck pieces, cover, and cook over low heat 30 minutes. Stir in the lemon juice, sugar, and jelly. If gravy looks too thick, add a little more water. Cook 20 minutes longer. Taste for seasoning. Skim the fat.

Arrange the duck on a heated platter, and cover with some of the gravy. Garnish with whole walnuts if you like. Serve the rest of gravy in a sauceboat.

Serves 4.

## Kufta
### MEATBALLS

MIDDLE EAST

2 tablespoons raw rice
3 tablespoons split peas
3 cups water
1 pound ground beef
1 cup chopped green onions
1 cup chopped parsley
1½ teaspoons salt
½ teaspoon pepper
1 egg, beaten
3 tablespoons butter
½ cup chopped onions
1½ cups beef broth
2 tablespoons tomato paste
1 tablespoon lemon juice

Cook the rice and split peas in the water 30 minutes. Drain well. Mix together the beef, green onions, parsley, salt, pepper, egg, and cooked rice and peas. Shape the mixture into 2-inch balls with wet hands.

Melt the butter in a skillet; sauté the onions 10 minutes. Stir in the broth, tomato paste, and lemon juice; bring to a boil and cook over low heat 10 minutes. Add the meatballs; cover, and cook over low heat 30 minutes. Shake the pan and baste occasionally.

Serves 4–6.

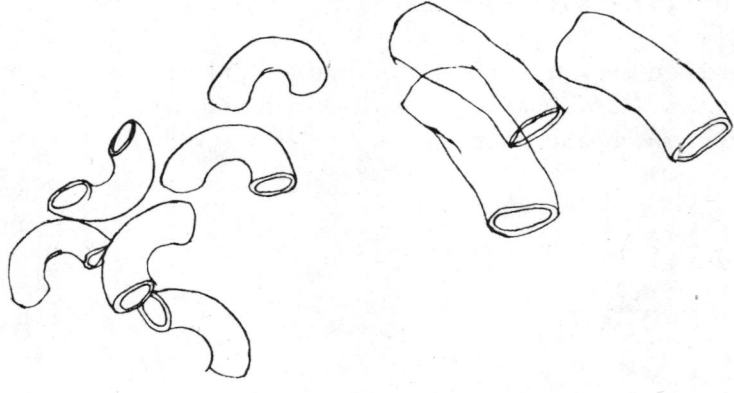

## *Pastichio*
## MACARONI CASSEROLE

GREECE

    3 tablespoons olive oil
    1 cup chopped onions
    1 pound ground beef
    ¾ cup peeled chopped tomatoes
    1½ teaspoons salt
    ½ teaspoon freshly ground black pepper
    ¼ teaspoon oregano
    ½ cup grated Parmesan cheese
    1 pound short-cut or elbow macaroni,
        cooked and drained

Heat the oil in a skillet; cook the onions and meat in it over high heat, stirring steadily, for 5 minutes. Mix in the tomatoes, salt, pepper, and oregano; cook over low heat 5 minutes. Mix in the cheese. Taste for seasoning.

In a buttered 2-quart casserole, spread half the macaroni. Spread the meat mixture over it and cover with the remaining macaroni. Cover with the following sauce:

    2 tablespoons butter
    1 tablespoon flour
    ½ teaspoon salt
    ⅛ teaspoon white pepper
    1 cup milk
    1 egg yolk
    ¼ cup grated Parmesan cheese

Melt the butter in a saucepan; gradually blend in the flour, salt, and pepper. Add the milk gradually, stirring steadily to the boiling point. Cook over low heat 5 minutes. Beat the egg yolk and cheese in a bowl; add the hot sauce slowly, stirring steadily, to prevent curdling. Pour over the macaroni. Bake in a 375° oven 30 minutes or until browned.

Serves 4–6.

## *Dolma*
## STUFFED CABBAGE ROLLS

IRAN

1 large head of cabbage
1 pound ground beef
1 cup chopped onions
½ cup chopped parsley
½ teaspoon cinnamon
2 teaspoons salt
½ teaspoon freshly ground black pepper
1½ cups beef broth
½ cup lemon juice
¼ cup sugar

Wash the cabbage, cover with water, bring to a boil and cook over low heat 15 minutes. Drain and carefully remove 24 leaves. Cut the leaves in half.

Mix together the beef, onions, parsley, cinnamon, 1 teaspoon salt, and ¼ teaspoon pepper. Put a heaping teaspoon of the mixture on each leaf. Fold in the opposite ends, then roll up into finger shapes. If there is any filling left, use a few more cabbage leaves.

Line the bottom of a deep skillet with cabbage leaves and arrange the rolls in it, placing more leaves between the layers. Add the broth, and the remaining salt and pepper. Cover and cook over low heat 30 minutes. Mix in the lemon juice and sugar. Cook 30 minutes; taste for seasoning. Drain. Serve hot or cold.

Makes about 48.

## *Stiffado*
## BEEF STEW

GREECE

    3 pounds eye round or chuck of beef, cut in 1-inch cubes
    3 teaspoons salt
    ½ teaspoon freshly ground black pepper
    1 teaspoon cinnamon
    ⅓ cup olive oil
    12 small white onions
    1 cup tomato sauce
    2 cups beef broth
    3 cups diced eggplant
    2 green peppers, cut in slivers
    ½ cup raw rice

Trim the fat from the meat. Season the meat with 2 teaspoons of the salt, the pepper, and cinnamon. Heat ¼ cup of the oil in a Dutch oven or heavy casserole and brown the meat. Remove the meat and set aside. In the oil remaining in the pan, sauté the onions until golden. Return the meat and add the tomato sauce and ½ cup of the broth. Cover and cook over low heat 1¼ hours.

Heat the remaining oil in a skillet; sauté the eggplant for 10 minutes. Sprinkle with the remaining salt and add to the meat with the green peppers, rice, and remaining broth. Re-cover and cook 30 minutes longer. Taste for seasoning.

Serves 6–8.

*Spanakopeta*  
SPINACH PIE

GREECE

    12 *phyllo* or strudel leaves (obtainable in specialty food shops)
    2 pounds spinach
    ½ cup chopped parsley
    ½ cup chopped dill
    2 cups chopped green onions
    1½ teasoons salt
    ¼ cup olive oil
    2 cups chopped onions
    ¼ teaspoon black pepper
    ½ pound Feta cheese, crumbled
    ¾ cup melted butter

Keep the pastry leaves covered, until ready to use.

Wash, clean, and discard the stems of the spinach. Drain and shred. Combine the spinach, parsley, dill, green onions, and salt in a bowl. Let stand 10 minutes, then drain, pressing out all the liquid.

Heat the oil in a skillet; sauté the chopped onions 10 minutes. Add to the spinach mixture, with the pepper and cheese. Mix well and let cool.

Brush an 11-by-14-inch baking pan with butter. Into it put 6 layers of pastry leaves, brushing each layer with melted butter. Spread the filling evenly, then cover with the remaining pastry leaves, again brushing each layer with melted butter. Brush the top layer heavily. With a sharp knife, trace the top layer into squares. Bake in a preheated 375° oven 30 minutes, or until golden brown. Cut through the squares and serve hot.

Serves 8.

## Dolmeh Felfel Sabz
## STUFFED PEPPERS

IRAN

8 green peppers
2½ cups water
¼ cup yellow split peas
¼ cup rice
4 tablespoons sesame or vegetable oil
¾ cup minced yellow onions
1 pound ground beef
½ teaspoon cinnamon
3 teaspoons salt
¾ teaspoon freshly ground black pepper
¼ cup chopped green onions
3 tablespoons minced parsley
2 cups peeled chopped tomatoes
Yogurt

Wash the peppers, cut a half-inch slice from the stem ends and reserve. Scoop out the seeds and fibers. Cover the peppers with water, bring to a boil, and cook over low heat 5 minutes. Drain well.

Bring the 2½ cups water to a boil. Add the split peas and rice. Cook 25 minutes. Drain.

Heat 2 tablespoons of the oil in a skillet. Add the yellow onions and beef. Cook over medium heat, stirring frequently, for 10 minutes. Mix in the cinnamon, 1½ teaspoons salt, ½ teaspoon pepper, the green onions, parsley, cooked split peas and rice. Stuff the peppers and replace the tops.

Heat the remaining oil in a deep skillet or casserole. Arrange the peppers in it in an upright position. Mix the tomatoes with the remaining salt and pepper; pour over the peppers. Bring to a boil, cover, and cook over low heat 35 minutes, or until the peppers are tender. Serve hot, topped with yogurt.

Serves 8.

## Coulebiac
### BEEF ROLL

RUSSIA

> 1 cup water
> ¼ pound (1 stick) butter
> 2 cups sifted flour
> ¼ teaspoon salt
> 5 eggs

Combine the water and butter in a saucepan; bring to a boil. When butter melts, remove from the heat and add all the flour and salt at once, stirring hard with a wooden spoon until smooth. Return to low heat and cook, stirring constantly, until mixture is dry and leaves the sides of the pan.

Remove from the heat and add 1 egg at a time, beating hard after each addition. Chill for 30 minutes. Meanwhile prepare the filling.

#### FILLING

> 2 tablespoons butter
> 1 cup finely chopped onions
> 1 pound ground beef
> 1½ teaspoons salt
> ½ teaspoon freshly ground black pepper
> 3 hard cooked eggs, chopped
> 2 tablespoons finely chopped dill or parsley
> 4 tablespoons sour cream
> 1 egg yolk, beaten
> 3 tablespoons melted butter

Melt the 2 tablespoons butter in a skillet; sauté the onion for 5 minutes. Add the beef; cook over high heat for 10 minutes, stirring almost constantly. Add the salt, pepper, eggs, dill or parsley, and sour cream, mixing lightly. Cool 30 minutes. Preheat oven to 400°.

Divide the paste in two, one piece larger than the other. Pat out the larger piece into a rectangle large enough to line the bottom and sides of a 12-inch loaf pan. Spread the filling in it. Roll out second piece of paste and cover filling, sealing the edges well. Make 2 slits in the top. Brush with the egg yolk.

Bake 40 minutes, or until browned. Pour the melted butter into the slits. Turn out carefully and slice.

Serves 4–6.

## *Imam Bayeldi*     MIDDLE EAST
### STUFFED EGGPLANT

2 eggplants
Salt
⅔ cup olive oil
3 (1 pound) onions, peeled and thinly sliced
2 green peppers, thinly sliced and seeded
1 cup chopped canned tomatoes, drained
¾ teaspoon freshly ground black pepper
½ cup minced parsley
8 cloves garlic
1 cup water

Try to buy long narrow eggplants, weighing about 1 pound each.

Wash and dry the eggplants, and cut off the stems. Cut each eggplant into quarters lengthwise. Make 2 long slashes in each quarter, on the cut side. Sprinkle the eggplant with 1 tablespoon salt and let stand for 30 minutes. Prepare the stuffing meanwhile.

Heat ¼ cup of the oil in a skillet; sauté the onions and green peppers for 5 minutes, stirring frequently. Add the tomatoes, pepper, ¼ cup of the parsley, and 1½ teaspoons salt. Cook 2 minutes.

Drain the eggplants well, as water will have oozed out. Pat dry, and arrange them, skin side down, in an oiled shallow baking pan. Force as much of the tomato mixture into the slashes as possible, and spread the remainder over the top. Place a garlic clove on each, and pour the remaining oil over the top. Pour the water into the pan, cover, and bake in a 375° oven 1¼ hours, removing the cover for the last 15 minutes. Cool in the pan and sprinkle with the remaining parsley.

Serves 4–8.

## Musaca cu Patlagele Vinete
## MEAT-EGGPLANT LAYERS

ROUMANIA

2 medium-sized eggplants
⅜ pound (1½ sticks) butter
3½ teaspoons salt
1½ cups chopped onions
1½ pounds lean ground beef
1 tablespoon tomato paste
⅓ cup dry red wine
½ teaspoon freshly ground black pepper
¼ teaspoon cinnamon
¼ cup chopped parsley
3 tablespoons flour
2 cups hot milk
1 cup cottage cheese, drained
2 eggs, beaten
⅛ teaspoon nutmeg
¾ cup dry bread crumbs
¾ cup grated Parmesan cheese

Peel the eggplants and cut into slices ½ inch thick. Melt 4 tablespoons of the butter in a skillet; brown the eggplant slices on both sides. Remove and sprinkle with 1 teaspoon of the salt.

In the same skillet, melt 4 tablespoons of the remaining butter; sauté the onions 10 minutes. Add the meat; cook 10 minutes, stirring frequently. Stir in the tomato paste, wine, pepper, cinnamon, parsley, and 1½ teaspoons of the remaining salt. Cook over low heat, stirring frequently until mixture is fairly dry. Taste for seasoning. Cool.

Melt the remaining butter in a saucepan; blend in the flour and remaining salt. Add the milk, stirring steadily to the boiling point, then cook 5 minutes longer. Remove from the heat, cool 5 minutes, then mix in the cottage cheese, eggs, and nutmeg.

Grease a baking pan measuring 8 x 12 inches and dust lightly with some bread crumbs. Arrange layers of the eggplant and meat, sprinkling each layer with bread crumbs and Parmesan cheese. Start and end with the eggplant. Pour the sauce over the top. Bake in a preheated 375° oven 1 hour, or until the custard top is set and golden brown. Let stand 30 minutes at room temperature before cutting into squares.

Serves 6–8.

*Fassolia me Arni*   GREECE
LAMB AND BEAN CASSEROLE

>2 cups dried white beans
>2 tablespoons olive oil
>1½ cups chopped onions
>2 pounds boneless lamb, cut in 1½-inch cubes
>2 teaspoons salt
>½ teaspoon freshly ground black pepper
>1 bay leaf
>1½ cups peeled chopped tomatoes
>2 cloves garlic, minced
>2 tablespoons parsley

Wash the beans, cover with water, and bring to a boil. Cook 5 minutes, remove from the heat, and let stand 1 hour. Drain; add fresh water to cover, bring to a boil, and cook over low heat 1½ hours. Drain, reserving 1½ cups liquid.

Heat the oil in a casserole; brown the onions in it. Add the lamb and cook until browned. Add the beans, bean liquid, the salt, pepper, and bay leaf. Cover and cook over low heat 1 hour. Add the tomatoes and garlic; re-cover and cook 1 hour longer or until beans and lamb are tender. Sprinkle with the parsley.

Serves 6–8.

## Yaprak Dolmasi
### STUFFED GRAPE LEAVES

TURKEY

1 quart jar grape leaves
½ cup sesame or vegetable oil
1 cup minced onions
½ pound ground beef
1 cup cooked drained rice
1½ teaspoons salt
¼ teaspoon freshly ground black pepper
3 tablespoons pine nuts or blanched slivered almonds
½ cup water
2 lemons, thinly sliced

Drain the grape leaves and drop them into boiling water. Remove the pan from the heat, let stand for 1 minute, then immediately drain the leaves and drop into cold water. Drain when cold. Carefully lift up each leaf separately and spread them out on paper towels, dull side up.

Heat 4 tablespoons of the oil in a skillet; sauté the onions in it for 5 minutes, stirring frequently. Add the beef, and cook, stirring steadily, until meat loses redness. Mix in the rice, salt, pepper, and nuts; cook 2 minutes, stirring steadily. Taste for seasoning. To stuff the leaves, place one at a time on a plate, dull side up. Put a tablespoon of the rice mixture on the center. Turn in the stem end, then fold over one side to the center, then the other. The filling should be covered at this point. Roll up the leaf from the stem end, until it looks like a cigar. Stuff about 40 leaves.

Use a heavy 2-quart casserole and cover the bottom with a layer of grape leaves. Arrange the stuffed grape leaves in a single layer over it. Put some plain grape leaves in another layer over them. Continue arranging the stuffed leaves over it. Sprinkle with the remaining oil, add the water, and arrange the lemon slices on top. Bring to a boil, cover and cook over low heat 1½ hours. Remove, cover, and let cool in the pan. Carefully transfer the stuffed leaves to a serving dish, and pour the liquid over them. Serve with a bowl of yogurt or sour cream.

Makes about 40.

## Sikbaj
### BEEF AND FIG CASSEROLE

IRAN

    3 pounds chuck, rump, or cross rib of beef
    2 tablespoons vegetable oil
    3 cups boiling water
    ¾ teaspoon crushed coriander seeds
    1 teaspoon cinnamon
    1½ cups sliced onions
    1 cup sliced carrots
    12 green onions, quartered lengthwise
    2 teaspoons salt
    ½ teaspoon freshly ground black pepper
    ¼ cup wine vinegar
    ½ cup honey
    1 cup sliced almonds
    1 17-ounce can figs, drained

  Cut the meat in 1½-inch cubes. Heat the oil in a Dutch oven or heavy casserole; lightly brown the meat in it. Add the water, coriander, cinnamon, onions, carrots, and green onions. Cook over low heat 1½ hours. Mix in the salt, pepper, vinegar, and honey. Cook 1 hour. Add the almonds and figs. Cover the pan, remove from the heat, and let stand 1 hour. Reheat just before serving.
  Serves 6–8.

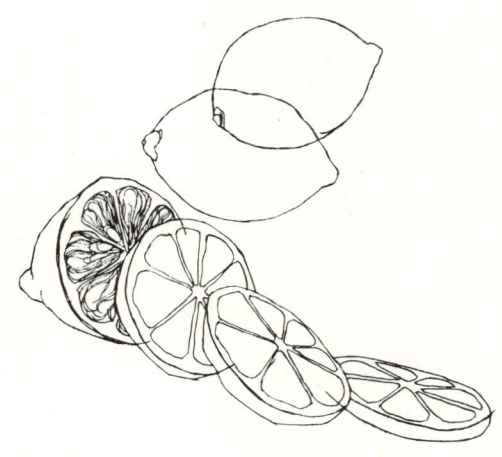

## Kibbe
### BAKED MEAT AND WHEAT

MIDDLE EAST

#### Filling

- 2 tablespoons sesame or olive oil
- ¾ cup chopped onions
- ½ pound ground lamb
- ½ teaspoon salt
- ¼ teaspoon freshly ground black pepper
- ¼ cup pine nuts

Heat the oil in a skillet; brown the onion in it. Add the meat, salt, and pepper. Cook, stirring frequently, for 5 minutes. Add the nuts. Cook, stirring frequently until browned.

#### Wheat Mixture

- 1 pound *borghul* (fine crushed wheat)
- 2 pounds lean twice-ground lamb
- ½ cup grated onions
- 2 teaspoons salt
- ½ teaspoon freshly ground black pepper
- ¼ teaspoon cinnamon
- ¼ cup ice water
- ½ cup melted butter

Soak the wheat in cold water to cover for 30 minutes, kneading it several times. Drain thoroughly, then mix in the lamb, onions, salt, pepper, and cinnamon. Knead for a few minutes, then put through the fine blade of a food chopper, adding ¼ cup ice water as you grind.

Pat half the wheat mixture into a greased 9-by-12-inch baking pan. Spread the filling over it. Cover with the remaining wheat mixture, pressing down until firm. With a sharp knife, cut diagonal lines across the top to form a diamond pattern. Pour the melted butter over the top. Bake in a preheated 400° oven 30 minutes. Reduce heat to 350° and bake 30 minutes longer. Cut into squares and serve hot or cold.

Serves 8–10.

## *Cholent*
## MEAT AND BEANS

ISRAEL

>2 cups dried lima beans
>6 tablespoons rendered chicken fat or oil
>1½ cups chopped onions
>2 pounds boneless lamb, cubed
>2-pound chicken, disjointed
>2 tomatoes, peeled and chopped
>¼ cup barley
>3 cups beef broth
>2 teaspoons salt
>½ teaspoon freshly ground black pepper
>2 teaspoons paprika
>1 tablespoon flour
>3 beef frankfurters, sliced ½ inch thick

Wash the lima beans. Place in a saucepan with water to cover, bring to a boil, then remove from heat and let soak 2 hours. Drain well; add fresh water to cover. Bring to a boil, cover saucepan, and cook over low heat 1½ hours. Drain.

Melt 4 tablespoons fat in a skillet. Sauté the onions 10 minutes; remove from skillet. Brown the lamb and chicken in the fat remaining in the skillet. Combine the beans, onions, browned meats, tomatoes, barley, broth, salt, pepper, paprika, and flour in a 4-quart Dutch oven or casserole. Sprinkle with the remaining fat; cover and bake in a 325° oven 2½ hours. Add a little boiling water from time to time if pan becomes too dry. Taste for seasoning. Remove cover, arrange frankfurters on top, and bake 20 minutes longer.

Serves 6–8.

## Moussaka
### LAMB AND EGGPLANT CASSEROLE
GREECE

2 1¼-pound eggplants
5 teaspoons salt
Flour
¾ cup olive or vegetable oil (approximately)
1 cup minced onion
2 cloves garlic, minced
2 pounds ground lamb
2 cups chopped canned tomatoes, drained
¾ teaspoon freshly ground black pepper
½ teaspoon cinnamon
½ teaspoon oregano

Wash, dry, and peel the eggplant. Cut into ¼-inch-thick slices. Arrange the eggplant slices on a flat surface, and sprinkle them with 3 teaspoons of the salt. Let stand for 20 minutes, then dry the slices with paper towels. Dip the slices in flour, coating them well, then shake them to remove the excess.

Heat ¼ cup of the oil in a large skillet; put the eggplant slices in it in a single layer and sauté them until golden brown on both sides. Remove the slices with a slotted spatula, and drain them on paper towels. Add a little more of the oil, and continue browning the remaining slices.

In the oil remaining, sauté the onions for 5 minutes, stirring frequently. Add the garlic and lamb, and cook, stirring frequently to prevent lumps from forming, until delicately browned. Add the tomatoes, pepper, cinnamon, oregano, and remaining salt. Cook over high heat, stirring frequently, until all the liquid is absorbed. Taste for seasoning.

#### SAUCE

4 tablespoons butter
4 tablespoons flour
½ teaspoon salt
2 cups milk, scalded
3 eggs
⅓ cup grated Parmesan cheese

Melt the butter in a saucepan. Remove from the heat and blend in the flour and salt. Very gradually, add the milk, stirring steadily. Return to medium heat, and cook, stirring steadily, to the boiling point, then cook over low heat 5 minutes, stirring frequently.

Beat the eggs in a bowl; very gradually, add half the sauce, stirring steadily to prevent curdling. Stir into the sauce in the pan, and cook 1 minute, but do not let boil. Mix in half the cheese.

Arrange half the eggplant slices on the bottom of a 3-quart casserole. Spread half the meat mixture over it, and repeat the layers. Pour the sauce over the top, and sprinkle with the remaining cheese. Bake in a preheated 350° oven 40 minutes, or until the top is golden brown. Let stand at room temperature for 10 minutes before serving.

Serves 6–8.

## Shashlik à la Karsky
### BROILED MARINATED LAMB

RUSSIA

2 whole loins of lamb
2 cups chopped green onions
½ cup chopped celery leaves
2 teaspoons salt
½ teaspoon freshly ground black pepper
¼ cup wine vinegar
¼ cup lemon juice
6 tablespoons butter
3 tablespoons flour
1½ cups beef broth
1 tablespoon tomato paste
1 cup thinly sliced onions
½ cup sliced carrots
¼ cup Madeira or dry sherry
12 very thin slices of lemon

Have the meat boned and each loin cut into four pieces. Put the lamb in a bowl and add the green onions, celery leaves, salt, pepper, vinegar, and lemon juice. Cover the bowl and let marinate for 4 hours at room temperature, or overnight.

Melt 3 tablespoons of the butter in a saucepan; blend in the flour until browned. Add the broth, stirring steadily to the boiling point. Mix in the tomato paste and cook over low heat while preparing the vegetables.

Melt the remaining butter in a skillet; sauté the onions and carrots 10 minutes. Add to the sauce and cook 30 minutes longer. Mix in the wine, and salt and pepper to taste. Strain.

Drain the lamb; arrange on a broiling pan. Broil in a hot broiler 15 minutes, turning to brown all sides. Garnish each piece of lamb with a lemon slice and serve the hot sauce in a sauceboat.

Serves 8.

*Limba cu Masline*  
TONGUE WITH OLIVES

ROUMANIA

5-pound pickled tongue
1 whole onion
1 stalk celery
3 tablespoons butter
1 cup chopped onions
1 clove garlic, minced
2 tablespoons flour
1 cup dry white wine
½ cup canned tomato sauce
3 tablespoons lemon juice
2 teaspoons sugar
½ teaspoon freshly ground black pepper
½ teaspoon ground ginger
1 teaspoon finely chopped bay leaf
1 cup sliced black olives

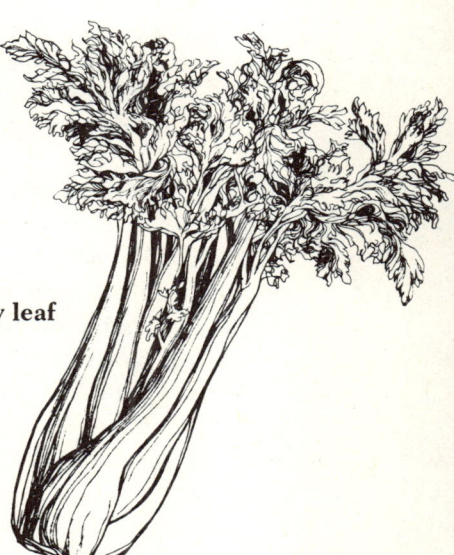

In a large saucepan, combine the tongue, whole onion, celery, and water to cover. Bring to a boil and cook over low heat 3 hours or until tender, adding boiling water from time to time to keep the tongue covered. Drain, reserving 1 cup stock. Skin the tongue, and discard root and connective tissues.

Melt the butter in a saucepan; sauté the chopped onions and garlic 10 minutes. Blend in the flour until browned; gradually add a combination of the stock, wine, and tomato sauce, stirring constantly to the boiling point. Mix in the lemon juice, sugar, pepper, ginger, bay leaf, and olives. Cook over low heat 5 minutes. Slice the tongue and heat in the sauce for 10 minutes. Taste for seasoning.

Serves 8–10.

## Basar Tz Aloouie
### SWEET AND SOUR MEAT

ISRAEL

> 4 pounds brisket or rump of beef
> 3 teaspoons salt
> 24 seedless raisins
> 2 tablespoons vegetable oil
> 1 cup chopped onions
> 3 cups boiling water
> ⅓ cup lemon juice
> 4 tablespoons brown sugar
> 4 gingersnaps, crushed

Rub the meat with 2 teaspoons of the salt, then make 24 little holes in it with a sharp knife and force a raisin into each.

Heat the oil in a heavy saucepan or Dutch oven and brown the meat in it over medium heat. Turn frequently, and don't worry if the raisins fall out. Add the onions and brown lightly. Pour off the fat. Add the remaining salt and 1 cup boiling water. Cover, and cook over low heat 2 hours, adding the remaining water from time to time. Stir in the lemon juice, sugar, and gingersnaps. Cook 20 minutes longer, or until the meat is tender. Taste for seasoning.
Serves 8–10.


## Moskovskaya Solyanka
### BEEF WITH SAUERKRAUT

RUSSIA

> 2 tablespoons vegetable oil
> 3 pounds cross rib or chuck of beef, cut in 2-inch cubes
> 1½ cups sliced onions
> 1½ teaspoons salt
> ½ teaspoon freshly ground black pepper
> 1½ pounds sauerkraut
> 1 bay leaf
> 1½ cups chopped canned tomatoes
> 6 frankfurters, cut in 2-inch slices
> 1 cup sour cream

Heat the oil in a casserole; brown the meat and onions in it. Sprinkle with the salt and pepper. Cover and cook over low heat 30 minutes. Watch carefully and add a very little water if necessary to keep from burning. Mix in the sauerkraut. Cook 10 minutes, stirring frequently. Add the bay leaf and tomatoes. Cover and cook 1 hour; add the frankfurters and cook 30 minutes longer or until the meat is tender. Discard the bay leaf, and mix in the sour cream.

Serves 6–8.


## *Cotletki*   RUSSIA
## VEAL CROQUETTES

3 slices white bread, trimmed
⅓ cup light cream
1½ pounds raw ground lean veal
½ teaspoon minced garlic
1½ teaspoons salt
¼ teaspoon white pepper
2 tablespoons melted butter
2 eggs, beaten
½ cup dry bread crumbs
6 tablespoons butter

Soak the bread in the cream; mash the undrained bread smooth. Mix with the veal, garlic, salt, pepper, and melted butter. Chop very fine. Form into 12 boat-shaped croquettes. Dip each croquette in the beaten eggs and then the bread crumbs, coating them well. Chill 1 hour.

Melt the butter in a large heavy skillet; arrange the croquettes in it in a single layer. Cook over low heat 10 minutes on each side or until browned and no pink remains inside. Serve with sautéed mushrooms or hollandaise sauce, if desired.

Serves 6.

## Khoubz Araby
### ARABIC BREAD

MIDDLE EAST

1¼ cups lukewarm water (approximately)
1 package active-dry yeast
Pinch of sugar
4 cups flour
1 teaspoon salt
2 tablespoons vegetable oil
½ cup white cornmeal
Sesame seeds, cumin seeds, or caraway (optional)

Pour ¼ cup of the water into a cup; add the yeast and sugar. Let stand 5 minutes, then stir until dissolved.

Put the flour and salt into a large bowl, and make a well in the center. Into it pour the oil, remaining water, and the yeast mixture. Mix the ingredients in the well, then work in the flour with the fingers until a dough is formed. If too stiff, add a little more warm water. If you have a dough hook attachment for your electric mixer, use it for 10 minutes, or until the dough is smooth and elastic. If not, turn out the dough onto a lightly floured surface, and knead until smooth and elastic, about 15 to 20 minutes. Shape the dough into a ball and place it in a lightly oiled bowl. Cover with a towel, and keep in a warm place until doubled in bulk, about 45 minutes.

Punch the dough down sharply with the hand, and divide into 6 pieces. Shape each piece into a ball, cover with the towel, and let stand 30 minutes.

Use three 14-by-17-inch baking sheets and sprinkle each with ⅓ of the cornmeal. If you have one oven, you'll have to bake one pan at a time. Roll each ball of dough into a thin circle, about 7 inches in diameter. Put two pieces on each baking sheet, allowing space between them. Sprinkle the tops with one of the seeds, if desired. Cover with a towel, and let stand for 30 minutes. Preheat the oven to 500°.

Bake the bread on the lowest level of the oven for 5 minutes, then raise to the next level and bake 5 minutes more, or until golden brown and puffed. Remove the breads from the pan, and wrap in foil. The resulting breads will be flat, but higher on the rim, and flat in the middle. Serve warm.

*Sabzi Salade*
MIXED SALAD

IRAN

> 1 head lettuce, preferably romaine
> 3 tomatoes, peeled and diced
> 2 cucumbers, peeled and thinly sliced
> 1 cup thinly sliced radishes
> ½ cup thinly sliced green onions
> ¼ cup minced parsley
> ¼ cup chopped dill
> ¾ cup sesame or olive oil
> ⅓ cup lemon juice
> ¾ teaspoon salt
> ¼ teaspoon freshly ground black pepper
> 1 clove garlic, minced
> ¼ pound Feta cheese, diced

Wash and dry the lettuce, and tear into bite-sized pieces. Combine in a bowl with all the vegetables and the herbs.

Beat together the oil, lemon juice, salt, pepper, and garlic. Just before serving, pour the dressing over the vegetables, and toss until coated, then toss in the cheese.

Serves 8.

## Tourlu Guvech
MIDDLE EAST
## PICKLED VEGETABLE SALAD

3 turnips
3 cups shredded cabbage
1 cup sliced celery
½ cup salt
3 cups water
3 cloves garlic
2 cups white vinegar
⅛ teaspoon Tabasco
2 tablespoons pickling spice
1 tablespoon sugar

Wash and pare the turnips. Cut in half lengthwise, then slice and dry on paper towels. Mix with the cabbage and celery.

Dissolve the salt in the water. In a large glass jar, put the vegetables and peeled garlic. Mix the vinegar, Tabasco, pickling spice, and sugar with the salt solution and fill the jar. Cover the jar with the lid tightly and let stand 3–4 days. Chill before serving.

Makes about 1½ pints.


## Pilaf Ali Pasha
TURKEY
## RICE WITH CURRANTS AND NUTS

¾ cup dried black currants
3 cups converted rice
¼ pound (1 stick) butter
¾ cup minced onions
1 cup pine nuts or blanched slivered almonds
6 cups boiling chicken broth
1½ teaspoons salt
½ teaspoon freshly ground black pepper
¼ teaspoon ground allspice
1 tablespoon tomato paste
1 cup thinly sliced green onions
Chopped fresh dill or parsley

Wash the currants, cover with boiling water, and let soak for 30 minutes. Drain, and spread out on paper towels to dry.

Wash the rice under cold running water, until the water runs clear. Drain and dry.

In a heavy pan, melt the butter. Sauté the onions 5 minutes, stirring frequently. Add the rice and nuts; sauté 3 minutes, stirring steadily. Mix in half the broth, then the salt, pepper, allspice, tomato paste, and green onions. Cover tightly, and cook over low heat 10 minutes. Add the remaining broth, re-cover, and cook 10 minutes longer. Sprinkle the currants over the top, re-cover, and place pan on an asbestos pad or flame tamer and keep over low heat for 45 minutes. Toss the rice with two forks, and turn into a heated serving dish. Sprinkle with the dill or parsley.

Serves 8–10.

## *Kukuye Sabzi*          IRAN
## VEGETABLE PIE

1 pound spinach, chopped, or 1 package frozen spinach, thawed
2½ cups chopped green onions
1 cup chopped lettuce
1½ cups chopped parsley
2 tablespoons flour
1½ teaspoons salt
¼ teaspoon freshly ground black pepper
½ cup chopped walnuts
8 eggs, beaten well
4 tablespoons butter
Yogurt

Wash the fresh spinach and drain well, or drain the uncooked thawed spinach. Mix together the spinach, green onions, lettuce, parsley, flour, salt, pepper, and nuts. Mix in the eggs.

Melt the butter in an 11-inch pie plate. Pour the vegetable mixture into it. Bake in a preheated 325° oven 1 hour or until top is brown and crisp. Serve hot or cold, with yogurt as a topping.

Serves 4–6.

## Taratoor
### SESAME SAUCE

MIDDLE EAST

  1 cup canned sesame *tahini* (paste)
  3 cloves garlic, put through a press or finely minced
  ½ cup lemon juice
  1 teaspoon salt
  ¾ cup ice water

Put the *tahini* and garlic in a bowl, and using a whisk or electric beater, mix well. Still beating, add the lemon juice, salt, and ½ cup of the water. Continue beating, and add 1 tablespoon of the remaining water at a time, until the mixture is the consistency of thick mayonnaise. It may not be necessary to add all the water, or it may take a little more, to achieve the proper consistency. Store refrigerated in a jar, and use as directed in other recipes.

Makes about 1½ cups.


## NOODLE CUSTARD PUDDING

ISRAEL

  3½ cups milk
  ½ pound fine noodles
  ½ cup sugar
  ⅛ teaspoon salt
  ¼ pound (1 stick) butter
  5 egg yolks
  ¼ cup chopped candied orange peel or seedless raisins
  4 egg whites
  ¼ cup dry bread crumbs

Bring the milk to a boil in a saucepan. Gradually add the noodles, stirring constantly. Mix in the sugar, salt and all but 1 tablespoon butter. Cook over low heat 20 minutes.

Beat the egg yolks in a bowl. Gradually add the undrained noodle mixture, mixing steadily to prevent curdling. Cool 10 minutes. Mix in the orange peel. Beat the egg whites until stiff, but not dry. Fold into the noodle mixture. Rub a baking dish with the remaining butter and dust with the bread crumbs. Pour the noodle mixture into it.

Place the dish in a pan. Add enough hot water to reach half way up the dish. Bake in a 350° oven 30 minutes, or until pudding is browned and firm to the touch. Serve hot or cold.

Serves 6–8.

## *Sirniki*     RUSSIA
## CHEESE PANCAKES

¼ pound cream cheese, softened
2 egg yolks
½ teaspoon salt
2 tablespoons sugar
1 cup cottage cheese, drained
½ cup sifted flour
2 egg whites, stiffly beaten
6 tablespoons butter

Mash the cream cheese smooth. Beat in the egg yolks, salt, and sugar, then the cottage cheese and flour. Fold in the egg whites.

Heat 2 tablespoons of the butter in a skillet until it sizzles. Drop the batter into it by the heaping tablespoon. Fry until browned on both sides. Keep warm while preparing the balance, and add more butter as needed. Serve hot with sour cream.

Makes about 30.

## Vatroushkis
### CHEESE PASTRIES

RUSSIA

>2 cups sifted flour
>½ teaspoon salt
>½ pound (2 sticks) butter
>⅓ cup sour cream

Sift the flour and salt into a bowl. Cut-in one third of the butter with a pastry blender or two knives, until the mixture looks like coarse cornmeal. Stir in the sour cream, mixing with the hand until a ball of dough is formed.

Roll out the dough on a lightly floured surface. Form the remaining butter into a square and place in the center of the dough. Fold ends of the dough over the butter and chill 30 minutes. Roll the dough into an oblong; fold into thirds and roll out again. Fold into thirds, wrap in foil, and chill for 3 hours.

#### FILLING

>1 pound cream cheese
>2 eggs
>¾ cup sour cream
>2 tablespoons melted butter
>3 tablespoons sugar
>½ teaspoon salt
>1 egg yolk

Beat the cheese until light and fluffy, using a machine if possible. Add the eggs, sour cream, melted butter, sugar, and salt, beating until smooth.

Roll out the dough ¼ inch thick on a lightly floured surface. Cut into 3-inch circles. Place a tablespoon of the cheese mixture in the center of each and pinch the edges together slightly to form a cup, leaving the center exposed. Brush pastry with the egg yolk.

Place on a baking pan or cookie sheet. Bake in a preheated 375° oven 20 minutes, or until delicately browned. Serve warm.

Makes about 2 dozen.

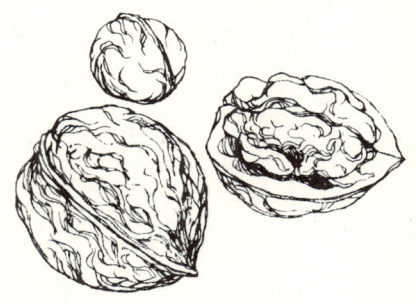

*Kourambiedes*  
WALNUT COOKIES

GREECE

1¼ cups shelled walnuts
½ pound (2 sticks) butter, at room temperature
¼ cup confectioners' sugar
1 teaspoon baking powder
1 cup flour

Put half the nuts in an electric blender, and blend until they look like flour. Repeat with the remaining nuts, or put the nuts through a mouli grater or nut grinder.

Cream the butter, then with a spoon beat in the confectioners' sugar and baking powder. Sift the flour into it, a little at a time, beating after each addition. Mix in the nuts thoroughly. Shape into a ball and chill 1 hour.

Break off about 2 tablespoons of dough at a time, and on a lightly floured surface, roll it with your palm into a rope about 6 inches long and ¼ inch in diameter. Form into an S shape, or circle, if you prefer. Arrange the cookies on a large baking sheet, leaving about 1 inch between each.

Bake in a preheated 350° oven, on the middle level, for 15 minutes, or until delicately browned. Transfer the cookies to a cake rack with a spatula, and when cool, sprinkle the tops with confectioners' sugar.

Makes about 2 dozen.

## Mazourka
### WALNUT CAKE

RUSSIA

> 1 pound shelled walnuts
> 9 egg yolks
> 2 cups sugar
> 2 tablespoons lemon juice
> 5 egg whites
> 2 cups sifted cake flour
> ½ pound candied fruit peel, ground

Put the nuts through an electric blender, a nut grinder, or mouli grater–the ground nuts should look like flour.

Rub an 8-by-12-inch baking pan with butter, then dust with flour.

Beat the egg yolks in a bowl; add the sugar and beat until light and fluffy. Beat in the lemon juice.

Beat the egg whites until stiff, but not dry, and fold into the yolk mixture. Fold in the flour and walnuts, then the fruit peel. Turn into the pan. Bake on the lower level of a preheated 325° oven 30 minutes, or until a cake tester comes out clean. Dust with powdered sugar. This rather firm cake will be about 1 inch high and should be served in long, thin slices.

## Oladyi
### WALNUT PANCAKES

RUSSIA

> ¼ pound (1 stick) butter
> ¾ cup shelled walnuts
> 6 eggs
> ⅓ cup sugar
> ¼ cup cognac
> 2 tablespoons flour
> 1 teaspoon grated lemon rind
> Confectioners' sugar

Melt half the butter. Grind the walnuts in an electric blender or put through a mouli grater.

Beat the eggs well, then beat in the sugar until light and thick. Mix in the cognac, flour, nuts, lemon rind, and melted butter.

Melt about 2 teaspoons of the remaining butter in a 6-inch skillet. Pour about 2 tablespoons of the batter into it, rotating the pan quickly to coat the bottom. Bake until delicately browned on both sides. Turn out and roll up immediately. Keep warm while preparing the balance. Serve warm, sprinkled with confectioners' sugar.

Serves 6–8.

*Gozleme*                                                                IRAN
**FRIED CRULLERS**

    ½ cup water
    ⅛ teaspoon salt
    ¼ pound (1 stick) butter
    ⅔ cup sifted flour
    3 eggs
    3 tablespoons currants or seedless raisins
    2 tablespoons finely chopped candied fruits
    1 tablespoon rose water
    Vegetable oil for deep frying
    Confectioners' sugar

Combine the water, salt, and butter in a saucepan. Bring to a boil and cook until butter melts. Add the flour all at once, beating vigorously with a wooden spoon until mixture forms a ball and leaves the sides of the pan. Remove from the heat and add 1 egg at a time, beating until smooth and glossy after each addition. Beat in the raisins, fruits, and rose water.

Heat the oil for 370°. Drop the paste into it by the teaspoon. Fry until browned on all sides. Don't crowd the pan, so crullers can turn themselves. Drain and sprinkle with confectioners' sugar. Serve hot or cold.

Makes about 24.

## Halva
### ALMOND DESSERT

MIDDLE EAST

>1 cup sugar
>1 cup honey
>2 cups water
>½ teaspoon cinnamon
>¼ pound (1 stick) butter
>½ cup finely ground almonds
>1 cup raw cream of wheat

Combine the sugar, honey, water, and cinnamon in a saucepan. Bring to a boil and cook over low heat 20 minutes. While the syrup is cooking, melt the butter in a skillet; add the almonds and cream of wheat. Cook over low heat, stirring steadily, until browned.

Add to the syrup (after syrup has cooked 20 minutes), mix well, cover, and cook 15 minutes, stirring occasionally. Pour into a buttered 8-by-10-inch buttered shallow pan. Cool. Cut into squares and sprinkle with confectioners' sugar or cinnamon.

Makes 20 2-inch squares.


## Shir Berenj
### RICE-FRUIT CUSTARD PUDDING

IRAN

>½ cup raw rice
>3 cups milk
>3 cups heavy cream
>¾ cup sugar
>¼ teaspoon salt
>¼ teaspoon ground cardamom seeds
>3 eggs
>¾ cup chopped candied fruit

Mix the rice, milk, 1 cup of the cream, the sugar, salt, and cardamom in the top of a double boiler. Cover, place over hot water, and cook 1 hour, stirring frequently.

Beat the eggs in a bowl; gradually add the hot rice mixture, stirring steadily to prevent curdling. Return to double boiler and cook, stirring steadily until mixture coats the spoon. Remove from heat and stir in the fruit. Cool.

Whip the remaining cream, and fold into the rice mixture. Turn into a serving dish and chill.

Serves 8–10.

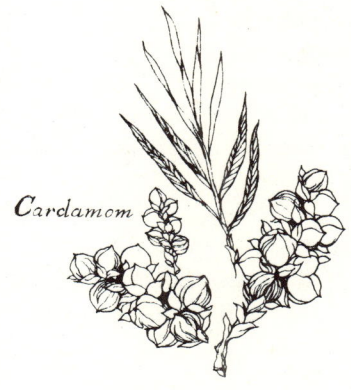

*Fereni*     IRAN
## RICE FLOUR CANDY DESSERT

½ cup sesame or vegetable oil
1 cup rice flour
4 cups milk
¼ cup rose water
½ cup granulated sugar
1 teaspoon ground cardamom seeds
½ cup sifted confectioners' sugar
1 cup chopped pistachio nuts

Heat the oil in a saucepan; stir in the rice flour until lightly browned. Gradually add the milk, stirring until smooth over low heat. Add the rose water, granulated sugar and cardamom. Cook over heat, stirring constantly, until thickened. Mix in the confectioners' sugar, stirring until dissolved.

Rinse a shallow pan with cold water, and pour the mixture into it to a depth of 1 inch; sprinkle with the nuts and let stand until firm. Cut in oblong pieces.

Serves 8–10.

## Keskul
### RICE-RAISIN DESSERT

TURKEY

> 3 tablespoons butter
> 1½ cups raw long-grain rice
> ½ teaspoon salt
> ¼ cup sugar
> 2 teaspoons cinnamon
> ¼ teaspoon mace
> ½ cup seedless raisins
> 2½ cups hot light cream
> ½ cup pistachio nuts or sliced toasted almonds

Melt the butter in a heavy saucepan; stir in the rice until coated. Add the salt, sugar, cinnamon, mace, raisins, and cream. Cover and cook over low heat 25 minutes, or until rice is tender and dry. Serve warm or cold, sprinkled with the nuts.
Serves 4–6.

## Baklava
### FLAKY NUT PASTRY

IRAN

> 4 cups finely chopped blanched almonds or walnuts
> 2 cups sugar
> ½ teaspoon ground cardamom seeds
> 1 pound (4 sticks) butter, melted
> 16 *phyllo* leaves or 4 packages strudel leaves

Mix together the almonds, sugar, and cardamon. Rub a 13-by-9-inch baking pan with a little of the butter. Separate the pastry leaves and cover them with a damp cloth while assembling the layers. Put a layer of pastry leaves in the pan, brush heavily with butter, cover with another layer of pastry leaves, brush with butter, then make as many successive layers as possible of the nut mixture and pastry leaves, brushing each layer with butter. Reserve 2 pastry leaves for the top. Brush top with butter, and cut the pastry in diamond shapes, but not through to the bottom.

Pour any remaining butter over the top. Bake in a preheated 350° oven 35 minutes or until golden brown. While the pastry is baking, prepare the syrup.

> 2 cups sugar
> 1 cup water
> 2 tablespoons rose water

Cook the sugar and water until very thick and syrupy, about 20 minutes. Mix in the rose water. Cool slightly, and when pastry is baked, pour the syrup over it. Cut through the pastry to the bottom.

Serves 10–12.

# *MIDDLE EUROPE*

GERMANY
AUSTRIA
HUNGARY
POLAND
CZECHOSLOVAKIA

SOME geographical areas can be readily agreed upon. There is no doubt as to the precise boundary lines of California, for example, which can be ascertained by looking at a map. Other land areas are more ephemeral, such as the limits of the Near or Middle East. Similarly that vast continental expanse known as Middle Europe is somewhat difficult to define with precision, but is generally regarded as containing most of that area to the east of France and to the west of Russia, including Germany, Austria, Hungary, Poland, and Czechoslovakia. The histories of these countries have overlapped on many occasions, and they have at times loved or hated one another, or co-existed for a time in an uneasy truce. Borderlines and national boundaries have ebbed and flowed regularly, like the tide. Monarchies, kingdoms, and dukedoms have come and gone. Armies have trampled across them from east to west, from west to east, and they have this in common—cuisines influenced by their neighbors and invaders.

In matters culinary they have all drawn from one another. For example, German cooking is commonplace in Austria, although perhaps the opposite statement—that Austrian cooking is commonplace in Germany—holds equally true. Moving eastward from Austria, Hungary has a cuisine which is reasonably close to that of Austria in certain respects, and so it goes.

Germany's cooking style tends to be hearty, sober, and satisfying, with heavy soups, dumplings, solid meat dishes, and calorific stews. Some of the young people of Germany are turning away from this serious and comparatively ponderous way of cooking, and tend to favor lighter preparations. Nevertheless, this trend is not true of the entire country. Furthermore, not all German cooking is quite the same; it differs from north to south, with a tendency toward lighter dishes in the south. Even the language of food differs in various parts of the country; for instance, a potato is called a *kartoffel* in the north, and an *erdapfel* (earth apple) in the south. Besides the potato, which is a staple food throughout the nation, Germans love herring, sausages, dark breads, beer (although wine is enormously popular), sweet-and-sour preparations, game meat and birds, and late afternoon pastries and coffee.

The soups are typically thick and satisfying: to mention a few — split pea, lentil, and potato. Also highly regarded are turtle, oxtail, wine and beer, and fruit soups, although these last are only prepared locally. Thick, fatty stews are liked; often the Germans call these *ragoûts*, in the French manner. When autumnal game is in season, it is rare to find a menu that doesn't list venison, rabbit, grouse, or partridge.

With most dishes, a large bowl of boiled potatoes is usually offered. Not infrequently, a hearty diner will consume a half dozen at a time. Otherwise, it is routine to serve another starchy preparation, such as dumplings, noodles, or perhaps something made from potatoes — potato pancakes, potato salad, or the like. The favorite vegetables, in all probability, are the ubiquitous potato, cabbage, and mushrooms.

Sausages constitute a cult approaching the mystic in Germany.

They are dearly beloved by most people, perhaps even held in awe and reverence. A visit to a *wurst* store reveals a bewildering array of sizes, colors, shapes, and ingredients from which to choose. To name a few: *Leberwurst; Blut Schwartemagen; schlachtwurst; Kalbsleberwurst; Fleischwurst; Koch Bratwurst; Stuttgarter Presskopf; Kalbsroulade; Schinkenwurst; Bierwurst; und so weiter*. The fried doughnuts are marvels of perfection as are the cakes and cookies, to be had in seemingly endless variations. The country's white wines are delicate and the finest are nothing short of exquisite; the red wines, alas, are barely passable, if that. Beer is brewed in scores of different styles—dark, light, bitter, or even sweet, aged or comparatively fresh, top-or-bottom fermented, and so forth. A great beer novelty is the distinctive Berliner Weisse, a champagne-like beer made from wheat, usually served with a splash of raspberry syrup, odd as that may sound.

Austrian and German cuisines have much in common, as previously mentioned; after all, the countries were once politically as well as geographically affiliated. Perhaps Austrian cooking is a trifle more refined that that of Germany, but in common with most generalizations, there are exceptions. Because of its unfortunate central position on the European continent, armies have marched across Austria's lovely territory over the past thousand or more years, wars have been fought and battles have raged, sieges have been endured. The nation once had great power and enormous territories, but now finds itself reduced to the merest shadow of its former empire, its territories ravaged and taken from it. But the Austrians have, in a sort of culinary retaliation, stolen from their plunderers, not in the form of land or gold, but from the cuisines of the invaders. From the Italians, they took many of the rice and pasta dishes now a firm part of the Austrian cuisine; from Switzerland, they learned the use of cheese in cooking; from Hungary, dishes made with the red gold of paprika; the Poles brought (and left behind) their love of sour cream, mushrooms, and cucumbers; grilled meats are attributed to the Balkan nations; and the Bohemians (of present-day Czechoslovakia) showed them how to make *mehlspeise*, that is, desserts made with flour; if made without flour, they are *süss-speise*. Between the wars and the sieges and the invasions, the Austrians managed to eat six times daily (three regular meals, plus a second breakfast, afternoon tea or coffee and cakes, and bedtime snacks). It has been said that the present-day tendency is to cut down (say, to five meals) but that trend, if in fact true, isn't noticeable to the casual observer. Everything still remains very *Gemütlich*.

Meals often begin with a soup. Perhaps a beef consomme is the most popular, but rest assured that it will have something added—tiny meatballs, liver dumplings, semolina mixtures, or perhaps thin slices of shredded omelets or pancakes. Not having a seacoast, the fish is always freshwater, such as carp, pike, and also the *fogash* (or *fogas*) of Hungary.

Among the main courses, many people regard boiled beef as the single favorite of the country, constituting almost a mania, although nowadays the fine distinctions among the various cuts of meat are almost completely gone. *Gulash* (which is sometimes spelled *gulyás* as in Hungary) is well liked, as is veal, usually cut into a *schnitzel*, a thin cutlet. *Wiener schnitzel* is the Viennese version, but there are dozens of similar variations upon this culinary theme. Chicken is often served as a *paprikás*, that is, prepared with paprika; or possibly it may appear as *Wiener Backhandl*, much like Maryland fried chicken. If a dish isn't accompanied by a bowl of boiled potatoes, most diners would return it to the kitchen, unless of course it came with dumplings, usually made of potatoes or bread. Perhaps the largest mouthful of all is a chopped pork-and-beef ball, covered with dough and boiled, which bears up as best it can under the overwhelming title of *Oberoesterreichische Fleischknoedeln*.

Ah, the delightful desserts and pastries of Austria, especially those of Vienna! They are a world unto themselves, and a happy one. Just to mention a few outstanding creations, there's *Zwetschenknoedeln* (plums covered with dough, boiled and served with breadcrumbs and melted butter); *Kaiserschmarrn* (a sort of pancake-omelet, sweetened and filled with raisins, and cut into sections); *Linzer Torte* (a rich almond and apricot cake); *Dobostorte* (a chocolate cake made with pastry layers); *Sachertorte* (a chocolate cake containing spongecake and jam, typically served with whipped cream!); *Palatschinken* (thin dessert pancakes);

*strudel* (but perhaps from Hungary); and *Salzburger Nockerl* (a type of soufflé).

The wines of Austria are so-so, and nothing to compare with those of Germany. Among the whites, Gumpoldskirchner is good, and Voeslauer is satisfactory among the reds. The Viennese have loved coffee ever since the Turks (one of many invaders) besieged Vienna, only to retreat, leaving behind them bags of the well-flavored brown beans. In Vienna's coffee houses (unhappily now disappearing under a tidal wave of espresso bars), the beverage can be ordered in a score of ways. One way, rest assured, is *mit Schlag*, with a large dollop of snowy whipped cream.

Hungarian food follows the Austrian way of doing things in many respects, but carries it one step further. It is brighter, spicier, more colorful and less restrained, and indeed, constitutes a remarkably original national culinary style. The Turks, invading from the east, controlled Hungary for a century and a half, bringing with them coffee, and more than likely paprika. In fact, in parts of Europe even now paprika is called Turkish pepper. Hungarian royalty married French and Italian women of noble blood; when they arrived with their entourages (always including chefs and pastry-makers), the Hungarian cuisine was soon modified. After Hungary became a part of the Austro-Hungarian Empire, both German and Austrian styles of cooking were introduced. Some of the distinctive features of the Hungarian culinary style include the colorful paprika, of course, as well as sour cream, goose liver, the use of lard and bacon, and the custom of serving some form of starchy dumplings or noodles with main courses. Incidentally, Hungarian paprika (available in hot and sweet types) is quite different from Spanish or American paprika, and should always be bought fresh, when called for in the recipes, for the flavor deteriorates with age.

The classic dish of the country is the *gulyás*; goulash in English, a paprika-flavored-and-colored stew, usually of beef. Other similar preparations are called *pörkölt* (which contains more onions and is richer and fattier than a *gulyás*); the *tokány* (narrow strips of meat are used and sour cream is added); and the *paprikás* (in which meat is cut into larger chunks than for the *gulyás*). Now that the differences and variations have been described, it is only fair to mention that there are exceptions galore. Much like the *gulyás* is a hearty soup, outstandingly delicious, called *gulyásleves*, that is, goulash soup.

With but one major lake, Balaton by name, and several rivers, only freshwater fish appear on the menu. Outstanding is the *fogas*, a unique variety of fish which is a cross between a pike and a perch, a pike-perch if you will, noted for its white flesh and having a fine taste.

Noodles and pastas, without which no Hungarian meal would be complete, come in a dazzling series of shapes and sizes, plus an assortment of ingredients and textures. Fresh vegetables, those best liked by the people are cabbage and kohlrabi, are often stuffed with meat and flavored by a sauce made of sour cream, bacon, and caraway seeds. So great is the country's love of paprika that they combine white liptói cheese with capers, mustard, caraway seeds, and paprika, to create *körözött liptói*, a spicy, reddish cheese spread.

The desserts are delicious, notably the cakes and pastries. Perhaps the single most famous (and popular) item is *rétes*, which the Hungarians claim to have invented. The Austrians respectfully beg to differ, pointing out that their designation for the same pastry as *strudel* has become firmly attached to this delicious filled confection. The national wines of Hungary are good, certainly better than those of Austria. Of course, the single most famous wine of the country is Tokay, which comes in many types, always white. Among the red wines, perhaps Egri Bikaver is the best.

Poland is an enormous land of vast plains and seemingly endless winters, with heavy snows and chilling winds. Because of the severe cold weather, lasting into April each year, when spring finally arrives, everyone is bewitched by the first early growths of the season—mushrooms, young greens, and wild berries.

The cuisine, as in most of Middle Europe, shows the influence of those who have passed across its soil, sometimes in peace, but more often as invaders, plunderers, and despoilers. Soups are particularly good here, and mention should be made of some of them. *Barszczyk* is a fine, hearty beet soup (although there are many variations) similar to Russia's *borscht*. *Krupnick* is a very good barley and mushroom soup. In warm weather, the Poles often serve *chlodnik*, a cold, sourish soup containing an odd mixture of flavors—pickle juice, clabbered milk, and crayfish.

With its bitter, long-lasting winters, the Poles love rich, warming, fatty stews. Perhaps the best known is *bigos*, the hunter's stew, made with meat and mushrooms. Indeed, mushrooms play a large part in the national cookery style, as well as *kasza* (buckwheat groats), sour cream, herbs (especially dill), and freshwater fish (notably carp). The Poles are fond of *pierozhki*, small envelopes of dough stuffed with various fillings, greatly resembling the *ravioli* of Italy, or Jewish-style *kreplach*. Two of the best pastries, popular throughout the country, are the *baba* (sometimes called *babka*), a yeast cake, and the *mazurek*, a nut cake. Russian vodka and Polish *wodka* are similar and the Polish product is excellent.

Czechoslovakia, much like its neighbor Austria, has frequently found itself in the unwelcome position of being center stage for warfare. Time and again, troops have marched across its land. Just as Austria has absorbed from the invaders something of their cuisine, so have the Czechs. The love of soups brings to mind Poland; the craze for sausages reminds one of Germany; the national dish of boiled beef recalls Austria's similar taste; and the delight the Czechs find in flour-based dumplings and noodles is reminiscent of Hungary.

The people of this central European land are inordinately fond of sausages—frankfurters, if you prefer that generic term. Perhaps the single favorite is the *párky*, picked up in the fingers and dipped in horseradish or mustard. But there are other types, such as *vuršty*, *klobásy*, *jelita*, and *jaternice*. Also, because of the habit of munching a sausage in the late afternoon (they eat them with equal delight in midmorning and late evening), appetizers aren't too important a part of the national cuisine. Meals typically begin with a soup—perhaps potato, mushroom, meat, or the like. If fish is served, the chances are that it will be carp, or possibly trout. As mentioned before, the national dish of Czechoslovakia is boiled beef, *hovezy maso*. Next in popularity would be poultry, roast goose, and duck. With many dishes, the custom is to serve *knedlíky*, dumplings large and small, heavy and light. The more substantial ones are cut with a string, never a knife.

*Knedlíky* are also served sweetened, as a dessert. Dumplings are filled with fruits, cottage cheese, poppy seeds, and jam (especially *povidla*, plum jam). The yeast cakes and pastries are delicious, inevitably prepared with a light hand. Czech wines are, well, mediocre might be the kindest word. Contrarily the beer is nothing short of superb, surely among the best in the world. The classic brew is a light Pilsener, although dark and smoky types are also produced. *Slivovice*, plum brandy, has its adherents.

## Marinierte Krebse
## MARINATED SHRIMP

GERMANY

2 pounds raw shrimp, shelled and deveined
3 cups water
¼ cup mixed pickling spice
¼ cup chopped celery leaves
3½ teaspoons salt
1 pound onions, sliced
6 bay leaves
1 cup olive oil
⅔ cup tarragon or wine vinegar
2 tablespoons capers
2 teaspoons celery seed

Wash the shrimp. In a saucepan, combine the water, pickling spice, celery leaves, and 2 teaspoons of the salt. Bring to a boil, add the shrimp, and cook over low heat 4 minutes. Drain thoroughly, and put half on the bottom of a glass or pottery deep oblong dish. Separate the sliced onions into rings, and put half over the shrimp, and distribute half the bay leaves over the onions. Repeat the layers.

Beat together the oil, vinegar, capers, celery seed, and remaining salt. Pour over the top, cover, and let marinate in the refrigerator for at least 24 hours—they may be kept up to a week. Serve as a first course, or on picks, as an hors d'oeuvre.

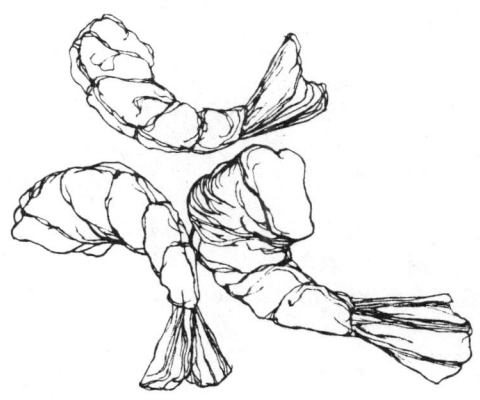

MIDDLE EUROPE

*Krebspfannkuchen*  GERMANY
## SHRIMP PANCAKES

    ¾ cup flour
    ½ teaspoon salt
    ½ cup light cream, at room temperature
    2 egg yolks, beaten
    1 tablespoon melted butter
    1 tablespoon grated onion
    ½ cup grated Parmesan cheese
    ½ pound cooked shrimp, cleaned and chopped
    ¼ teaspoon freshly ground black pepper
    2 egg whites, beaten stiff
    Butter

Sift the flour and salt into a bowl; mix in the cream until smooth, then beat in the egg yolks, melted butter, onion, and 2 tablespoons of the grated cheese. Chill for 30 minutes. Mix in the shrimp and pepper, then fold in the egg whites.

Heat a griddle or heavy skillet, and rub generously with butter. Drop the batter onto it by the tablespoon. Cook until delicately browned on both sides. Arrange on a serving dish; sprinkle with the remaining cheese, and dot with butter. Place under the broiler until butter melts.

Serves 4–6, as an appetizer.


*Käsepudding*  GERMANY
## CHEESE PUDDING SOUFFLÉ

    4 tablespoons flour
    1½ cups light cream
    2 cups freshly grated Parmesan cheese
    ½ teaspoon salt
    ¼ teaspoon white pepper
    1 teaspoon paprika
    6 egg yolks
    6 egg whites

Sift the flour into a saucepan; blend in a little of the cream until smooth, then mix in all the cream. Cook over low heat, stirring steadily to the boiling point, then cook 5 minutes longer, mixing occasionally. Stir in the salt, pepper, and paprika.

Beat the egg yolks in a bowl; very gradually add the hot mixture, stirring steadily to prevent curdling. Cool.

Beat the egg whites until stiff but not dry. Add about ¼ the beaten egg white to the cheese mixture, and mix thoroughly, then fold in the remaining egg whites carefully. Turn into a 1½-quart buttered soufflé dish or casserole. Bake on the lower level of a preheated 400° oven 35 minutes, or until golden on top and puffed. Serve at once, as a first course, luncheon, or supper dish.

Serves 6.

*Hühnerleberragout*  AUSTRIA
CHICKEN LIVER RAGOUT

> 1 pound chicken livers
> 6 tablespoons butter
> ½ cup minced onions
> 1 teaspoon salt
> ¼ teaspoon freshly ground black pepper
> 1 teaspoon paprika
> 3 tablespoons dry white wine
> ¼ cup chopped parsley
> ¼ pound button or sliced mushrooms, sautéed
> 1 cup tiny canned green peas, drained
> ½ pound noodles, cooked and drained

Wash the livers, and cut away any discolored areas. Dry on paper towels. Melt 2 tablespoons of the butter in a skillet; sauté the onions 5 minutes. Remove the onions, and melt the remaining butter in the skillet; add the livers and cook over high heat until browned, but still pink inside, about 4 minutes. Sprinkle with the salt, pepper, and paprika, and toss. Add the wine, and bring to a boil; remove from the heat and toss in the parsley, mushrooms, and peas. Taste for seasoning and heap on the noodles.

Serves 4.

*Ryby Marinované*  CZECHOSLOVAKIA
## MARINATED FISH

> 6 slices (about 3 pounds) pike, salmon, tuna, or mackerel
> 3 teaspoons salt
> ½ teaspoon freshly ground black pepper
> 4 tablespoons butter
> 1½ cups water
> ½ cup fish stock or clam juice
> ½ cup cider vinegar
> 1 cup sliced onions
> 6 peppercorns
> 2 cloves
> 1 allspice
> 1 bay leaf
> 2 teaspoons chopped capers
> 1 dill pickle, chopped
> ¼ cup vegetable oil

Wash and dry the fish. Sprinkle with the pepper and 2 teaspoons of the salt. Melt the butter in a skillet. Add the fish, and cook 10 minutes on each side. Cool.

While the fish is cooking, prepare the marinade.

In a saucepan, combine the water, fish stock, vinegar, onions, peppercorns, cloves, allspice, bay leaf, and remaining salt. Bring to a boil, and cook over low heat 30 minutes. Cool to room temperature, and mix in the capers, pickle, and oil.

Put the fish in a bowl and pour the marinade over it. Cover, and let marinate in the refrigerator at least 24 hours.

Serves 6–12.

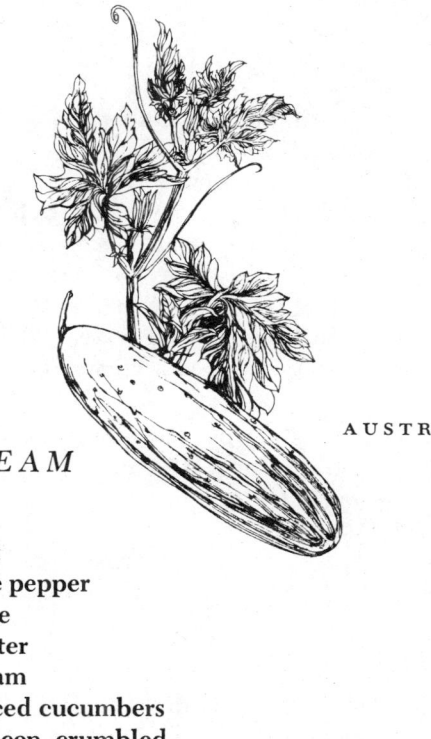

*Wiener Fischfilets*
FISH IN SOUR CREAM

AUSTRIA

    6 fillets of sole
    1½ teaspoons salt
    ½ teaspoon white pepper
    ⅓ cup lemon juice
    2 tablespoons butter
    1½ cups sour cream
    ¾ cup peeled, diced cucumbers
    6 slices cooked bacon, crumbled
    3 teaspoons capers
    1 tablespoon prepared mustard
    ¼ cup grated Parmesan cheese

Wash and dry the fillets, and season with the salt and pepper. Let stand 15 minutes, then sprinkle with the lemon juice.

Rub an oblong baking dish with butter, and put 2 fillets on the bottom. Spoon ½ cup of the sour cream over them, and sprinkle with ⅓ of the cucumbers, bacon, and capers. Arrange 2 more fillets over it. Mix the mustard with half the remaining sour cream, and spread over the fillets, then half the remaining cucumbers, bacon, and capers. Repeat the layers, and sprinkle with the grated cheese. Bake in a preheated 375° oven 30 minutes. To serve, cut down through the layers with a sharp knife into six pieces.

Serves 6.

## Szegedi Pontyhalaszle
## PAPRIKA FISH

HUNGARY

6 slices (about 3 pounds) fish (carp, whitefish, cod, or halibut)
2 teaspoons salt
6 tablespoons lard or butter
1 pound onions, peeled and chopped
2 tablespoons hot Hungarian paprika
2 teaspoons flour
¾ cup boiling water
1½ cups sour cream

Wash and dry the fish slices; sprinkle with the salt.

Melt the lard or butter in a 12-inch skillet. Sauté the onions in it until golden. Remove from the heat and blend in the paprika and flour; gradually add the water. Return to the heat, and stirring constantly, bring to a boil, then cook 10 minutes. Arrange the fish in the skillet; cover loosely, and cook over low heat 20 minutes, or until the fish flakes easily when tested with a fork. Taste for seasoning. Just before serving, transfer the fish to a hot serving dish. Stir the sour cream into the gravy, and heat, but do not let boil. Pour over the fish.

Serves 6.

## Gombaleves
## MUSHROOM SOUP

HUNGARY

4 tablespoons butter
1 pound mushrooms, chopped
¾ cup chopped onion
1 clove garlic, minced
1½ teaspoons salt
1 teaspoon paprika
3 tablespoons flour
6 cups chicken broth
Csipetke (see recipe) or egg barley (a small type of egg noodle)
1 cup sour cream

Melt the butter in a 2-quart saucepan; sauté the mushrooms and onions in it until browned. Blend in the garlic, salt, paprika, and flour. Cook 2 minutes, stirring constantly. Add the broth gradually, stirring constantly to the boiling point. Cook over low heat 10 minutes. Add the *Csipetke* and cook 12 minutes. Just before serving, stir in the sour cream.

Serves 6–8.

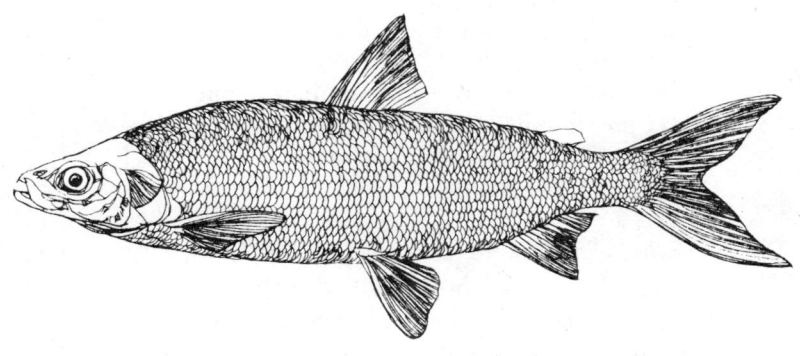

*Káposztaleves*    HUNGARY
BROWNED CABBAGE SOUP

> 4 slices bacon
> 3 cups shredded cabbage
> ½ cup chopped onion
> 2 teaspoons salt
> 1½ teaspoons paprika
> 5 cups water
> 3 cups peeled cubed potatoes
> ¾ cup peeled chopped tomatoes

In a 2-quart saucepan, brown the bacon. Remove the bacon and reserve. To the fat in the saucepan, add the cabbage, onion, salt, and paprika. Cook until the cabbage browns, stirring frequently. Add the water, potatoes, and tomatoes. Bring to a boil and cook over low heat 20 minutes. Crumble the bacon and add it to the soup.

Serves 6–8.

## Barszczyk
### BEET-BEEF SOUP

POLAND

2 pounds brisket or plate of beef
1 marrow bone, cracked
3 quarts water
1 cup chopped onions
8 large beets, peeled and halved
1 cup canned tomatoes
1½ pounds cabbage, shredded
2 teaspoons salt
½ teaspoon freshly ground black pepper
1 pound lima beans, shelled or 1 package, frozen
2 tablespoons minced parsley
2 tablespoons minced dill

Wash the meat and bone, and put in a kettle or large saucepan with the water. Bring to a boil, and skim the top. Cook over medium heat 1 hour. Skim the top. Add the onions, beets, and tomatoes. Cover and cook 30 minutes. Add the cabbage, salt, and pepper. Re-cover and cook 30 minutes. Add the lima beans, and cook 20 minutes longer. Remove the beets, grate half of them, and return the grated beets to the soup. Stir in the parsley and dill; taste for seasoning, and bring to a boil. Remove the meat and bone. The meat may be cut into cubes and served in the soup, or sliced and served separately.

Serve the soup with *Piroshki* (see recipe) or a boiled potato.
Serves 6–8.

## Korhelyleves
### SAUERKRAUT SOUP

HUNGARY

1½ pounds sauerkraut
6 slices bacon
2 cups chopped onions
2 tablespoons flour
½ pound smoked sausages
¼ cup sour cream

Buy barrel sauerkraut if possible, and ask for some juice. If canned sauerkraut is used, drain it, and reserve the juice. Put the sauerkraut in a colander or sieve, and rinse it under cold running water for a few minutes. Measure the juice, and add enough water to make 6 cups. Combine this with the sauerkraut in a 2-quart saucepan. Bring to a boil and cook over low heat while preparing the remaining ingredients.

Brown the bacon in a skillet. Remove the bacon and reserve. Pour off all but ¼ cup of the fat; sauté the onions until browned. Blend in the flour until browned. Mix in a little of the soup, then add this to all the soup. Slice the sausages and brown them. Drain, and add the sausages to the soup. Cook over low heat 45 minutes. Taste for seasoning. Crumble the bacon into the soup, then stir in the sour cream.

Serves 6–8.

## *Kartoffelsuppe Mit Käse*              GERMANY
## POTATO CHEESE SOUP

2 pounds potatoes, peeled and diced
1 cup diced onions
6 cups chicken broth or water
2 tablespoons butter
2 tablespoons flour
1 tablespoon minced dill
3 tablespoons minced chives or green onions
¼ teaspoon white pepper
½ pound cream cheese, at room temperature
Minced parsley

In a large saucepan, combine the potatoes, onions, and broth or water. Bring to a boil, and cook over low heat 15 minutes. In a small saucepan, melt the butter; blend in the flour. Add about 1 cup of the soup, stirring steadily to the boiling point. Stir into all the soup, and add the dill, chives, and pepper. Cook 5 minutes, and taste for seasoning.

Force the cheese through a sieve, divide among six heated soup plates, and pour the soup over it. Sprinkle with parsley.

Serves 6.

*Gulyásleves*  HUNGARY
# GOULASH SOUP

### Soup

2 pounds stewing beef
3 tablespoons beef suet or butter
2 cups chopped onion
2 tablespoons hot Hungarian paprika
1 teaspoon caraway seeds
1 cup grated raw potato
2 teaspoons salt
1 tablespoon tomato purée
8 cups beef broth
2 cups peeled diced potatoes
Salt
1 small hot green pepper (optional)

Cut the beef in bite-sized pieces. Cook the suet until melted, or melt the butter in a heavy 3-quart saucepan. Add the onions and sauté until golden. Stir in the paprika, then add the beef, caraway seeds, grated potato, and salt. Cover, and cook over low heat 10 minutes, stirring two or three times. Mix in the tomato purée, and ½ cup of the broth. Re-cover, and cook over low heat 1 hour. Watch carefully to prevent burning. Add the potatoes and the remaining broth. Bring to a boil, and cook over low heat 20 minutes. Add salt to taste. If you're using the green pepper, slice it as thin as possible, and discard the seeds. Sprinkle on top of the soup. While the soup is cooking, prepare the dumpling dough.

### Csipetke
Dough Dumplings

1 cup flour
½ teaspoon salt
2 eggs

Sift the flour and salt into a bowl. Work in the egg and knead until a stiff dough is formed. Flatten the dough between the palms and break off bean-sized pieces. Drop into the soup and cook 12 minutes.

Serves 8–10.

Note: There should be a definite paprika flavor to the soup. If the paprika you're using isn't very fresh it will not have the proper flavor, so add some more, when tasting the soup. Also, if you don't use the hot variety of paprika, add a dash of cayenne pepper or Tabasco.

## *Balkanishe Chlodnik*                      AUSTRIA
### SHRIMP-BEET SOUP, VIENNESE VARIATION

> 2 16-ounce cans julienne-cut beets
> 3 cups water
> 2 tablespoons grated onion
> 1½ teaspoons salt
> 1½ pounds cooked shelled shrimp
> ¾ cup peeled, seeded, chopped cucumbers
> 2 hard-cooked eggs, sieved
> 3 tablespoons minced dill
> 1 cup dry white wine
> 2 cups sour cream
> 8 thin slices lemon

In a saucepan, combine the undrained beets, the water, onions, and salt. Bring to a boil, and cook over low heat 20 minutes. Purée the beets in an electric blender, or force through a food mill. Cool.

Chop the shrimp, reserving 8 whole ones. Add the chopped shrimp to the soup, with the cucumber, eggs, and dill. Blend the wine into the sour cream, and stir into the soup. Taste for seasoning and chill. Serve in soup cups, with a slice of lemon and a whole shrimp in each.

Serves 8.

## Bableves
### BEAN SOUP

HUNGARY

    2½ cups dried white beans
    3 slices bacon
    1 cup chopped onions
    2 tablespoons flour
    ½ cup grated carrots
    4 cups boiling water
    4 cups beef broth
    2 teaspoons salt
    2 teaspoons paprika
    ¾ teaspoon freshly ground black pepper
    2 bay leaves
    1 cup sour cream
    2 tablespoons minced parsley

    Wash the beans, cover with water, and bring to a boil. Cook 1 minute, remove from the heat, and let soak 2 hours. Drain.

    In a 3-quart saucepan, cook the bacon until browned. Remove the bacon and crumble it. Reserve. To the bacon fat, add the onions; sauté until golden. Blend in the flour, stirring until browned. Mix in the carrots, then gradually add the boiling water, stirring steadily to the boiling point. Mix in the broth, salt, paprika, pepper, bay leaves, and beans. Bring to a boil again, and cook over low heat 2 hours, or until the beans are tender. Discard the bay leaves; add the bacon to the soup. Just before serving, mix in the sour cream, and sprinkle with the minced parsley.

    Serves 8–10.

*Paprikahuhn*                                                            AUSTRIA
## CHICKEN PAPRIKASH

2 2-pound broiling chickens
1 whole onion
2½ cups water
2½ teaspoons salt
6 tablespoons butter
1 cup chopped onions
2 tablespoons paprika
¾ cup peeled, seeded, chopped tomatoes
2 cups warm sour cream
1 tablespoon flour
¼ cup heavy cream

Have the chicken cut into quarters, and the wing tips removed. Wash and dry the chicken and the giblets. In a saucepan, combine the wing tips, necks, giblets, onion, water, and 1 teaspoon salt. Bring to a boil, and cook over low heat 1 hour. Strain, and reduce the broth to ¾ cup. Prepare the chicken while the broth is cooking.

Sprinkle the chicken quarters with the remaining salt. Melt the butter in a large deep skillet with an ovenproof handle; sauté the onions in it until golden. Blend in the paprika, and arrange the chicken in it. Cover, and cook over low heat 20 minutes, turning the chicken a few times. Add the tomatoes; re-cover, and bake in a preheated 375° oven 10 minutes. Mix in the sour cream; re-cover, and bake 15 minutes longer, or until chicken is tender. Transfer the chicken to a hot serving dish and keep hot.

Mix the flour with the heavy cream, until smooth. Stir into the pan juices with the broth; cook over direct heat, stirring steadily, to the boiling point, then cook 5 minutes longer. Taste for seasoning. Pour some of the sauce over the chicken, and serve the rest in a sauceboat. Serve with *Spätzle* (see recipe) or noodles.

Serves 4–8.

## Gefülte Gans
### STUFFED GOOSE

GERMANY

20 pitted prunes
1 cup Port wine
6 apples, peeled, quartered, and cored
3 tablespoons sugar
10–12 pound goose
2 teaspoons caraway seeds
3 teaspoons salt
1 teaspoon freshly ground black pepper
¾ cup minced onion
1 cup fresh bread crumbs
1 cup ice water

Wash the prunes, and soak in the Port overnight. Bring to a boil and cook 20 minutes. Remove from the heat, and mix in the apples and sugar.

Wash and dry the goose well. Combine the caraway seeds, salt, and black pepper. Rub into skin and cavity of goose. (If possible, season the goose the day before.) Combine the fruit with the onion and bread crumbs. Stuff the goose with fruit mixture and close opening with skewers or thread. Place on a rack in a shallow roasting pan and roast in a 350° oven 2 hours, pouring off the fat from time to time. Remove the rack. Pour the ice water over the goose and continue roasting 1 hour longer, basting occasionally. The skin should be crisp and brown. Transfer the goose to a platter, and pour off the fat from the pan. Pour the pan juices into a saucepan.

#### SAUCE

1 tablespoon arrowroot or cornstarch
1 cup Port wine
2 tablespoons prepared French-style mustard
½ cup lemon juice
2 tablespoons grated lemon rind

Mix the arrowroot with a little of the Port, until smooth, then add all the Port. Blend the mustard into the pan juices, then add the Port and lemon juice. Bring to a boil, stirring constantly, add the lemon rind and then cook over low heat 3 minutes. Serve in a sauceboat.

Serves 6–8.

*Wiener Backhendl*
FRIED CHICKEN

AUSTRIA

    2 2-pound broiling chickens
    2 cups flour
    2½ teaspoons salt
    3 eggs, beaten
    2 cups sifted bread crumbs
    Lard, vegetable shortening, or vegetable oil for deep frying
    ½ cup melted butter

Viennese fried chicken is customarily prepared in quarters, but you may have the chickens disjointed, if you prefer. Wash and dry the pieces. Sift the flour and half the salt onto a large piece of waxed paper or a flat plate; roll the pieces in the mixture, coating them well. Dip into the eggs and roll in the bread crumbs, coating the pieces evenly. Chill for 20 minutes.

In a large skillet, put enough of the selected frying fat to reach 2 inches up the side. Heat to 350° and put some of the chicken pieces in it so that they don't touch. Fry the quarters 30 minutes, or if chickens are disjointed, 20 minutes, turning them once with tongs, to prevent piercing the breading. Drain on paper towels as the pieces are fried, and arrange in a baking pan. When all the pieces are finished, pour the melted butter over them and bake in a 350° oven 15 minutes.

Serves 4–8.

## Bigos Myśliwski
### HUNTERS' STEW

POLAND

This is a famous Polish dish, once served at royal banquets or after a royal hunting expedition. Because the *bigos* requires a variety of meat, the quantity may be too much, unless you're having a large dinner party. However, it freezes well, so if there is too much for your immediate needs, pack the leftovers in freezer containers and freeze it for future use. Then reheat the stew when you want to serve it.

> 1 pound top round or chuck of beef
> 1 pound boneless lamb
> ½ pound ham
> 1 pound boneless pork
> 1 whole chicken breast
> 4 Polish sausages or knockwurst
> 4 dried mushrooms
> ¼ pound salt pork
> 1½ cups chopped onions
> 2 tablespoons flour
> 2 teaspoons salt
> ½ teaspoon freshly ground black pepper
> 2 teaspoons sugar
> 3 pounds sauerkraut
> 1 cup Madeira or medium sherry

Cut the beef, lamb, ham, and pork into ½-inch cubes. Remove the skin and bones of the chicken, and cut it into ½-inch cubes. Slice the sausages.

Wash the mushrooms, cover with water, and let soak 15 minutes. Drain and cut in narrow strips.

Dice the salt pork, and brown it in a large Dutch oven or heavy saucepan. Remove the browned pieces with a slotted spoon. Add all the cubed meat and the chicken; cook until browned. Add the onions, and cook until browned. Mix in the flour, salt, pepper and sugar. Add the sauerkraut and mushrooms. Cover, and cook over low heat 30 minutes, stirring occasionally. Brown the sau-

sages in a skillet, pour off the fat, and add to the stew, then cook 30 minutes. Add the wine, bring to a boil, and cook 5 minutes. Keep the pan covered, until ready to serve.
Serves 10–12.

*Rindfleisch in Bier*  AUSTRIA
BOILED BEEF IN BEER

>5 pounds brisket or rump of beef
>2 teaspoons salt
>½ teaspoon freshly ground black pepper
>6 slices bacon
>3 (1 pound) onions, peeled and sliced
>1 cup grated carrots
>Sliced peel of ½ lemon
>2 bay leaves
>6 cups beer
>8 peppercorns
>3 tablespoons gin
>2 tablespoons butter
>2 tablespoons flour

Wash and dry the meat; rub it with salt and pepper. Cover the bacon with water, and bring it to a boil. Cook 5 minutes; drain and dry. In a Dutch oven or large casserole, arrange the bacon on the bottom. Spread the onions and carrots over it, then the lemon peel and bay leaves. Put the meat on top, and add the beer, peppercorns, and gin. Bring to boil, and cook over low heat 3 hours, or until the meat is tender. Remove the meat, and strain the broth, skimming the fat.

Melt the butter in a saucepan; blend in the flour, then gradually add 2 cups of the beer broth, stirring constantly to the boiling point. Cook 5 minutes.

Slice the meat, and put it in a hot casserole or deep serving dish. Pour the gravy over it.
Serves 8–12.

## *Erdélyi Rakott Kapusta*
## SAUERKRAUT-MEAT CASSEROLE

POLAND

>2 pounds sauerkraut
>2½ pounds boneless beef or pork
>4 slices bacon
>2 teaspoons salt
>½ teaspoon freshly ground black pepper
>1½ cups minced onion
>2 cloves garlic, minced
>2 tablespoons paprika
>1 pound Polish or Hungarian sausages, sliced
>1½ cups chicken broth
>1½ cups sour cream

If fresh sauerkraut is used, drain it well. If canned, place it in a colander or sieve, and rinse under cold running water for 5 minutes. Drain. Cut the meat into ½-inch cubes. Lightly brown the bacon in a skillet; remove the bacon, crumble, and reserve. To the fat remaining in the skillet, add the meat; cook, mixing frequently, until browned on all sides. Season with the salt and pepper, and with a slotted spoon, transfer it to a bowl. To the fat remaining, add the onion; cook until golden, mixing frequently. Remove from the heat, and mix in the garlic and paprika. Add to the meat, and toss. Brown the sausages in the skillet, drain, and add to the meat. Stir 1 cup of the broth into the skillet, and bring to a boil, scraping the bottom of any browned particles. Add to the meat, and mix thoroughly.

In a greased 3-quart casserole, spread one third of the sauerkraut. Spread half the meat mixture over it, then half the remaining sauerkraut, the remaining meat mixture, and finally the remaining sauerkraut. Mix the sour cream with the remaining broth, and pour it over the top. Cover and bake in the middle level of a preheated 400° oven for 45 minutes. Remove the cover, sprinkle the top with the reserved bacon, reduce the heat to 350°, and bake 30 minutes longer.

Serves 8–10.

## *Sztufada*
## BEEF RIBS AND NOODLES

POLAND

    4 pounds short ribs of beef
    1½ teaspoons salt
    ½ teaspoon freshly ground black pepper
    2 strips bacon, diced
    1½ cups chopped onions
    ½ teaspoon thyme
    2 tablespoons caraway seeds
    ⅓ cup wine vinegar
    1 cup boiling beef broth or water
    1 head cauliflower or 1 package cauliflower, thawed
    3 cups cooked, hot, fine noodles

Cut the short ribs into serving-sized pieces and sprinkle with the salt and pepper. In a Dutch oven or casserole, cook the bacon until it begins to brown. Pour off the fat. Add the onions and short ribs; cook over medium heat 10 minutes, stirring frequently. Mix in the thyme, caraway seeds, vinegar, and broth. Cover, and bake in a 350° oven 2 hours. Baste frequently, and add a little boiling water if pan becomes dry.

If fresh cauliflower is used, wash it thoroughly, and break it into flowerets. Skim the fat off the stew and add the fresh or frozen cauliflower; bake 10 minutes longer. Taste for seasoning. Arrange the ribs and cauliflower on a heated serving dish and surround with the noodles. Pour the gravy over the top.

Serves 4–6.

## Wienersaft Gulyás
### GOULASH, VIENNESE STYLE
AUSTRIA

⅜ pound (1½ sticks) butter
1 teaspoon crushed caraway seeds
1 teaspoon crushed marjoram
1 teaspoon grated lemon rind
1 clove garlic, minced
1 teaspoon tomato paste
1½ pounds onions, peeled and thinly sliced
2 tablespoons paprika
3 pounds chuck or rump of beef, cut in 2-inch cubes
2 teaspoons salt
1½ cups boiling water
1 cup julienne-cut green peppers, lightly sautéed

Melt the butter in a Dutch oven or heavy casserole. Stir in the caraway seeds, marjoram, lemon rind, garlic and tomato paste. Add the onions and cook them over low heat until soft, stirring occasionally. Blend in the paprika for a few seconds. Add the meat; cover, and cook over low heat 15 minutes, stirring occasionally. Add the salt and 1 cup of the water, re-cover and cook 1½ hours, or until the meat is tender. Add the remaining water, and bring to a boil. Taste for seasoning. Turn into a hot, deep serving dish, or serve directly from the casserole, garnished with the green peppers, and with noodles or *Spätzle* (see recipe).
Serves 6–8.


## Wiener Rostbraten
### STEAK WITH ONIONS
AUSTRIA

1½ pounds onions
1 teaspoon salt
4 ½-inch thick boneless shell steaks
6 tablespoons butter
2 tablespoons vegetable oil
Freshly ground black pepper

Buy medium-sized yellow onions. Peel and slice them very thin, then into strips. Pound the steaks lightly to flatten them.

Melt 4 tablespoons of the butter in a large skillet. Add the onions and sauté over medium heat, until golden and crisp, about 10 minutes. Sprinkle with salt. About 4 minutes before the onions will be ready, prepare the steaks.

Heat the oil and remaining butter in a heavy 12-inch skillet; put the steaks in it in a single layer, and cook over high heat 1 minute on each side for very rare, 2 minutes on each side for medium. Transfer the steaks to a hot platter, season with salt and pepper, and mound the onions over them.

Serves 4.

## *Gulyás*        GOULASH
HUNGARY

> 3 pounds chuck or cross ribs of beef
> 6 tablespoons butter
> 2 pounds onions, chopped
> 2 tablespoons hot Hungarian paprika
> 2 teaspoons salt
> ½ teaspoon freshly ground black pepper
> 1 clove garlic, minced
> 2 green peppers, seeded and coarsely chopped
> 1 8-ounce can tomato sauce
> 1 cup sour cream

Cut the meat into 2-inch cubes.

Melt 4 tablespoons of the butter in a Dutch oven or heavy saucepan; sauté the onions 15 minutes, stirring frequently. Remove the onions and set aside. Melt the remaining butter in the pan and brown the meat well on all sides; sprinkle with the paprika, salt, and pepper. Return the onions to the pan with the green peppers, garlic, and tomato sauce. Cover, and cook over low heat 2½ hours, stirring occasionally. Mix in sour cream; heat but do not boil.

Serves 6–8.

## Eszterházy Rostélyos
## BRAISED STEAK

AUSTRIA

> 6 top round steaks, cut ¾ inch thick
> ⅓ cup flour
> 2 teaspoons salt
> ½ teaspoon freshly ground black pepper
> 4 tablespoons butter
> 2 cups minced onion
> ½ cup grated carrots
> 1 clove garlic, minced
> 2 cups beef broth or water
> ¼ teaspoon thyme
> 2 bay leaves
> 3 sprigs parsley
> ⅛ teaspoon ground allspice
> 2 tablespoons lemon juice
> 1 cup sour cream
> 1 cup crisp-fried sliced onions

Pound the steaks lightly to flatten, then dip them in a mixture of the flour, salt, and pepper. Pound the surfaces. Melt the butter in a 12-inch skillet or Dutch oven. Put the steaks in it in a single layer, and brown both sides. Remove the steaks. To the fat remaining add the onion, garlic, and carrots; cook until golden, stirring frequently. Stir in the broth and bring to a boil, scraping the bottom of any browned particles. Add the thyme, bay leaves, parsley, allspice, and lemon juice. Arrange the meat in the pan; cover loosely and cook over low heat 1 hour. Taste for seasoning. Arrange the steaks on a heated platter and keep warm.

Force the gravy through a sieve into a saucepan. Skim any fat from the surface, then blend the sour cream into the gravy. Heat, but do not let boil. Pour the gravy over the steaks, and garnish with the fried onion.

Serves 6.

*Bográcy Gulyás*  HUNGARY
MIXED MEAT GOULASH

    1 pound boneless beef
    1 pound boneless veal
    1 pound boneless pork
    4 tablespoons butter
    3 cups thinly sliced onions
    1 cup thinly sliced green peppers
    2 teaspoons salt
    ½ teaspoon freshly ground black pepper
    3 tablespoons paprika
    ½ teaspoon caraway seeds
    2 tablespoons tomato paste
    1 cup beef broth
    1½ cups sour cream
    2 cups peeled cubed potatoes, half-cooked and drained

Cut the beef, veal, and pork into 1½-inch cubes.

Melt the butter in a casserole; sauté the onions 10 minutes. Add the green pepper, beef, veal, and pork; cook over medium heat until browned. Stir in the salt, pepper, paprika, caraway seeds, tomato paste, and ¼ cup broth. Cover, and cook over low heat 30 minutes. Add the remaining broth and cook 1½ hours longer. Add the potatoes; cook 10 minutes. Stir the sour cream into the pan juices. Heat, but do not boil.

Serves 6–8.

*Sauerbraten*                                                            GERMANY
## MARINATED POT ROAST

- 5 pounds top round or rump of beef
- 2 teaspoons salt
- ½ teaspoon freshly ground black pepper
- 1 cup thinly sliced onions
- 1 carrot, sliced thin
- 1 stalk celery, chopped
- 4 cloves
- 4 peppercorns, crushed
- 2 bay leaves
- 1 cup red wine vinegar
- 1 cup dry red wine
- 2½ cups water
- 2 tablespoons vegetable oil
- 5 tablespoons butter
- 1 cup minced onion
- ½ cup grated carrots
- ¼ cup flour
- 1 tablespoon sugar
- ¾ cup gingersnap crumbs

Wipe the meat with a damp cloth, then rub with the salt and pepper. Place in a bowl (not metal). Combine the onions, carrot, celery, cloves, peppercorns, bay leaves, vinegar, wine, and water in a saucepan. Bring to a boil, then cool it. Pour over the meat. Cover and let marinate in the refrigerator 4 days. Turn meat once or twice a day.

Drain the meat and dry thoroughly; strain and heat the marinade. Heat the oil and 1 tablespoon butter in a Dutch oven. Brown the meat in it on all sides. Remove the meat. In the fat remaining, sauté the onion and carrots for 5 minutes. Add 2 cups of the heated marinade, and return the meat. Bring to a boil, cover, and cook over low heat 2 hours, adding the remaining marinade after 1 hour.

Melt the remaining butter in a skillet; blend in the flour, then the sugar until browned. Mix in a little gravy, then stir into the remaining gravy. Re-cover and cook 30 minutes longer, or until the meat is tender. Transfer the meat to a heated platter. Stir the gingersnaps into the gravy; cook over medium heat 5 minutes or until smooth. Slice the meat and pour some of the gravy over it and put the rest in a sauceboat. Serve with potato dumplings or boiled potatoes.

Serves 8–10.

## *Schweinebraten*  GERMANY
## ROAST FRESH HAM

> 6-pound leg of pork
> 2 teaspoons salt
> 1 teaspoon freshly ground black pepper
> 1 teaspoon crushed caraway seed
> 2 cloves garlic, minced
> 1 pound onions, peeled and sliced
> 2 carrots, sliced
> 3 cloves
> 2 bay leaves
> 1½ cups dry white wine
> 1 cup sour cream

Wash and dry the leg of pork. Cut gashes on the skin side, in a crisscross pattern. Rub the leg with a mixture of the salt, pepper, caraway, and garlic.

Use a shallow roasting pan, and on the bottom spread the onions, carrots, cloves, and bay leaves. Put the leg in the pan, skin side down, and roast in a preheated 350° oven 30 minutes. Pour 1 cup of the wine over the pork, and roast 1 hour, basting frequently. Turn the pork skin side up, and roast 2 hours longer, basting frequently. Transfer the pork to a hot platter.

Strain the pan juices into a saucepan, pressing through as much of the vegetables as possible. Add the remaining wine; bring to a boil, taste for seasoning and cook 5 minutes. Just before serving, blend in the sour cream. Serve in a sauceboat. Sauerkraut and dumplings make excellent accompaniments.

Serves 6–8.

## *Rindslendenragout*
## PORK CASSEROLE

AUSTRIA

4 pounds loin of pork
3½ teaspoons salt
1 teaspoon freshly ground black pepper
¼ pound (1 stick) butter
3 cups sliced white onions
3 (1¼ pounds) potatoes, peeled and thinly sliced
2 carrots, julienne cut
1½ cups grated cabbage
1½ teaspoons caraway seeds
1½ cups chicken broth

Bone the pork, and cut the meat into 1-inch cubes; toss with 2 teaspoons of the salt, and ½ teaspoon of the pepper. Melt half the butter in a skillet. Brown the pork in it. Remove the pork. In the butter remaining, sauté the onions until golden.

On the bottom of a 3-quart buttered casserole, arrange the potato slices. Now make alternate layers of the pork, the onions, carrots, and cabbage, sprinkling each layer with caraway seeds, and some of the remaining salt and pepper. Cover with the remaining potatoes and season them.

Melt the remaining butter in the skillet, scraping the bottom. Pour over the potatoes. Add the broth, cover the casserole tightly, and bake in a preheated 375° oven 1¼ hours. Remove the cover and bake 30 minutes longer, or until the potatoes brown. Serve directly from the casserole.

Serves 4–6.

## Székely Gulyás
## PORK AND SAUERKRAUT GOULASH

HUNGARY

    1 pound sauerkraut
    2 cups shredded cabbage
    3 pounds boneless pork
    3 tablespoons lard or butter
    1½ cups minced onions
    1 clove garlic, minced
    2 tablespoons paprika
    2 teaspoons salt
    1 teaspoon caraway seeds
    ¾ cup peeled, chopped tomatoes
    2 cups water
    1 cup sour cream

Try to buy barrel sauerkraut. If canned sauerkraut is used, put it in a colander or strainer, and let cold water run over it for 5 minutes. Drain well. Mix the cabbage with the sauerkraut. Cut the pork into 1-inch cubes.

Melt the lard in a Dutch oven or heavy casserole; sauté the onion in it until golden. Stir in the garlic, paprika, and salt. Add the pork and toss until well coated; cook over low heat 10 minutes, stirring frequently. Spread the sauerkraut over the pork, and sprinkle with the caraway seeds and tomatoes. Add the water, bring to a boil, cover, and cook over low heat 1½ hours, shaking the pan frequently and adding more water if necessary. Stir in the sour cream, and cook 10 minutes longer, but do not let it boil. Serve with dumplings or boiled potatoes.

Serves 6–8.

*Wieprzowina z Kapusta*                                      POLAND
## SPARERIBS WITH SAUERKRAUT AND BARLEY

> 2 racks spareribs
> 1 pound sauerkraut
> 2 tablespoons vegetable oil
> 2 cloves garlic, minced
> 1½ cups coarsely chopped onions
> 1 bay leaf
> 1½ teaspoons salt
> ½ teaspoon freshly ground black pepper
> 2 cups boiling water
> 2 apples, peeled, cored and chopped
> ½ cup fine barley
> 1 teaspoon caraway seeds

Cut the spareribs into individual ribs. Try to buy barrel sauerkraut, but if you can't, use canned sauerkraut and rinse it under cold running water.

Heat the oil in a Dutch oven or large saucepan; brown the ribs in it over high heat. Pour off the fat. Add the garlic and onions; cook over low heat 10 minutes. Add the bay leaf, salt, pepper, and half the water and cook 30 minutes, stirring occasionally. Add the apples, sauerkraut, barley, caraway seeds, and remaining water. Mix well, cover, and cook 1 hour longer. Watch carefully, and add a little more boiling water if pan becomes dry. Taste for seasoning and discard the bay leaf.

Serves 4–6.

## *Paprika Rahmschnitzel*     AUSTRIA
## SAUTÉED VEAL IN PAPRIKA SAUCE

### Sauce

4 tablespoons butter
¾ cup minced onion
½ teaspoon salt
2 tablespoons paprika
1 tablespoon flour
1 cup chicken broth
¼ cup dry white wine

Melt the butter in a saucepan; sauté the onions until yellow and soft. Blend in the salt, paprika, and flour; gradually add the broth, stirring steadily to the boiling point. Mix in the wine, and cook over low heat 10 minutes.

### Veal

6 veal cutlets (about 2½ pounds)
1¼ teaspoons salt
½ teaspoon white pepper
¼ cup flour
6 tablespoons butter
½ cup sour cream
Gherkins
Lemon wedges

Pound the veal cutlets as thin as possible. Dip them in a mixture of salt, pepper, and flour. Melt the butter in a large skillet. Put the veal cutlets in it in a single layer. Sauté until delicately browned on both sides. Add the sauce, and cook over low heat 10 minutes, turning the veal once or twice. Remove the veal, and arrange it on a hot platter. Add the sour cream to the sauce remaining in the skillet; heat, stirring constantly, but do not let boil. Pour over the veal, and garnish with the gherkins and lemon wedges.
Serves 6.

## Kalbsgulyás
## VEAL GOULASH

AUSTRIA

> 3 pounds boneless shoulder or leg of veal
> 3 tablespoons butter
> 1 pound onions, peeled and thinly sliced
> 2 tablespoons paprika
> 2 teaspoons salt
> 1 cup boiling beef broth
> 1½ cups peeled, diced, seeded tomatoes
> ½ teaspoon crushed caraway seeds

Cut the veal into 1½-inch cubes.

Melt the butter in a Dutch oven or heavy casserole; sauté the onions in it for 10 minutes, stirring frequently. Blend in the paprika, and add the veal. Cook 10 minutes, stirring frequently. Sprinkle with the salt, and add the broth. Cover, and cook over low heat 45 minutes. Mix occasionally. Add the tomatoes, and cook 30 minutes longer, or until the veal is tender. Mix in the caraway seeds, and taste for seasoning. Serve with *Spätzle* (see recipe) or noodles.

Serves 6–8.

## Weiner Schnitzel
## BREADED VEAL CUTLET

AUSTRIA

> 6 veal cutlets, cut from the leg (about 2 pounds)
> ½ cup lemon juice
> ½ cup dry white wine
> 4 slices white bread, toasted
> 1½ teaspoons salt
> ½ teaspoon freshly ground black pepper
> 2 eggs
> 2 tablespoons water
> Flour
> 4 tablespoons vegetable oil
> 6 tablespoons butter
> Lemon wedges

Have the veal cut ¼ inch thick, then pound lightly to flatten. In a glass or pottery dish, combine the lemon juice and wine; place the veal in it, and spoon the liquid over it several times. Let stand 1 hour. Break the toast into little pieces, and run in an electric blender until crumbs are formed. Or grate the toast, or put through a food grinder. If you want to use packaged bread crumbs, sift them. You'll need about 1 cup. Remove the veal from the marinade, and dry with paper towels. Sprinkle the slices with salt and pepper. Beat the eggs with the water, dip the slices into it, and then into flour. Shake off any excess flour, then dip them into the crumbs. Chill for 30 minutes.

If possible, use two 12-inch skillets. Heat some oil in each, then add some butter and heat until it foams up. Put 2 slices of veal in each skillet, in a single layer, and cook over medium heat 4 minutes on each side. Use tongs for turning, to prevent breaking the breading. Drain, and if necessary keep warm while preparing the remaining veal. Serve garnished with lemon wedges.

Serves 6.

Variations:

*With Anchovy Butter:*

> ¼ **pound (1 stick) sweet butter**
> ¼ **cup drained minced anchovies**

Melt the butter in a small skillet; mix in the anchovies with a wooden spoon, and cook over low heat 3 minutes.

*A la Holstein:*

Put a fried egg and 2 anchovy fillets in a crisscross design on each veal cutlet. Sprinkle capers over all.

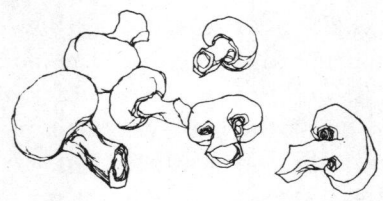

## Kalbsbraten
### ROAST VEAL WITH MUSHROOM SAUCE
GERMANY

6 pounds boned rolled loin of veal
2 teaspoons salt
½ teaspoon freshly ground black pepper
¼ pound (1 stick) butter
1 stalk celery, sliced
3 sprigs parsley
1 bay leaf
½ teaspoon thyme
¾ cup chicken broth
¼ cup dry white wine
1 cup sour cream
½ pound mushrooms, sliced
2 teaspoons arrowroot or cornstarch
1 cup heavy cream

Rinse and dry the veal, rub with the salt and pepper, then with 6 tablespoons of the butter. Put the veal in a shallow roasting pan, and around it the celery, parsley, bay leaf, and thyme. Roast in a 400° oven 20 minutes. Add the broth and wine; reduce the heat to 350° and roast 1 hour, basting frequently. Stir the sour cream into the gravy, and roast 45 minutes longer, or until the veal is tender. Baste frequently. While the veal is roasting, sauté the mushrooms in the remaining butter.

Put the roast veal on a heated platter. Strain the gravy into a small saucepan, and skim the fat. Mix the arrowroot with a little of the heavy cream, then all the cream. Add to the pan juices, stirring steadily to the boiling point, then cook 5 minutes longer. Mix in the mushrooms, and taste for seasoning. Carve the veal, and serve the sauce in a sauceboat.

Serves 6–8.

MIDDLE EUROPE 221

*Sülze*　　　　　　　　　　　　　　　　　　　　　　GERMANY
## JELLIED PIGS' KNUCKLES

>6 pigs' knuckles
>½ cup white vinegar
>7 cups water
>1 tablespoon salt
>8 peppercorns
>1 bay leaf
>½ teaspoon thyme
>1 onion
>3 cloves garlic
>1 teaspoon freshly ground black pepper
>¼ cup minced parsley
>⅛ teaspoon sugar
>1 envelope (tablespoon) gelatin
>¼ cup dry white wine
>½ cup chopped dill pickle
>¼ pound cooked tongue, cut julienne
>3 hard cooked eggs, sliced
>1 tablespoon capers

Wash the pigs' knuckles and combine them in a kettle with the vinegar, water, salt, peppercorns, bay leaf, thyme, onion, and garlic. Bring to a boil and cook over low heat 2 hours, or until the meat falls away from the bones. Remove the knuckles from the broth, and cut the meat away from the bones, then into narrow strips. Sprinkle it with the pepper and parsley. Strain the broth into a clean saucepan, and cook over medium heat 30 minutes. Skim the fat, and stir the meat and sugar into the broth; cook 15 minutes. Taste for seasoning.

Sprinkle the gelatin into the wine, let stand 5 minutes, and stir into broth.

Spread the meat on the bottom of an 11-by-16-inch glass or pyroceram dish. Over it arrange the pickle, tongue, eggs, and capers. Very slowly pour in the broth. Chill for at least 6 hours, or until set. Serve with chopped onion and lemon wedges or vinaigrette sauce.

Serves 8–10 as a first course.

Note: Calves' feet may be used instead of pigs' knuckles.

## Töltött Káposzta
### STUFFED CABBAGE ROLLS

HUNGARY

> 3-pound head cabbage
> ½ pound ground pork or veal
> ½ pound ground beef
> ½ cup half-cooked rice
> 1 clove garlic, minced
> 4 teaspoons salt
> 1 teaspoon freshly ground black pepper
> 2 tablespoons minced parsley
> 1 teaspoon paprika
> 1 pound sauerkraut
> 3 onions, thinly sliced
> 3 cups canned tomatoes
> 1 tablespoon caraway seeds
> 1 cup sour cream

Cover the cabbage with boiling water and let stand 10 minutes. Carefully remove 24 large leaves. Shred the remaining cabbage.

Mix together the meat, rice, garlic, 2 teaspoons of the salt, ½ teaspoon of the pepper, the parsley and the paprika. Place some of the mixture on each cabbage leaf, turn ends in and roll up. Mix the shredded cabbage with the sauerkraut and spread about ⅓ on the bottom of a greased Dutch oven or heavy saucepan. Arrange the cabbage rolls over it, and spread the remaining sauerkraut mixture over them, then cover with the onions. Mix the tomatoes with the remaining salt and pepper; pour over the onions. Sprinkle the caraway seeds over all. Cover and cook over low heat 3 hours, shaking the pan frequently. Stir the sour cream into the gravy, heat, and serve.

Serves 8–12.

*Eierpflanze*  
STUFFED EGGPLANT

GERMANY

    3 1-pound eggplants
    3 teaspoons salt
    3 tablespoons butter
    1 cup chopped onions
    1½ pounds ground beef
    2 cloves garlic, minced
    ½ teaspoon freshly ground black pepper
    ¾ teaspoon thyme
    1 cup cooked egg barley (a small type of egg noodle)
    ½ cup cottage cheese, drained
    1 29-ounce can tomatoes, drained and chopped

Wash the eggplants and place on a baking pan. Add water to a depth of ¼ inch. Bake in a 400° oven 20 minutes. Cool slightly, discard stems, and cut each in half lengthwise. Scoop out the pulp and chop; sprinkle the cavities with 1½ teaspoons of the salt, and let stand, cut side down, while preparing the filling.

Melt the butter in a skillet; sauté the onions 5 minutes. Add the meat; cook over high heat 5 minutes, stirring almost steadily. Mix in the garlic, pepper, thyme, chopped eggplant, and remaining salt; cook over low heat 10 minutes. Mix half the meat mixture with the egg barley, cheese, and ¾ cup of the tomatoes. Taste for seasoning. Stuff the eggplant halves with the meat-barley mixture. Spread the remaining tomatoes and meat mixture in a greased baking dish. Arrange the eggplant halves over it. Bake in a 400° oven 20 minutes.

Serves 6.

*Töltött Kalarábé*  HUNGARY
## STUFFED KOHLRABIES

12 medium-sized young kohlrabies and leaves
½ pound ground veal
½ pound ground beef
2 eggs
Dash nutmeg
½ teaspoon white pepper
1½ teaspoons salt
6 tablespoons butter
½ cup chopped onion
1 clove garlic
1 tablespoon paprika
2 cups chicken broth
3 tablespoons flour
1 cup dry white wine
1 cup sour cream
¼ cup grated Parmesan cheese
2 tablespoons minced parsley

Peel the kohlrabies. Wash half the leaves (discard the rest). Cook the kohlrabies in boiling salted water for 5 minutes. Remove and cool. Drop the washed leaves into the boiling water, and remove. Cut a ¼-inch slice off the root end of the kohlrabies and carefully scoop out the pulp, leaving a ¼-inch-thick shell. Chop the pulp, and the leaves.

Mix together the veal, beef, eggs, nutmeg, and half the pepper and salt. Stuff the kohlrabies, and mound the filling slightly above the top of the vegetable.

Melt half the butter in a 2-quart casserole. Sauté the onions in it for 5 minutes. Stir in the garlic, paprika, and the chopped pulp and leaves. Arrange the kohlrabies in it in an upright position.

Pour the broth around them. Bring to a boil, and bake in a preheated 350° oven 30 minutes. Prepare the sauce meanwhile.

Melt the remaining butter in a saucepan; blend in the flour and the remaining salt and pepper. Gradually add the wine, stirring steadily to the boiling point.

Cook over low heat 5 minutes. Cool slightly, then stir in the sour cream, cheese, and parsley. At the end of the 30 minutes cooking time, spoon the sauce over the tops of the kohlrabies. Raise the heat to 450°, and bake 10 minutes longer.

Serves 4 as a main course, or 12 as a first course.

*Töltött Zoldpaprika*  HUNGARY
STUFFED PEPPERS

> 12 medium sized green peppers
> 2 pounds ground beef or pork
> ½ cup grated onions
> ½ cup cooked rice
> 2 eggs, beaten
> 2 tablespoons cold water
> 2½ teaspoons salt
> ½ teaspoon freshly ground black pepper
> 2 tablespoons vegetable oil
> 1 cup chopped onions
> 3 8-ounce cans tomato sauce

Cut a 1-inch piece from the stem ends of the peppers and reserve. Scoop out the seeds and fibers.

Mix together the meat, grated onions, rice, egg, water, 1½ teaspoons of the salt, and ¼ teaspoon of the pepper. Stuff the peppers and replace the tops.

Heat the oil in a Dutch oven or heavy saucepan; sauté the chopped onions 10 minutes. Mix in the tomato sauce and the remaining salt and pepper; arrange the peppers in an upright position. Cover and cook over low heat 1¼ hours or until the peppers are tender. Taste for seasoning.

Serves 6 as a main course, or 12 as a first course.

## *Ungarishes Bohnengulyás*
## DRIED BEAN GOULASH

AUSTRIA-HUNGARY

>1 pound dried white beans
>2 tablespoons vegetable oil
>1 cup chopped onions
>½ pound cooked ham, diced
>2 cloves garlic, minced
>1 tablespoon flour
>1 tablespoon paprika
>6 cups beef broth or water
>2 tablespoons tomato paste
>½ teaspoon rosemary
>1½ teaspoons salt
>1 cup cooked diced potato

Wash beans thoroughly, cover with water, bring to a boil, and cook 2 minutes. Remove from heat and let soak 1 hour. Drain.

Heat the oil in a large saucepan; sauté the onions until golden. Mix in the ham, garlic, flour, and paprika, then the broth or water. Add the beans, bring to a boil, and cook over low heat 2 hours. Mix in the tomato paste, rosemary, and salt. Cook 30 minutes longer, or until the beans are tender. Taste for seasoning. Turn into a deep serving dish, and sprinkle with the potatoes. Serve as a supper or dinner dish.

Serves 4–6.

## *Paprikás Burgonya*
## POTATOES IN PAPRIKA SAUCE

AUSTRIA-HUNGARY

>2 pounds potatoes
>4 tablespoons lard or butter
>1 cup chopped onions
>1 cup chopped green pepper
>1 tablespoon paprika
>1 teaspoon salt
>1 cup peeled chopped tomatoes
>1½ cups chicken broth
>½ cup sour cream

Peel the potatoes, and cut in eighths lengthwise. Keep in cold water while preparing the sauce.

Melt the lard or butter in an 11-inch skillet; sauté the onions and green pepper 10 minutes, stirring frequently. Blend in the paprika and salt. Drain the potatoes, and dry them on paper towels. Add to the skillet, tossing until well coated. Add the tomatoes and broth. Bring to a boil, cover, and cook over low heat 25 minutes, shaking the pan frequently. Stir in the sour cream just before serving. Serve with roast or boiled meat or poultry.

Serves 6–8.

*Kartoffelklösse*　　　　　　　　　　　　　　　　　　　GERMANY
POTATO DUMPLINGS

>2 pounds potatoes
>3 egg yolks, beaten
>3 tablespoons cornstarch
>3 tablespoons farina (not quick-cooking)
>1½ teaspoons salt
>½ teaspoon white pepper
>¼ teaspoon nutmeg
>1 cup toasted white bread cubes
>Flour

Scrub the potatoes and cook in boiling water until tender. Drain, peel, and put through a ricer or mash very smooth. Beat in the egg yolks, cornstarch, farina, salt, pepper, and nutmeg. Form about 2 tablespoons into a ball, between floured hands, and drop into a deep pot of boiling salted water. This is a test to see if dumpling holds together. If it doesn't, add a little flour. If it does, shape the mixture into 1-inch balls and press a few bread cubes in the center of each, and press the opening together. Roll lightly in flour, and drop into the boiling salted water. Don't crowd the pot. Cook 15 minutes, or until they rise to the surface. Remove with a slotted spoon, draining them well. Serve with melted browned butter.

Makes about 20.

## Spätzle
### EGG DROP DUMPLINGS
AUSTRIA

    2 cups flour
    ½ teaspoon salt
    3 eggs, lightly beaten
    ½ cup milk (about)

Sift the flour and salt into a bowl; beat in the eggs. Then very gradually add just enough of the milk to make a soft dough. Beat until smooth.

Bring 2 quarts of well-salted water to a boil in a large saucepan. There are two ways to make the *spätzle*. Put a colander with large holes over the saucepan, and with a spoon force the dough through the holes, a few tablespoons at a time, into the boiling water. Or, put the dough on a board, shape into pencil-thick lengths, and with a sharp knife cut off ½-inch-long pieces directly into the water. In either case, stir, to prevent sticking. Don't crowd the pan. Cook over high heat 7 minutes. Taste one to see if it is tender. If not, cook 1 minute longer. Drain in a colander. Serve with browned melted butter, if no gravy is accompanying them.

Makes about 3 cups.


## Leberknödel
### LIVER DUMPLINGS
GERMANY

    3 slices white bread, trimmed
    ¼ cup milk
    2 tablespoons butter
    ¼ cup minced onion
    ¼ cup minced parsley
    1 pound calf's liver
    1½ teaspoons salt
    ¼ teaspoon freshly ground black pepper
    4 tablespoons flour
    2 egg yolks, beaten
    2 egg whites, beaten stiff

Crumble the bread, and soak in the milk for 10 minutes. Drain thoroughly, and mash the bread.

Melt the butter in a skillet, sauté the onion and parsley until lightly browned, stirring frequently. Cool.

Wash the liver, removing any fibrous tissues. Grind the raw liver, or chop to a paste. Mix in the salt, pepper, flour, bread, and sautéed onion mixture. Beat in the egg yolks, then fold in the egg whites.

Bring about 3 quarts of salted water to a boil. Make a test dumpling. Pick up 1 tablespoon of the batter, and with another tablespoon, shape into a ball, then drop it carefully into the boiling water. Cook 10 minutes, and drain. If it holds together, proceed shaping and cooking the dumplings. If it separates, add a little more flour to the liver mixture. Don't crowd the pan when cooking the dumplings, and use a slotted spoon to remove them. Let drain on a napkin. Serve with browned melted butter and sauerkraut. The dumplings are particularly good with roast meat or poultry, and may also be served in soup.

Makes about 36.

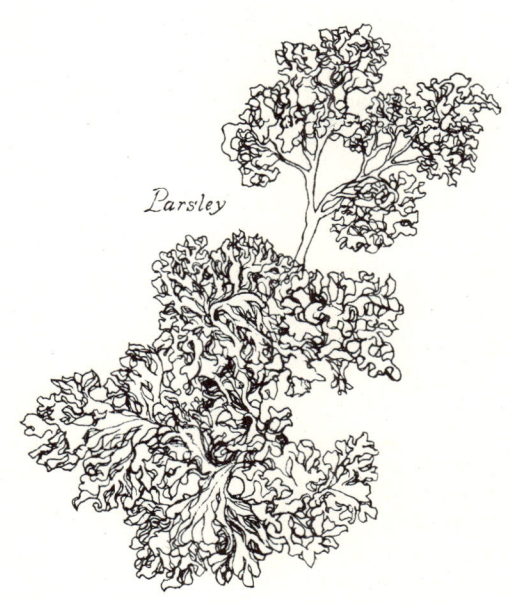
Parsley

## Salzburger Nöckerl
### MERINGUE SOUFFLÉ

AUSTRIA

5 egg whites
¾ cup sugar
4 tablespoons butter
¼ cup heavy cream
1 tablespoon flour
3 egg yolks, beaten
Confectioners' sugar

It's important to have everything measured and assembled before you begin the preparation of the dish. If you have an oblong or oval flat flameproof dish, about 12 inches long, use it. If not, an 11-inch skillet can be used. Preheat the oven to 350°.

Beat the egg whites until fairly stiff, then gradually beat in the sugar, continuing to beat until very stiff.

Put the butter and cream in the selected pan, and place over low heat until the butter melts, and mixture is foamy.

Very gently fold the flour and egg yolks into the beaten whites. Pick up about a third of the meringue at a time with a large spoon, and drop it into the pan, forming three *nöckerl*. Keep the pan over direct medium heat for 1 minute, then place on the middle level of the oven for 12 minutes, or until tops are delicately browned. Sprinkle with confectioners' sugar, and serve at once. Serves 6.

## Gsusztatott Palacsinta
### WALNUT PANCAKES WITH CHOCOLATE CREAM

HUNGARY

#### PANCAKES

3 eggs
1½ cups milk
¾ cup sifted flour
¼ teaspoon salt
2 tablespoons vegetable oil
Butter

In a bowl, beat the eggs; stir in the milk, then beat in the flour, salt, and oil, until smooth. Chill for 1 hour, and beat again.

Heat a 7-inch skillet, and rub with a little butter. Pour in about 2 tablespoons of the batter, turning the pan quickly to coat the bottom. Cook until delicately browned on both sides. Turn out onto a napkin and stack while preparing the balance of the pancakes. Keep warm.

### Filling

1½ cups shelled walnuts
½ cup sugar
1 teaspoon cinnamon
1 teaspoon vanilla extract
¾ cup heavy cream (about)

Pulverize the nuts in an electric blender, or put through a mouli grater or nut grinder. Mix in the sugar, cinnamon, vanilla extract, and just enough of the cream to make a spreadable mixture.

### Sauce

¾ cup sugar
1 cup milk
8 squares (ounces) unsweetened chocolate

Combine the sugar and milk in a saucepan; cook over low heat, stirring constantly, until sugar dissolves. Add the chocolate, and stir over low heat until chocolate melts and mixture is smooth.

Spread some of the nut mixture on each pancake, and fold over. Serve the chocolate sauce in a sauceboat.

Serves 6–8.

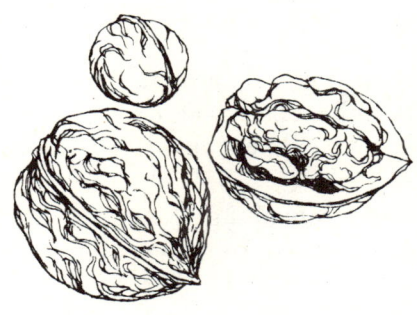

## *Topfenpalatschinken*
## PANCAKES IN CUSTARD SAUCE

AUSTRIA

### PANCAKES

3 eggs
⅓ cup bubbly club soda
1 cup milk
3 tablespoons sugar
1 cup sifted flour
¼ teaspoon salt
1 teaspoon vanilla extract
Butter

Beat the eggs in a bowl, then beat in the club soda and milk. With a spoon, mix in the sugar and flour until smooth, then mix in the salt and vanilla. Chill 30 minutes.

Heat a 7-inch skillet, and rub it with a little butter. Pour in about 2 tablespoons of the batter, and turn pan quickly from side to side to coat the bottom evenly. Cook until delicately browned on both sides. Turn out onto a napkin, and stack while preparing the balance.

### FILLING AND SAUCE

¼ pound (1 stick) butter
1⅓ cups sugar
2 egg yolks, beaten
1 teaspoon vanilla extract
1 cup cottage cheese, drained
¾ cup sour cream
2 whole eggs
2½ cups milk

Cream the butter, gradually adding ¾ cup of the sugar. Beat in the egg yolks, vanilla, cheese, and sour cream. Spread some of the cheese mixture on each pancake, roll up, and arrange in a buttered baking dish.

Beat the eggs and remaining sugar together until light and thick, then beat in the milk. Pour over the pancakes and bake in a preheated 350° oven 25 minutes, or until the custard is set and lightly browned.

Serves 6–8.

*

## *Kaiserschmarn*                 AUSTRIA
### RAISIN OMELET PANCAKE

¼ cup seedless raisins
¼ cup cognac
4 eggs yolks
⅛ teaspoon salt
¼ cup sugar
1 cup sifted flour
1 cup light cream
4 egg whites, beaten stiff
6 tablespoons butter
Confectioners' sugar

Soak the raisins in the cognac for 20 minutes. Drain well. Beat the egg yolks and salt until thick and light. Beat in the sugar. Add the flour, alternately with the cream, mixing until smooth. Mix in the raisins. Fold in the egg whites, carefully but thoroughly, so no trace of white remains.

Melt 2 tablespoons butter in a 9-inch skillet (use 2 pans if possible), pour in half the batter, and cook over low heat until browned on the bottom. Place on the upper level of a preheated 450° oven and bake 5 minutes, or until puffed and browned. Turn out onto a plate. If you've used only one pan, repeat with remaining batter.

Tear the browned pancakes into pieces with two forks. Melt the remaining butter in a skillet; add the pancake pieces. Sauté over low heat 2 minutes, stirring constantly. Sprinkle with confectioners' sugar and serve hot.

Serves 4–6.

*Rétes*    AUSTRIA-HUNGARY
STRUDEL

### Dough

2½ cups flour
½ teaspoon salt
2 teaspoons vinegar
¼ cup vegetable oil
1 egg
½ cup warm water (about)

Sift the flour and salt together into a bowl, and make a well in the center. Into it put the vinegar, 2 tablespoons of the oil, and the egg. Gradually work in the flour; add just enough of the warm water to make a soft dough. It may not be necessary to add all the water. Knead well; raise the dough and slap it down several times until it loses its stickiness. This will take 10–15 minutes. (Use an electric dough hook, if you have one.) Form into a ball, brush with oil, and cover with a warm bowl for 30 minutes.

Spread a cloth over a large table and dust with flour. Roll out the dough in a circle, turning it several times. Brush with oil. Flour both hands heavily and begin stretching the dough from underneath with the backs of the hands. Work carefully and brush with more oil occasionally. Don't worry if the dough tears; it should be almost transparent. Cut off the thick edges. Let dry for 5 minutes.

### Poppy Seed Filling

½ pound poppy seeds
¼ pound (1 stick) butter
½ cup honey
1½ cups coarsely chopped walnuts or pecans
½ cup seedless raisins
¼ cup heavy cream
1 tablespoon grated orange rind
4 tablespoons melted butter

If possible, have the poppy seeds ground at the store. If not, cover with boiling water and let soak 2 hours. Drain well and grind twice, using the finest blade of the food chopper. Or use an electric blender.

Cream the ¼ pound butter; beat in the honey, nuts, raisins, cream, and orange rind. Mix in the poppy seeds. Spread over two-thirds of the strudel dough; roll up and place on a greased baking pan. Brush with the melted butter. Bake in a preheated 375° oven 45 minutes, or until delicately browned. Cut into 2-inch slices while still hot.

### APPLE FILLING

3 tablespoons butter
1½ cups fresh bread crumbs
¾ cup melted butter
¾ cup ground walnuts
4 cups peeled sliced apples
1 cup seedless raisins (optional)
2 teaspoons grated lemon rind
⅔ cup sugar
1 tablespoon cinnamon

Melt the 3 tablespoons butter in a skillet; sauté the bread crumbs in it until lightly browned. Cool.

Brush the strudel dough generously with melted butter. Sprinkle with the bread crumbs and walnuts. Spread the apples in a 2-inch strip along one end of the dough. Brush with melted butter and sprinkle with the raisins, lemon rind, sugar, and cinnamon. Fold in opposite sides of the dough. Starting from the apple end, lift up the cloth, and roll up like a jelly roll. Transfer the roll to a greased baking sheet. (If roll is too long for the pan, turn ends in.) Brush with melted butter. Bake in a preheated 350° oven 50 minutes or until delicately browned. Brush with melted butter a few times during the baking period. Sprinkle top with sugar. Serve warm, cut into 2-inch pieces.

### Cheese Filling

¼ pound (1 stick) butter
¾ cup sugar
6 egg yolks
1¾ cups sour cream
2 teaspoons grated lemon rind
1 pound cream cheese
½ cup seedless raisins (optional)
4 egg whites, beaten stiff

Melt half the butter and brush the dough with it.

Cream the remaining butter; gradually add the sugar. Add the egg yolks, beating until light and fluffy. Add the sour cream and lemon rind. Force the cheese through a sieve. Combine with previous mixture, beating until thoroughly smooth. Add the raisins, if desired. Fold in the egg whites. Spread the cheese mixture over two-thirds of the dough. Turn opposite sides in and roll up loosely. Brush with melted butter. Place on a buttered baking sheet. Bake in a preheated 375° oven 45 minutes, or until delicately browned. Cut into 2-inch slices while hot.

*Lomanci z Makom*     POLAND
## POPPY SEED CANDY PASTRIES

1¼ cups flour
½ teaspoon salt
¼ pound (1 stick) butter
4 tablespoons sour cream
¼ pound poppy seeds (about 1¼ cups), ground
¼ cup milk
1½ cups honey
½ cup seedless raisins
½ cup nuts (filberts, walnuts, or almonds)

Sift the flour and salt into a bowl; work in the butter with the hand. Mix in sour cream until a dough is formed. Chill at least 3 hours, or overnight, if you prefer. Roll out the dough ⅛ inch thick on a lightly floured surface and fit it into an 11-inch pie plate or 8-inch square pan. Prick in several places with a fork. Bake in a preheated 375° oven 20 minutes. Cool, and cut into ½-inch squares.

Soak the poppy seeds in the milk until they absorb all the liquid, about 10 minutes. In a saucepan combine the poppy seeds with the honey, raisins, and nuts; cook over low heat 10 minutes. Cool 10 minutes. Pour into a serving bowl; add the pastry squares and mix lightly and carefully. Put a serving spoon in the dish, and let each person serve himself, as is the custom in Poland.

Serves 8–10.

*Diósrétes* HUNGARY
## NUT STRUDEL

> 4 eggs
> ⅓ cup sugar
> 2 cups ground walnuts
> 2 tablespoons lemon juice
> 1 tablespoon grated lemon rind
> ½ cup seedless raisins (optional)
> Strudel Dough (see recipe)
> ¼ cup bread crumbs

Separate the eggs. Beat the yolks well and add the sugar, beating until light and creamy. Mix in the nuts, lemon juice and rind, and raisins. Beat the egg whites until stiff and fold in. Sprinkle dough with bread crumbs and spread the nut filling evenly over one third of the dough. Lift up the cloth or sheet and carefully roll the dough over as for a jelly roll. Oil a baking sheet and carefully arrange strudel on it (cut in half if it is too large to fit on sheet). Brush with remaining melted butter and bake in a preheated 400° oven 35 minutes or until brown on top. Slice while hot. Serve hot or cold.

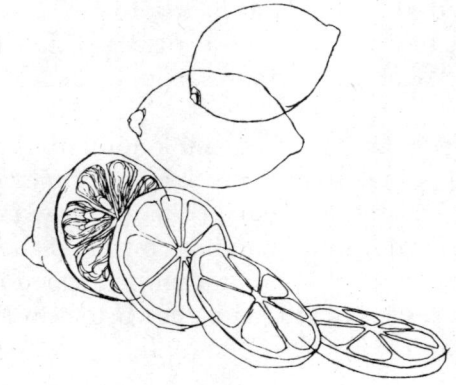

*Rigo Torte*  HUNGARY
## CHOCOLATE TORTE

### Pastry

1½ cups flour
¼ teaspoon salt
¼ pound (1 stick) sweet butter
2 egg yolks
2 tablespoons sugar
1 teaspoon grated lemon rind

Sift the flour and salt onto a board. Cut the butter into small pieces, and work it into the flour with the fingers. Make a well in the center, and into it put the egg yolks, sugar, and lemon rind. Blend the flour mixture into it with the fingers, until a smooth dough is formed. Shape into a ball, and chill 3 hours. Roll out the dough on a lightly floured surface, and fit on the bottom of a 10-inch spring form. Prick the bottom in several places, and bake in a preheated 375° oven, 20 minutes, or until delicately browned. Cool, then brush the sides of the pan with a little vegetable oil.

### Praline

1 cup sugar
1 tablespoon lemon juice
¾ cup chopped toasted filberts

Combine the sugar and lemon juice in a small heavy skillet. Cook over low heat, stirring constantly with a wooden spoon, until caramel color. Stir in the nuts, and pour into a well-oiled 9-inch skillet or pan. Let stand until cold and brittle; break into pieces, and pulverize a few pieces at a time in an electric blender, or put through a nut grinder. Reserve.

### Filling

1 pound (4 sticks) sweet butter
2 cups sugar
1 pound semi-sweet chocolate, grated
1 teaspoon cognac
1 teaspoon vanilla extract
1 cup finely ground toasted filberts

Cream the butter until fluffy, then gradually beat in the sugar, until very light. Add the chocolate, a little at a time, beating steadily. Then beat in the cognac and vanilla. Spread the mixture over the cooled pastry, and put in the refrigerator until filling is set. Mix the ground filberts with the reserved praline, and spread over the filling.

### Icing

½ pound semi-sweet chocolate bits
1 cup strong-brewed coffee
1 tablespoon butter

Combine the coffee and chocolate in a small saucepan. Cook over low heat, until chocolate melts. Mix in the butter, then cook over low heat, stirring steadily, for 5 minutes, or until thickened and smooth. Cool 15 minutes, then very slowly spoon evenly over the nut topping. Refrigerate until icing sets.

Serves 10–12.

## *Rahmstrudel*
## VIENNESE CREAM PIE

AUSTRIA

### Pastry

2 cups flour
½ teaspoon salt
½ pound (2 sticks) sweet butter
6 tablespoons sour cream

Sift the flour and salt into a bowl. With the hand, work in the butter. Add the sour cream, mixing until a dough is formed. Wrap in foil or waxed paper and chill 3 hours.

### Filling

¼ pound (1 stick) butter
1 cup sugar
3 eggs, separated
¾ cup sour cream
¼ cup seedless raisins, white if available (optional)

In an electric mixer, cream the butter; gradually add ½ cup of the sugar. Add 1 egg yolk at a time, beating until very light and fluffy. (Without an electric mixer, use a large bowl and wooden spoon.) Stir in the sour cream. Beat the egg whites until peaks begin to form, then gradually beat in the remaining sugar until very stiff. Fold into the sour cream mixture. Mix in the raisins lightly, if used.

Roll out half the pastry, and line a deep 9-inch (with fluted edge) pie plate with it. Pour the sour cream mixture into it, and cover with the remaining pastry. Seal the edges.

Bake in a preheated 425° oven 15 minutes. Reduce heat to 375° and bake 10 minutes longer, or until the pastry is golden brown. Serve warm.

Serves 8.

## Nustorte
## NUT CAKE

AUSTRIA

    1½ cups toasted walnuts or filberts
    6 eggs
    1 cup sugar
    ¾ cup flour
    ¼ cup melted butter

Pulverize the nuts in an electric blender, or put through a mouli grater or nut grinder. The resulting nuts should look like flour, and should measure 1½ cups.

Grease a 9-inch spring-form pan, and dust lightly with flour.

Beat the eggs, gradually adding the sugar; beat until very light and fluffy. Mix in the nuts and flour only until blended, then fold in the melted butter. Turn into the pan. Bake in a preheated 325° oven 40 minutes, or until a cake tester comes out clean. Cool, then remove from the pan, and split the cake. While the cake is baking, prepare the filling and icing.

### FILLING

    1½ cups finely ground nuts (same kind as used in cake)
    ½ cup sugar
    ⅓ cup milk
    2 tablespoons rum

In a saucepan, mix together the nuts, sugar, and milk. Bring to a boil, stirring occasionally. Stir in the rum, and let cool. Spread between the layers.

### ICING

    ¾ cup sifted confectioners' sugar
    5 teaspoons warm milk
    ½ teaspoon vanilla extract

Stir all of the ingredients together, until smooth. Spread over the top of the cake.

*ITALY*

ITALY is a glorious land of magnificent scenery, hot yellow sunshine, motor scooters, *bel canto* singing, intolerable traffic, and with a most original and colorful cuisine.

Italian food may be compared to Italian music, and particularly to the opera of that melodic country. Opera, especially those written by certain composers, has bold music colorations, an unbelievable story line, and often, rather obvious musical themes. To hear the lovely compositions of Vincenzo Bellini, Gioacchino Rossini, Gaetano Donizetti, and Giacomo Puccini is to comprehend that a country which produced this style of music could only possess a similar, florid cuisine. The man who wrote *La Bohème* could only have done so by nourishing himself with Italian food. The same composer, living on German liver dumplings, would have written something on the order of *Götterdämmerung*.

The food of this brilliantly lit, sunny and expansive land is brighter in color and more definite in character than that of France. Which, in and of itself, is not necessarily complimentary, because the Italian cuisine is noticeably less subtle than that of its Gallic neighbor. Unlikely food colors appear frequently upon Italian tables. Bright green is commonplace on dinner plates— green *gnocchi*, *lasagne verdi*, the peas and rice of Venice. Iridescent reds may be found in the fish soups, clam preparations, and aromatic tomato sauces. The French would tone down these excesses (in their opinion), as they do with other sauces, making them smooth and unctuous to the palate; in Italy, as often as not, they are brightly colored, full bodied, and not infrequently a trifle lumpy. Italian food, nonetheless, is not merely a lesser and imitative version of French cookery.

The cuisine of France, as exemplified by home and restaurant cooking of the grand class, has almost totally resisted the onslaughts of foreign dishes, remaining aloof, serene and not a little smug, secure in the excellence of its own culinary style. In Italy this has not been completely true, and some French dishes and sauces have gradually made their way into Italian homes, and found a place on Italian menus. Not to such an extent, however, as to displace Italian regional dishes, which still constitute ninety-five percent, or more, of the preparations in homes and restaurants.

The Roman predecessors of present-day Italy, those legendary conquerors of two millennia ago, grew fat on the riches of overpowered lands, from which they exacted staggering tributes of money and foodstuffs. In a city where the equivalent of a few pennies could buy a good meal, there were numerous millionaires even by today's standards. Soon the art of fine and elaborate dining became the hallmark of a civilized citizen of Rome; to be called a gourmet was the highest possible praise. Later, the calculated delights of dining were replaced by what can only be called gluttony. Of course, all of this has been frequently related, with repetitious tales of excesses in food and drink some two thousand years ago, when chefs vied to create new and more bizarre creations, at fantastic expense. It was a period which didn't last too long, as history goes, for the Goths and Vandals, barbarians in animal skins, destroyed the falling Roman Empire in comparatively short

ITALY 245

order. Civilization came to a shuddering halt, and the gracious arts of cookery and dining disappeared, while the survivors concerned themselves with mere survival. No longer were there thoughts or plans of banquets costing thousands of dollars for each guest. Within about a century, the only recipes remaining were in handwritten notebooks or manuscripts stored in the musty archives of a few remote, overlooked, and inconveniently located abbies and monasteries, which the barbarians did not find.

Centuries and still more centuries shuffled by on leaden feet, but then, like a beam of sunlight, came the Renaissance of Italy. First there was a re-awakening of painting and writing; later, of the applied and creative arts of daily life, including cookery. Beginning with the fifteenth century, fine food began to be appreciated once more, and notebooks of recipes, dusty with the accumulation of a thousand endless and cloistered years, were eagerly passed from hand to hand. The culinary arts became what today would be called a cultural happening. But truly good food, as the Romans once learned, costs money. It was only the city-state of Venice, swollen with the riches of its control of the sea, monopoly of trade, and the plunder of other areas by its invincible navy, that possessed the required surplus of funds. The Venetians, when not plotting to assassinate an interminable series of short-lived Doges, were soon preoccupied in making desserts using that wonderful sweetener, sugar. A skilled pastry-cook, in enormous demand by the wealthy, soon became a secondary sort of aristocrat, whose confections were praised to the heavens. The Venetians introduced the fork to the table, and also brought glassware to the heights of perfection, primarily for their wines. Indeed, it was the Italians who married off Catherine de Medici in 1533 to the prince who later became Henry II of France. Included in Catherine's dowry were cooks and chefs and confectioners, who taught the French court, and later the French people, how to cook. The French subsequently went off from there, in new directions, in the Gallic fashion.

Many Americans tend to generalize, erroneously in this case, about Italian food, thinking of it as consisting primarily of tomato sauce, garlic, olive oil, and spaghetti. That is, until they visit Italy. It is then recognized as one of the world's truly great cookery styles, unique and original in scope. Italians often use many ingredients which are known but not commonly used in the United States—*pignoli* (pine nuts), dried mushrooms, salted anchovies, freshly grated hard cheeses, *ceci* (chick-peas), truffles, and tomato paste (a reduction of tomatoes on a one-to-seven ratio). Although anchovies and olive oil are found not infrequently in American kitchens, the Italians use both items regularly, rather than rarely. Italian peasants and chefs are equally devoted to the use of herbs —fresh when available, if not, dried. The favorite herbs include wild and sweet marjoram, thyme, rosemary, sweet basil, sage, oregano, fennel, parsley, and bay leaves. Of course, herbs are far from unknown in America, but their use is generally limited, and typically only the dried form is commonplace.

A mental adjustment must also be made with respect to the availability of foodstuffs within Italy. In our own country, when California asparagus (for example) raise their pointed green heads above the soil, they are soon available all over the nation, rushed by planes and refrigerated trucks. This is not so, even today, in much of Italy, which still lacks the complex transportation system required to make this a reality. Except for the eternal city of Rome, which draws the best food from the entire nation, local specialties are truly local. Thus, in Naples, seafood preparations are superb, aromatic with herbs and garlic—but you won't find much fresh fish in Florence brought there from the Mediterranean. Similarly a cut of steak in Florence is usually memorable, but can often be inedible when served along the Naples waterfront.

Many of the regional dishes of Italy, although occasionally obtainable elsewhere, are best in their provincial homeland. In the north, where pastas are merely tolerated or regarded patronizingly, rice-based dishes, *risottos,* are superb, as typified by *risotto alla Piemontese,* a rice and chicken affair. Northerners also prefer cornmeal, as used in *polenta,* to the spaghetti of the south. A rather interesting dish, which illustrates the Italian willingness to draw upon its neighbors' cuisines (in this case, Austria) is *polenta con krauti a Luganighe,* cornmeal cooked with sausages and sauerkraut, found in the Alto Adige area of north Italy. In Tuscany, where Florence nestles beside the Arno River, the people are devoted to beans and beef. Bologna, surely the gastronomic capital of Emilia-Romagna, and perhaps entitled to that title in all of Italy, cooks with butter, olive oil, and pork fat. This is exceptional, for generally speaking, butter is used in the north and olive oil is the classic cooking fat of the south. Not surprisingly, Bolognese cooking is strong on rich and fatty sauces, typified by the ever-present *ragu*. In and around Rome, the cuisine, as in all great capital cities, draws the best and finest ingredients from the provinces. The food tends to be bland and less full-flavored than elsewhere in this long land. Indeed, garlic rarely appears in Roman dishes, except perhaps for one favorite, spaghetti with clam sauce, *spaghetti con vongole*. Two other typical dishes of Rome, both pastas, include *gnocchi*, dumplings made of semolina flour or potatoes, and *fettucine al burro*, thin strands of pasta, rich with cream, sweet butter, and cheese. Toward the French border, Genoa loves to use *il pesto*, a flavoring mixture made of garlic, fresh basil, and cheese. Milan, inland and surrounded by farming areas, features fresh vegetables in its cookery style.

South of Rome, beginning with the seaport of Naples and its stupendous harbor, the food truly becomes hearty, robust and earthy. This is the land of Italian culinary clichés—enormous bowls of macaroni or other pasta, unstrained tomato sauce, garlic, pizza—all the preconceived ideas many people still have of the food of all Italy. To many people, Neapolitan cookery is the *vera cucina Italiana*, the real thing—just what they expected to find. On the triangular island of Sicily the food is more or less in the southern style, but with Mediterranean touches added. Typical of Sicilian dishes that combine local ingredients plus the traditional pasta is *spaghetti con le sarde*, that is, with sardines. Don't plan on having it at home, because it requires a pound or so of fresh fennel.

In retrospect, Italian food has its good points, but also its share of weaknesses. The fish is fine if consumed along the seacoasts, or in Rome; otherwise it is often best avoided. The country, as a nation, tends to overcook meat of all types. Beef, compared to American beef, is never great, except in Florence, where it reaches its peak. The veal is outstanding, being among the finest in the world. Lamb can be very good, particularly if you encounter *abbacchio,* very young lamb, so that a dozen chops constitute a portion. Pork is good when young, but not so when older. Of course, when ham is salted and dried, as in *prosciutto,* it is exceptionally good. The poultry, alas, is only mediocre, and sometimes tough and sinewy as only a senior rooster can be. Nevertheless, poultry dishes are very popular and preparation imaginative. Italian cheeses are excellent; to mention the obvious ones, there are *Fontina, Tallegio, Gorgonzola, Bel Paese, Parmigiano, Pecorino, Ricotta,* and *Mozzarella.* Italian fruit in season can also be called superb, as good as fruit can ever hope to be. The wines of the country are what's often called drinkable—the sort of wines you drink in large gulps, rather than sipping and tasting, and the reds are far better, on the average, than the whites. This is not meant to be patronizing, but to distinguish the gulf that lies between great German and French wines, and the lesser (but equally enjoyable) products of the Italian soil.

*Sardine alla Veneto*
## SARDINE ANTIPASTO

> 2 green peppers
> 3 tablespoons butter
> 1 clove garlic, minced
> 1 cup peeled, seeded, chopped tomatoes
> ½ teaspoon salt
> ⅛ teaspoon freshly ground black pepper
> ¼ teaspoon sage
> ⅛ teaspoon sugar
> 3 3¾-ounce cans skinless and boneless sardines
> 3 hard-cooked egg yolks, sieved

Wash the peppers, and broil as close to the heat as possible, until skin blisters, or pierce with a fork, and hold over a flame. Peel off the skin, and cut in narrow strips, discarding the seeds and fibers.

Melt the butter in a small saucepan; stir in the garlic for 1 minute. Add the tomatoes, salt, pepper, sage, and sugar. Cook over low heat 20 minutes, stirring frequently. Cool.

Drain the sardines, and arrange them on a serving dish. Pour the sauce over them, and garnish with the peppers and eggs.

Serves 6–8.

## Zuppa di Vongole
## CLAM SOUP

60 little-neck clams
½ cup olive oil
2 whole cloves garlic
3 anchovy fillets, chopped
½ cup dry red wine
1 tablespoon tomato paste
½ cup warm water
½ teaspoon freshly ground black pepper
¼ teaspoon oregano
8 slices Italian bread, sautéed
2 tablespoons minced parsley

Wash the clams and scrub the shells well with a brush. Wash again. Heat the oil in a large saucepan; add the garlic, let brown, and remove. Mix the anchovies and wine into the oil; cook 5 minutes. Add the tomato paste, water, and pepper; cook 5 minutes. Add the clams and oregano; cover pan and cook 5 minutes, or until all the shells are open. (Discard those that don't open.) Taste for seasoning. Place 2 slices bread in each soup dish, pour the clams and sauce over them, and sprinkle with the parsley.
Serves 4–6.

## Gamberetti Fra Diavolo
### SHRIMP WITH WINE AND TOMATOES

2 pounds raw shrimp
¼ cup olive oil
¼ cup minced onions
2 cloves garlic, minced
1 cup dry white wine
1½ pounds tomatoes, peeled, seeded, chopped, and drained
1 teaspoon salt
¼ teaspoon dried ground red peppers
1 teaspoon crushed oregano
2 tablespoons parsley

Wash the shrimp, slit the backs, and remove the veins, but leave the shells on. Wash again and dry.

Heat the oil in a large skillet. Add the shrimp, and cook over high heat 3 minutes, turning them once. Remove the shrimp. (If you like, at this point, remove the shells.) Pour off all but about 1 tablespoon of the oil. To the oil remaining, add the onions; cook over medium heat 5 minutes. Stir in the garlic for 1 minute. Add the wine, and cook over high heat until reduced to half its original quantity. Add the tomatoes, salt, red peppers, and oregano. Bring to a boil, stirring frequently, then cook over low heat 10 minutes. Return the shrimp, and add the parsley. Cook 5 minutes. Taste for seasoning.

Serves 6–8.

## Gamberetti alla Griglia
### BROILED GARLIC SHRIMP

30–36 large raw shrimp, shelled and deveined
1 teaspoon salt
¼ teaspoon freshly ground black pepper
¼ cup olive oil
6 tablespoons butter
3 anchovies, mashed to a paste
2 cloves garlic, minced
¼ cup brandy
1 tablespoon prepared mustard
2 tablespoons lemon juice

Wash and dry the shrimp; season with the salt and pepper. Pour 2 tablespoons of the oil into a broiling pan, arrange the shrimp in it, and sprinkle with the remaining oil.

Broil the shrimp 8 minutes, turning them and basting midway.

While the shrimp are broiling, prepare the sauce. Cream 4 tablespoons of the butter; blend in the anchovies. Melt the remaining butter in a saucepan; stir in the garlic for 1 minute. Add the brandy. Cook over high heat, until reduced to half its original quantity. Remove from the heat, and beat in the mustard, lemon juice, and anchovy butter.

Transfer the shrimp to a heated serving dish, and pour the sauce over them.

Serves 6–8.

## Gamberetti alla Crema
### SHRIMP IN TOMATO-CREAM SAUCE

    3 tablespoons olive oil
    3 tablespoons butter
    ½ cup minced onions
    2 tablespoons grated carrot
    1 bay leaf, finely chopped
    1½ pounds raw shrimp, shelled and deveined
    ⅓ cup warm brandy
    1 cup peeled, seeded, chopped tomatoes
    1 teaspoon salt
    ¼ teaspoon freshly ground black pepper
    1 tablespoon lemon juice
    ¾ cup fish stock or bottled clam juice
    1 tablespoon flour
    ¾ cup heavy cream

Heat the oil and 2 tablespoons butter in a skillet; sauté the onion and carrot 10 minutes. Add the bay leaf and shrimp; sauté 3 minutes. Pour the warm brandy over the shrimp and set it aflame. When flames die, add the tomatoes, salt, pepper, lemon juice, and fish stock. Cook over low heat 6 minutes.

Transfer the shrimp to a warm serving dish. Cook the sauce over high heat 3 minutes. Blend the flour with the remaining butter and add to the sauce with the cream. Cook over low heat 3 minutes, stirring steadily. Pour over the shrimp.

Serves 4–6.

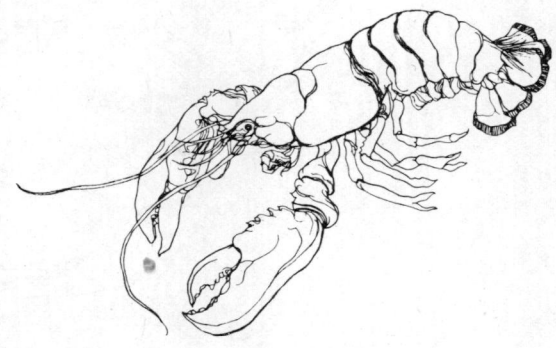

*Aragosta Piccante*
## LOBSTER IN PIQUANT SAUCE

> 2 1½-pound lobsters or 4 lobster tails
> ⅓ cup butter
> ⅓ cup olive oil
> ⅓ cup minced shallots or green onions
> 1 clove garlic, minced
> ¼ cup brandy
> ¼ cup gin
> ½ cup dry white wine
> 2 cups heavy cream
> 2 teaspoons salt
> ½ teaspoon white pepper
> 1 tablespoon lemon juice

Wash the lobster or tails and cut into sections in the shell. If there is any coral in the live lobsters, set it aside.

Heat the butter and oil in a deep skillet; cook the lobster over high heat until they turn red. Pour off the fat; add the shallots, garlic, brandy, and gin; cook until all the liquid is evaporated. Add the wine; cook again until no liquid remains. Add the cream, salt, and pepper; cover and cook over low heat 15 minutes. Remove the meat from the lobster shells, place on a heated serving dish, and keep warm. If there is any coral reserved, mix it into the sauce with the lemon juice; if not, just add the lemon juice. Reduce the sauce to 1 cup. Strain over the lobster meat.

Serves 2–4.

*Spigola alla Livornese*
## SEA BASS IN TOMATO SAUCE

>6 slices sea bass (3 pounds)
>½ cup flour
>2½ teaspoons salt
>½ teaspoon freshly ground black pepper
>½ cup olive oil
>¾ cup minced onions
>2 cloves garlic, minced
>2 pounds tomatoes, peeled and chopped
>½ cup dry white wine
>1 cup sliced black olives
>2 tablespoons capers
>3 tablespoons minced parsley

Wash and dry the fish, then dip in a mixture of the flour, 1½ teaspoons of the salt, and ¼ teaspoon of the pepper.

Heat half the oil in a saucepan; sauté the onions and garlic 3 minutes. Add the tomatoes, wine, and the remaining salt and pepper; cook over low heat 30 minutes. While the sauce is cooking, heat the remaining oil in a skillet; brown the fish in it on both sides. Add to the sauce and cook 15 minutes. Add the olives and capers; cook 2 minutes. Sprinkle with the parsley.

Serves 6.

Note: Any firm fleshed fish can be prepared in the same manner.

## *Fettuccine alla Papalina*
## NOODLES WITH EGG SAUCE

### Noodles

3½ cups sifted flour
5 eggs
1 tablespoon olive oil
1 teaspoon salt

Put the flour on a board in a mound. Make a well in the center, and into it put the eggs. Beat lightly with a fork, and stir in the oil and salt. With the fingers, mix in the flour until a dough is formed, then knead, until smooth and elastic. (If you have an electric mixer with a kneading attachment, use it.) Wrap the dough in a damp cloth and let it stand 30 minutes.

Divide the dough into two pieces, and roll each piece very thin. Cut into ¼-inch-wide strips and let stand for 30 minutes. Cook in a deep pot of boiling salted water 8 minutes. Prepare the sauce meanwhile.

### Sauce

8 egg yolks
½ cup heavy cream
¼ pound butter, broken into small pieces
1 teaspoon salt
1½ teaspoons freshly ground black pepper
½ cup grated Parmesan Cheese

Beat the egg yolks in a saucepan. Add the cream, butter, salt, pepper, and cheese. Mix well. Add the fettuccine, tossing lightly over very low heat until butter melts and fettuccine is well coated.

Serves 4–6.

Note: If you don't want to make your own noodles use 1 pound of medium egg noodles instead.

*Lasagne alla Partenope*
## LASAGNE WITH SAUSAGE

¾ pound sweet Italian sausages
⅓ cup olive oil
2 cloves garlic, minced
1 29-ounce can Italian-style tomatoes, chopped
1 6-ounce can tomato paste
½ teaspoon basil
1 teaspoon salt
½ teaspoon freshly ground black pepper
1 pound mushrooms, sliced
1 pound *lasagne* cooked and drained
1 pound ricotta cheese
¾ pound mozzarella cheese, sliced
6 hard-cooked eggs, sliced
¼ cup grated Parmesan cheese

Remove the skin of the sausage and chop the meat. Lightly brown the sausage meat in a skillet; drain well. Heat 4 tablespoons of the oil in a saucepan. Stir in the garlic for 1 minute, then add the tomatoes, tomato paste, basil, salt, and pepper. Bring to a boil and cook over low heat 45 minutes, stirring frequently. Taste for seasoning.

Heat the remaining oil in a skillet; sauté the mushrooms in it for 5 minutes. In a shallow oiled oblong baking dish, arrange a layer of *lasagne*, then layers of ricotta, sausage, mozzarella, egg slices, mushrooms, and sauce. Continue the order until all the ingredients are used up, ending with the sauce. Sprinkle with the Parmesan cheese. Bake in a 400° oven 30 minutes, or until lightly browned on top.

Serves 4–6.

*Spaghetti Marinara*
## SPAGHETTI WITH FRESH TOMATO SAUCE

⅓ cup olive oil
2 cloves garlic, minced
4 cups peeled diced tomatoes
2 tablespoons chopped parsley
1½ teaspoons salt
¼ teaspoon freshly ground black pepper
½ teaspoon basil
1 pound spaghetti, cooked and drained
Freshly grated Parmesan cheese

Heat the oil in a saucepan; sauté the garlic 1 minute. Add the tomatoes, parsley, salt, and pepper; cook over low heat 30 minutes. Mix in the basil; cook 15 minutes longer. Taste for seasoning.

Pour the sauce over the spaghetti, mix lightly, and serve with the grated chese.
Serves 4.

*Gnocchi di Patate*
## POTATO DUMPLINGS

2 pounds potatoes
1 cup flour
3 egg yolks
2 teaspoons salt
¼ teaspoon white pepper
1 tablespoon butter

Cook the potatoes in their skins until tender. Peel, and return to a saucepan; shake over low heat until dry. Beat the potatoes in an electric mixer or mash very smooth—it is important that no lumps remain. Mix in the flour, egg yolks, salt, pepper, and butter. Knead on a floured surface until smooth. If dough doesn't hold its shape, work in a little more flour. Break off a portion of the dough and roll into a piece measuring about ¾ of an inch thick and about an inch in length. Drop the sample piece into deep boiling salted water to test the consistency. If it holds its shape, you can continue making up the remainder of the dough into *gnocchi*. If it doesn't hold its shape, add a little more flour and try again. (This is required because potatoes differ greatly at various times of the year.)

Drop the *gnocchi* singly into the boiling water; don't crowd them. Cook 10 minutes, or until they rise to the surface. Remove with a slotted spoon. Serve with melted butter and grated cheese, or any sauce you wish, particularly tomato or meat sauce.

Serves 4–6.

*Pasticcio de Maccheroni*
## MACARONI PIE

2 cups flour
1 teaspoon salt
¾ cup shortening
1 egg, beaten
3 tablespoons cold water
¾ pound elbow macaroni, cooked and drained
1 cup ricotta or cottage cheese
1½ cups grated mozzarella cheese
½ teaspoon freshly ground black pepper
3 tablespoons melted butter

Sift the flour and salt into a bowl; cut in the shortening with a pastry blender or two knives. Mix the egg and water, add, and toss until a dough is formed. Form into two balls, one slightly larger than the other. Wrap in waxed paper and chill 1 hour.

Roll out the larger piece of the dough and line an 11-inch pie plate with it. Mix together the macaroni, cheeses, pepper, and melted butter. Spread in the lined pie plate. Cover with the remaining thinly rolled dough. Cut a few slits in the top. Bake in a preheated 400° oven 30 minutes, or until pastry is browned. Serve hot, cut in wedges.

Serves 6–8.

## 260 ITALY

*Spaghetti alla Boscaiola*
### SPAGHETTI WITH TUNA FISH SAUCE

>¼ cup olive oil
>1 cup chopped onions
>1 clove garlic, minced
>1 29-ounce can Italian-style tomatoes, chopped
>1¼ teaspoons salt
>½ teaspoon freshly ground black pepper
>1 teaspoon oregano
>2 7-ounce cans tuna fish, drained and broken into chunks
>¼ cup capers, drained
>1 can anchovies, minced
>½ cup sliced Italian olives
>1 pound spaghetti, cooked and drained

Heat the oil in a saucepan; sauté the onions 5 minutes. Mix in the garlic, tomatoes, salt, black pepper, and oregano. Bring to a boil and cook over low heat 30 minutes. Add the tuna fish, capers, anchovies, and olives. Cook 5 minutes longer. Pour over hot spaghetti.
Serves 4–6.

*Spaghettini Zingarella*
### THIN SPAGHETTI WITH WHITE CLAM SAUCE

>36 small, hard-shell clams
>¼ cup olive oil
>4 whole cloves garlic
>¼ teaspoon freshly ground black pepper
>¼ teaspoon oregano
>2 tablespoons minced parsley
>¼ teaspoon basil
>1 pound spaghettini, cooked and drained

Scrub the clams and rinse under cold running water until water runs clear.

Heat the oil in saucepan; brown the garlic cloves in it, then discard. Add the clams, pepper, oregano, parsley, and basil. Cover the pan and cook over low heat 10 minutes. Remove from the heat and let stand 5 minutes, before pouring over the hot drained spaghettini.

Serves 4–6.

## Ragu
### BOLOGNESE SAUCE

2 tablespoons butter
¼ pound ham, cut julienne
¾ cup chopped onions
¼ cup chopped celery
½ cup grated carrots
¾ pound ground beef
½ pound calf's liver, diced
1½ tablespoons tomato paste
1¼ cups dry white wine
1 cup water
1 teaspoon salt
½ teaspoon freshly ground black pepper
⅛ teaspoon nutmeg
1 cup heavy cream

Melt the butter in a saucepan; sauté the ham, onions, celery, and carrots 10 minutes, stirring frequently. Add the beef; cook over medium heat, stirring almost constantly, until browned. Stir in the liver; cook 2 minutes. Blend in the tomato paste, then stir in the wine, water, salt, pepper, and nutmeg. Cover and cook over low heat 45 minutes, stirring frequently. Stir in the cream and taste for seasoning. Serve with *pastas* or use as a sauce for broiled or roast meat.

Makes about 3 cups.

262   ITALY

*Spaghetti all'Amatriciana*
SPAGHETTI WITH BACON-TOMATO SAUCE

> ¼ pound bacon
> ½ cup chopped onion
> 1 pound tomatoes, peeled and chopped
> ¾ cup dry white wine
> 1 teaspoon salt
> ⅛ teaspoon dried crushed red peppers
> 1 pound spaghetti, cooked and drained
> 1 cup freshly grated Pecorino or Parmesan cheese

Cook the bacon in a saucepan until lightly browned; remove the bacon, drain, and break into small pieces. Pour off half the fat. Add the onion and sauté 5 minutes. Add the tomatoes, wine, salt, and red peppers; bring to a boil and cook over low heat 10 minutes. Add the bacon. Taste for seasoning, pour over the spaghetti, and sprinkle with the cheese. Mix and serve.
Serves 4.

*Polenta Pasticciata*
CORNMEAL PIE

> 1 quart water
> 3 teaspoons salt
> 1 cup yellow cornmeal
> 6 tablespoons butter
> 3 tablespoons flour
> ¼ teaspoon white pepper
> ⅛ teaspoon nutmeg
> 3 cups milk
> ¾ cup grated Parmesan cheese
> ¾ pound mushrooms, thinly sliced

Bring the water and 2 teaspoons of the salt to a boil; stir in the cornmeal until it begins to thicken. Cook over low heat 20 minutes, stirring frequently.

Melt 4 tablespoons of the butter in a skillet; blend in the flour, pepper, nutmeg, and ½ teaspoon salt. Add the milk, stirring steadily to the boiling point. Cook over low heat 15 minutes. Mix in ½ cup cheese until melted. Sauté the mushrooms in the remaining butter 5 minutes. Season with the remaining salt.

In a buttered shallow baking dish, spread one-third of the cornmeal, then one-fourth of the sauce and one-third of the mushrooms. Repeat the layers twice more, ending with the sauce. Sprinkle with the remaining cheese. Bake in a 375° oven 30 minutes or until browned.

Serves 6–8.

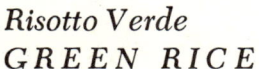

## Risotto Verde
### GREEN RICE

> 2 tablespoons olive oil
> 4 tablespoons butter
> 1 cup minced green onions
> 1 cup minced parsley
> 1½ cups finely chopped raw spinach
> 2 cups raw Italian or long-grain rice
> 3½ cups hot chicken broth
> 1½ teaspoons salt
> ¼ teaspoon white pepper
> Freshly grated Parmesan cheese

Heat the oil and 2 tablespoons of the butter in a heavy saucepan; mix in the green onions, parsley, and spinach. Cover and cook over low heat 5 minutes. Mix in the rice until translucent. Add 2 cups of the broth, the salt and pepper; cover, cook over low heat 20 minutes, adding the remaining broth after 10 minutes. Lightly mix in the remaining butter with a fork. Serve with the grated cheese.

Serves 6–8.

*Fegato con Risotto*
## CALF'S LIVER WITH RICE

>3 tablespoons olive oil
>1 cup chopped onions
>1 clove garlic, minced
>1½ cups raw rice
>4 cups chicken broth
>1 teaspoon tomato paste
>¼ teaspoon freshly ground black pepper
>1½ pounds calf's liver
>6 tablespoons butter
>1 8-ounce can tiny green peas
>2 tablespoons minced parsley

Heat the oil in a deep skillet; sauté the onions 5 minutes. Add the garlic and rice; cook over low heat 5 minutes, stirring frequently. Add the broth, tomato paste, and pepper, bring to a boil, cover, and bake in a 350° oven 35 minutes.

Cut the liver in finger-length strips. Melt the butter in a skillet; brown the liver in it. Add to the rice with the peas; re-cover and bake 10 minutes longer or until the rice is tender and dry. Taste for seasoning. Sprinkle with the parsley.

Serves 4–6.

*Minestra di Riso e Prezzemolo*
## RICE AND PARSLEY SOUP

>3 tablespoons olive oil
>1 cup minced onions
>2 cups grated raw potatoes
>6 cups chicken broth
>½ cup minced parsley
>½ cup raw rice
>Salt
>Freshly ground black pepper
>3 tablespoons butter
>½ cup freshly grated Parmesan cheese

Heat the oil in a saucepan; add the onions, and cook until yellow. Mix in the potatoes, broth, and half the parsley. Bring to a boil, stir in the rice, cover, and cook over low heat 20 minutes. Season to taste with salt and pepper, then stir in the butter, cheese, and remaining parsley.

Serves 6–8.

*Pasta e Fagioli*
## MACARONI AND BEAN SOUP

> 2 cups dried white beans
> 1 beef bone
> 2 quarts water
> ¼ cup olive oil
> ¾ cup minced onions
> 2 cloves garlic, minced
> ½ teaspoon rosemary
> 1 tablespoon flour
> 2 teaspoons tomato paste
> 2 cups beef broth
> 2 teaspoons salt
> ½ teaspoon freshly ground black pepper
> 2 tablespoons minced parsley
> 1 cup small elbow or shell macaroni

Wash the beans, cover with water, bring to a boil, turn off heat, and let soak 1 hour. Drain. Add the bone and the 2 quarts water. Bring to a boil, cover loosely, and cook over low heat 2 hours.

Heat the oil in a saucepan; sauté the onions and garlic 5 minutes. Blend in the rosemary, flour, and tomato paste, then stir in the broth, salt, and pepper. Cook, stirring steadily, until mixture boils. Add to the beans. Cook 1 hour longer. Discard the bone. Mix in the parsley and macaroni. Cook 10 minutes longer, or until macaroni is tender. This is a very thick soup, so don't expect as much liquid as there usually is.

Serves 6–8.

## Minestrone
### VEGETABLE-BEAN SOUP

1 cup dried white beans
2½ quarts water
3 slices bacon
2 tablespoons olive oil
1 cup thinly sliced onions
1 carrot, diced
1 cup diced potatoes
2 cups diced zucchini
1 cup peeled, diced tomatoes
3 cups shredded cabbage
1 tablespoon salt
½ teaspoon freshly ground black pepper
1 clove garlic, minced
½ teaspoon basil
¼ cup raw rice
3 tablespoons minced parsley
½ cup freshly grated Parmesan cheese

Wash the beans, cover with water, and bring to a boil. Let soak 1 hour, drain, and add the 2½ quarts water. Bring to a boil and cook over low heat 1½ hours. While the beans are cooking, prepare the vegetables.

In a skillet, lightly brown the bacon. Pour off the fat and crumble the bacon. To the skillet, add the oil and onions. Sauté 5 minutes. Mix in the carrot, potatoes, and zucchini; sauté 5 minutes, stirring frequently. Add to the cooked, undrained beans the tomatoes, cabbage, salt, pepper, garlic, and basil. Cook over low heat 1¼ hours. Mix in the rice, sautéed vegetables, and parsley; cook 20 minutes longer. Just before serving, stir in the cheese. Serve with additional grated cheese.

Serves 8–10.

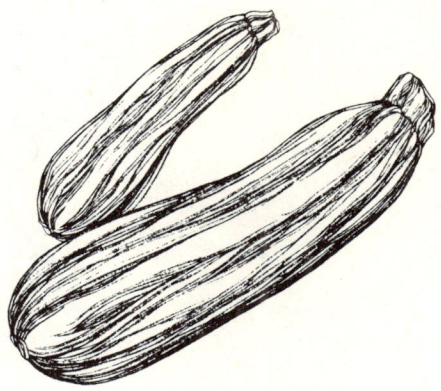

## *Minestra di Ceci alla Tuscana*
## CHICK-PEAS, TUSCAN STYLE

    2 cups dried chick-peas
    3 quarts water
    1 teaspoon rosemary
    1 cup peeled chopped tomatoes
    1 bay leaf
    2 teaspoons salt
    ½ teaspoon freshly ground black pepper
    ¼ cup olive oil
    ¼ cup finely chopped onions
    2 cloves garlic, minced
    1 cup shell-shaped macaroni
    3 tablespoons minced parsley

Wash the chick-peas, cover with water, and bring to a boil. Turn off heat and let soak 1 hour. Drain. Add the 3 quarts water and the rosemary, tomatoes, and bay leaf. Bring to a boil and cook over low heat 2½ hours. Discard the bay leaf. Purée half the chick-peas in an electric blender or force through a sieve. Return to the balance of the soup; mix in the salt and pepper.

Heat the oil in a skillet; sauté the onions 10 minutes. Mix in the garlic; sauté 1 minute. Add to the soup with the macaroni and parsley. Cook 15 minutes. Taste for seasoning.

Serves 6–8.

*Spezzatino di Pollo*
## GARLIC FRIED CHICKEN

    2 3-pound frying chickens
    3 eggs, beaten
    ¾ cup flour
    2 teaspoons salt
    ½ teaspoon freshly ground black pepper
    3 cloves garlic, minced
    ½ cup vegetable oil
    ½ cup olive oil
    4 whole cloves garlic
    Lemon wedges

Have the chickens chopped up bones and all into 1-inch pieces. Wash and dry the pieces. Dip in the eggs. Mix together the flour, salt, pepper, and minced garlic. Dip the chicken pieces in the mixture. Let stand a few minutes to dry.

Heat the oils in a skillet; add the whole cloves of garlic, brown, and remove. Add the chicken pieces. Fry until browned and tender. Drain. Serve garnished with lemon wedges.

Serves 6–8.

## *Pollo in Fricassea*
## CHICKEN FRICASSEE WITH WINE

    3-pound frying chicken, disjointed
    1½ cups dry red wine
    1½ teaspoons salt
    ¼ teaspoon freshly ground black pepper
    2 cloves garlic, minced
    ½ teaspoon thyme
    ½ teaspoon marjoram
    Flour
    ¼ cup olive oil
    2 tablespoons butter
    ¾ cup chopped onions
    ½ cup chicken broth
    2 egg yolks

Wash and dry the chicken. Mix together the wine, salt, pepper, garlic, thyme, and marjoram; marinate the chicken in the mixture for 3 hours, or overnight, in the refrigerator, if you prefer. Baste and turn frequently.

When ready to cook, remove the chicken pieces, and dry them. Reserve the marinade. Dust the chicken pieces with flour. Heat the oil in a deep skillet; brown the chicken pieces in it on all sides. Remove the chicken, and pour off the oil. Melt the butter in the skillet; add the onions, and sauté until browned. Add the marinade and broth; bring to a boil and cook over high heat 10 minutes. Return the chicken, and cook over low heat 30 minutes.

Beat the egg yolks in a bowl; gradually add a little of the hot sauce, stirring steadily to prevent curdling. Stir into the pan, and heat, but do not let boil.

Serves 4.

## Pollo alla Cacciatora
### CHICKEN, HUNTER'S STYLE

    3-pound frying chicken, disjointed
    3 tablespoons olive oil
    4 tablespoons butter
    Salt
    Freshly ground black pepper
    ½ cup chopped onions
    ½ cup dry white wine
    1 tablespoon flour
    1 cup boiling chicken broth
    2 tablespoons brandy
    1½ cups peeled, seeded, chopped tomatoes
    1 tablespoon chopped parsley
    ½ teaspoon tarragon
    ½ pound mushrooms, sliced

Wash and dry the chicken pieces. Heat the oil and 2 tablespoons of the butter in a skillet; add the chicken pieces in a single layer, and brown well on all sides. Sprinkle with salt and pepper, then cover, and cook over low heat 15 minutes. Remove the chicken pieces, and keep warm.

To the fat remaining, add the onions; sauté until golden. Stir in the wine, and cook until evaporated. Blend in the flour, then the broth. Heat the brandy, set it aflame, and pour into the pan. When flames die, add the tomatoes, parsley, tarragon, and salt and pepper. Cook over low heat 10 minutes. While the sauce is cooking, sauté the mushrooms in the remaining butter for 5 minutes. Add to the sauce and return the chicken. Cook 10 minutes, or until the chicken is tender.

Serves 4.

## *Pollo alla Siciliana*
## SAUTÉED CHICKEN, SICILIAN STYLE

¾ pound small white onions, peeled
3½-pound frying chicken, disjointed
¼ cup olive oil
2 tablespoons butter
1½ teaspoons salt
½ teaspoon freshly ground black pepper
1 clove garlic, minced
1 cup dry white wine
1½ cups peeled, seeded, diced tomatoes
3 tablespoons minced parsley
½ teaspoon basil
½ cup chicken broth
½ pound sweet Italian sausages

Cook the onions in boiling water 5 minutes; drain and dry. Wash and dry the chicken. Heat the oil and butter in a skillet; brown the chicken and onions in it. Add the salt, pepper, garlic, and wine; cook over medium heat until almost all the wine is evaporated. Mix in the tomatoes, parsley, basil and broth. Cover and cook over low heat 30 minutes.

While the chicken is cooking, cut the sausages in 1-inch slices. Brown them in a skillet, drain, and add to the chicken after it has cooked 30 minutes. Cook 10 minutes longer, or until the chicken is tender.

Serves 4–6.

*Cappone alla Siciliana*
CAPON AND EGGPLANT

    16 small white onions, peeled
    5-pound capon, disjointed
    ½ cup olive oil
    ½ teaspoon freshly ground black pepper
    1 clove garlic, minced
    ¾ cup Marsala or sweet sherry
    2½ teaspoons salt
    1 cup peeled, diced tomatoes
    3 tablespoons minced parsley
    1 small eggplant, peeled and sliced
    ⅓ cup flour

Cook the onions in boiling water 5 minutes; drain and dry. Wash and dry the capon pieces. Heat 4 tablespoons of the oil in a skillet; brown the capon and onions in it. Add the pepper, garlic, wine, and 1½ teaspoons of the salt; cook over medium heat until almost all the wine is evaporated. Mix in the tomatoes and parsley. Cover and cook over low heat 30 minutes, or until the capon is tender. Taste for seasoning.

Dip the eggplant slices in the flour, then sauté in the remaining oil until browned on both sides. Sprinkle with the remaining salt. Arrange the eggplant slices over the capon; cook 10 minutes longer.

Serves 4–5.

## *Anitra Farcita e Arrostita*
## ROAST STUFFED DUCK

    5-pound duck
    2 teaspoons salt
    ½ teaspoon freshly ground black pepper
    2 cloves garlic, minced
    2 tablespoons olive oil
    ¾ cup minced onions
    ½ pound sweet Italian sausages or sausage meat
    1 cup diced toasted bread
    ⅛ teaspoon crushed dried red peppers
    ½ teaspoon rosemary
    ½ cup chopped black olives
    1 cup Marsala wine or medium sherry

    Wash and dry the duck; rub inside and out with the salt, pepper, and garlic.
    Heat the oil in a skillet; sauté the onions 5 minutes. If sausages are used, remove the casings and chop the meat. Add the chopped sausages or sausage meat to the onions; let brown. Pour off the fat. Mix in the diced toast, red peppers, rosemary, and olives. Stuff the duck with the mixture. Close the opening with skewers or sew it.
    Place duck breast side down on a rack in a roasting pan. Roast in a 425° oven 30 minutes. Pour off the fat, and turn duck on its side. Reduce heat to 350°. Roast 1 hour. Pour off the fat, and turn breast side up. Pour the wine over the duck; roast 1 hour longer, or until tender, basting frequently.
    Serves 4–5.

## 274 ITALY

*Bistecca alla Fiorentina*
### TUSCAN-STYLE STEAK

    4 club steaks, cut 2 inches thick
    6 tablespoons olive oil
    3 tablespoons lemon juice
    2 cloves garlic, minced
    3 tablespoons minced parsley
    Salt
    Freshly ground black pepper
    3 tablespoons butter

Brush the steaks with a mixture of the oil, lemon juice, garlic, and parsley. Let stand 1 hour at room temperature. Broil the steaks 6 minutes on each side (for medium rare) or to desired degree of rareness. Sprinkle with salt and pepper and put dots of the butter on each steak before serving.
Serves 4.


*Bistecca Parmigiana*
### BREADED STEAK

    6 club steaks, cut ¾ inch thick
    2 eggs, beaten
    ⅓ cup freshly grated Parmesan cheese
    ⅓ cup dry bread crumbs
    2 tablespoons olive oil
    ¾ cup chopped onions
    1 teaspoon salt
    ¼ teaspoon freshly ground black pepper
    ½ teaspoon oregano
    2 cups Marinara Sauce (see recipe)
    3 tablespoons butter
    ¼ cup dry white wine
    ½ pound mozzarella cheese, sliced thin

Remove any bone, and all the fat, from the steaks. Dip the steaks in the eggs, then in a mixture of the grated cheese and bread crumbs. Let stand while preparing the sauce.

Heat 2 tablespoons of the oil in a skillet; sauté the onions 5 minutes. Mix in the salt, pepper, oregano, marinara sauce, and wine. Bring to a boil and cook over low heat 20 minutes. Taste for seasoning.

Melt the butter in a skillet; quickly brown the steaks in it on both sides over high heat. Arrange the steaks in a single layer in a shallow baking dish. Pour ¾ of the sauce over the steaks and arrange the sliced cheese over the sauce. Pour the remaining sauce on top.

Bake in a preheated 425° oven 10 minutes, or until the cheese is melted.

Serves 6.


*Filetto Ripieno*
## STUFFED FILLETS OF BEEF

> 6 fillets of beef, cut 1 inch thick
> 6 slices proscuitto ham
> 6 thin slices mozzarella cheese
> 1½ teaspoons salt
> ½ teaspoon freshly ground black pepper
> ½ cup flour
> 2 eggs, beaten
> ¾ cup dry bread crumbs
> 6 tablespoons butter

Cut the steaks horizontally through the middle, leaving one side attached. Open like a book and pound each side lightly to flatten. Put a slice of ham and a slice of cheese on each, then close up, pressing the edges together firmly. Be sure the ham and cheese are completely enclosed. Season with the salt and pepper, dip in the flour, then in the eggs, and finally in the bread crumbs.

Melt the butter in a skillet; sauté the steaks 4 minutes on each side, or to desired degree of rareness.

Serves 4.

## Stufatino alla Romano
### POT ROAST IN RED WINE

3 pounds eye round of beef
3 tablespoons flour
2 teaspoons salt
½ teaspoon freshly ground black pepper
½ teaspoon rosemary
2 slices salt pork, minced
2 tablespoons butter
1 cup thinly sliced onions
2 cloves garlic, minced
1 cup dry red wine
1 tablespoon tomato paste
½ cup boiling water

Have the meat tied, to help hold its shape.

Rub the meat with a mixture of the flour, salt, pepper, and rosemary. Lightly brown the salt pork in a heavy casserole. Pour off all but 2 tablespoons of the fat. Add the butter, onions, and garlic; sauté 5 minutes. Add the meat; cook over medium heat until browned on all sides. Stir in the wine; cook over high heat 5 minutes. Blend in the tomato paste and water. Cover and cook over low heat 2½ hours. Taste for seasoning. Skim the fat from the gravy, and serve gravy in a sauceboat.

Serves 6–8.

## Manzo in Salsa di Prezzemolo
### BEEF WITH PARSLEY SAUCE

3 pounds eye round of beef
3 tablespoons olive oil
6 anchovy fillets, chopped
2 cloves garlic, minced
½ cup chopped parsley
1¼ cups dry white wine
¾ teaspoon salt
½ teaspoon freshly ground black pepper

Cut the meat into slices about 1½ inches thick, then pound with a mallet or cleaver. Heat the oil in a skillet; brown the beef slices on both sides. Mix in the anchovies, garlic, and parsley; cook over low heat 5 minutes. Add the wine, salt, and pepper. Cover and cook over low heat 45 minutes or until meat is tender.

Serves 6–8.

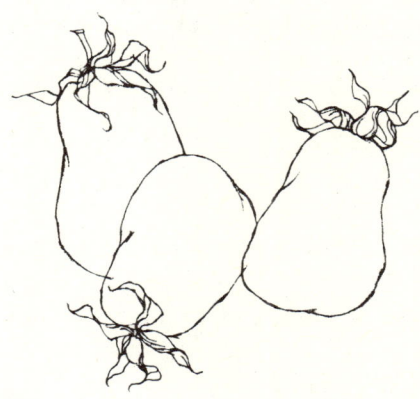

*Bistecca alla Pizzaiola*
## STEAK WITH PEPPERS AND TOMATOES

    4 club steaks, cut 1 inch thick
    4 tablespoons butter
    2 tablespoons olive oil
    2 cloves garlic, minced
    2 green peppers, cut in narrow strips
    1½ cups peeled chopped tomatoes
    2 teaspoons salt
    ½ teaspoon freshly ground black pepper
    ½ teaspoon oregano
    2 tablespoons chopped parsley

Trim most of the fat from the steak. Heat the butter and oil in a skillet. Brown the steaks in it over high heat 2 minutes on each side. Add the garlic, pepper strips, tomatoes, salt, pepper, and oregano. Cook over low heat, turning the steaks a few times, for 10 minutes. Sprinkle with the parsley.

Serves 4.

## Manzo Peperonata
### FILLET OF BEEF WITH PEPPER SAUCE

    6 fillets of beef, cut ¾ inch thick
    3 tablespoons olive oil
    ¾ cup thinly sliced onions
    1½ pounds tomatoes, peeled and diced
    6 red or green peppers, cut in ½-inch slices
    1½ teaspoons salt
    ¼ teaspoon freshly ground black pepper
    1 clove garlic, minced
    2 tablespoons butter

Pound the fillets lightly to flatten.

Heat the oil in a skillet; sauté the onions 10 minutes, stirring frequently. Add the tomatoes; cook over low heat 10 minutes. Mix in the peppers, salt, pepper, and garlic. Cook over low heat 20 minutes.

In a separate skillet, melt the butter. Brown the fillets over high heat 3 minutes on each side. Pour the sauce over the meat and cook 2 minutes longer, or to desired degree of rareness.

Serves 6.

## Arangini
### RICE-MEAT BALLS

    5 tablespoons vegetable oil
    ¼ cup chopped onions
    ¼ cup chopped green pepper
    1 clove garlic, minced
    1½ pounds ground beef
    ½ cup raw long-grain rice
    1½ teaspoons salt
    ¼ teaspoon freshly ground black pepper
    2 cups Marinara Sauce (see recipe)
    1 teaspoon sugar
    1 bay leaf
    ⅛ teaspoon ground allspice

Heat 2 tablespoons of the oil in a skillet; sauté the onions, pepper, and garlic 5 minutes. Mix the sautéed vegetables with the beef, raw rice, salt, and pepper. Shape into 1½-inch balls.

Heat the remaining oil in the skillet; brown the beef balls in it on all sides, shaking the pan to turn them. Add the marinara sauce, sugar, bay leaf, and allspice. Cover, and cook over low heat 20 minutes. The finished balls should look somewhat like a porcupine, with the rice sticking up around the meat.

Serves 4–6.

*Manzo al Vino Bianco*
## BEEF IN WHITE WINE

> 4 pounds chuck or rump of beef
> 2½ teaspoons salt
> ½ teaspoon freshly ground black pepper
> 1 clove garlic, minced
> 3 tablespoons butter
> 1 cup thinly sliced onions
> ½ cup sliced carrots
> ¼ cup wine vingear
> 1½ pounds tomatoes, peeled and chopped
> 2 bay leaves
> ¼ teaspoon sugar
> 1½ cups dry white wine
> ¼ cup heavy cream

Have the beef tied, to help hold its shape.

Mix together the salt, pepper, and garlic; rub into the meat. Melt the butter in a Dutch oven or heavy saucepan; add the meat, onions, and carrots. Cook over medium heat until meat browns on all sides. Add the vinegar, tomatoes, bay leaves, sugar, and wine. Cover and cook over low heat 3 hours. Taste for seasoning, skim the fat, and stir in the cream.

Serves 8–10.

## Spezzatino
## GROUND MEAT STEW

>2 slices bacon, chopped
>¾ cup chopped onions
>1 carrot, sliced
>1 pound ground beef
>1 pound ground veal
>1 teaspoon salt
>¼ teaspoon freshly ground black pepper
>1 teaspoon tomato paste
>½ cup beef broth
>1 cup chopped mushrooms
>3 chicken livers, diced
>¼ cup heavy cream

Combine the bacon, onions, and carrots in a deep skillet; sauté until lightly browned. Pour off the fat. Add the beef and veal; cook over medium heat, stirring almost constantly, until meat browns. Stir in the salt, pepper, tomato paste, and broth. Cover, and cook over low heat 1 hour, stirring frequently. Add the mushrooms and livers; re-cover and cook 10 minutes longer. Stir in the cream; taste for seasoning.

Serves 6–8.

## Agnello Arrosto
## MARINATED ROAST LAMB

>5-pound leg of lamb
>1 tablespoon salt
>¾ teaspoon freshly ground black pepper
>2 cloves garlic, minced
>1 teaspoon rosemary
>¼ cup olive oil
>3 tablespoons wine vinegar
>1 cup dry red wine

Remove the fell (skin) of the lamb. Prick the lamb in numerous places and rub with a mixture of the salt, pepper, garlic, and rosemary. Mix together the oil, vinegar, and wine, and pour over the lamb. Let marinate 4–6 hours, turning the meat frequently. Drain, reserving the marinade.

Place the lamb in a roasting pan. Roast in a 400° oven 25 minutes. Pour off the fat; add the marinade and reduce heat to 325° Roast 1½ hours longer or until tender, basting frequently.

Serves 6–8.


*Saltimbocca Romana*
## VEAL AND PROSCIUTTO MEDALLIONS

>12 slices leg of veal, cut ½ inch thick
>1¼ teaspoons salt
>¼ teaspoon freshly ground black pepper
>12 fresh sage leaves or ½ teaspoon dried sage
>12 slices prosciutto ham
>6 tablespoons butter
>1 cup dry white wine

Have the veal pounded thin, or do it yourself by placing each slice between two sheets of waxed paper, and pounding it with a cleaver or heavy knife. Season the veal with the salt and pepper. Put a sage leaf on each, or sprinkle with the dried sage. Fit a slice of prosciutto over each piece of the veal, then fold the slices in half. Fasten with toothpicks.

Melt the butter in a skillet; place the veal in it in a single layer, and cook over high heat 2 minutes on each side; then reduce the heat to low, and cook 5 minutes, or until the veal is tender.

Transfer the veal to a heated serving dish, remove the toothpicks, and keep warm. Stir the wine into the skillet, scraping the bottom and sides of any browned particles. Cook over high heat until reduced to half its original quantity, and pour over the veal.

Serves 6.

## *Pasticceria con Vitello*
## VEAL PASTRIES

### Pastry

2 cups instantized flour
1 teaspoon salt
¼ pound (1 stick) butter
1 egg yolk
⅓ cup ice water (about)

Mix the flour and salt in a bowl; cut the butter into small pieces, and cut it in with a pastry blender or two knives. Beat the egg yolk with 2 tablespoons of the ice water, and mix it in with a fork. If the dough holds together, don't add any more water—if it doesn't, add just enough of the remaining water to make a dough. Form into a ball, wrap in waxed paper, and chill 2 hours.

### Veal

6 oval slices leg of veal, cut ½ inch thick
4 dried mushrooms
¼ pound (1 stick) butter
1½ teaspoons salt
¾ teaspoon freshly ground black pepper
¾ cup chopped onions
¼ pound fresh mushrooms, chopped
½ cup dry sherry
6 slices prosciutto ham
1 egg yolk
2 tablespoons milk

Pound the veal lightly. Soak the dried mushrooms in warm water for 30 minutes, drain and chop. Melt 4 tablespoons of the butter in a large skillet; brown the veal in it for about 4 minutes on each side. Season with 1 teaspoon of the salt and ½ teaspoon of the pepper, and transfer to a plate. Cool.

Melt the remaining butter in the skillet; add the onions. Sauté 5 minutes. Add the dried and fresh mushrooms. Cook 5 minutes, stirring frequently. Stir in the sherry, and remaining salt and pepper; cook over high heat until almost all the wine evaporates. Taste for seasoning, and cool.

Roll out the dough into an oblong ⅛ inch thick, and cut into six pieces, each large enough to completely enclose the veal. Place a slice of prosciutto in the center of each, spread some mushroom mixture over it, and put a piece of veal on top. Fold over the dough, pressing all the edges together firmly to seal.

Rinse a baking sheet with cold water, and arrange the pastries on it, seam side down. Beat the egg yolk with the milk, and brush the pastries with the mixture. Bake in a preheated 400° oven 20 minutes, or until browned. Serve hot.

Serves 6.

## Gnocchi di Vitello
### VEAL DUMPLINGS

> 1 pound ground veal
> ¼ pound prosciutto or cooked ham, finely chopped
> 2 eggs, beaten
> 2 teaspoons salt
> 1 cup grated Parmesan cheese
> 1 cup dry bread crumbs
> 6 tablespoons butter
> 4 tablespoons dry vermouth
> 1 pound tomatoes, peeled and chopped
> ¼ teaspoon freshly ground black pepper

Mix together the veal, prosciutto, eggs, 1 teaspoon of the salt and 4 tablespoons of the cheese. Shape tablespoons of the mixture into little balls. Roll in the bread crumbs.

Melt the butter in a skillet; brown the balls in it. Add the wine; cook until absorbed, then add the tomatoes, pepper, and remaining salt; cook over low heat 30 minutes. Taste for seasoning. Put the remaining cheese in a small bowl, and serve with the dumplings.

Serves 4–6.

## 284  ITALY

*Vitello Tonnato*
## VEAL IN TUNA FISH SAUCE

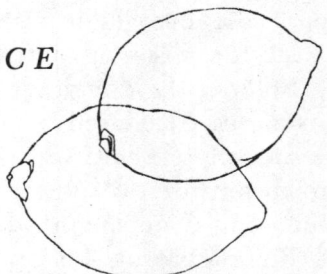

3½ pounds leg of veal
12 anchovy fillets
1 orange
1 cup olive oil
1 cup sliced onions
1 cup grated carrots
2 cloves garlic
2 bay leaves
½ teaspoon thyme
2 cups dry white wine
3 cups chicken broth
1½ teaspoons salt
½ teaspoon freshly ground black pepper
1 7-ounce can tuna fish, drained
1 egg yolk
2 tablespoons lemon juice
2 tablespoons capers, rinsed and drained

Have the veal boned and tied up into a firm shape. Make six slits in the veal. Rinse 6 anchovies, and insert them into the slits.

Wash the orange, cut in quarters, and remove the pits.

Heat ¼ cup of the oil in a Dutch oven or heavy saucepan; lightly brown the veal in it. Pour off the fat. Add the orange, onions, carrots, garlic, bay leaves, thyme, wine, broth, salt, and pepper. Cover, and cook over low heat 2 hours or until tender. Let the meat cool in the gravy. Remove the veal. Cook the gravy over high heat for 10 minutes. Strain ½ of a cup of the gravy.

If you have a blender, use it. Put the tuna fish, egg yolk, lemon juice, and the remaining olive oil and anchovies into the blender, and run at high speed until the mixture is puréed. Turn into a small bowl, and gradually mix in the reserved ½ cup gravy. The sauce should now be the consistency of very heavy cream. Taste for seasoning, and stir in the capers.

If you don't have a blender, mash the tuna fish and anchovies, then put through a fine sieve. Beat the egg yolk in a bowl with an electric mixer or whisk, and still beating, add the lemon juice and tuna mixture. Add the oil, by the half teaspoon, still beating, and when ¼ is used up, add it in a slow steady stream. Continue as directed for the blender method.

Cut the meat in thin slices. Cover the bottom of a serving dish with a thin layer of the sauce, and arrange the veal slices over it. Pour the rest of the sauce over it, and smooth it so as to cover each slice. Cover the dish with plastic wrap, and chill overnight, or for at least 4 hours. Let stand at room temperature for 30 minutes before serving. Garnish with lemon slices, black olives and capers.

Serves 8–10 as a first course.

## *Stufatino*
## BRAISED BREAST OF VEAL

> 5-pound breast of veal
> ⅓ cup olive oil
> 2 cloves garlic, minced
> 1 bay leaf
> ½ teaspoon thyme
> ½ teaspoon oregano
> 2 teaspoons salt
> ½ teaspoon freshly ground black pepper
> 1 cup dry white wine
> 2 cups peeled, seeded, diced tomatoes
> ½ cup boiling water
> 3 tablespoons chopped parsley
> 2 teaspoons grated lemon rind

Have the veal cut up into serving-sized pieces, bone and all.

Heat the oil in a Dutch oven or heavy saucepan; add the meat and brown on all sides. Pour off most of the fat. Mix in the garlic, bay leaf, thyme, oregano, salt, pepper, and wine; cook over low heat until wine is absorbed. Add the tomatoes and water; cover and cook 1½ hours, or until meat is tender. Discard the bay leaf, and mix in the parsley and lemon rind.

Serves 6–8.

# ITALY

Sage

*Involti di Vitello*
## VEAL BIRDS

2 pounds sliced leg of veal (6 slices)
½ pound ground veal
1 clove garlic, minced
¼ cup finely chopped parsley
⅛ teaspoon nutmeg
½ cup dry white wine
2 teaspoons salt
½ teaspoon freshly ground black pepper
⅓ cup flour
6 tablespoons butter
¼ teaspoon sage

Have the veal cutlets pounded very thin, or do it yourself by putting each between waxed paper and pounding with a cleaver or knife. Mix together the ground veal, garlic, parsley, nutmeg, 2 tablespoons of the wine, ¾ teaspoon of the salt, and ¼ teaspoon of the pepper. Spread some of the mixture on each of the cutlets, roll up, and tie with white thread.

Mix the flour with the remaining salt and pepper; dip the rolled meat in the mixture. Melt the butter in a skillet; add the sage, and veal birds. Cook over medium heat until browned on all sides. Add the remaining wine, and cook over low heat 20 minutes, or until tender. Baste and turn several times.

Serves 6.

## *Ossi Buchi*
## BRAISED VEAL KNUCKLES

>6 veal knuckles, about 4 inches long
>½ cup flour
>2 tablespoons olive oil
>2 tablespoons butter
>2 teaspoons salt
>½ teaspoon freshly ground black pepper
>¼ teaspoon rosemary
>¾ cup chopped onions
>2 whole cloves garlic
>¼ cup grated carrots
>1 stalk celery, chopped
>½ cup dry white wine
>1½ cups peeled, seeded, chopped tomatoes
>1½ cups beef broth
>1 tablespoon grated lemon rind
>1 tablespoon grated orange rind
>1 clove garlic, minced
>2 tablespoons parsley

Roll the veal knuckles lightly in the flour.

Heat the oil and butter in a Dutch oven or heavy saucepan; brown the knuckles in it. Sprinkle with the salt, pepper, and rosemary. Add the onions, whole cloves of garlic, carrots, and celery. Cook 5 minutes. Add the wine, tomatoes, and broth. Place the knuckles upright, so that the marrow won't run out. Cover and cook over low heat 1½ hours, or until tender. Add small amounts of boiling water from time to time if necessary. Mix together the lemon and orange rind, garlic, and parsley; stir into the gravy. Cook 5 minutes longer. Serve the knuckles covered with the sauce.

Serves 6.

## *Piccata di Vitello Venezia*
## VEAL SCALOPPINE WITH ZUCCHINI

12 veal scallops, cut ¼ inch thick
Salt
Freshly ground black pepper
Flour
⅜ pound (1½ sticks) butter
½ pound mushrooms, sliced
¼ pound prosciutto ham, minced
1 cup chopped onions
1 clove garlic, minced
1 pound tomatoes, peeled, seeded, and chopped
1½ pounds small zucchini, washed and thinly sliced
2 eggs, beaten
4 tablespoons olive oil
1 cup Marsala or dry sherry

Have the veal pounded as thin as possible, or do it yourself by placing a piece of veal between two sheets of waxed paper, and pounding it with a cleaver. Season the veal with salt and pepper, and dip lightly in flour.

Melt 4 tablespoons of the butter in a skillet; sauté the mushrooms 5 minutes. Stir in the prosciutto, and cook 2 minutes. Season with salt and pepper and keep warm.

Melt 2 tablespoons of the butter in a saucepan; sauté the onions and garlic 5 minutes. Add the tomatoes, and some salt and pepper. Cook over low heat 10 minutes, or until fairly dry.

Toss the zucchini with some flour, and dip the slices in the eggs. Heat the oil in a skillet, and fry the zucchini until lightly browned. Drain, sprinkle with salt, and keep warm.

Melt the remaining butter in a large skillet, and put the veal in it in a single layer. Cook about 2 minutes on each side, or until browned and tender. Transfer to a heated serving dish, and keep warm. Stir the wine into the skillet, and cook over high heat, until reduced to three-quarters its original quantity. Add the mushroom mixture and cook 1 minute. Pour over the veal, and make small mounds of the tomatoes and zucchini around it.

Serves 6.

## Carciofi Borghese
### STUFFED ARTICHOKES

    4 medium-sized artichokes
    1 cup dry bread crumbs
    ½ cup chicken broth
    ¼ pound sausage meat
    ½ cup finely chopped onion
    2 tablespoons chopped parsley
    ½ teaspoon oregano
    ¼ pound mushrooms, finely chopped
    3 tablespoons olive oil
    1 tablespoon flour
    ¾ teaspoon salt
    ¼ teaspoon freshly ground black pepper
    4 slices lemon

Cut off the stem and ½ inch of the top of the artichokes and remove about 2 layers of the hard outer leaves. Plunge, stem end down, into rapidly boiling salted water and cook 30 minutes, or until the outer leaves can be detached easily. Drain, and turn upside down, pressing to remove water. Place right side up and cut out the chokes (fuzzy centers).

Mix together the bread crumbs, broth, sausage meat, onion, parsley, oregano, and mushrooms. Heat 2 tablespoons of the oil in a skillet and sauté the mixture until light brown. Blend in the flour, salt, and pepper. Stuff the center of each artichoke with the mixture. Arrange the artichokes in an oiled casserole and bake in a 350° oven 30 minutes. Serve with lemon slices.

Serves 4.

## Risi e Bisi
## RICE AND PEAS

        4 tablespoons olive oil
        4 tablespoons butter
        ¾ cup chopped onions
        2 cups raw Italian or long-grain rice
        3 tablespoons Marsala or dry sherry
        2 pounds peas, shelled, or 2 packages, frozen, thawed
        1½ teaspoons salt
        ¼ teaspoon white pepper
        4 cups hot chicken broth
        ¼ cup grated Parmesan cheese

Heat the oil and 2 tablespoons of the butter in a heavy saucepan; add the onions and cook 5 minutes, but don't let them brown. Mix in the rice until translucent. Add the wine, cook over low heat 1 minute. Add the peas, salt, pepper, and 2 cups of the broth. Cover, bring to a boil and cook over low heat 10 minutes. Add the remaining broth, re-cover and cook 10 minutes (frozen peas, 5 minutes) longer, or until rice is tender and dry. Taste for seasoning; mix in the cheese and remaining butter with a fork.
    Serves 6–8.


## Piselli alla Romana
## PEAS AND HAM

        4 tablespoons butter
        ¾ cup chopped onions
        3 tablespoons flour
        1½ teaspoons salt
        ¼ teaspoon freshly ground black pepper
        2 cups chicken broth
        3 pounds peas, shelled, or 3 packages, frozen, thawed
        ½ pound cooked ham, cut julienne

Melt the butter in a skillet; sauté the onion 10 minutes. Blend in the flour, salt, and pepper; gradually add the broth, stirring

steadily to the boiling point. Add the peas and ham. Cover and cook over low heat 20 minutes for fresh peas, 10 minutes for frozen.
 Serves 6–8.

## Funghi Ripieni
### STUFFED MUSHROOMS

>24 large mushrooms
>4 tablespoons olive oil
>¼ cup chopped onions
>1 clove garlic, minced
>½ cup chopped green pepper
>½ teaspoon salt
>¼ teaspoon freshly ground black pepper
>3 tablespoons grated Parmesan cheese
>2 tablespoons chopped capers
>2 tablespoons dry bread crumbs

Wash, dry, and remove the stems of the mushrooms. Chop the stems. Heat 2 tablespoons oil in a skillet; sauté the onions, garlic, and green pepper 5 minutes. Add the chopped mushroom stems; sauté 3 minutes. Mix in the salt, pepper, cheese, capers, and bread crumbs; stuff the mushrooms. Place in an oiled baking dish and sprinkle with the remaining oil. Bake in a 375° oven 15 minutes.
 Serves 6, or pierce with cocktail picks and serve as an hors d'oeuvre.

## Crema di Formaggio
### RICH CHEESE DESSERT

¾ pound softened cream cheese
¾ pound ricotta or cottage cheese
¾ cup sugar
6 egg yolks, beaten
3 tablespoons heavy cream
3 tablespoons Strega or cognac
Raspberries or strawberries

Beat the cheeses in an electric mixer, blender, or rotary beater until very smooth. Blend in the sugar until smooth; add the egg yolks, cream, and liqueur, beating until very smooth and thick. Pour into a serving dish and chill. Garnish with raspberries or strawberries.
Serves 8–10.

## Gnocchi alla Crema
### SWEET GNOCCHI

6 egg yolks
3 tablespoons sugar
3 tablespoons cornstarch
1 cup sifted flour
¼ teaspoon salt
¼ teaspoon nutmeg
1¼ cups heavy cream
½ pound (2 sticks) butter
1 tablespoon grated orange rind
4 tablespoons melted butter
¼ cup sifted confectioners' sugar
1 teaspoon cinnamon
¼ cup vanilla cooky crumbs

Beat the egg yolks lightly in the top of a double boiler. Mix in the sugar, cornstarch, flour, salt, and nutmeg. Gradually add the cream, stirring steadily, then add the ½ pound butter. Cook over low heat, beating steadily with a whisk, until smooth and thick, about 10 minutes. Add the orange rind. Pour the mixture onto a well-floured surface and smooth with a hot knife until it's an oblong about ½ inch thick. Cool, until it's solid, then cut into ½-inch squares. Rub an ovenproof baking dish with a little of the melted butter. Arrange the gnocchi in layers, sprinkling each layer with the confectioners' sugar, cinnamon, crumbs, and melted butter. Place in a preheated 450° oven for 10 minutes, or until delicately browned. Serve hot.

Serves 6–8.


*Gato di Castagne*
## CHILLED CHESTNUT DESSERT

>1 pound chestnuts
>2 eggs
>½ cup sugar
>1 cup milk
>1 cup light cream
>1 square (ounce) unsweetened cholocate, grated
>3 tablespoons brandy
>1 teaspoon vanilla extract
>1 cup heavy cream

Cut a crisscross on the flat side of the chestnuts. Cover with water, bring to a boil, and cook over low heat 40 minutes. Drain, cool slightly, peel, and remove inner skin. Purée the chestnuts in an electric blender or force through a sieve.

Beat the eggs and sugar in the top of a double boiler. Stir in the milk, cream, and the chocolate. Place over hot water and cook, stirring constantly until thickened. Beat the mixture into the chestnuts, with 1 tablespoon brandy and the vanilla. Cool slightly, then turn into a well-greased 7-inch tube pan. Chill 4 hours or until firm. Carefully unmold onto a chilled serving dish. Whip the cream, and mix in the remaining brandy. Fill the center of the mold with it.

Serves 6–8.

# THE LATIN COUNTRIES

SPAIN
PORTUGAL
SOUTH AMERICA
MEXICO

A<small>N</small> ancient group of people called the Mauretanians, who lived some thousands of years ago in what is now Morocco, North Africa, moved across the Mediterranean and into Europe, for reasons unknown. They settled on that fair-sized body of land called the Iberian peninsula, which today includes Spain and Portugal. Many centuries later, the Moors of Africa invaded and conquered this portion of Europe, and their continuing influence upon the subjugated people may still be observed by a present-day visitor. In more modern times, comparatively speaking, the two Iberian nations of Spain and Portugal were in the vanguard of nations equipping voyages of discovery and exploration to the New World. For various reasons, but probably because it was thought there was gold in South America, most of the voyages headed in that direction. They explored and conquered, and subdued those Indian tribes reckless enough to fight, all in the name of their majesties of Spain and Portugal, but always with the hope of finding vast treasures of gold and silver. The conquistadors came and ultimately married Indian women. As a result, almost every present-day country in Central and South America, and Mexico as well, speaks Spanish, except for Brazil, where Portuguese is the language. (The only other exceptions are in the small enclaves of Guiana on the northeastern coast of the continent, where French, English, and Dutch are spoken.) The conquering explorers brought their cooking styles with them, but over the past centuries these have been modified by the local foodstuffs available and by the native cooking styles. Many unique and original dishes have been created, dishes to be found only in various parts of South America.

The romantic land of Spain and of its folk hero, Don Quixote, is not all hot sunshine, sere land, olive trees, decaying castles, synthetic gypsies, and hordes of camera-laden tourists milling about the Alhambra. The nation covers a wide range of temperature variations and climatic areas. It is one thing to swelter in the incredible midsummer temperatures of Andalusia; it is something startlingly different to shiver in the chill winter winds of Galicia and Asturias, where no amount of clothing is sufficient to maintain bodily warmth. As a result, the food of Spain encompasses dishes suitable for the two extremes of climate. For example, in wintertime there is the steaming soup-stew called the *cocido,* a filling meal in itself. Equally, there is *gazpacho,* the iced summer soup, so cooling and refreshing on a hot day.

The basis of the Spanish cuisine is undoubtedly the use of olive oil as a cooking fat as opposed to butter, probably because the latter is so much more perishable during the many hot months of the year. Iberian food, unhappily, can be oily and heavy when not properly prepared. However, it is certainly not spicy or hot to the palate as many people think, Spanish food being confused with that of Mexico. The food served on the Iberian peninsula is usually unspiced, but often heavily flavored with garlic.

The appetizers include such items as shrimp cooked in olive oil and garlic, a wide choice of olives prepared in many different fashions, and notably the raw air-dried ham called *jamón serrano.*

This last is exceptionally good with a green-and-gold slice of Spanish melon, ripened in the sun. Fish preparations are particularly fine and often quite imaginative, with special emphasis on shellfish preparations. Mixed seafood creations, typified by the *zarzuela de mariscos*, a sort of seafood soup or chowder, somewhat like France's *bouillabaisse*, is quite delicious. Incidentally, the term *zarzuela de mariscos* literally means a "musical comedy of seafood."

A national soup of Spain is the previously mentioned *cocido*, made in a dozen or more different fashions. Various combinations and permutations are known, in different parts of the nation, as *pote Gallego, olla podrida,* or *caldo.* The net effect is that of the rich broth of a New England boiled dinner, with or without the meat or vegetables. To repeat once again, the other classic soup is the *gazpacho*, which appears in so many varying guises and styles that it would appear that no two Spaniards have the same recipe.

Another firm pillar in the structure of Spanish cookery is a series of rice dishes of which the *paella* is the best known, although it's sometimes called *arroz a la Valenciana*, particularly around Valencia, as its chauvinistic citizens insist. It is typically made with chicken, seafood, saffron, ham or sausages, vegetables, the whole affair intermixed with plenty of rice. Similar to the *paella* is *arroz con pollo*, made primarily with chicken and certainly without seafood. The range of Spanish rice dishes, wide and imaginative, includes preparations using clams, artichokes, beans, and so on, in seemingly endless variations upon a basic theme, that of rice.

The wines of Iberia are passing fair, except for Spain's classic wine, sherry, which is a marvel. The three principal types are *fino*, quite dry to the taste, having the palate dryness of a martini, *amontillado*, somewhat sweeter, and probably the favorite of Americans; and *oloroso*, the sweetest of all, exemplified by Harvey's Bristol Cream.

It appears that the food of Spain and Portugal are quite similar in style. Obviously, however, that statement cannot stand unchallenged, and the comparison is merely skin deep and subject to exceptions galore. For one thing, the food of Portugal seems to be more influenced than that of Spain by the culinary arts of France and Italy.

The typical Portuguese dish, if indeed there is such a creation, is prepared with garlic, olive oil, tomatoes, and onions. Fish is frequently prepared with these ingredients, to be illustrative. Fresh fish, in point of fact, is one of the delights of a vacation in this ancient land. One shellfish worthy of special notice is *ameijoas*, clams, which are particularly delicious here, and made into a wide variety of dishes, some of which might be anticipated; others are of startling originality. For example, cubes of pork are combined with tiny clams to create a most unusual but very palatable combination. The shrimp is remarkably good, as is the lobster, which has become prohibitively expensive in recent years. As a nation, and for all of their fresh seafood, the people of Portugal apparently have a taste for dried codfish, *bacalau*. In many parts of the country it is served almost daily, in one form or another, with eggs, vegetables, and so forth.

Portugal has some very good soups. One is the *caldo verde*, a vegetable soup made with sausages and kale. Another good preparation is the *cozido*, Portugal's version of Spain's *cocido*, a meal-in-one dish. *Sopa à Portuguésa* is a tasty fish chowder, thickened with almonds ground fine. If the cuisine of this small country has a fault, it may lie in its meat preparations, which are not distinguished for their excellence. *Bife à Portuguésa* is a cut of steak cooked with garlic and red wine, and better than average. Other interesting meat dishes include tripe cooked with ham and sausages, pork pickled in vinegar, and calf's liver sautéed in olive oil and garlic.

Portugal's sister nation in South America is Brazil, which still retains strong emotional ties to the homeland, despite some troubled relations during the past century or so. Even in such an everyday matter as the mosaic sidewalks of Rio de Janeiro, the relationship may be seen at a glance, for they resemble those of Lisbon. The food of the giant of the New World, covering a large portion of the southern continent of the Americas, has a similar identity with that of Portugal, but Brazil has certain unique creations. *Empadinhas* are small unsweetened pies, filled with meat, shrimp, or almost anything the cook has on hand, and constitute a delicious snack or appetizer. The Brazilians like to broil foods over open fires or charcoal, a *churrasco*. The meats are then sprinkled with *mandioca*, a starchy flour made from cassava roots.

The national dish of the country, unquestionably, is *feijoada*, a bean preparation containing assorted meats, rice, and almost anything in the way of pork products, including a few items most Americans would rather not learn about. A unique foodstuff is *palmito*, heart of palm, which is obtained by cutting down a young tree and removing the center, which is a tender young green vegetable. It is very delicate in taste, ideal in salads, and has a nutty flavor. Regretfully, the tree dies.

In Argentina the national dish is the *puchero criolla*, the local version of Spain's *cocido*, although with some improvements and variations. Basically it remains a type of boiled dinner, but it is often served most attractively in the shell of a giant squash.

The food of neighboring Uruguay is quite like that of Argentina, with some Italian touches, for much of the country was settled during the past century by immigrants from that Mediterranean country. Otherwise, the emphasis in Uruguay is upon beef, usually broiled over charcoal.

Chile, on the continent's west coast, is a long narrow land fronting on the Pacific. The seafood is extraordinary, for the fishing is remarkably successful, chiefly because of the Humboldt Current that flows northward carrying enormous numbers of fish in its chilly, swiftly moving waters. As might be anticipated, fish soups and stews, in addition to simple preparations, are superb. Particularly memorable is the *chupe de mariscos*, a seafood chowder to end all seafood chowders. The *carbonada*, a meat stew, may be found all over the continent, but the Chilean version of this classic dish is generally excellent. Of course, the wines of Chile are the best on the continent, although the Argentineans may object to that statement. The white wines and champagne of Chile are particularly good, the red considerably less so. There is also *chacolí*, a fermented grape cider.

Paraguay, inland and quite isolated, has some interesting river fish preparations. They also like cakes and breads, and consume vast quantities of preserved fruits in syrup as the end to a substantial meal. The national drink is *maté*, sometimes called Paraguayan tea, which is similar to that of Asia, but more astringent to the taste. *Maté* is also popular in Argentina and Chile.

Peru prepares some good *chupes*, those remarkable seafood soups, using scallops, shrimp, and various other shellfish, including *locos* (which actually means "crazy ones"), a variety unique to South America's west coast. All the versions are excellent and imaginative. A favorite snack food is *anticuchos*, usually made with beef heart, but it may equally be prepared with chunks of beef; it is the standard food offered at railway station stops.

Bolivia, a volatile country high in the Andes, has cold weather most of the year and is always cold at night even during the warm weather season. Perhaps for this reason, spicy foods are particularly well liked. There are *ajís* and *picantes*, all suitably burning to the taste. Farther north is Ecuador, the land of perpetual spring, although a trifle cooler on the average than most people imagine spring should ideally be. Particularly good is the *ajiaco*, a potato soup. Also worthy of particular note is *locro*, a vegetable soup made in a score of different fashions.

Colombia, on the north coast of the continent, has some hearty soups, too, suited to the cool climate of the mountainous interior of the nation. Most of the other dishes of the country, and the food in general, tends to be filling and quite substantial. The desserts here are worthwhile, but the fresh fruits are truly remarkable.

Nowadays, Venezuela is extremely modern and prosperous. As a corollary, the people are beginning to move away from their national dishes in favor of what is usually called French-Continental food. A few old preparations have retained their national popularity, including *hallacas*, a Venezuelan cornmeal dish which is somewhat difficult to prepare in North American homes.

The basis of Mexico's native cuisine is corn, which is ground finely and made into a staple food, the *tortilla*, a thin pancake. A *tortilla* filled with beans or meat is called a *taco*; when deep fried, it becomes a *tostado*, and so forth. Another basic food is dried beans, *frijoles*, and of course, rice. One of the most interesting dishes unique to Mexico is the *mole de guajolote*, turkey in a *mole* sauce, a complicated sauce using many different ingredients, but including the surprising one of chocolate. Some wines are produced, but with only a moderate degree of success; on the other hand, the beers are excellent. Mexico prepares three types of liquor, all made from that all-purpose cactus plant called the maguey. The only one of interest to Americans is *tequilla,* a strong clear liquid of considerable potency. The coffee is just fine here, although somewhat strong to American tastes. Many Mexicans still have a cup of chocolate for breakfast, for this beverage originated here.

## Empanadas de Camarónes
### SHRIMP PASTRIES

SOUTH AMERICA

1½ cups flour
1½ teaspoons salt
¾ cup shortening
1 egg, beaten
¼ cup ice water
3 tablespoons olive oil
½ cup chopped onions
1½ cups peeled chopped tomatoes
¾ pound cooked cleaned shrimp, coarsely chopped
½ teaspoon freshly ground black pepper
2 hard-cooked egg yolks, chopped
¼ cup chopped black olives
2 tablespoons minced parsley
1 egg yolk, beaten
2 tablespoons milk

Sift the flour and ¾ teaspoon salt into a bowl; cut in the shortening with a pastry blender or 2 knives. Stir in the egg and water until a ball of dough is formed. Chill 2 hours.

Heat the oil in a skillet; sauté the onions 5 minutes. Add the tomatoes; cook over low heat 10 minutes. Mix in the shrimp, pepper, and remaining salt; cook over low heat 5 minutes. Remove from heat and blend in the egg yolks, olives, and parsley. Taste for seasoning and let stand until cool.

Roll out the dough on a lightly floured surface ⅛ inch thick. Cut into 5-inch circles. Place a tablespoon of the shrimp mixture on each, and fold over the dough, sealing the edges with a little water. Arrange on a buttered baking sheet. Brush the tops with the egg yolk mixed with the milk. Bake in a preheated 400° oven 15 minutes, or until browned. Serve hot.

Makes about 2 dozen.

## *Empanadas de Queso*
## CHEESE PASTRIES

SOUTH AMERICA

2½ cups instantized flour
½ teaspoon salt
½ teaspoon sugar
1 teaspoon baking powder
¾ cup shortening
4 egg yolks
½ cup milk
2 eggs whites
2 cups grated cheddar cheese
1 teaspoon Spanish paprika

Combine the flour, salt, sugar, and baking powder in a bowl; cut in the shortening with a pastry blender or 2 knives. Beat the egg yolks and milk together; stir into the flour mixture until a ball of dough is formed. Chill for 1 hour.

Beat the egg whites until frothy; stir in the cheese and paprika. Roll out the dough as thin as possible on a lightly floured surface. Cut into 3-inch circles. Place a heaping teaspoon of the cheese mixture on half the circles and cover with the remaining circles; moisten the edges with a little water and press together firmly. Arrange on a baking sheet. Bake in a preheated 375° oven for 15 minutes, or until browned. Serve hot, as an appetizer.

Makes about 3 dozen.

## Tortilla de Banana
## BANANA OMELET

SOUTH AMERICA

    4 firm bananas
    4 tablespoons butter
    6 eggs, separated
    ¼ cup light cream
    1 teaspoon salt
    2 tablespoons chopped parsley
    Dash of cayenne pepper

Peel the bananas and slice thin. Melt the butter in a skillet; add the bananas in a single layer and sauté 5 minutes, stirring frequently but gently.

Beat the egg yolks, cream, and salt in a bowl. Beat the egg whites stiff and fold them into the yolks. Pour into a well-buttered 12-inch skillet (with an ovenproof handle) or baking dish and arrange the bananas on top. Bake in a preheated 350° oven 20 minutes, or until set and lightly browned on top. Transfer to a heated platter, sprinkle with the parsley and cayenne pepper. Slice and serve as a first luncheon or supper dish.

Serves 3–6.

## Escabeche de Camarónes
## MARINATED SHRIMP

MEXICO

    2 pounds raw shrimp, shelled and deveined
    ¾ cup olive oil
    ½ cup chopped onions
    2 cloves garlic, minced
    ½ teaspoon freshly ground black pepper
    1 teaspoon Spanish paprika
    2 teaspoons salt
    ½ cup cider vinegar
    ¼ teaspoon dry mustard
    1 teaspoon crushed cumin seed
    ¼ teaspoon dried ground chili peppers
    2 onions, thinly sliced

Wash and dry the shrimp. Heat ¼ cup oil in a skillet; sauté the onions and garlic 5 minutes. Add the shrimp, pepper, paprika, and 1 teaspoon salt; sauté 5 minutes. Cool 10 minutes.

Mix together the vinegar, mustard, cumin seed, chili peppers, and the remaining oil and salt. Arrange layers of the shrimp and sliced onions in a bowl or jar and pour the marinade over all. Marinate in the refrigerator 48 hours before serving on shredded lettuce as an appetizer, or pierced with cocktail picks as an hors d'oeuvre.

Serves 6–8 as a first course.

## *Camarões Fritos*     PORTUGAL
## BATTER FRIED SHRIMP

    4 tablespoons lemon juice
    ¼ teaspoon freshly ground black pepper
    6 tablespoons olive oil
    1½ teaspoons salt
    1½ pounds raw shrimp, shelled and deveined
    1 cup flour
    2 egg yolks, beaten
    ⅔ cup beer
    2 egg whites, stiffly beaten
    Vegetable oil for deep-frying
    Minced parsley
    Lime or Lemon wedges

Mix together the lemon juice, pepper, 4 tablespoons of the oil, and 1 teaspoon of the salt. Marinate the shrimp in the mixture for 2 hours. While the shrimp are marinating, prepare the batter.

Sift the flour and remaining salt into a bowl. Blend in the egg yolks and beer until smooth. Stir in the remaining oil; let stand 1 hour. Fold in the egg whites. Drain the shrimp and dip them in the batter one by one. Heat the fat to 370°; fry the shrimp in it until browned. Sprinkle with parsley and serve with lime or lemon wedges.

Serves 4–6, or serve as a hot hors d'oeuvre on cocktail picks.

## *Camarónes con Salsa de Almendras*
## SHRIMP IN ALMOND SAUCE

ECUADOR

> 2 pounds raw shrimp
> 1 stalk celery
> ½ teaspoon pickling spice
> 1½ cups water
> 2 teaspoons salt
> 5 slices homemade type white bread, trimmed
> 1½ cups milk
> 4 tablespoons butter
> 2 cloves garlic, minced
> 1 cup minced onions
> 1 teaspoon Spanish paprika
> ½ teaspoon freshly ground black pepper
> ¼ teaspoon dried ground chili peppers
> ½ cup olive oil
> 1 cup ground almonds

Wash the shrimp and combine in a saucepan with the celery, pickling spice, water, and 1 teaspoon of the salt. Bring to a boil and cook over medium heat 5 minutes. Let cool in the liquid for 15 minutes. Remove the shrimp and cook the liquid until reduced to ¾ cup. Strain and reserve. Shell the shrimp and remove the black vein. Soak the bread in the milk 5 minutes. Mash smooth.

Melt the butter in a skillet; sauté the garlic, onions, paprika, pepper, chili peppers, and remaining salt for 10 minutes. Add the bread and sauté 5 minutes, stirring frequently. Gradually stir in the oil. Mix in the almonds. Very gradually mix in the reserved stock, then add the shrimp. Cook over low heat 5 minutes.

Serves 8 as a first course.

## Bacalao à la Argentina
### CODFISH, ARGENTINA STYLE

ARGENTINA

>2 pounds dried codfish (salt cod)
>1 whole onion, peeled
>1 bay leaf
>¾ cup olive oil
>1½ cups thinly sliced onions
>1 clove garlic, minced
>1 can chick-peas, drained
>3 eggs
>3 tablespoons lemon juice
>⅛ teaspoon dried ground chili peppers
>3 tablespoons grated Parmesan cheese
>4 tablespoons minced parsley
>¾ cup dried bread crumbs
>2 tablespoons butter
>Pitted black olives

Wash the codfish and soak in water to cover overnight; change the water twice. Drain and cover with fresh water; add the onion and bay leaf. Bring to a boil and cook over low heat 30 minutes. Drain and flake. Heat ¼ cup of the oil in a skillet; sauté the onions and garlic 5 minutes. Mix in the codfish and cook 5 minutes, stirring frequently. Mix in the chick-peas. Cook 2 minutes. Spread the mixture in a buttered baking dish.

Beat the eggs; gradually add the remaining oil, beating steadily. Stir in the lemon juice, chili peppers, cheese, and parsley. Pour over the fish. Sprinkle with the bread crumbs and dot with the butter. Bake in a preheated 350° oven 20 minutes or until browned. Garnish with olives.

Serves 6–8.

## Vatapá
## SHRIMP COCONUT STEW

BRAZIL

Fresh coconut or 3 cups flaked coconut and
   3 cups milk
4 tablespoons olive oil
1½ cups finely chopped onions
2 cloves garlic, minced
½ teaspoon dried ground chili peppers
1 cup peeled, seeded, chopped tomatoes
2 cups water
2 teaspoons salt
1 tablespoon grated ginger root or
   1 teapsoon ground ginger
2 bay leaves
2 pounds snapper, halibut, etc., cut in 2-inch pieces
1½ pounds raw shrimp, shelled and deveined
¼ pound dried shrimp, finely minced
2 cups ground peanuts
½ cup yellow cornmeal
3 tablespoons butter

Buy a coconut which has water in it—shake it to test. With an ice pick or screw driver, make holes through the dark spots of the coconut. Pour off the liquid into a cup. Put the coconut in a 425° oven for 15 minutes. Immediately hit the coconut with a hammer, to remove it from the shell. Peel off the brown skin, and cut the meat into small pieces. Put a little at a time with some of the liquid into a blender, and blend until fine. If you don't have a blender, grate the coconut, then mix in the liquid. You should have about 3 cups.

If the dried variety is used, rinse the coconut under cold running water. Combine the coconut and milk; bring to a boil and let soak 30 minutes. Blend in an electric blender and strain, squeezing out all the milk, and reserve.

Heat the oil in a saucepan; sauté the onions, garlic, and chili peppers 5 minutes. Add the tomatoes; cook 5 minutes. Add the water, salt, ginger, and bay leaves. Bring to a boil; add the fish and raw shrimp. Cook over low heat 10 minutes. Remove the fish and shrimp; strain the stock.

Combine the coconut milk with the dried shrimp and peanuts. Bring to a boil and cook over low heat 15 minutes. Strain.

Combine the reserved stock with the peanut mixture; bring to a boil and stir in the cornmeal. Cook over low heat 25 minutes, stirring frequently. Stir in the butter and return the fish and shrimp. Taste for seasoning. Serve in deep bowls, with rice.

Serves 8–10.

## *Albondigas de Pescado*     SOUTH AMERICA
### FRIED FISH CROQUETTES

> 3 pounds fillet of mackerel
> ¼ pound (1 stick) butter
> 2 cups chopped onions
> 2 cloves garlic, minced
> 3 eggs
> 1½ teaspoons salt
> ½ teaspoon freshly ground pepper
> ½ cup dry bread crumbs

Wash the fish, and pull out any bones which may remain. Grind the fish in a food chopper, or chop very fine.

Melt 2 tablespoons of the butter in a skillet, sauté the onions and garlic until browned. Cool, add to the fish, and chop together until well blended. Beat in 1 egg at a time, then mix in the salt and pepper. Chill for 30 minutes.

Using about 2 tablespoons of the mixture at a time, shape it into croquettes between wet hands. Dip lightly in the bread crumbs.

In a large skillet, melt half the remaining butter. Put in a single layer of croquettes, and fry over low heat until browned on both sides. Transfer the croquettes to a serving dish, and continue frying the remaining croquettes, adding butter as needed. Serve hot or cold.

Serves 6–8.

*Chupe de Mariscos*     PERU-CHILE
SEAFOOD CASSEROLE

* 2 1½-pound lobsters or 4 large African lobster tails
1 quart water
2 cups dry white wine
2 tablespoons salt
2 pounds raw shrimp
24 clams
24 mussels
6 tablespoons butter
1 tablespoon Spanish paprika
¾ cup chopped onions
2 cups fresh soft bread crumbs
1½ cups milk
¾ cup grated mozzarella cheese
3 egg yolks
⅛ teaspoon cayenne pepper
4 hard-cooked eggs, cut in half

Wash the lobsters. Bring the water, wine, and salt to a boil. Drop the lobsters into it and cook 20 minutes. Drain. Drop the shrimp into the boiling liquid and cook 5 minutes. Drain, reserving the liquid.

Scrub the clams and mussels with a brush, and cut off the beards of the mussels. Put them in a pan with ½ cup of the reserved liquid. Cover and steam until the shells open. Drain and discard the shells, also any whose shells don't open.

Remove the meat of the lobsters and cut into 2-inch pieces. Shell and devein the shrimp. Put all the seafood into a greased 3-quart casserole.

Melt the butter in a saucepan; stir in the paprika and onions.

Cook over low heat 5 minutes. Add the bread crumbs, milk, and 1½ cups of the reserved liquid. Bring to a boil and cook over low heat 10 minutes.

In a bowl, mix together the mozzarella cheese, egg yolks, and cayenne pepper. Add the hot sauce, stirring steadily to prevent curdling. Taste for seasoning. Pour over the seafood. Bake in a 350° oven 30 minutes. Remove cover and place under the broiler until top browns. Garnish with the eggs. Serve with French bread and rice.

Serves 8.

## *Huachinango Relleno*    MEXICO
### STUFFED FISH FILLETS

> 3 tablespoons butter
> 3 tablespoons flour
> ¾ cup chicken broth
> ¾ cup light cream
> ⅛ teaspoon mace
> 1½ teaspoons salt
> ½ teaspoon white pepper
> 6 fillets of red snapper or sole
> 12 shucked oysters
> ¼ pound mushrooms, sliced and sautéed

Melt the butter in a saucepan; blend in the flour. Add the broth and cream, stirring steadily over low heat until smooth and thickened. Add the mace, 1 teaspoon of the salt, and ½ teaspoon pepper and cook 5 minutes longer.

Rinse and dry the fish fillets; sprinkle with the remaining salt and pepper. Dip the oysters in the sauce and place two on each fillet. Divide the mushrooms among the fillets, then roll up like a jelly roll. Arrange in a single layer in a shallow buttered baking dish and pour the remaining sauce over them. Bake in a 375° oven 25 minutes, or until the fish flakes easily when tested with a fork.

Place under the broiler until top is delicately browned. Serve garnished with cooked green peas and parsley.

Serves 6.

## Zarzuela de Mariscos
### SEAFOOD SOUP STEW

SPAIN

12 hard-shell clams
12 mussels
1 pound scallops
1 1½-pound live lobster or 2 large African lobster tails
1½ pounds large shrimp (8 to a pound if possible)
½ cup blanched almonds
¼ cup olive oil
1 cup chopped green peppers
1 cup minced onion
3 cloves garlic, minced
⅛ pound proscuitto ham, chopped
2 pounds tomatoes, peeled, seeded, and chopped
2 teaspoons salt
½ teaspoon freshly ground black pepper
1 tablespoon finely chopped bay leaf
¼ teaspoon crushed saffron
1½ cups dry white wine
2½ cups water
Parsley

Wash and scrub the clams with a brush under cold running water until the water runs clear. Wash and scrub the mussels in the same manner, and cut off the beards. Wash the scallops—if bay scallops are used, leave them whole; cut sea scallops in half. Cut off the tail section of the live lobster, then cut it into 1-inch pieces crosswise. (If lobster tails are used, cut them in the same way.) Crack the claws of the live lobster. Shell and devein the shrimp. Refrigerate all the seafood until ready to use.

Pulverize the almonds in an electric blender, or put through a mouli grater or food mill.

Heat the oil in a 6-quart casserole or Dutch oven. Add the green pepper, onions, and garlic. Cook over low heat 10 minutes, stirring frequently. Stir in the ham, tomatoes, almonds, salt, pepper, bay leaf, and saffron. Bring to a boil over high heat, then cook over medium heat 10 minutes. Add the wine and water. Bring to a boil and cook 5 minutes, stirring frequently. Add the lobster;

cover and cook 10 minutes. Add the shrimp, clams, and mussels; cook 3 minutes. Add the scallops; cover, and cook 5 minutes. Taste for seasoning, and look over the clams and mussels, to be sure they have all opened—if any haven't, discard them. Sprinkle with parsley, and serve from the pot, if you like. Serve with garlic-rubbed toasted French or Italian bread.

Serves 6–8.

*Seviche Chileño*
MARINATED RAW FISH

CHILE

    2 pounds raw fresh fillets of sole, snapper, or halibut
    2 red onions
    1 cup lime or lemon juice
    1 cup orange juice
    ¼ teaspoon Tabasco
    1¼ teaspoons salt
    ⅛ teaspoon dried ground chili peppers
    1 cup peeled chopped tomatoes

The fish used for *Seviche* must be fresh, not frozen. Rinse the fish, and cut it into 1-inch pieces. Place it in a glass or pottery bowl.

Peel the onions, and slice them very thin, then separate into rings. Mix together the lime juice, orange juice, Tabasco, salt, chili peppers, and onions. Pour the mixture over the fish and mix well. Cover and marinate in the refrigerator overnight, or for at least 4 hours. Check the color of the fish—it should look white and opaque, much as it would look if it were cooked. Mix in the tomatoes, and marinate 1 hour longer.

Serve the *Seviche* in lettuce cups. The customary garnish is a piece of sweet potato and a piece of corn on the cob.

Serves 8–10.

### Langosta Criolla
### LOBSTER IN TOMATO SAUCE
SOUTH AMERICA

2 1½-pound live lobsters or 4 large African lobster tails
⅔ cup olive oil
1 cup chopped onions
2 cups canned drained tomatoes
2 cloves garlic, minced
1½ teaspoons salt
½ teaspoon freshly ground black pepper
½ teaspoon oregano
3 tablespoons cognac
2 tablespoons minced parsley

The lobster may be prepared in the shell, in which case have them chopped up. Or have the lobsters split, remove the meat and cut up. The tails may be cooked in the shell or meat removed, too.

Heat half the oil in a saucepan; sauté the onions 10 minutes. Add the tomatoes, garlic, salt and pepper, and oregano. Cover, and cook over low heat 30 minutes.

Heat the remaining oil in a skillet; cook the lobster in it until the shells turn red, or cook meat 5 minutes. Heat the cognac, pour over the lobster and set aflame. When flames die, add the lobster to the tomato sauce. Cook over low heat 15 minutes. Mix in the parsley and taste for seasoning.

Serves 2–4.

Note: Shrimp prepared in this manner are equally good. Follow the cooking time for lobster meat.

## Gazpacho Andaluz
SPAIN
## COLD VEGETABLE SOUP

1½ pounds tomatoes, peeled and seeded
1 cucumber, peeled and sliced
2 green peppers, seeded and sliced
½ sliced onion
1 clove garlic
¼ cup olive oil
3 tablespoons wine vinegar
4 slices white bread, trimmed and cubed
4 cups water
1½ teaspoons salt
½ teaspoon freshly ground black pepper
½ teaspoon crushed cumin seeds

Use an electric blender, if possible, and purée small amounts of all the ingredients at a time. Empty into a bowl (not metal) as each batch is finished. If you don't have a blender, put the ingredients through a food mill. (If you are using a food mill, it is not necessary to seed the tomatoes.) Chill 4 hours. Just before serving, check consistency. The soup should be thick, but not solid. Add a little ice water if necessary. Serve in soup cups with an ice cube in each. Put the garnishes in small individual bowls, and pass them.

### Garnish

**Croutons**
**Chopped green onions**
**Diced cucumbers**
**Diced green peppers**

Serves 8–10.

*Ajiaco*     COLOMBIA
## POTATO, CORN, AND AVOCADO SOUP

    4 tablespoons butter
    1½ cups finely chopped onions
    3 cups peeled diced potatoes
    4 cups chicken broth
    ¼ teaspoon dried ground chili peppers
    ⅛ teaspoon saffron
    3 cups milk
    1 cup cooked or canned corn kernels
    ¼ pound cream cheese
    3 eggs
    2 avocados, peeled and thinly sliced

Melt the butter in a saucepan; sauté the onions until browned. Add the potatoes, broth, chili peppers, and saffron. Bring to a boil and cook over low heat 20 minutes. Mash some of the potatoes against the sides of the pan. Mix in the milk and corn; cook 10 minutes.

Beat the cream cheese smooth, then beat in the eggs. Gradually add about 2 cups soup, stirring steadily to prevent curdling. Return to balance of soup, mixing steadily. Heat, but do not let boil. Taste for seasoning. Place a few slices of avocado in each soup plate and pour the soup over them.

Serves 6–8.

*Sopa de Pescado*                                                                   PERU
## SHRIMP AND SCALLOP SOUP

    1 pound raw shrimp, shelled and deveined
    1 pound scallops
    6 tablespoons butter
    1 cup finely chopped onions
    4 cups fish stock or bottled clam juice
    4 cups dry white wine
    ½ teaspoon white pepper
    1 cup diced homemade type white bread
    1 cup milk
    ⅛ teaspoon dried ground chili peppers
    ½ cup ground almonds
    1 cup heavy cream
    ½ teaspoon Spanish paprika
    2 hard-cooked eggs, sieved

Wash the shrimp, cover with water and bring to a boil; drain. Cut each in quarters, crosswise. Wash the scallops—if bay scallops are used, leave them whole; quarter sea scallops.

Melt the butter in a saucepan; sauté the onions until soft and lightly browned. Mix in the fish stock, wine, and pepper; bring to a boil and cook over low heat 30 minutes. Soak the bread in the milk and mash smooth; add to the saucepan and cook over low heat 10 minutes. Add the shrimp, scallops, and chili peppers. Cook 5 minutes. Blend in the almonds, cream, paprika, and eggs. Cook 5 minutes longer. Taste for seasoning.

Serves 8–10.

## Canja
### THICK CHICKEN-RICE SOUP
BRAZIL

> 5-pound fowl, disjointed
> 1 tablespoon salt
> ½ teaspoon freshly ground black pepper
> 2 tablespoons olive oil
> 1 cup sliced onions
> 1 clove garlic, minced
> 2 quarts boiling water
> 1 cup peeled diced tomatoes
> 1 bay leaf
> 2 sprigs parsley
> ⅛ teaspoon marjoram
> ¾ cup raw long-grain rice
> 1 cup diced cooked ham
> 2 tablespoons minced parsley

Wash and dry the chicken pieces; season with the salt and pepper. Heat the oil in a skillet; lightly brown the chicken, onions, and garlic in it. Transfer the chicken and onions to a saucepan. Add the boiling water, tomatoes, bay leaf, parsley, and marjoram. Cover and cook over low heat 1 hour. Stir in the rice and cook 30 minutes. Remove the chicken and cut the meat from the bones, then return chicken to soup. Add the ham, and cook 5 minutes. Discard the bay leaf. Taste for seasoning. Serve the soup in deep plates or bowls, sprinkled with parsley.

Serves 6–8.


## Sopa de Espuma
### SOUP WITH FLUFFY DUMPLINGS
MEXICO

> ¾ cup sifted flour
> 1 teaspoon baking powder
> ¼ cup melted butter
> 3 eggs
> ¼ cup freshly grated Parmesan cheese
> 2 quarts chicken broth

Sift together the flour and baking powder, then stir in the melted butter. Add 1 egg at a time, beating until well blended after each addition. Stir in the cheese.

Bring the broth to a rolling boil and drop the batter into it by the teaspoon. Cover, and cook over medium heat for 10 minutes without raising the cover. Serve hot in consommé cups.

Serves 8–10.

*Potaje de Garbanzos*
CHICK-PEA SOUP

SPAIN

    1 pound dried chick-peas
    1 pound boneless beef, cut in ½-inch cubes
    1 beef bone
    2½ quarts water
    ¼ pound bacon, chopped
    1½ cups chopped onions
    3 potatoes, peeled and diced
    2 teaspoons salt
    ½ teaspoon freshly ground black pepper
    ⅛ teaspoon saffron
    3 Spanish (*chorizos*) or other spicy sausages, sliced thin

Soak the chick-peas in salted water overnight. Drain. Combine the chick-peas with the beef, bone, and the 2½ quarts of water. Bring to a boil and cook over low heat 1½ hours. Purée half the chick-peas in an electric blender, or force through a sieve, and return to the soup.

Sauté the bacon and onions together for 10 minutes. Drain. Add to the soup with potatoes, salt, pepper, and saffron. Cook over low heat 15 minutes. While the soup is cooking, brown the sausages, and drain. Add to the soup, and cook 5 minutes longer. Taste for seasoning, and discard the bone.

Serves 6–8.

## Sopa de Frijoles Meturado
## MIXED BEAN SOUP

SOUTH AMERICA

1½ pounds mixed dried beans
4 quarts water
2 bay leaves
2 beef bones, cracked
2 whole onions
4 tablespoons olive oil
1½ cups chopped onions
2 cloves garlic, minced
2½ teaspoons salt
⅛ teaspoon dried ground red peppers
1 teaspoon Spanish paprika
½ pound Spanish sausages, sliced

Buy as many different kinds of beans as you can—black, small red, chili beans, white, chick-peas, pigeon peas, and black-eyed peas, for example. Wash them thoroughly. Cover with water, bring to a boil, cook 2 minutes, remove from the heat and let soak 1 hour. (Or soak in cold water overnight.) Drain, add the 4 quarts water, the bay leaves, bones, and whole onions. Bring to a boil and cook over low heat 2 hours, or until beans are tender. Discard the bay leaves and bones. Purée about 3 cups of the beans in an electric blender, or force through a sieve. Return to the saucepan.

While the beans are cooking, heat the oil in a skillet; sauté the chopped onions and garlic 10 minutes. Add to the soup with the salt, red peppers, and paprika. Cook over low heat 20 minutes. If soup is too thick, add a little beef broth. Brown the sausages, drain and add to the soup. Cook 10 minutes longer. Taste for seasoning.

Serves 10–12.

SOUTH AMERICA

*Mondongo*
PEPPER POT

1½ pounds tripe
Veal knuckle
4 quarts water
1 lemon, sliced
½ pound dried chick-peas
½ teaspoon thyme
1 tablespoon salt
½ teaspoon freshly ground black pepper
1 cup chopped onions
2 cloves garlic, minced
2 cups peeled diced tomatoes
3 carrots, sliced
2 sweet potatoes, peeled and diced
1½ pounds yellow squash, peeled and cubed
2 cups shredded cabbage
⅛ teaspoon Tabasco
2 teaspoons Worcestershire sauce

Wash and scrape the tripe. Have the veal knuckle cracked. Wash the chick-peas, cover with water, and bring to a boil. Let soak 2 hours, then drain.

Cut the tripe into inch-wide strips. Combine in a saucepan with the veal knuckle, the 4 quarts of water, and the lemon. Bring to a boil and cook over low heat 4 hours. Add the drained chick-peas, the thyme, salt, pepper, onions, garlic, tomatoes, carrots, sweet potatoes, squash, and cabbage. Cover and cook over low heat 2 hours. Stir in the Tabasco and Worcestershire sauce. Taste for seasoning and discard the veal knuckle.

Serves 8–10.

## Paella                                                              SPAIN

### SPANISH NATIONAL RICE DISH

There are literally dozens of methods for preparing *Paella*. This is one prepared as it is at the Restaurant Gurea, in Barcelona, one of the best I've ever eaten.

- 12 clams or mussels, or a combination
- 2½-pound frying chicken, disjointed
- 1 clove garlic, minced
- 2½ teaspoons salt
- ¾ teaspoon freshly ground black pepper
- 8 tablespoons olive oil
- ⅛ pound smoked ham, cut julienne
- 2 Spanish (*chorizos*) or other spicy sausage, sliced and parboiled 10 minutes
- 1 cup chopped onions
- ½ cup coarsely chopped green pepper
- 2½ cups raw long-grain rice
- 1 cup peeled, seeded, chopped tomatoes
- 3½ cups boiling water
- 1½ cups beer
- ¼ teaspoon saffron, finely crushed
- 1 pound raw shrimp, shelled and deveined
- 1 8-ounce can tiny peas
- ½ pound cooked lobster meat, cut into bite-sized pieces
- 1 package frozen artichoke hearts, cooked and drained
- 3 pimentos, cut julienne

Wash the clams or mussels; scrub with a brush, rinse and dry. Place in a skillet with a little water, cover, and cook over high heat until shells open. Discard any that do not open.

Wash and dry the chicken pieces; rub with a mixture of the garlic, 1½ teaspoons of the salt, ½ teaspoon of the pepper, and 2 tablespoons of the oil. Heat 4 tablespoons of the remaining oil in a deep skillet; brown the chicken in it over low heat. Add the ham, sausage, onions, and green pepper. Cook over low heat 20 minutes, stirring frequently. In a separate skillet, heat the remaining oil. Add the rice; cook 5 minutes, stirring frequently. Mix in the tomatoes, water, beer, saffron, and remaining salt and pepper.

Cover and cook over medium low heat 5 minutes. Turn the mixture into a *Paella* pan or large fairly flat casserole. Arrange the chicken pieces and shrimp on it, and pour over it the pan juices, sausage, onions, and peppers. Place the pan on the lower level of a preheated 400° oven and bake 15 minutes. Scatter the peas over the top, and arrange the lobster, artichokes, and clams or mussels on the rice. Bake 5 minutes longer. Garnish with the pimentos. Serves 6–8.

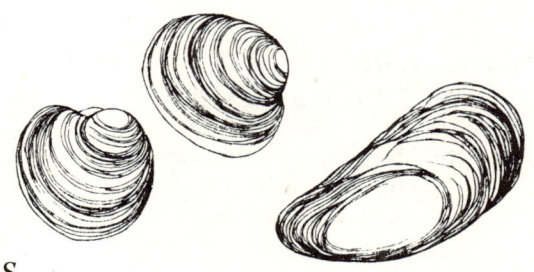

## TORTILLAS                                                MEXICO

    3 cups instant Masa Harina
    1¼ teaspoons salt
    1⅔ cups water (about)

*Masa Harina* is available in packages put up by Quaker Oats. If you can't find it, use a very fine cornmeal, and half flour. (Put the cornmeal in an electric blender, to make it even finer, or sift it through a fine sifter.) Combine the Masa Harina and salt in a bowl. Gradually add 1¼ cups of the water, stirring constantly, then knead with the fingers, and spoon by spoon, add just enough of the remaining water, until a firm, but not sticky, dough is formed. Break off walnut-sized balls, and press them into 5-inch circles between two sheets of waxed paper. Stack between sheets of waxed paper.

Heat a 7-inch heavy skillet, or griddle, and put one tortilla at a time on it. Cook over medium heat 2 minutes, turn over with a spatula, and cook 2 minutes longer. Stack the tortillas on foil, cover, and keep warm in a 250° oven while preparing the balance. Makes about 16.

Note: Frozen and canned tortillas are available, and can be used for making Enchiladas and Tostados.

## *Enchiladas de Pollo*     MEXICO
## CHICKEN-STUFFED FRIED TORTILLAS

    3 tablespoons seedless raisins
    3 tablespoons olive oil
    ¾ cup chopped onions
    2 cups peeled chopped tomatoes
    1 cup chopped green peppers
    1¼ teaspoons salt
    ⅛ teaspoon Tabasco
    1½ cups coarsely chopped cooked chicken
    ½ cup chopped pimento-stuffed olives
    16 Tortillas (see recipe)
    3 eggs, beaten
    1½ cups vegetable oil
    Freshly grated Parmesan cheese

    Soak the raisins in hot water for 15 minutes; drain and dry.

    Heat the oil in a saucepan; sauté the onions 5 minutes. Add the tomatoes, green peppers, salt, and Tabasco. Bring to a boil and cook over low heat 15 minutes, stirring frequently.

    Mix together the chicken, olives, and raisins. Place a tablespoon of the mixture on one side of each tortilla, fold over, and fasten with toothpicks. Dip the tortillas, one by one, in the beaten eggs. Heat the oil in a 7-inch skillet and fry each one until browned on both sides. Drain, and arrange them in a baking dish. Pour the tomato sauce over them and sprinkle with the cheese. Bake on the middle level of a preheated 425° oven 10 minutes or until bubbly and the cheese melted and lightly browned.

    Serves 8–16.

## Frango ao Môlho Pardo
### CHICKEN IN BROWN SAUCE

BRAZIL

    2 4-pound roasting chickens, disjointed
    2½ teaspoons salt
    ½ teaspoon freshly ground black pepper
    ¼ pound chicken livers
    2 tablespoons olive or vegetable oil
    2 tablespoons butter
    1 cup chopped onions
    1 bay leaf
    1 stalk celery and leaves
    10½-ounce can chicken broth
    1 cup boiling water
    16 very small white onions (see note below)
    1 tablespoon cornstarch
    2 teaspoons Kitchen Bouquet
    3 tablespoons cold water

Wash and dry the chicken pieces; season with the salt and pepper. Purée the livers in an electric blender, or chop to a paste. Refrigerate until needed.

Heat the oil and butter in a Dutch oven or heatproof casserole; brown the chicken pieces in it very well. Add the chopped onions and let brown. Add the bay leaf, celery, broth and boiling water. Cover, and cook over low heat 1 hour. Add the white onions, and cook 30 minutes longer.

Mix the cornstarch, Kitchen Bouquet, and cold water to a smooth paste. Stir into the gravy. Cook 5 minutes, and taste for seasoning. Just before serving, stir the livers into the gravy. Heat, but do not let boil. Serve with rice.

Serves 8.

Note: If fresh small onions aren't available, use the canned variety, but add them only 10 minutes before end of cooking time.

## Ají de Gallina
### CHICKEN IN SPICY BREAD SAUCE

BOLIVIA

1 teaspoon dried ground chili peppers
6 slices homemade type white bread
1 cup milk
¾ cup olive oil
2 3-pound fryers, disjointed
1 cup chopped onions
1 clove garlic, minced
¾ cup peeled, diced tomatoes
3 cups chicken broth
1½ teaspoons salt
½ teaspoon freshly ground black pepper
¼ cup freshly grated Parmesan cheese
4 hard-cooked eggs, sliced
Ripe black olives

Soak the chili peppers in warm water for 15 minutes. Drain. Trim the bread of the crusts and break up the bread into small pieces. Soak in the milk, then mash very smooth.

Heat half of the oil in a Dutch oven or heavy saucepan; brown the chicken in it very well. Remove chicken. Add the remaining oil; heat, and sauté the onions and garlic 5 minutes, or until soft and yellow. Mix in the tomatoes, chili peppers, and mashed bread; cook over high heat 2 minutes, stirring steadily. Add the broth, salt and pepper. Bring to a boil and return the chicken. Cover and cook over low heat 1 hour, or until tender. Stir in the cheese. Serve garnished with the eggs and olives, and with baked sweet potatoes.

Serves 8–10.

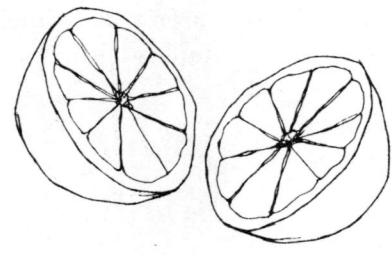

*Pato com Môlho de Laranja*   BRAZIL
DUCK IN ORANGE SAUCE

> 2 5-pound ducks
> ¼ cup lemon or lime juice
> 3 teaspoons salt
> 1 teaspoon freshly ground black pepper
> 4 cups orange juice
> 3 tablespoons grated orange rind
> 2 bay leaves
> ¼ cup rum
> 6 bananas, peeled and quartered
> 2 tablespoons cornstarch
> ¼ cup curaçao
> ½ cup ground Brazil nuts
> Whole Brazil nuts
> 1 cup currant jelly, cut into cubes

Wash the duck, and remove as much fat as possible. Sprinkle the ducks with the lemon juice and rub with salt and pepper. Place the ducks, breast side down, on a rack in a roasting pan and roast in a 425° oven 20 minutes. Pour off the fat. Reduce heat to 350° and roast 50 minutes. Pour off fat. Turn breast side up and pour 3 cups of the orange juice over the ducks. Sprinkle with the orange rind. Add the bay leaves and rum; roast 30 minutes, basting frequently. Add the bananas and roast 30 minutes. Remove the ducks and bananas. Skim the fat from pan juices and strain.

Mix the cornstarch and the remaining orange juice in a saucepan; add the strained pan juices and cook, stirring constantly to the boiling point. Mix in curaçao and ground Brazil nuts and cook over low heat 5 minutes. Carve the ducks and arrange on a platter surrounded with the bananas, whole nuts, and currant jelly. Pour a little sauce over the ducks and serve the rest in a sauceboat.

Serves 6–8.

## Pastel de Mole
### STUFFED PATTY SHELLS

MEXICO

1 can *Mole Poblano* (see note)
3 tablespoons olive oil
¾ cup peeled, seeded, chopped tomatoes
1 teaspoon sugar
2 cups chicken broth
3 cups diced cooked turkey or chicken
12 heated patty shells (baked, frozen, or from pastry shop)

Heat the oil in a saucepan; stir in the Mole and cook, stirring almost constantly for 2 minutes. Add the tomatoes and sugar; cook over low heat 3 minutes. Gradually add the broth, stirring constantly. Cook over low heat 20 minutes. Mix in the chicken and cook 5 minutes longer. Fill the shells and serve hot.
Serves 12.
Note: *Mole Poblano* is available in Mexican, Spanish, or specialty food shops.

## Pato con Azeitunas
### BRAISED DUCK WITH OLIVES

SPAIN

5-pound duck, disjointed
2 teaspoons salt
½ teaspoon freshly ground black pepper
2 slices blanched bacon, diced
¾ cup chopped onions
¼ pound mushrooms, sliced
1 cup sliced green peppers
1 clove garlic, minced
1 cup heated dry red wine
1 bay leaf
2 tablespoons minced parsley
24 small pimento-stuffed green olives

Wash and dry the duck; remove as much fat as possible. Season the duck with the salt and pepper. Fry the bacon in a Dutch oven or casserole. Add the duck and brown on all sides; pour off the fat. Stir in the onions, mushrooms, green peppers, and garlic. Cook until browned. Add the wine, bay leaf, and parsley. Cover, and cook over low heat for 1¼ hours, or until tender. Skim the fat, taste for seasoning, and add the olives. Cook 5 minutes longer.

Serves 4.

## Mole de Guajolote                                      MEXICO
### TURKEY WITH MOLE SAUCE

>  8-pound turkey, cut into serving-sized pieces
>  6 cups water
>  3 teaspoons salt
>  ½ cup olive oil
>  1 slice dry white toast
>  2 tablespoons sesame seeds
>  6 cloves garlic
>  3 green peppers, seeded
>  8 tomatoes
>  ½ cup blanched almonds
>  ¼ teaspoon freshly ground black pepper
>  ½ teaspoon cinnamon
>  2 ounces (squares) unsweetened chocolate, grated
>  2 tablespoons chili powder

Combine the turkey pieces, water, and 2 teaspoons salt in a saucepan. Bring to a boil and cook over medium heat until almost tender, about 1½ hours. Drain well. Reserve 2 cups stock.

Heat ¼ cup olive oil in a skillet; brown the turkey well on all sides. Transfer the turkey to a casserole. Pour the stock over it.

Grind together the toast, sesame seeds, garlic, green peppers, tomatoes, and almonds. Mix in the pepper, cinnamon, chocolate, chili powder, and remaining salt. Heat the remaining oil in the skillet and add the ground mixture; cook over low heat 5 minutes, stirring constantly. Spread over the turkey. Cover and cook over low heat 2 hours, stirring occasionally. Serve hot with boiled rice.

Serves 8.

*Peru al Jerez*     SPAIN
## MARINATED BRAISED TURKEY

    8-pound turkey, disjointed
    3 cloves garlic, minced
    1 tablespoon salt
    ½ teaspoon freshly ground black pepper
    ½ cup wine vinegar
    1 cup dry sherry
    2 cups peeled cubed tomatoes
    2 cups julienne-cut green peppers
    ½ cup chopped parsley
    ¾ cup olive oil
    ½ cup water
    ¼ pound prosciutto or cooked ham, cut julienne

Wash and dry the turkey pieces, then rub with a mixture of the garlic, salt, and pepper. Let stand for 1 hour. In a glass or pottery bowl, mix together the vinegar, sherry, tomatoes, green peppers, parsley, and ½ cup of the oil. Marinate the turkey in the mixture in the refrigerator overnight. Baste and turn turkey frequently.

Remove the turkey from refrigerator 2 hours before cooking time and baste a number of times. Drain and dry the turkey, reserving the marinade. Heat the remaining oil in a Dutch oven or casserole; brown the turkey pieces in it. Add the marinade and water. Bring to a boil, cover, and cook over low heat 1 hour, or until turkey is almost tender. Add the ham; cook uncovered 20 minutes longer. Taste for seasoning.

Serves 6–8.

## Estouffat
### BRAISED BEEF AND BEANS

SPAIN

>4 Spanish (*chorizos*) or other spicy sausage
>4 pounds rump or eye round of beef
>2 tablespoons wine vinegar
>½ cup flour
>¼ pound salt pork, diced
>16 small white onions, peeled
>3 carrots, cut in eighths
>2 cloves garlic, minced
>1½ cups peeled, chopped tomatoes
>2 teaspoons salt
>½ teaspoon freshly ground black pepper
>2 cloves
>2 teaspoons finely chopped bay leaves
>½ teaspoon thyme
>4 cups dry red wine
>2 cups cooked or canned dried white beans
>2 tablespoons minced parsley

Cut the sausages into 1-inch slices. Brown in a skillet; drain and reserve.

Cut the beef into 2-inch cubes, then toss with the vinegar and roll in the flour.

Brown the salt pork in a Dutch oven or casserole; drain off all but 3 tablespoons fat. Add the beef, onions, and carrots; brown lightly. Mix in the garlic, tomatoes, salt, pepper, cloves, bay leaves, thyme, and 2 cups of the wine. Cover, and bake in a 300° oven 3 hours, adding the remaining wine after 2 hours. Add the beans, sausages, and parsley. Taste for seasoning and bake 30 minutes longer.

Serves 8–10.

## Anticuchos
### MEAT SKEWERS

PERU

    3 pounds beef heart or sirloin steak
    1½ teaspoons salt
    ½ teaspoon dried ground chili peppers
    6 peppercorns
    2 teaspoons crushed cumin seeds
    ¼ teaspoon saffron
    3 cloves garlic, minced
    1 cup red wine vinegar
    ¼ cup water
    2 tablespoons olive oil

 Wash and trim the heart, and cut it into 1-inch cubes, or cut the steak into 1-inch cubes. In a bowl, mix together the salt, chili peppers, peppercorns, cumin, saffron, garlic, vinegar, and water. Add the meat and let marinate overnight in the refrigerator.

 Drain the meat; reserve the marinade. Thread the meat on 6 or 8 skewers; brush with olive oil. Broil as close to the heat as possible, 5 minutes, or to desired degree of rareness, turning and basting frequently with the marinade.

 Serves 6–8.


## Carne en Salsa Negra
### BEEF WITH OLIVES

SPAIN

    4 pounds eye round of beef
    ¼ cup olive oil
    1½ cups sliced onions
    2½ teaspoons salt
    ¼ teaspoon freshly ground black pepper
    ⅓ cup lemon juice
    ½ cup currants or seedless raisins
    2 tablespoons brandy
    3 cups water
    4 carrots, quartered
    1 cups sliced black olives
    2 teaspoons capers

Trim the meat of the fat.

Heat the oil in a casserole; brown the meat in it very well. Pour off the fat; add the onions, and let brown. Add the salt, pepper, lemon juice, currants, brandy, and water. Cover, and cook over low heat 2 hours. Add the carrots, olives, and capers; cook 30 minutes longer, or until the meat is tender. Taste for seasoning. Slice the meat, and arrange it on a hot platter, with the carrots around it. Pour some of the gravy over it, and serve the rest in a sauceboat.

Serves 8–10.

## *Cariucho*                                   COLOMBIA
### STEAK WITH PEANUT SAUCE

    4 tablespoons olive oil
    1½ cups chopped onions
    1 cup chopped green peppers
    1½ cups peeled chopped tomatoes
    2 teaspoons salt
    ¼ teaspoon dried ground chili peppers
    1 teaspoon Spanish paprika
    1½ cups ground peanuts
    2 cups chicken broth
    ½ cup heavy cream
    6 shell steaks (Delmonico, club)

Heat the oil in a skillet; sauté the onions and green peppers 5 minutes. Add the tomatoes, salt, chili peppers, and paprika; cook over low heat 5 minutes. Mix in the peanuts and broth; cook 30 minutes. Stir in the cream; taste for seasoning.

Broil the steaks to desired degree of rareness; transfer to a heated platter and pour sauce over them. Serve with boiled potatoes.

Serves 6.

## *Lomo à la Huancaina*   PERU
## STEAK WITH CHILI-CHEESE SAUCE

### Sauce

¼ cup lemon juice
1½ teaspoons salt
1 teaspoon dried ground chili peppers
2 red onions, peeled and sliced thin
¼ pound Münster or mozzarella cheese
¼ pound cream cheese
1 teaspoon turmeric
½ cup heavy cream
2 hard-cooked egg yolks, mashed
⅓ cup olive oil

In a bowl, mix together the lemon juice, 1 teaspoon of the salt, and ½ teaspoon of the chili peppers. Separate the sliced onions into rings, and add to the marinade. Mix well, and let stand 1 hour.

Grate the Münster or mozzarella cheese, and put in the bowl of an electric blender. Break the cream cheese into small pieces, and put it in the blender bowl with the turmeric, cream, egg yolks, and remaining salt and chili peppers. Blend until smooth. If you don't have a blender, mash the cheeses very fine, and beat in the cream and other ingredients with a rotary beater until smooth.

Heat the oil in a skillet; add the cheese sauce, and cook over low heat, stirring frequently, until thickened.

### Steak

6 shell steaks (Delmonico, club)
3 hard-cooked eggs, quartered lengthwise
12 black olives

Broil the steaks to desired degree of doneness. While they're broiling, drain the onion rings. Arrange the steaks on a platter, and pour the sauce over them. Scatter the onion rings on top. Garnish with the quartered eggs and olives.

Serves 6.

SOUTH AMERICA

## *Carne Asado*
## MARINATED ROAST BEEF

    3-rib roast beef
    2 teaspoons salt
    1 teaspoon freshly ground black pepper
    2 cloves garlic, minced
    1½ cups dry red wine
    ½ cup red wine vinegar
    ¼ cup olive oil
    2 cups chopped onions
    1 cup chopped green peppers
    2 cups peeled diced tomatoes
    1 bay leaf

Have the meat boned and tied.

Rub the meat with a mixture of the salt, pepper, and garlic. Mix together the wine and vinegar in a bowl (not metal). Put the meat in it and marinate in the refrigerator 24 hours, turning and basting a few times. Remove from refrigerator 2 hours before roasting.

Drain and dry the meat; reserve the marinade. Heat the oil in a shallow roasting pan over direct heat; brown the meat in it on all sides. Pour off half the fat. Add the onions, green peppers, tomatoes, bay leaf, and half the marinade. Roast the meat in a 350° oven 1¼ hours or to desired degree of rareness, basting frequently and adding the remaining marinade from time to time. Transfer the meat to a hot platter. Discard the bay leaf; skim the fat and purée the gravy in an electric blender, or force through a sieve. If too thick, add a little water. Taste the gravy for seasoning, heat and serve in a sauceboat.

Serves 6–8.

## Feijoada Completa
## MIXED MEATS AND BLACK BEANS

BRAZIL

1 pound dried beef
3-pound smoked tongue
4 cups dried black beans
1 pound raw corned beef
¼ pound salt pork
4 pounds loin of pork
1½ teaspoons salt
½ teaspoon freshly ground black pepper
2 cups orange juice
3 tablespoons olive oil
2 cups chopped onions
2 cloves garlic, minced
½ pound Spanish (*chorizos*) or other spicy sausages, sliced
¼ teaspoon dried ground chili peppers

Soak the dried beef and tongue separately in cold water for 2 hours. Drain. In separate pots, cover the tongue and beef with fresh water and bring to a boil. Cook the beef 15 minutes. Drain and cut in small pieces. Cook the tongue 2½ hours while preparing the other ingredients.

Wash the beans, cover with water and bring to a boil. Cook 2 minutes and remove from the heat; let soak one hour. Drain, add fresh water to cover and bring to a boil; add the dried beef and cook over low heat 2½ hours. While the beans are cooking, prepare the other meats. Combine the corned beef and salt pork in a saucepan. Add water to cover. Bring to a boil; cover, and cook over low heat 2½ hours.

Season the pork with the salt and pepper; roast in a 375° oven 2 hours. When the beans are tender, drain the corned beef and salt pork and add to the beans. Remove 1 cup of the beans and purée them in an electric blender or mash to a paste. Return to the remaining beans with the orange juice. Cook over low heat 1 hour.

Heat the oil in a skillet; sauté the onions and garlic 5 minutes. Add to the beans. Brown the sausages in the skillet; drain. Add to the beans with the chili peppers. Cook 30 minutes. Taste for seasoning. Drain the tongue; trim away the root ends and peel off the skin.

Slice all the meats and arrange on a platter. Put the beans in a deep bowl. Serve with rice, sliced oranges, and pickled onions. Serves 10–12.

*Sobrebarriga* COLOMBIA
ROLLED STUFFED STEAK

    1 flank steak, about 2½ pounds
    ½ pound ground pork
    ½ cup chopped onions
    ¼ cup chopped green peppers
    3 tablespoons minced pimentos
    2 tablespoons cider vinegar
    ¼ teaspoon dry mustard
    1 teaspoon Worcestershire sauce
    3 teaspoons salt
    ¾ teaspoon freshly ground black pepper
    3 tablespoons butter
    8 small white onions
    2 cloves garlic, minced
    1 cup chopped tomatoes
    1 teaspoon crushed cumin seeds
    1 cup boiling water

Have the meat pounded as thin as possible, or do it yourself between two sheets of waxed paper. Mix together the pork, chopped onions, green peppers, pimentos, vinegar, mustard, Worcestershire sauce, 1 teaspoon of the salt, and ¼ teaspoon pepper. Spread over half the meat and roll up like a jelly roll. Tie with string at both ends, and in the middle.

Melt the butter in a Dutch oven or heavy saucepan; brown the meat in it on all sides. Add the white onions and let brown. Mix in the garlic, tomatoes, water, cumin, and remaining salt and pepper. Cover and cook over low heat 2¼ hours, or until tender. Remove the fastenings and slice the steak in rounds. Arrange on a heated platter. Skim the fat from the gravy and pour over the meat.

Serves 4–6.

## Carbonada Criolla
### MEAT AND FRUIT STEW

ARGENTINA-URUGUAY

    3 pounds chuck or rump of beef
    2 tablespoons olive oil
    4 tablespoons butter
    1½ cups diced onions
    ½ cup coarsely chopped green peppers
    1½ cups dry white wine
    1 tablespoon tomato paste
    1 bay leaf
    2 teaspoons salt
    ½ teaspoon freshly ground black pepper
    ½ teaspoon thyme
    2 cups beef broth
    3 cups peeled, cubed sweet potatoes
    3 pears, peeled and cubed
    3 peaches or apples, peeled and sliced
    3 tablespoons currants or seedless raisins
    ½ cup bananas

Optional:

    1 large pumpkin (about 10 pounds)
    ¼ pound (1 stick) butter
    2 tablespoons sugar

    Cut the meat into 1-inch cubes. Heat the oil and butter in a Dutch oven or heavy casserole; brown the beef in it. Remove the meat. Brown the onions and green pepper in the fat remaining in the pan. Stir in the wine, tomato paste, bay leaf, salt, pepper, thyme, and broth; bring to a boil and return the meat. Bring to a boil again, cover, and cook over low heat 1 hour. Add the sweet potatoes; re-cover and cook 20 minutes. Carefully mix in the pears, peaches or apples, and raisins. Cook uncovered 10 minutes longer. Taste for seasoning. Turn into a heated serving dish and sprinkle with the bananas, or, as is customary in Argentina, turn into a pumpkin.
    To prepare pumpkin, wash and scrub it under cold running water. Cut a 3-inch piece off the stem and scrape out the seeds

and fibers. Rub the butter all over the inside, and sprinkle with the sugar. Put the top of the pumpkin back in place, then place the pumpkin in a baking pan. Bake in a preheated 375° oven for 45 minutes. Pour the meat mixture into it, replace the top of the pumpkin, and bake 10 minutes longer. To serve, put the pumpkin on a serving dish and spoon out the mixture.

Serves 6–8, with or without the pumpkin.

## *Puchero Argentino*           ARGENTINA
### ARGENTINE BOILED DINNER

- 3 quarts water
- 3½-pound chicken, disjointed
- 2 pounds short ribs of beef
- ½ pound lean salt pork, sliced
- 3 *chorizos* (Spanish sausages) or other spicy sausage
- 6 whole carrots, peeled
- 3 cloves garlic, minced
- 6 whole onions, peeled
- 6 tomatoes
- 1 small zucchini or yellow squash, peeled and sliced
- 1 green pepper, chopped
- 6 potatoes, peeled
- 6 leeks or green onions
- 1 small cabbage, cut in eighths
- 2 tablespoons chopped parsley
- 2 cups cooked or canned chick-peas, drained

Bring the water to a boil in a large saucepan. Add the chicken, beef, and pork. Cover, and cook over medium heat 1½ hours. Add the sausages and carrots, and cook 30 minutes. Add the garlic, onions, tomatoes, squash, green pepper, potatoes, leeks, cabbage, parsley, and chick-peas. Cook 30 minutes, or until potatoes are tender. Taste for seasoning. (No salt is specified in the recipe because of the salt pork and sausage; you may or may not need to add salt.)

Remove the meats and arrange on a platter. Surround with the vegetables. Serve the soup in deep plates.

Serves 8–10.

# THE LATIN COUNTRIES

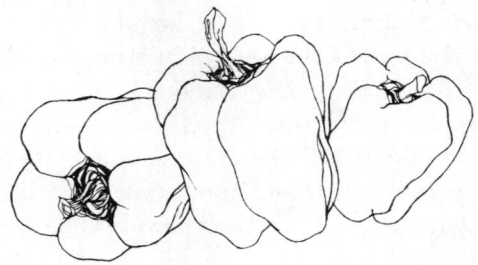

*Sopa Seca*
## PORK AND RICE

SOUTH AMERICA

½ cup olive oil
2½ cups chopped onions
2 pounds boneless pork, cut in ½-inch cubes
2 cloves garlic, minced
2 cups peeled, chopped tomatoes
2 cans chick-peas, drained
¼ teaspoon dried ground chili peppers
3½ teaspoons salt
2 cups raw long-grain rice
1 cup chopped green peppers
3 cups boiling water
1 cup dry white wine
½ teaspoon freshly ground black pepper
½ teaspoon oregano
½ cup seedless raisins
½ cup sliced almonds

Heat half the oil in a large deep skillet; brown half the onions in it. Add the pork and half the garlic. Cook until browned. Add the tomatoes, chick-peas, chili peppers, and 1½ teaspoons of the salt. Cover, and cook over low heat 45 minutes. Prepare the rice meanwhile.

Heat the remaining oil in a saucepan; sauté the rice, green peppers, and remaining onions until browned. Mix in the boiling water, wine, pepper, oregano, and the remaining salt and garlic. Cover, and cook over low heat for 15 minutes. Mix in the raisins and almonds and combine with the chick-pea mixture. Cook 10 minutes longer. Taste for seasoning.

Serves 6–8.

*Lomo de Puerco en Salsa Raja*　　　　　　　　　　　　　MEXICO
## MARINATED LOIN OF PORK WITH PEPPER SAUCE

>8-rib loin of pork
>2 teaspoons ground cumin seeds
>¾ teaspoon freshly ground black pepper
>2½ teaspoons salt
>¼ cup wine vinegar
>¾ cup dry white wine
>3 cloves garlic, minced
>4 Spanish (*chorizos*) or other spicy sausages, sliced
>5 tablespoons olive oil
>1½ cups chopped onions
>1½ cups peeled chopped tomatoes
>1½ cups beef broth
>6 green peppers, seeded and thinly sliced
>2 onions, thinly sliced
>3 tomatoes, cut in wedges

Trim most of the fat from the pork, and rub it with a mixture of the cumin seeds, ½ teaspoon of the pepper, and 2 teaspoons of the salt. In a bowl, mix together the vinegar, wine, and garlic. Put the pork in it, and baste. Cover, and let marinate at room temperature for 4 hours, basting and turning several times.

Brown the sausages, drain, and reserve. Remove the pork from the marinade, and gently pat it dry with paper towels. Heat 3 tablespoons of the oil in a Dutch oven or casserole; brown the pork in it on all sides. Pour off the fat. Add the sausages, chopped onions, chopped tomatoes, broth, and the marinade. Cover, and cook over low heat 2½ hours, or roast in a 350° oven for the same length of time. Baste and turn several times.

Heat the remaining oil in a skillet; sauté the green peppers and sliced onions 10 minutes. Season with the remaining salt and pepper.

When the pork is cooked, transfer it to a hot platter. Skim the fat from the gravy and taste for seasoning. Carve the pork, pour the gravy over it, and spread the peppers and onions on top. Arrange the tomato wedges around it.

Serves 4–6.

## Porco com Amêjoas à Alentejana  PORTUGAL
## PORK AND CLAMS, ALENTEJANA

2 pounds boneless pork
2½ teaspoons salt
½ teaspoon freshly ground black pepper
2 cloves garlic, minced
½ cup dry white wine
1 bay leaf
24 small hard-shelled clams (see note below)
3 tablespoons olive oil
1½ cups chopped onions
⅛ teaspoon crushed dried red peppers
2 tablespoons minced cilantro (fresh coriander, Chinese parsley) or parsley
3 pimentos, cut julienne

Cut the pork into 1-inch cubes. Mix together the salt, pepper, and garlic. Toss the pork cubes in the mixture, then place the cubes in a bowl, and add the wine and bay leaf. Cover, and let stand for 1 hour at room temperature.

Scrub the clams under cold running water, then place the clams in a skillet. Cover and cook over low heat 5 minutes or until the clams open, discarding any whose shells don't open. Discard all the shells, and strain and reserve any remaining pan liquids.

Drain and dry the pork cubes, reserving the marinade. Heat the oil in a deep skillet; add the pork and cook over medium heat until browned on all sides. Add the onions and red pepper; cook 5 minutes, stirring frequently. Add the marinade and cook until it is almost absorbed. Stir in the clams and juice. Cook 3 minutes; don't overcook. Mix in the cilantro or parsley. Serve garnished with the pimentos.

Serves 6–8.

Note: Small whole canned steamed clams may be used, if fresh clams are not available. Merely drain them, remove from the shells, and add at the time the recipe specifies.

## *Picadillo*
## MIXED MEAT HASH

SOUTH AMERICA

½ cup olive oil
1½ cups chopped green peppers
1½ cups chopped onions
2 cloves garlic, minced
1 cup canned tomato sauce
⅛ teaspoon dried ground chili peppers
1½ pounds ground beef
1 pound ground pork
1½ teaspoons salt
½ teaspoon freshly ground black pepper
¼ cup dry white wine
½ cup seedless raisins
1 cup sliced pimento stuffed olives
¼ cup capers, rinsed and drained
½ cup pine nuts or sliced almonds

Heat half the oil in a large skillet; sauté the green peppers, onions, and garlic 5 minutes. Add the tomato sauce and chili peppers; cook over low heat 15 minutes.

Heat the remaining oil in a skillet; add the beef and pork. Cook over medium heat, stirring almost constantly, until browned. Mix in the salt, pepper, wine, and raisins; cover, and cook over low heat 15 minutes, stirring frequently. Stir in the tomato mixture. Cook, uncovered, 10 minutes. Stir in the olives, capers and nuts; cook 5 minutes longer. Serve with rice.

Serves 6–8.

Note: All beef or all pork can be used, if you prefer.

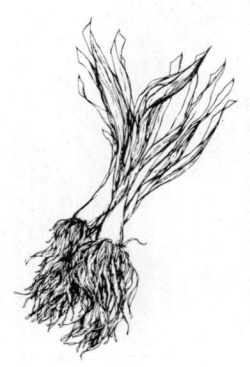

## *Chiles Rellenos con Puerco*
## PORK-STUFFED PEPPERS

MEXICO

    12 medium-sized green peppers
    1½ pounds boneless pork
    1 cup chopped onions
    2 cloves garlic, minced
    1½ teaspoons salt
    ¼ teaspoon freshly ground black pepper
    1 cup water
    ¼ cup pine nuts or slivered almonds
    ¼ cup seedless raisins
    1½ cups flour
    4 eggs
    Vegetable oil for deep-frying

Wash the peppers; cover with water, bring to a boil, and cook over low heat 10 minutes. Drain, cool, and cut the peppers in half lengthwise. Scoop out the seeds and fibre.

Cut the pork into small pieces and combine in a saucepan with the onions, garlic, salt, pepper, and water; bring to a boil and cook over low heat for 30 minutes. Chop or grind the undrained mixture. Mix in the nuts. Soak the raisins in hot water for 10 minutes. Drain, and add to the pork mixture. Taste for seasoning.

Stuff the peppers with the pork mixture and roll in the flour. Separate the eggs; beat the egg whites until stiff, then beat in the egg yolks. Dip the peppers in the eggs, coating them well.

Heat the oil to 365°; fry 2 pepper halves at a time until delicately browned. Drain and keep warm while preparing the balance.

Serves 6–12.

## Pastel de Choclo
### MEAT-CORN PUDDING

CHILE

    2 pounds top sirloin
    ½ cup seedless raisins
    3 tablespoons olive oil
    3 cups chopped onions
    1 tablespoon flour
    ¼ teaspoon dried ground chili peppers
    3 teaspoons salt
    ¼ cup beef broth
    ¾ cup sliced stuffed olives
    2 teaspoons ground cumin seed
    2 tablespoons butter
    2 cups canned corn kernels
    2 egg yolks
    ¼ cup heavy cream

Cut the meat in very small dice.

Soak the raisins in hot water while preparing the meat. Heat the oil in a skillet; add 2½ cups of the onions and sauté 5 minutes. Mix in the meat until browned. Sprinkle with the flour, chili peppers, and 2 teaspoons of the salt. Stir in the broth. Cook over low heat 5 minutes, stirring frequently. Remove from heat and mix in the olives, cumin, and drained raisins. Turn into a 10-inch buttered pie plate.

Melt the butter in the skillet; sauté the remaining onions 5 minutes. Mix in the corn and remaining salt. Cool 5 minutes. Beat the egg yolks and cream; gradually add the corn mixture, stirring well. Pour over the meat and bake in a 350° oven 20 minutes, or until the custard is firm.

Serves 4–6.

## Mollejas al Jerez
### SWEETBREADS IN SHERRY

SPAIN

>3 pair parboiled sweetbreads
>3 tablespoons flour
>6 tablespoons butter
>1 cup chopped onions
>1 teaspoon salt
>⅛ teaspoon white pepper
>1 cup dry sherry
>6 shallots, sliced

Cut the sweetbreads into small cubes, then toss with the flour. Melt the butter in a skillet; lightly brown the sweetbreads. Add the onions, salt, and pepper; sauté 5 minutes. Mix in the sherry; cook over low heat 5 minutes. Stir in the shallots; cook 5 minutes. Taste for seasoning. Serve with green peas and sautéed bread. Serves 3–6.


## Pastelitos de Coco
### COCONUT PASTRIES

SOUTH AMERICA

>2 cups instantized flour
>½ teaspoon salt
>½ teaspoon baking powder
>⅜ pound (1½ sticks) butter
>2 tablespoons orange liqueur
>¼ cup orange juice
>1½ cups flaked coconut
>1 tablespoon cornstarch
>½ cup sugar
>¾ cup light cream
>2 egg yolks
>3 tablespoons melted cooled butter
>1 egg white

Combine the flour, salt, and baking powder in a bowl; cut in the butter with a pastry blender or 2 knives until the consistency of coarse cornmeal. Mix in the liqueur and orange juice until a ball of dough is formed. Chill 1 hour.

Mix together the coconut, cornstarch, sugar, and cream. Cook over low heat, stirring constantly for 5 minutes. Beat the egg yolks and melted butter in a bowl; gradually add the hot mixture, stirring constantly to prevent curdling. Return to saucepan and stir over low heat for 2 minutes. Cool.

On a lightly floured surface, roll out the dough as thin as possible. Cut into 3-inch circles with a cooky cutter. Place a tablespoon of the coconut mixture on half the circles and cover with the remaining circles. Seal the edges with a little water. Arrange on a baking sheet and brush with the egg white. Bake in a preheated 425° oven 15 minutes, or until delicately browned. Cool on a cake rack.

Makes about 2 dozen.

## Torta de Almendras
### ALMOND TORTE

SPAIN

2 cups shelled blanched almonds
1¼ cups (2½ sticks) butter
1¼ cups sugar
1 egg
1½ cups sifted cake flour
1 teaspoon almond extract

Grind the nuts in an electric blender, or put through a mouli grater, or fine blade of a food chopper. (You'll now have more than 2 cups, so measure.)

Cream the butter until soft; beat in the sugar until fluffy. Mix in the egg, then the flour, almond extract, and 2 cups of the ground almonds until smooth. Turn into a buttered 9-inch spring form. Sprinkle with the remaining almonds. Bake in a preheated 325° oven 50 minutes, or until delicately browned and a cake tester comes out clean. Cool thoroughly on a cake rack before removing from pan.

Serves 8–10.

## Torta de Chocolate
## CHOCOLATE TORTE

MEXICO

#### Layers

1½ cups instantized flour
½ cup sifted unsweetened cocoa
½ teaspoon salt
½ pound (2 sticks) sweet butter
⅓ cup sour cream

In a bowl, mix together the flour, cocoa, and salt. Break the butter into small pieces, and cut into the flour mixture with a pastry blender or two knives. With the hand, work in the sour cream until a ball of dough is formed. Form into three balls, wrap, and chill 2 hours.

On a lightly floured surface, roll out each piece into a 10-inch square. Place on a wet baking sheet and bake in a preheated 400° oven on the middle level, for 10 minutes. Loosen from the pan with a spatula carefully, and cool on a cake rack.

#### Filling

1 pound semi-sweet chocolate
¼ cup light cream
5 egg yolks
¼ pound sweet butter, at room temperature
1 teaspoon vanilla extract

Break the chocolate into small pieces, and combine with the cream in the top of a double boiler. Place over hot water until melted, stirring frequently. Beat the egg yolks in a bowl; gradually add a little of the melted chocolate, stirring steadily to prevent curdling, then return to all the chocolate. Beat well for 1 minute. Remove from the heat, and beat in small pieces of butter at a time, then the vanilla. Let stand until cold, beating occasionally.

To assemble, spread the pastry layers with the chocolate, reserving a little for the top, and put together in layers. Be careful when spreading the filling, for the layers are very fragile. Cut small squares, as the torte is very rich.

Serves 10–12.

## Buñuelos
### TINY CRULLERS IN BROWN SUGAR SAUCE

SOUTH AMERICA

> 3 tablespoons butter
> ½ cup sugar
> 1 cup water
> 1 tablespoon grated lemon rind
> ⅞ cup sifted flour
> 3 eggs
> Vegetable oil for deep-frying

In a saucepan put the butter, sugar, and water. Bring to a boil, stirring until the sugar dissolves. Stir in the lemon rind and remove from the heat. Add the flour all at once, and beat very hard. Return to low heat, and cook, stirring constantly, until the dough leaves the sides of the pan and forms a ball. Remove from the heat.

Beat in 1 egg at a time, beating well after each addition. Continue beating until the dough is shiny and smooth.

Heat deep oil to 375°. Drop the dough into it by the teaspoon, being careful not to crowd the pan. Fry about 5 minutes, or until delicately browned, turning them once. Drain on paper towels.

#### SAUCE

> 3 tablespoons flour
> 1 cup packed dark brown sugar
> 1 cup water
> 1 tablespoon butter
> 2 tablespoons heavy cream
> 1 tablespoon rum or brandy

In a saucepan, combine the flour and brown sugar. Gradually stir in the water until smooth. Cook over medium heat stirring constantly to the boiling point, then cook until thick, stirring occasionally. Beat in the butter, cream, and rum. You may serve it hot, or cold, whichever you prefer. Put the crullers in a deep dish, and pour the sauce over them.

Serves 6–8.

*FRANCE*

L*A cuisine française* exists on three separate levels, and possibly even on a fourth plateau. Although the food of France is generally discussed as if it consisted of merely one style, this is really not accurate. There are surely these three categories—*haute cuisine, la cuisine bourgeoise,* and *la cuisine régionale.* The fourth classification, that of international-style French food, may or may not be included, depending upon one's point of view.

To begin with, when French culinary excellence is being discussed, the vast majority of people are thinking in terms of that nation's *haute cuisine.* Unfortunately, this term is not readily translatable into colloquial English, for its literal meaning of high cooking, or high culinary art, doesn't convey the precise meaning. It refers, of course, to the sort of exceptional food found in a handful of great restaurants, typically awarded two or three rosettes by Michelin, that red-faced guide to food, wines, and accommodations in France. Although not completely error free, Michelin at least makes a determined effort to be reliable in its recommendations. The overwhelming number of restaurants proudly flaunting two or three rosettes usually do serve dishes of the *haute cuisine,* although they often also offer dishes from the other two categories listed above. Almost always, except perhaps with the notable exception of a restaurant in the city of Lyons, the actual kitchen preparation is by men, rather than by women—a fact so far overlooked by the Women's Liberation Movement—who may yet charge into kitchens demanding equal rights for their sex. The food served in restaurants of this type is almost always expensive —it has to be in these inflationary times—and the total number of diners served is not great, in relation to the total population of France and its hordes of visitors.

Very roughly speaking, this situation is approximated with respect to *haute couture,* high fashion, another art practiced superbly in France. The leading couturiers, such as Dior, Givenchy, and St. Laurent, represent merely a tiny fraction of all the stylists and dressmakers to be found in that country. Only a very few of the so-called beautiful people, armed with enormous amounts of money and psychologically driven to be included in the descriptions of smart gatherings, are in a position to purchase the actual and original creations of the great designers. The rest of the world, no matter how fashion hungry they may be, must make do with copies, imitations, and the handiwork of less talented dressmakers or manufacturers. The identical situation applies to food classified as *haute cuisine* in France, where a mere handful of restaurants serve these dishes properly, as they were intended by such great and original chefs as Escoffier and Carême; the other restaurants, thousands of them, merely imitate this culinary style as best they can. Often, as in a copied evening gown, the results may be very satisfactory. Not infrequently they may be somewhat less so, for one reason or another. In French homes there are often naturally talented and skilled amateur chefs, men and women, who can prepare certain dishes of top quality most of the time. As a rule, however, they generally lack the necessary practice of having prepared the dish enough times to be able to repeat it flawlessly each and every time.

The second category of French cuisine is generally referred to as *bourgeois* cooking, that is, the food of the middle class. It is the average food of the average family in medium financial circumstances—people who are devoted deeply to fine food, and think of it lovingly, but must give equal regard to the high cost of the finest quality ingredients. Bourgeois cooking is the daily fare of tens of millions of French people, including the small shopkeeper of Nice, the concierge of a Paris apartment house, and the factory worker in Mauberge.

It is tasty, home-style food prepared far better than home-style food anywhere else in the world—on the average—although that of China might be given some consideration. Certainly in the western world, the average French family in modest circumstances eats far better than its counterpart in any other nation. Such fine dishes as *daube* (pot roast), *blanquette de veau* (a veal stew), and *pot-au-feu* (a classic soup with meat) are surely bourgeois food, although many *haute cuisine* restaurants serve them. This sort of home cookery is typically undertaken by women, rather than men. Their training has not been professional, but may have been imparted by their mothers. Quite naturally, as might be anticipated, they vary a great deal in skills and in their ability to re-create a particular dish from one time to another.

The third category of French food, *regional* cookery, is of exceptional interest to the curious and enterprising gastronome. These specialties of the provinces are often remarkable dishes, prepared with considerable care and skill in the various districts of the nation, and often are of astonishing variety and versatility. It should be remembered that France once consisted of some two dozen politically separate areas, dukedoms, and kingdoms, each distrusting the other in a very Gallic fashion. As a result, provincial culinary styles developed, completely independent of those of neighboring areas. Also contributing to this enormous inventiveness and richness was the fact that the country we now call France consists of regions which are different from one another. For example, think of the moist fertile land of sea-girt Brittany in the north, rich with dairy products, and compare it with the aromatic sun-scorched earth of Provence in the south, spicy with garlic, herbs, and olive oil, almost Italian in nature. Indeed, some experts have attempted to divide the cooking of France into categories based upon the type of fat used in cooking—oil, butter, and lard. Some regional dishes have remained purely regional, and may be found in a particular locality of the French provinces, and almost nowhere else. Other dishes have made their way across the nation, and may be encountered almost anywhere in France. For example, *tripes à la mode de Caen*, tripe as prepared in Caen and a specialty of that city, may be found in Paris, or for that matter, in Montpelier. Contrarily, it would be somewhat difficult to locate *petits pois de Cérons*, green peas cooked with pork, except in the Bordeaux region, where it is a specialty.

Lastly, and somewhat problematically, is that rather miscellaneous assortment of dishes classified as international cuisine, consisting mostly of French-based or French-originated dishes, which have almost completely lost their character in the inept hands of partly trained chefs and hotel managers dedicated to pleasing every guest. The menu of a first-class hotel in Bangkok or Rio de Janeiro can almost surely be anticipated in advance before setting foot in the door; there are always such preparations as sautéed veal, string beans with almonds, and the like. The menus are prepared for travelers, usually people of some means and more likely elderly than not, who have reached a stage of their lives in which their doctors have told them to avoid foods with spices, or too much fat, or prepared with cream. You'll almost never find, on international French menus, anything on the order of snails, frogs' legs, or garlic-flavored dishes. Instead, there will be bland preparations that only vaguely resemble their Gallic originals. However, the menu will list them in hotel-style French.

It has been said, with a degree of truth, that it is impossible to be served a poor meal in any restaurant in France. That statement seems removed from actual fact, but meals in France are far better than anywhere else in the world on an overall basis. But why?

Probably it is because the French people, as a nation, are rugged individualists, the last of a vanishing breed of self-centered and opinionated people, in these days of prefabricated thoughts and reactions. They are often very thrifty, and never more annoyed than when money has to be wasted on mediocre food. Americans think it rude to complain about food, whereas Frenchmen habitually lose their tempers and return unsatisfactory dishes to the kitchen. Obviously the French have profited by their actions, and Americans have been the losers. Also, Frenchmen are individualistic and creative, experimenting and producing new dishes constantly. They are inclined to improvise in the kitchen, using considerable imagination, with whatever ingredients are at hand. Furthermore, the French are curious about food and think about it a great deal. If a country receives the politicians it deserves, then equally a nation receives the type of food it deserves. France hasn't had much luck with politicians, but its food is just fine. The nation has also been fortunate in having the soil and climate necessary to produce the world's best wines. Inasmuch as wine tastes best with food, good wines tend to accompany good food, which constitutes a double encouragement. Furthermore, French cheeses are the finest in the world, credit being given partly to nature, and partly to the skill of Frenchmen.

Another important factor is that the people of this country are willing to spend a larger proportion of their national income on food than are the people of any other nation in the world. By placing importance on what is served at a family meal, the French family group has developed a tradition of excellence. It is customary for a family in France to discuss what is being served with appropriate comments, whereas in America, for example, there was a long period of time in which it was thought crude to discuss the meal.

But, after all is said and done, it is the people who create and maintain the standards of cuisine of a country. Although not every Frenchman is a gourmet, more of them regard themselves as fastidious with respect to matters of food than do the people of other countries. A French *routier*, a truck driver, will drive kilometers out of his way to dine at a roadside place noted for its *andouillettes*; his American counterpart will also drive out of his way, but more likely than not because the waitress has blond hair and is buxom.

## Terrine de Foie de Volaille
### CHICKEN LIVER MOUSSE

> 1 pound chicken livers
> ½ pound (2 sticks) butter, at room temperature
> ¼ teaspoon thyme
> 2 tablespoons minced shallots or green onions
> 1¼ teaspoons salt
> ½ teaspoon freshly ground black pepper
> 3 tablespoons Port wine or sweet sherry
> 3 egg whites

Wash the livers; cutting away any discolored spots. Melt 4 tablespoons of the butter in a skillet; add the livers and thyme. Cover over high heat 3 minutes. Add the shallots, salt, and pepper. Cook 3 minutes longer. Select 4 livers and reserve. Purée the remaining livers with the wine in an electric blender, or chop, and then force through a sieve. Beat in remaining butter; taste for seasoning.

Beat the egg whites until stiff but not dry and fold them into the chicken liver mixture. Rub a 1-quart terrine or loaf pan with butter or oil, and spread half the liver mixture in it. Arrange the reserved whole livers on it, then cover with the remaining liver mixture. Cover with plastic wrap and then the cover, if it has one, or foil. Chill for 24 hours. The paté may be sliced, or spooned out.
Serves 6–8.

## Brioche à la Moëlle
### BRIOCHE WITH MARROW AND FOIE GRAS

This is a fairly complicated dish, but well worth the trouble, for it is one of the most sensational first courses I have ever tasted.

> Marrow bones
> 8 brioche
> 8 slices foie gras
> 2 cups Sauce Espagnole (see recipe)
> 2 truffles, minced
> ¾ cup Hollandaise Sauce (see recipe)

Ask the butcher to crack a fairly good quantity of marrow bones —you'll need at least a cup of marrow, but the more, the better. With a sharp knife, push out the marrow. Put it in a bowl, and cover it with cold salted water; let soak (refrigerated) overnight, or for at least 2 hours. Drain the marrow and wrap it in cheesecloth. Lower the marrow into simmering salted water and cook 4 minutes. Drain, and put the marrow on a napkin to dry.

Cut the tops off the brioche, and scoop out the insides. Put a slice of foie gras in each, then divide the marrow among them. Combine the Sauce Espanole with the truffles, then spoon into the brioche. Cover the tops with Hollandaise sauce. Put the brioche on a baking pan, and place in a 400° oven for 10 minutes. Serve hot.

Serves 8.

## *Caviar au Gratin*
## CAVIAR CUSTARD

> ⅔ cup heavy cream
> ⅔ cup fresh white bread crumbs
> 6 eggs
> ¼ cup minced chives or green part of green onion
> 8 ounces black caviar
> 3 tablespoons butter

Heat the cream until bubbles begin forming around the edges, then pour it over the bread crumbs and let stand 5 minutes. Mash smooth. Beat the eggs, and then beat them into the bread-crumb mixture. Stir in the chives and caviar.

You can bake the custard in 6 individual buttered custard cups, or in one 1½-quart buttered soufflé dish or baking dish. Bake in a preheated 325° oven 15 minutes for the individual ones, or 25 minutes for the large one, or until a knife inserted in the center comes out clean.

Serves 6.

Note: The better the quality of the caviar, the better the custard, but the inexpensive Danish Caviar may be used as a substitute for the more expensive varieties.

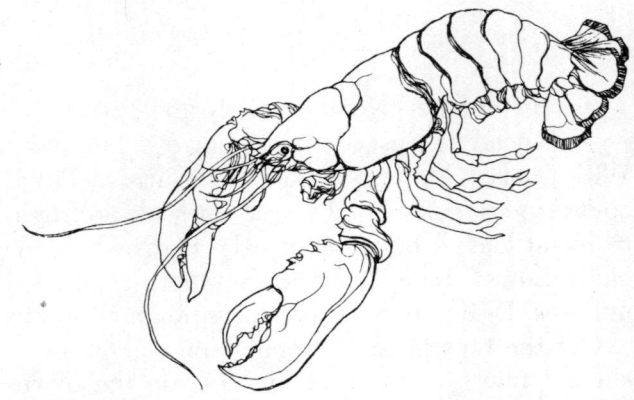

## Croustade de Langouste Bonne Auberge
## LOBSTER IN PUFF PASTRY

### Pastry

½ pound (2 sticks) sweet butter
2 cups instantized flour
½ teaspoon salt
½ cup ice water

Place the butter in a bowl of very cold water. Knead it very well until smooth. Wrap in a clean towel and press out all the water.

Put the flour and salt in a bowl. Add 3 tablespoons of the butter, working it into the flour with the fingers. Add the ½ cup ice water gradually, mixing lightly with the fingers until a dough is formed.

On a lightly floured surface, roll out the dough into a ¼ inch thick rectangle. Form the remaining butter into a smaller rectangle, ½ inch thick. Place in the center of the dough. Fold one side over the butter and then the other side, pressing all sides down carefully. Chill 20 minutes.

Place the dough, with the open edge facing you, on a lightly floured surface. Roll as thin as possible into a rectangle. Fold one side toward the center, and cover with other side. Roll again in the same manner, fold again, and chill 20 minutes. Repeat entire process 3 more times. Roll out the dough ¼ inch thick. Cut into twelve 4-by-6-inch rectangles. Place 6 on a baking sheet. Brush the tops lightly with water. Place remaining 6 rectangles over them, pressing down very lightly.

Bake in a preheated 450° oven 5 minutes. Reduce heat to 350° and bake 25 minutes longer, or until delicately browned and dry to the touch.

### Lobster Filling

2 cups water
1 cup dry white wine
2½ teaspoons salt
1 stalk celery
1 carrot
1 bay leaf
3 peppercorns
2 1½-pound lobsters, split or 4 African lobster tails
6 tablespoons butter
5 tablespoons flour
2 cups heavy cream
½ teaspoon white pepper
2 truffles, sliced thin (optional)
¼ pound mushrooms, sliced

In a saucepan combine the water, wine, 1 teaspoon of the salt, the celery, carrot, bay leaf, and peppercorns. Bring to a boil. Add the lobsters and cook over medium heat 15 minutes. Remove lobsters, reserving ½ cup of the stock. Cool 15 minutes. Carefully remove the meat from the shells and cut into cubes.

Melt 4 tablespoons of the butter in a saucepan. Add the flour, stirring until smooth. Gradually add the cream, stirring constantly, to the boiling point. Add the pepper, remaining salt, and reserved stock. Cook over low heat 5 minutes. Add the truffles. Cook 2 minutes.

Melt the remaining butter in a skillet. Sauté the mushrooms in it 5 minutes. Add to sauce with the lobster meat. Cook 2 minutes. Taste for seasoning. Pour over the hot pastries and serve immediately.

Serves 6.

Note: If you don't want to make the pastry, buy frozen patty shells, bake according to the directions, and fill with the lobster mixture.

## Gratin de Crevettes
## SHRIMP RAMEKINS

2 pounds raw shrimp
3 cups water
1 cup dry white wine
2 carrots, sliced
1 onion, sliced
1 bay leaf
⅛ teaspoon thyme
4 peppercorns
3 sprigs parsley
1 clove garlic
2 teaspoons salt
6 tablespoons butter
½ pound mushrooms, chopped
2 tablespoons flour
½ cup heavy cream
2 tablespoons cognac
3 egg yolks
Cayenne pepper
¼ cup fine dry bread crumbs
¼ cup grated Swiss cheese

Shell, devein and wash the shrimp; reserve the shells.

Combine the shells, water, wine, carrots, onion, bay leaf, thyme, peppercorns, parsley, garlic, and 1 teaspoon of the salt in a saucepan. Bring to a boil and cook over low heat 20 minutes. Strain into another saucepan; add the shrimp and cook 4 minutes. Remove the shrimp; and cook the stock until reduced to 2 cups.

Melt 2 tablespoons of the butter in a skillet; sauté the mushrooms 5 minutes; season with ½ teaspoon of the salt. Melt the remaining butter in a saucepan; blend in the flour, then very gradually add the stock, stirring steadily to the boiling point. Stir in the cream and cognac; cook over low heat 5 minutes longer. Beat the egg yolks in a bowl, and very gradually add the hot sauce, stirring steadily to prevent curdling. Return to the saucepan, and cook, stirring steadily until thickened. Add Cayenne pepper, and salt, to taste.

You may prepare the gratin in one large baking dish, or individual ones. In either case, spread the mushrooms on the bottom, arrange the shrimp over them, and cover with the sauce. Mix the bread crumbs with the cheese, and sprinkle on top. Place on the upper level of a preheated 450° oven for 5 minutes or until delicately browned, and bubbly hot.

Serves 6.

## Mousseline de Poisson
### FISH MOUSSE

1½ pounds salmon or halibut
½ cup water
½ cup dry white wine
1 onion
1 stalk celery
1 bay leaf
2 teaspoons salt
¼ teaspoon white pepper
½ pound (2 sticks) sweet butter
4 tablespoons flour
1¼ cups light cream
2 tablespoons dry sherry
4 tablespoons heavy cream

Combine the fish, water, wine, vegetables, bay leaf, salt, and pepper in a deep skillet. Bring to a boil and cook over low heat 20 minutes. Let fish cool in the stock. Drain. Remove the skin and bones and flake the fish.

Melt 4 tablespoons butter in a saucepan; blend in the flour. Gradually add the light cream, stirring to the boiling point, then cook over low heat 5 minutes. Cool. Cream the remaining butter until fluffy. Beat in the fish until smooth. Add the sherry, heavy cream, and cooled white sauce. Beat until smooth and light. Taste for seasoning. Turn into a buttered 1-quart fish or other mold and chill 5 hours or until firm.

Serves 6.

## Crevettes à l'Américaine
## SHRIMP IN SPICY TOMATO SAUCE

3 pounds raw shrimp, shelled and deveined
¼ cup olive oil
1½ teaspoons salt
½ teaspoon freshly ground black pepper
3 tablespoons butter
½ cup chopped onions
1 carrot, grated
¼ cup cognac, warmed
1 cup peeled chopped tomatoes
1 clove garlic, minced
½ teaspoon thyme
¾ cup dry white wine
1 bay leaf

Wash and dry the shrimp.

Heat the oil in a skillet; add the shrimp, salt and pepper, and cook over medium heat 2 minutes.

Melt the butter in a heavy casserole. Sauté the onions and carrot 5 minutes. Add the shrimp. Heat the cognac in a ladle; set it aflame and pour over the shrimp. When flames die, mix in the tomatoes, garlic, thyme, wine, and bay leaf. Cover tightly and cook over low heat 10 minutes. Taste for seasoning.

Serves 8–10.


## Croûtes aux Champignons
## MUSHROOMS ON TOAST

1 pound mushrooms
4 slices white bread
¼ pound (1 stick) butter
¼ cup minced green onions
1 teaspoon salt
¼ teaspoon freshly ground black pepper
6 tablespoons sour cream
¼ cup grated Swiss cheese

Select 4 large mushroom caps, and reserve them. Chop the remaining mushrooms. Trim the crusts off the bread. Melt half the butter in a skillet; brown the bread in it, remove, and keep warm.

Melt 2 tablespoons of the butter in the skillet; sauté the mushroom caps 3 minutes. Remove. Melt the remaining butter in the skillet. Add the chopped mushrooms and green onions; cook 3 minutes. Mix in the salt, pepper, and sour cream. Taste for seasoning, and heat, but do not let boil.

Arrange the bread slices in a baking dish, and spread the mushroom mixture on each. Top with a mushroom cap, and sprinkle with cheese. Bake on the upper level of a preheated 400° oven 5 minutes, or until the cheese melts. Serve hot.

Serves 4.

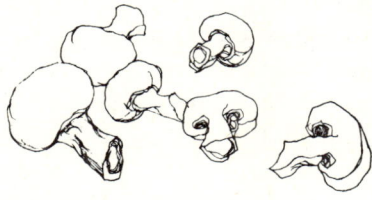

*Soupe à l'Oignon Gratinée*
## ONION SOUP WITH CHEESE CRUSTS

> 3 tablespoons butter
> 3 cups diced onions
> 2 tablespoons flour
> 6 cups beef broth
> ¼ teaspoon freshly ground black pepper
> Slices of French bread, lightly toasted
> 1 cup grated Gruyère or Swiss cheese

Melt the butter in a saucepan; sauté the onions over low heat until browned and soft. Blend in the flour. Gradually add the broth, stirring steadily, then the pepper. Cook over low heat 30 minutes. Taste for seasoning.

Use 6–8 pottery ovenproof marmites or bowls, and place a slice of bread in each; sprinkle each slice with cheese. Pour the soup around the bread. Set under a hot broiler until cheese melts. Serve with grated Parmesan cheese, if desired.

Serves 6–8.

## Le Fond Blanc
## CHICKEN BROTH

Chicken broth might appear to be too simple to include in French recipes, but it is an ingredient needed for other recipes, and should be made properly, which is the reason for its being given. Canned chicken broth is an adequate, but not perfect, substitute. If canned broth is used, reduce the salt specified in a recipe, and taste before serving—then, and only then, add more salt if needed.

> 4-pound fowl, plus additional back and necks, if possible
> 3 quarts water
> 1 clove
> 2 onions
> 2 carrots, sliced
> 1 parsnip, sliced
> 3 celery stalks and leaves, sliced
> 3 leeks or 6 green onions, sliced
> 2 teaspoons salt

Wash the chicken and parts, if used. Split the chicken in half, combine in a large pot or kettle with the water. Bring to a boil and skim the fat. Stick the clove in an onion, and add with all the vegetables and the salt. Bring to a boil again, cover loosely and cook over low heat 3 hours. Remove the chicken and use in other dishes. Strain the broth and remove the fat.

## BEEF BROTH

Substitute 2 pounds stewing beef and 2 pounds cracked beef bones for the chicken.

## *Pot-au-Feu*
## BEEF SOUP

>2 pounds rump or chuck of beef
>1 pound oxtail, cut into 2-inch pieces
>1 marrow bone, cracked
>2 onions
>2 cloves
>4 quarts water
>1 tablespoon salt
>3 carrots, sliced
>6 leeks, sliced
>2 whole cloves garlic
>2 stalks celery, sliced
>1 turnip, diced
>3 peppercorns
>1 bay leaf
>½ teaspoon thyme
>2 tablespoons minced parsley
>1 2-pound head cabbage
>2 tablespoons butter
>Dried French bread slices

Wash the meat and bone. Put one unpeeled onion in a hot oven until the onion skin turns dark, and use it for the soup, still unpeeled. Peel the other onion and stick the cloves in it.

In a deep saucepan or kettle, combine the beef, oxtail, bone, and water. Bring to a boil, skim the top, add the onions and salt; cook over low heat 2 hours. Add the carrots, leeks, garlic, celery, turnip, peppercorns, bay leaf, thyme, and parsley. Cook 1 hour. Skim the fat.

Cut the cabbage in eighths and sauté in the butter for 5 minutes. Add to the soup. Cook 30 minutes longer. Strain and skim the fat; taste for seasoning. Return the cabbage to the soup.

Serve the soup from a tureen—the meat may be sliced and placed in it, or put on a separate platter. Place a slice of dried bread in each soup plate and pour the soup and vegetables over it. Parmesan cheese may be sprinkled on top.

Serves 6–8.

*Potage Crème à la Nivernaise*
## CREAM OF CARROT SOUP

> 6 tablespoons butter
> 8 carrots, peeled and thinly sliced
> 1 teaspoon sugar
> 1 teaspoon salt
> ½ cup water
> 2 tablespoons flour
> ¼ teaspoon freshly ground white pepper
> 3 cups chicken broth
> 2½ cups milk
> ½ cup heavy cream
> 2 egg yolks, beaten

Melt 3 tablespoons of the butter in a heavy saucepan; add the carrots, sugar, ½ teaspoon salt, and the water. Cover, and cook over low heat for 20 minutes. Dice a few slices, and set aside for garnish.

Melt the remaining butter in a saucepan and blend in flour, pepper, and the remaining ½ teaspoon salt. Gradually add the broth and milk, stirring to the boiling point; then cook 5 minutes, stirring occasionally. Add the sliced carrots, and cook over low heat 45 minutes. Purée the soup in an electric blender or force through a fine sieve.

Mix the cream with the egg yolks, and very gradually add some of the hot soup, stirring steadily to prevent curdling. Return to the balance of the soup with the diced carrots, and heat, but do not let boil.

Serves 6–8.

## *Soupe au Pistou*
## VEGETABLE-HERB SOUP

½ cup olive oil
1½ cups chopped onions
8 cups water
1 bay leaf
1 pound green beans, cut into 1-inch lengths
3 potatoes, peeled and cubed
3 tomatoes, peeled and cubed
¼ pound vermicelli, broken in half
1½ teaspoons salt
¼ teaspoon freshly ground black pepper
2 tablespoons fresh basil or 1 teaspoon dried
2 tablespoons fresh tarragon or 1 teaspoon dried
3 cloves garlic, minced
1 tablespoon tomato paste
Grated Parmesan cheese

Heat half of the olive oil in a large saucepan. Sauté the onions 15 minutes, stirring frequently. Add the water, bay leaf, beans, potatoes, and tomatoes. Cook over medium heat 15 minutes. Add the vermicelli, salt and pepper. Cook over low heat 15 minutes. Discard the bay leaf.

If dried herbs are used, soak them in lukewarm water for 10 minutes. Drain. Pound the garlic into a paste. Add the herbs and pound until very smooth. Mix in the tomato paste, then gradually add the remaining oil, mixing steadily. Serve the soup with a tablespoon of the herb mixture in each plate. Serve the grated cheese separately.

Serves 8–10.

## Bisque de Homard
### LOBSTER BISQUE

    2 1½-pound live lobsters
    6 tablespoons butter
    ¼ cup chopped onions
    ¼ cup grated carrots
    ¼ cup cognac
    1 cup dry white wine
    1 tablespoon tomato sauce
    5 cups fish stock or bottled clam juice
    ¼ teaspoon thyme
    4 tablespoons flour
    ½ teaspoon salt
    Dash cayenne pepper
    1½ cups heavy cream

Have the live lobsters cut into 4 sections and the claws cracked. Melt 3 tablespoons butter in a saucepan; sauté the onions and carrots 5 minutes. Remove from the pan. Add the lobster; sauté 5 minutes, or until lobster turns red. Warm the cognac, pour over the lobster and set aflame. When flames die, return the vegetables. Stir in the wine, tomato sauce, 1 cup fish stock, and the thyme. Cover and cook over low heat 15 minutes. Remove lobster; reserve the sauce. Scoop out the lobster meat and chop coarsely. Break up the lobster shells and pulverize in an electric blender with 2 tablespoons sauce or put through a food chopper.

Melt the remaining butter in a saucepan; blend in the flour. Gradually add the remaining fish stock; stirring steadily to the boiling point. Add the salt, cayenne, reserved sauce, and pulverized shells. Cover and cook over low heat 1 hour. Strain. Stir in the cream and lobster meat. Heat, taste for seasoning, and serve.

    Serves 6–8.

## Crème St. Jacques
### CREAM OF SCALLOP SOUP

> 4 cups water
> 1 cup clam juice
> 1 cup dry white wine
> 1 pound potatoes, peeled and quartered
> 1 cup chopped onions
> ⅛ teaspoon minced garlic
> 1 small bay leaf
> ¼ teaspoon thyme
> 1¼ teaspoons salt
> ¼ teaspoon freshly ground white pepper
> 1 pound scallops, coarsely chopped
> 2 egg yolks
> ½ cup heavy cream

Bring the water, clam juice, and wine to a boil; add the potatoes, onions, garlic, bay leaf, thyme, salt, and pepper. Cook over low heat 45 minutes. Add the scallops and cook 5 minutes longer. Remove about ¼ cup of the scallops and reserve.

Discard the bay leaf; purée the soup in an electric blender or force through a food mill.

Beat together the egg yolks and cream; gradually add about 1 cup of the soup, stirring steadily to prevent curdling. Return to the saucepan. Taste for seasoning; heat but do not boil. Serve garnished with the reserved scallops.

Serves 8.

## Velouté Aurore
## CREAM OF TOMATO AND AVOCADO SOUP

> 3 tablespoons butter
> 1 cup minced onions
> ½ teaspoon minced garlic
> 4 cups chicken broth
> 2 cups peeled, seeded, chopped tomatoes
> Salt
> Cayenne pepper
> 1 avocado
> 2 egg yolks
> ¼ cup heavy cream

Heat the butter in a saucepan; add the onions and garlic. Cook over low heat, stirring frequently until soft and yellow, but not brown. Add the broth and tomatoes; bring to a boil, and cook over low heat 20 minutes. Season to taste with salt and cayenne pepper, then cook 10 minutes longer. Purée the soup in an electric blender, or force through a sieve.

While the soup is cooking, peel the avocado, and mash very smooth. Beat the egg yolks and cream together, then stir into the avocado. Very gradually add some of the hot soup, stirring steadily, then return to all the soup. Taste for seasoning again, and heat, stirring constantly, but do not let boil.

Serves 4–6.


## Sauce Hollandaise
## HOLLANDAISE SAUCE

> ¼ pound (1 stick) sweet butter
> 4 egg yolks
> 1 tablespoon lemon juice
> ⅛ teaspoon salt
> 2 tablespoons heavy cream

Divide the butter in 3 pieces. In the top of a double boiler, beat the egg yolks and lemon juice with a wooden spoon. Add one piece of butter, place over hot water and cook, stirring constantly until butter melts. (Never let the water boil; add a little cold water to keep it under the boiling point, if necessary.) Add the second piece of butter, still mixing steadily, until melted and absorbed, then add the third piece. When thickened, remove from heat and stir in the salt and cream.

Makes about 1¼ cups.

For blender Hollandaise, melt the butter. Put the yolks, lemon juice, and salt in the blender bowl, and turn it on for a few seconds. With the motor still on, add the melted butter in a slow, steady stream. When all the butter is added, pour in the cream. If the sauce is not to be used immediately, turn it into a small bowl, and place over hot water.

*Sauce Espagnole*
BROWN SAUCE

> ½ cup beef fat
> 1 carrot, sliced
> 1½ cups diced onions
> ⅓ cup flour
> 2 quarts beef broth
> 1 bay leaf
> 2 sprigs parsley
> ¼ teaspoon thyme
> 3 tablespoons canned tomato sauce

Melt the fat in a heavy saucepan; sauté the carrot and onions until browned. Sprinkle with the flour and stir until dark brown, but be careful not to burn it. Slowly add the broth, stirring constantly to the boiling point. Add the bay leaf, parsley, and thyme; cook over low heat 2 hours. Mix in the tomato sauce and cook 1 hour longer. Strain and season to taste. Use as a base for sauces.

Makes about 5 cups.

## Moules à la Crème
### MUSSELS IN WINE-CREAM SAUCE

This is a creamy version of Moules Marinières, from Normandy.

60 mussels
1½ cups dry white wine
3 tablespoons minced shallots or green onions
¼ teaspoon freshly ground black pepper
2 sprigs parsley
1 egg yolk
½ cup heavy cream
2 tablespoons flour
3 tablespoons butter

Wash the mussels, and scrub each one with a brush, until shells are clean. Discard any whose shells are slightly open, or broken. Snip off the beards, that is, the fuzzy part that clings to the shells. Keep the mussels in cold water until needed, at all times, and be sure they are free of sand before cooking. If they are not, continue washing them under cold running water until the water runs clear.

Use a large kettle, and into it put the mussels, wine, shallots, pepper, and parsley. Cover and cook over high heat until the shells open, then reduce the heat as low as possible, and cook 5 minutes. Be sure to discard any whose shells do not open. Remove the mussels, and keep warm.

Strain the pan juices into a saucepan through several layers of cheesecloth, or a very fine sieve. Cook over high heat for 3 minutes. Mix together the egg yolk, cream, and flour; add a little of the hot liquid, stirring steadily to prevent curdling, then return it to the saucepan. Cook, stirring steadily to the boiling point. Remove from the heat, and blend in the butter. Strain over the mussels.

Serves 4–6.

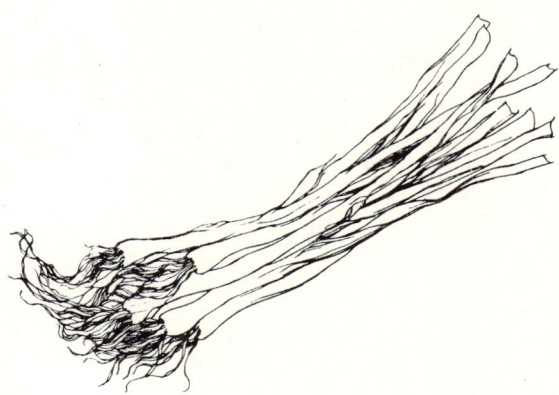

*Poisson Carcassonne*
## FISH IN NUT SAUCE

    4 pounds salmon or halibut steaks, cut ¾ inch thick
    2 teaspoons salt
    ½ teaspoon white pepper
    4 tablespoons butter
    1 cup finely chopped onions
    ½ cup chopped celery
    1 bay leaf
    3 sprigs parsley
    ¾ cup dry white wine
    ¾ cup water
    1 cup finely chopped almonds or walnuts

Cut the fish into six serving-sized pieces. Season with the salt and pepper. Melt 1 tablespoon butter in a skillet; sauté the onions 5 minutes. Arrange the fish in the skillet and add the celery, bay leaf, parsley, wine, and water. Bring to a boil, cover loosely, and cook over low heat 20 minutes or until fish flakes easily when tested with a fork. Transfer the fish to a serving dish and strain the stock.

Melt the remaining butter in a skillet; stir in the nuts. Cook over low heat, stirring steadily until browned. Blend in the reserved stock; bring to a boil, taste for seasoning, and pour over the fish.

Serves 6–8.

## Darne de Saumon à la Montpellier
### SALMON IN GREEN BUTTER

#### Fish

3 pounds salmon, in one piece
2 cups water
1 cup dry white wine
1 onion, sliced
½ carrot, sliced
3 whole peppercorns, crushed
1½ teaspoons salt
Bouquet garni (bay leaf, 1 sprig parsley, 1 sprig thyme, celery stalk with leaves, tied together)

Buy a center cut of salmon. Rinse and dry it, then wrap it in cheesecloth, to help retain its shape.

Combine the water, wine, onion, carrot, peppercorns, salt, and bouquet garni in a deep saucepan. Bring to a boil, reduce heat, and simmer 20 minutes. Cool 10 minutes. Lower the salmon into the court bouillon. Simmer over low heat 30 minutes or until fish flakes easily when tested with a fork. Cool in the liquid, then remove carefully, and skin. Pat dry, and chill.

#### Green Butter

1 quart water
1 bunch watercress
4 sprigs parsley
5 lettuce leaves
Handful of spinach leaves
Leaves from 1 stalk celery
1 small dill pickle, finely chopped
12 capers, finely chopped
4 anchovy fillets, finely chopped
1 teaspoon dried tarragon leaves
1 teaspoon dried basil leaves
½ teaspoon Dijon-style mustard
1 clove garlic, finely chopped
Salt
Freshly ground white pepper
½ pound (2 sticks) sweet butter

Bring the water to a boil in a saucepan; add the washed watercress, parsley, lettuce, spinach, and celery leaves. Cover pan tightly and allow greens to stand 3 minutes. Drain well. Place greens in a towel and squeeze out any water. Purée the greens in an electric blender, or chop and force through a fine sieve.

Chop the pickle, capers, anchovy fillets, tarragon, basil, mustard, garlic, and salt and pepper to taste, until very smooth. Cream the butter until very light and fluffy and add the puréed mixture; mix until well blended.

Spread on the top and sides of the salmon. Put the salmon on a platter, and surround with watercress or parsley. Chill for 30 minutes.

Serves 6–8.

*Maquereaux aux oignons*
## MACKEREL IN ONION SAUCE

4 fillets of mackerel
¾ cup flour
2 teaspoons salt
½ teaspoon freshly ground black pepper
4 tablespoons butter
2 cups thinly sliced onions
¼ cup water
1 tablespoon minced parsley
2 tablespoons capers
2 tablespoons chopped pimentos

Cut the fillets in half crosswise and dip each piece in a mixture of the flour, salt, and pepper.

Melt the butter in a skillet; sauté the onions until browned. Arrange the fish over the onions and cook 10 minutes on each side. Add the water; cover, and cook over low heat 5 minutes. Sprinkle with the parsley, capers, and pimentos. Cook 1 minute.

Serves 4.

*Poisson en Papillote*
## BAKED FISH IN PAPERS

    12 shucked oysters
    6 fillets of pompano, sole, or whitefish
    3 teaspoons salt
    ¾ teaspoon freshly ground black pepper
    4 tablespoons olive oil
    6 tablespoons butter
    ½ pound mushrooms, chopped
    ½ cup chopped onions
    ½ pound shrimp, cooked, cleaned, and chopped
    ⅓ cup dry white wine
    ¼ teaspoon anchovy paste
    1 tablespoon lemon juice
    1 tablespoon minced parsley
    2 egg yolks, beaten
    2 tablespoons minced truffles (optional)

Cover the oysters with water, bring to a boil, drain, and chop. Wash and dry the fish; season with half the salt and pepper. Heat the oil in a skillet; lightly brown the fish in it. Cut 4 pieces of parchment paper or aluminum foil large enough to cover the fillets and place one fillet on each. Or use the new Brown-in-Bags, in which case assemble the fillets on a flat surface, then slip them into the bag.

Melt the butter in the skillet; sauté the mushrooms and onions 5 minutes. Remove from the heat and stir in the oysters, shrimp,

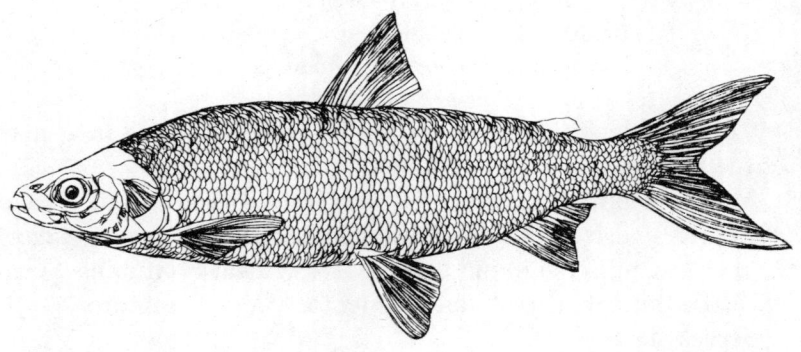

wine, anchovy paste, lemon juice, parsley, then very gradually the egg yolks. Return to very low heat and cook, stirring constantly, until thickened, but do not let boil. Add the truffles, if used, and the remaining salt and pepper. Spread the sauce over the fillets and fold the paper or foil like an envelope, or fold over the edges of the bags, sealing the edges. Arrange on a baking sheet; bake in a 375° oven 15 minutes. Put an envelope on a plate, slit the edges, and serve in the wrapping.

Serves 6.


*Alose à la Provençale*
## SHAD PROVENCALE

    4 fillets of shad (or bluefish or mackerel)
    2½ teaspoons salt
    ½ teaspoon freshly ground black pepper
    2 pounds sorrel (use spinach, if not available)
    3 tablespoons olive oil
    1 cup chopped onions
    1½ cups peeled chopped tomatoes
    2 cloves garlic, minced
    3 tablespoons dry bread crumbs
    3 tablespoons butter

Rinse and dry the fish; sprinkle with 1½ teaspoons of the salt, and ¼ teaspoon of the pepper and let stand while preparing the sorrel.

Wash the sorrel or spinach, drain well and shred. If frozen spinach is used, drain it thoroughly. Heat the oil in a skillet; sauté the onions 5 minutes. Mix in the sorrel or spinach, tomatoes, garlic, and remaining salt and pepper. Cook over low heat 10 minutes. Stir in the bread crumbs and taste for seasoning.

Melt the butter in a skillet; brown the fish in it on both sides. Spread half the vegetable mixture on the bottom of a buttered baking dish. Arrange the fish over it and cover with the remaining vegetable mixture. Bake in a 325° oven 45 minutes.

Serves 4–8.

## Quenelles de Brochet
## FISH MOUSSE BALLS

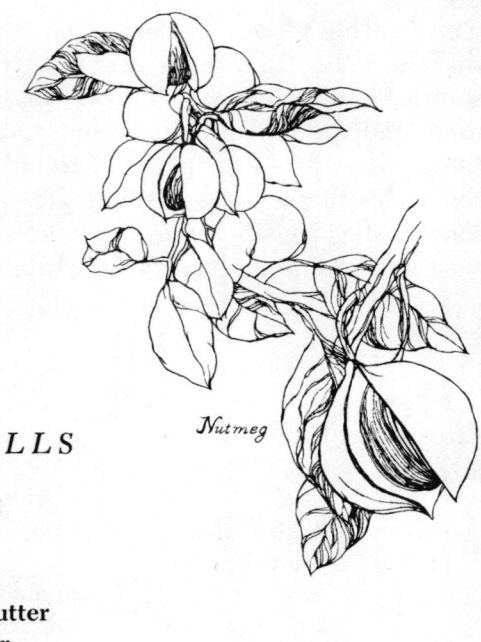

### Pastry Cream

1 cup water
1 teaspoon salt
4 tablespoons butter
1 cup sifted flour
2 eggs

Bring the water, salt, and butter to a boil, and stir until the butter melts. Remove saucepan from the heat, and with a wooden spoon, beat in the flour all at once. Return to low heat and cook, beating steadily until mixture forms a ball and leaves the sides of the pan. Remove from the heat and beat in 1 egg at a time, continuing to beat until smooth and glossy. Transfer to a mixing bowl.

### Fish Mixture

1½ pounds boneless pike (or halibut)
1¼ teaspoons salt
½ teaspoon white pepper
⅛ teaspoon nutmeg
¼ cup heavy cream
3 cups fish stock, or boiling salted water

Grind the fish three times in a meat chopper, or purée in an electric blender. Add to the pastry cream with the salt, pepper, and nutmeg. Beat with an electric mixer or wooden spoon until very smooth and light. Taste for seasoning. Chill 2 hours. Beat in the cream very gradually.

Bring the fish stock to a boil in a large skillet, then reduce heat to low. Use two wet round soup spoons to shape the *quenelles*. Pick up a spoonful of the mixture and smooth the top with the other spoon. Carefully drop it into the skillet. Dip the spoons in cold water and work quickly to shape remaining *quenelles*. Don't crowd skillet as the *quenelles* double in size when cooking. Cook over low heat 20 minutes. Remove with a slotted spoon and drain well on a napkin or kitchen towel.

SAUCE

½ cup cooked shrimp or lobster
2 tablespoons butter
2 tablespoons flour
1 cup hot fish stock or clam juice
¼ cup heavy cream

Chop half the shrimp to a paste, or purée in an electric blender. Coarsely chop the remaining shrimp.

Melt the butter in a saucepan; blend in the flour, then remove from the heat. Beat in the fish stock with a wire whisk until smooth. Return to the heat and cook, stirring steadily, until the boiling point, then cook over low heat 5 minutes longer.

Stir in the cream and all the shrimp. Taste for seasoning. Cook 5 minutes, but do not let boil.

Arrange the *quenelles* on a heated serving dish or individual plates, and pour the sauce over them.

Serves 6–8.

## Truite Poêle
### POACHED STUFFED TROUT

4 brook trout
2 cups water
1 cup dry white wine
1 cup sliced onions
1 carrot, sliced
1 bay leaf
¼ teaspoon thyme
3 teaspoons salt
½ teaspoon freshly ground white pepper
1½ cups fresh bread crumbs
1 cup heavy cream
¼ pound mushrooms, sautéed and chopped
¼ cup chopped green onions
2 tablespoons minced parsley
3 tablespoons butter
4 slices lemon

Have the trout split and the bones and heads removed. Combine the heads, bones, water, wine, onion, carrot, bay leaf, thyme, 2 teaspoons of the salt, and ¼ teaspoon of the pepper in a saucepan. Bring to a boil and cook over low heat 30 minutes. Strain and reserve.

Moisten the bread crumbs with ½ cup of the cream and mash smooth; mix in the mushrooms, green onions, parsley, and remaining salt and pepper. Stuff the fish with this mixture and close the openings with toothpicks or sew up. Melt the butter in a skillet and add the stock; arrange the fish in it. Cover loosely. Cook over low heat 25 minutes or until fish flakes easily when tested with a fork. Transfer fish to a hot serving platter. Cook the stock over high heat 5 minutes, then mix in the remaining cream. Garnish each trout with a lemon slice and pour the sauce over the fish. Serves 4.

Note: If frozen eviscerated trout are used, and there are no heads or bones, use 2 cups bottled clam juice in place of the water for making the stock, and don't use any salt in the stock.

## La Pochouse Bourguignonne
## MIXED FISH CHOWDER

> 4 pounds assorted freshwater fish (pike, whitefish, trout, and eel)
> 2 teaspoons salt
> ½ teaspoon freshly ground black pepper
> 2 strips bacon
> ¼ pound (1 stick) butter
> 2 cloves garlic, minced
> 2 quarts dry white wine
> 4 sprigs parsley ⎫
> 2 bay leaves     ⎬ tied together
> 2 stalks celery  ⎭
> ½ teaspoon thyme
> 4 tablespoons flour
> 1 teaspoon meat extract
> ½ cup cognac

The more types of fish you have, the more authentic the dish will be, so try to buy as many varieties as you can. The fish should weigh 4 pounds net, that is, after the heads and tails are removed. Have the fish cut into pieces about 1½ inches thick. Wash the fish, sprinkle with the salt and pepper.

Cover the bacon with water, bring to a boil, and cook 5 minutes, then drain, dry, and mince.

Melt half the butter in a deep saucepan. Add the bacon and cook until bacon browns. Add the garlic, wine, parsley bundle, and thyme. Bring to a boil, and cook over medium heat 20 minutes. Arrange the fish in the pan, and cook 20 minutes.

Knead the flour with the remaining butter and blend it into the liquid. Add the meat extract. Cook 5 minutes and taste for seasoning.

Warm the cognac in a ladle, set it aflame and pour it into the fish mixture, shaking the pan until the flames die.

Serve the soup from a toureen, with garlic rubbed, sautéed French bread slices.

Serves 8–10.

## Bouillabaisse Marseillaise
## FISH SOUP, MARSEILLE STYLE

In Marseille, Mediterranean fish are used for preparing this dish. Unfortunately, we don't have similar fish in the United States. As substitutes, use a combination consisting of mackerel, sea bass, whiting, and sole. Also eel if you can get it. When buying the fish, ask for the heads, bones, and skin for making the stock.

### Stock

3 pounds fish trimmings
3 tablespoons olive oil
1 cup chopped onions
2 stalks celery and leaves, cut up
2 carrots, sliced
4 sprigs parsley
½ teaspoon thyme
½ teaspoon rosemary
1 bay leaf
6 cups water
2 cups dry white wine

Wash the fish trimmings. Heat the oil in a large saucepan; add the onions, celery, carrots, parsley, thyme, rosemary, and bay leaf. Cook over very low heat for 10 minutes, stirring frequently. Add the water, wine, and fish trimmings. Bring to a boil, and cook over medium heat 1 hour. Strain, pressing down to extract all the liquid. Reserve the stock, and keep hot.

### Fish

3 pounds assorted sliced fish
1 pound eel, sliced
2 teaspoons salt
½ teaspoon freshly ground black pepper
½ teaspoon thyme
½ teaspoon rosemary
1 teaspoon powdered saffron

1 teaspoon crushed fennel seeds
¾ cup olive oil (about)
3 leeks or 6 green onions, sliced thin
1½ cups peeled, seeded tomatoes
2 pieces orange rind
2 1½-pound lobsters, cut up in the shells (optional)
Sliced French Bread

Wash and dry the fish and eel. Mix together the spices, herbs, and ¼ cup of the oil. Pour the mixture over the fish, and turn the pieces to coat them. Let stand 30 minutes.

In a large saucepan, heat 2 tablespoons of the oil. Add the leeks, and cook over low heat 5 minutes. Pour in the reserved boiling stock; add the firmer pieces of fish, the tomatoes, orange rind, and lobsters if you're using them. Bring to a boil, and cook over high heat 5 minutes. Add the remaining fish, and cook 15 minutes longer. Taste for seasoning and serve immediately as follows.

While the fish is marinating, put slices of French bread on a pan in a 300° oven and let them dry until crisp. Then, when ready to serve, put a slice or two in each deep soup bowl. Arrange the fish on a platter, and pour the soup into the soup bowls. Serve the fish and soup simultaneously.

Serves 6–8.

The following sauce may accompany the bouillabaisse and a tiny amount should be stirred into the soup and eaten with the fish:

2 cloves garlic, minced
½ teaspoon Tabasco
½ cup fresh bread crumbs, soaked and drained
¼ cup olive oil
½ cup fish soup

Mix together the garlic, Tabasco, and bread crumbs; very gradually beat in the olive oil, then the soup.

## FRANCE

*Poularde Demi-Deuil*
## POACHED STUFFED CHICKEN

The name, demi-deuil, literally means half-mourning, and is derived from the black of the truffles under the white skin of the chicken.

> 5-pound roasting chicken
> 1 extra chicken breast
> Truffles
> 2 teaspoons salt
> ½ teaspoon white pepper
> ½ teaspoon thyme
> 1 small bay leaf, crumbled
> ¼ pound ham
> ¼ pound foie gras, diced
> 2 quarts chicken broth
> 3 tablespoons butter
> 3 tablespoons flour
> 3 egg yolks
> ½ cup heavy cream

Wash the chicken, and dry it. Remove the skin and bones of the chicken breast. Slice the truffles, the more the better, but they're expensive, so if you just want to use one, slice it thin. Gently loosen the skin over the breast of the whole chicken and slide the truffle slices in. If you've used several truffles, cover more of the surface under the skin, and dice some for the stuffing. Sprinkle the cavity of the bird with half the salt and pepper, then put in the thyme and bay leaf.

Grind the ham and the chicken breast, and season with the remaining salt and pepper. Fold in the foie gras, and the truffles if you have some left. Stuff the bird, and close it with skewers and string, or sew it. Put the chicken in a Dutch oven or heavy casserole, and add the broth. Bring to a boil, cover, and cook over medium low heat for 1¼ hours, or until the chicken is tender. Lift the bird out carefully, put it on a hot serving platter, and keep warm.

Cook the broth over high heat until reduced to 3 cups. Melt the butter in a saucepan; blend in the flour, then gradually add the broth, stirring steadily to the boiling point. Cook over low heat 5 minutes longer. Beat the egg yolks and cream in a bowl; gradually add some of the hot sauce, stirring constantly to prevent curdling. Return to the balance of the sauce, and heat, but do not let boil.

Remove the strings and skewers from the chicken. Spoon a little of the hot sauce over the bird, and serve the rest in a sauceboat. Serves 4.

## *Bouillabaisse de Chapon*
### CAPON IN SPICY SAUCE

> 5-pound capon, disjointed
> 2 teaspoons salt
> ½ teaspoon freshly ground black pepper
> ¼ cup Pernod (licorice flavored liqueur)
> ¼ teaspoon crushed saffron
> ½ cup olive oil
> ½ teaspoon fennel seeds, crushed
> 1 cup chopped onions
> 4 cloves garlic, minced
> 2 pounds tomatoes, peeled, seeded, and chopped
> ¼ cup minced parsley
> 2 cups boiling water
> 1 pound potatoes, peeled and cut in eighths

Wash and dry the capon and season with the salt and pepper. (Cut up and reserve the liver for the sauce.) Put the capon pieces in a bowl (not metal). Mix together the Pernod, saffron, and half the oil. Pour over the capon, turning the pieces to coat them. Let stand 45 minutes, basting and turning a few times.

Heat the remaining oil in a Dutch oven or heavy casserole; add the fennel, onions, and garlic. Sauté 5 minutes. Add the tomatoes, and cook 5 minutes, stirring several times. Add the undrained capon. Cover and cook over low heat 15 minutes, turning the pieces once. Add the parsley and boiling water. Re-cover and cook 20 minutes. Add the potatoes, and cook 20 minutes longer. Taste for seasoning. Remove 2 pieces of the potato for the sauce and mash them smooth. Pour off ⅓ cup of the gravy for the sauce.

### Sauce

2 tablespoons butter
Reserved liver
1 clove garlic, minced
½ teaspoon dried ground red peppers
¼ cup olive oil

Melt the butter in a skillet; sauté the liver until no red remains, and mash it smooth. Beat together the garlic, red peppers, oil, liver, and potatoes until smooth, then blend in the ⅓ cup gravy.

Serve the capon from the casserole, or arrange in a deep dish and pour the gravy and vegetables over it. Serve the sauce separately.

Serves 4.

## *Canard aux Lentilles*
## DUCK WITH LENTILS

### Duck

5-pound duck
2 teaspoons salt
½ teaspoon freshly ground black pepper
2 cloves garlic, minced

Wash the duck, and remove as much fat as possible. Dry the duck, and rub it, inside and out, with the salt, pepper, and garlic. Let stand 1 hour. Prick the skin in several places.

### Lentils

2 cups lentils
4 tablespoons butter
¾ cup chopped onions
¼ cup chopped shallots or green onions
1 clove garlic, minced
½ cup grated carrots
1½ teaspoons salt
¼ teaspoon freshly ground black pepper
½ teaspoon thyme
1 bay leaf ⎫
4 sprigs parsley ⎬ tied together
1 stalk celery ⎭
Boiling water
¼ cup minced parsley

Wash the lentils, cover with water, and bring to a boil. Let stand 5 minutes, then drain.

Melt the butter in a heavy casserole or Dutch oven. Add the onions, shallots, garlic, and carrots; sauté until yellow, stirring frequently. Add the lentils, salt, pepper, thyme, the bouquet garni, and enough boiling water to barely cover the mixture. Cover, and place on the lower level of a preheated 375° oven for 1 hour.

At the same time, place the duck on a rack in a shallow roasting pan, and put it on the upper level of the oven (unless you have two, in which case use the lower level of the second oven) and roast 1¼ hours, turning the duck to brown all sides. At the end of the time, cut the duck into serving-sized pieces, holding it over a dish so as to catch the juices. Add the duck and juices to the lentils, and with two spoons, mix together. Re-cover and bake 30 minutes longer, removing the cover for the last 10 minutes. Discard the bouquet garni, taste for seasoning, and sprinkle with the parsley.

Serves 4.

## Canard aux Pêches
## DUCK WITH PEACHES

5-pound duck
2 teaspoons salt
½ teaspoon freshly ground black pepper
½ teaspoon ground ginger

Wash the duck, pull off as much fat as possible, and dry. Rub the duck, inside and out, with a mixture of the salt, pepper, and ginger. Let stand 1 hour.

Place the duck, breast side down, on a greased rack in a shallow roasting pan. Roast in a 450° oven for 45 minutes. Turn duck over, breast side up, and with a fork, prick the skin in several places, being careful to put the tines of the fork in so that they don't prick the meat. Roast 1¼ hours longer, or until duck is tender, browned, and crisp. While the duck is roasting, prepare the sauce.

SAUCE

2 cups Sauce Espagnole (see recipe) or canned beef gravy
1 cup bottled Melba Sauce
¼ cup orange juice
1 tablespoon lemon juice
½ cup cognac
1 29-ounce can peach halves (white, if possible)

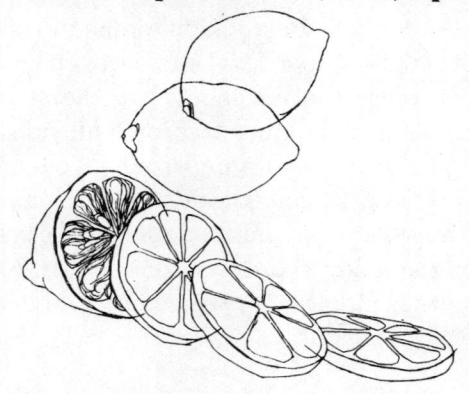

In a saucepan, mix together the Sauce Espagnole, Melba sauce, orange juice, lemon juice, and ¼ cup of the cognac. Heat, stirring frequently. Drain the peaches, and put them in a skillet; pour the remaining cognac over them, and heat slowly.

To serve, carve the duck, and arrange it on a platter. Spoon a little of the sauce over each piece, and surround with the peaches. Serve the remaining sauce separately.

Serves 4.

## *Navarin de Mouton*
## LAMB STEW

>3 pounds boned shoulder of lamb
>4 tablespoons vegetable oil
>4 tablespoons butter
>1½ cups diced onions
>1 cup diced carrots
>2 teaspoons salt
>½ teaspoon freshly ground black pepper
>2 tablespoons flour
>1 cup dry white wine
>2 whole cloves garlic
>½ teaspoon thyme
>1 bay leaf ⎱ tied together
>3 sprigs parsley ⎰
>1 cup peeled, seeded, chopped tomatoes
>2 cups raw potato balls

Cut the lamb into 1-inch cubes. Heat half the oil and butter in a casserole or Dutch oven; add the meat and brown on all sides. While the lamb is browning, heat the remaining oil and butter in a skillet, sauté the onions and carrots until golden. Add to the lamb. Sprinkle with the salt, pepper, and flour, stirring until lamb is coated. Add the wine, and enough water to barely cover. Add the garlic, thyme, bay leaf, parsley, and tomatoes. Bring to a boil, cover, and cook over low heat 1½ hours. Skim the fat, add the potatoes, and cook 15 minutes longer. Discard the bay leaf and parsley. Taste for seasoning and serve.

Serves 6–8.

## Ragoût d'Agneau à la Provençale
## LAMB STEW, PROVENCE STYLE

### Lamb

3 pounds lamb steaks
2 cloves garlic, minced
2 teaspoons salt
½ teaspoon freshly ground black pepper
3 tablespoons olive oil
18 small white onions
½ cup grated carrots
½ cup minced parsley
½ cup dry white wine
½ cup beef broth

Rinse and dry the lamb steaks. Season the steaks with a mixture of the garlic, salt, and pepper, then cut each in half. Let stand 30 minutes.

Heat the oil in a Dutch oven or heavy deep skillet; brown the meat in it well. Add the onions and carrots; cook until onions brown, stirring frequently. Pour off the fat; add the parsley, wine, and broth. Bring to a boil, cover, and cook over low heat 1½ hours. Prepare the vegetables meanwhile.

### Vegetables

1 medium-sized eggplant
2½ teaspoons salt
¼ cup olive oil
1 cup chopped onions
2 cloves garlic, minced
1 cup peeled, seeded, chopped tomatoes
1 cup thinly sliced green peppers
½ teaspoon freshly ground black pepper
½ teaspoon thyme
⅛ teaspoon fennel seeds, crushed
12 pitted black olives

Peel the eggplant, cut in half lengthwise, then slice crosswise. Sprinkle the eggplant with 1½ teaspoons of the salt, and let stand 45 minutes. Rinse and dry the slices.

Heat the oil in a deep skillet; add the eggplant, onions, and garlic. Cook 5 minutes, shaking the pan several times. Add the tomatoes, green peppers, pepper, thyme, fennels, and remaining salt. Cook over medium heat 15 minutes, stirring gently several times. Stir in the olives.

Heap the lamb on a heated serving dish, and surround with the vegetables.

Serves 6–8.

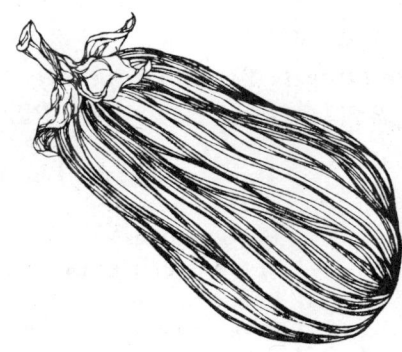

*Côtes de Porc Grillées*
## MARINATED BROILED PORK CHOPS

    4 pork chops, cut 1½ inches thick
    ¾ cup olive oil
    1 clove garlic, minced
    ½ teaspoon thyme
    ½ teaspoon rosemary
    ½ teaspoon sage
    1 bay leaf, crushed
    1½ teaspoons salt
    ½ teaspoon freshly ground black pepper

Trim the fat off the chops; rinse and dry. In a bowl (not metal) mix together the oil, garlic, thyme, rosemary, sage, and bay leaf. Marinate the chops in the mixture for 12 to 24 hours, basting and turning them several times.

When ready to cook, drain the chops, and season them with the salt and pepper. Arrange them on a broiling pan, and broil 6 inches from the source of heat, 15 minutes on each side, or until no pink remains in the meat.

Serves 4.

*Cotelettes de Porc en Papillote*
PORK CHOPS IN PAPER

        6 porks chops, cut 1 inch thick
        ⅓ cup olive oil
        1¾ teaspoons salt
        ¾ teaspoon freshly ground black pepper
        ½ cup minced parsley
        ½ pound chicken livers
        3 slices bacon
        2 cloves garlic, minced

Rinse and dry the chops. Mix together the oil, 1¼ teaspoons salt, ½ teaspoon pepper, and ¼ cup of the parsley. Marinate the chops in the mixture for 3 hours, turning them once or twice. Drain, reserving the oil, and arrange the chops on a pan. Bake in a 350° oven 20 minutes, turning them midway. Cool.

Wash and dry the livers. In a skillet, lightly brown the bacon. Remove the bacon. Pour off all but 2 tablespoons of the fat, and sauté the livers in the fat remaining until no red remains. Chop together the bacon, liver, garlic, and remaining salt, pepper, and parsley. Taste for seasoning.

Cut 6 pieces of aluminum foil or parchment paper, large enough to completely envelope the chops. Brush the foil with a little of the reserved oil, and place a chop on it. Spread some of the liver mixture on each chop, and fold over the foil so that it completely covers the chops (or use the new Brown-in-Bags). Arrange on a baking pan, and bake in a 400° oven for 15 minutes. Serve with the foil folded back, or slit the bags.

Serves 6.

## Boeuf Rôti à la Bordelaise
## MARINATED ROAST BEEF

>5-pound rump roast or cross rib of beef
>2 strips beef suet
>1 onion, sliced
>4 shallots, chopped
>4 sprigs parsley
>1 bay leaf
>½ teaspoon thyme
>½ cup olive oil
>1½ cups dry white wine
>2½ teaspoons salt
>½ teaspoon freshly ground black pepper
>1 tablespoon wine vinegar

Trim the fat from the meat and reserve with the suet. In a glass or pottery bowl, combine the onion, shallots, parsley, bay leaf, thyme, oil, and wine. Add the meat, and marinate overnight in the refrigerator, turning the meat several times.

Put half of the reserved beef fat and suet in the bottom of a roasting pan. Strain the marinade; use the vegetables to spread over the fat. Put the meat on top of the vegetables and season with the salt and pepper; place another piece of fat over the meat and add ¼ cup of the marinade. Roast in a 350° oven 1¼ hours, basting frequently. Transfer meat to a serving platter and keep hot.

Strain the pan juices and skim the fat, then combine in a saucepan with the remaining strained marinade. Cook over high heat 10 minutes. Add the wine vinegar, reheat, and serve separately as a sauce for roast.

Serves 8–10.

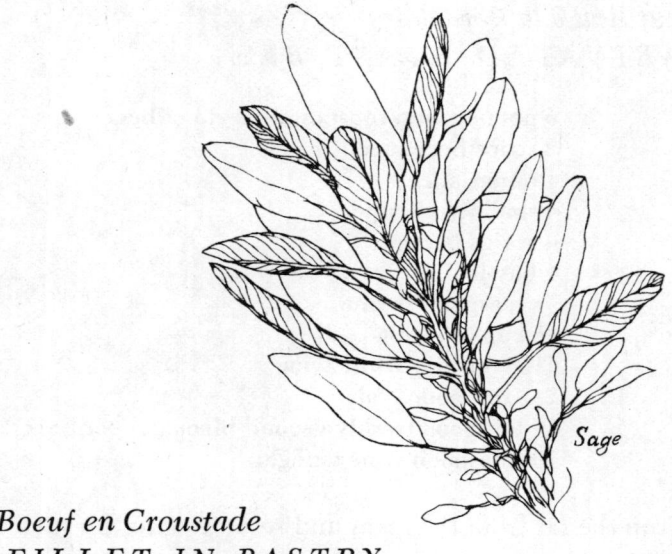

*Filet de Boeuf en Croustade*
BEEF FILLET IN PASTRY

Begin the preparation the day before you want to serve the fillet.

    5-pound fillet of beef
    3 tablespoons butter
    1 cup chopped onions
    2 carrots, sliced
    2 sprigs parsley
    1 bay leaf
    ⅛ teaspoon sage
    ¼ teaspoon thyme
    ⅛ teaspoon nutmeg
    1½ cups dry white wine
    ½ pound mushrooms, chopped and sautéed
    ¼ pound ham, chopped and sautéed
    2 slices crisp bacon, crumbled
    ¼ pound chicken livers, sautéed and chopped
    ½ teaspoon salt
    ¼ teaspoon freshly ground black pepper
    1 egg, lightly beaten
    1 tablespoon cognac
    Puff Paste (see recipe for Croustade de Langouste)
    2 tablespoons Madeira or sweet sherry

Have the butcher bard, that is, wrap thin strips of beef fat around the meat.

Melt the butter in a skillet; add the onion, carrots, parsley, bay leaf, sage, thyme, and nutmeg. Cover and cook over low heat 5 minutes. Mix in the wine. Place the mixture in a bowl (not metal). Add the fillet and marinate 24 hours in the refrigerator, basting with the marinade from time to time. Drain, dry, and roast in a 500° oven 20 minutes, turning to brown all sides. Cool.

When ready to prepare, mix together the sauteéd mushrooms, ham, bacon, and chicken livers and season with a little salt and pepper. Mix in the beaten egg and 2 tablespoons of the marinade. Add the cognac. Cover the meat completely with the chicken liver mixture. Roll out the pastry in a sheet large enough to completely cover the meat and wrap the meat in it. Moisten the edges of the pastry with a little water and seal carefully. Cut 2 small holes in the top. Place the meat in a baking pan. Bake in a preheated 425° oven for 10 minutes per pound for rare beef (15 minutes per pound for medium), pouring the Madeira through the holes in the crust 10 minutes before the end of the baking time. Let stand 15 minutes before cutting into 1-inch thick slices.

Serves 6–8.

## Boeuf à la Mode
## MARINATED POT ROAST

Begin the preparation of the dish the day before you want to serve it.

>    5 pounds cross rib or rump of beef
>    1 veal knuckle
>    ¾ cup sliced onions
>    2 cloves garlic, minced
>    1 bay leaf
>    2½ teaspoons salt
>    ½ teaspoon freshly ground black pepper
>    ¼ teaspoon thyme
>    ⅛ teaspoon nutmeg
>    2 tablespoons wine vinegar
>    4 tablespoons olive oil
>    4 cups dry red wine
>    3 tablespoons cognac
>    12 small white onions, lightly sautéed
>    4 carrots, quartered
>    12 mushroom caps
>    1 teaspoon Worcestershire sauce
>    2 teaspoons arrowroot or cornstarch
>    2 tablespoons Madeira or port

Have the butcher lard the meat, and crack the veal knuckle.

In a glass or pottery bowl, combine the sliced onions, garlic, bay leaf, salt, pepper, thyme, nutmeg, vinegar, 2 tablespoons of the oil, and 1½ cups of the wine. Marinate the meat in the mixture for 24 hours in the refrigerator, turning occasionally. Drain and reserve marinade. Dry the meat.

Heat the remaining oil in a skillet; brown the meat in it on all sides. Transfer the meat to a Dutch oven or deep heavy saucepan. Pour the marinade into the skillet and bring to a boil, scraping the brown particles from the bottom of the skillet. Add to the meat with the veal knuckle, cognac, and remaining wine. Cover and bring to a boil over direct heat, then roast in a 350° oven 2½ hours. Remove the knuckle and skim the fat from the gravy.

Add the white onions, carrots, and mushrooms; re-cover and roast 1 hour longer. Put the pan on direct heat. Mix together the Worcestershire sauce, arrowroot, and Madeira. Stir into the gravy until thickened. Taste for seasoning. Carve the meat and arrange it on a hot serving platter. Surround with the vegetables and pour some of the gravy over the meat. Serve the rest of the gravy in a sauceboat.

Serves 6–8.

## Boeuf à la Mode en Gelée

Prepare the meat as directed for *Boeuf à la Mode*. Arrange the cooked vegetables from the recipe above, with strips of pimentos and sliced olives, in an attractive design on the bottom of a mold or casserole.

Slice the cooked beef thinly and arrange the slices over the vegetables so that they overlap. Strain the gravy. Soften 1 envelope (1 tablespoon) gelatin in 2 tablespoons water and stir into the hot gravy until dissolved. Pour over the meat. Chill until firm. Carefully turn out of mold onto a chilled platter.

*Thyme*

## Filet aux Ris de Veau
### FILLET OF BEEF WITH SWEETBREADS

¼ cup olive oil
¾ cup chopped onions
1 clove garlic, minced
¾ cup grated carrots
2 slices bacon, half cooked and drained
1 tablespoon cornstarch
2 cups beef broth
¼ cup dry white wine
1 tablespoon tomato paste
1 bay leaf
3 tablespoons chopped parsley
2 pairs sweetbreads, parboiled
⅓ cup dry bread crumbs
2 teaspoons salt
½ teaspoon freshly ground black pepper
6 tablespoons butter
2 egg yolks
6 fillets of beef, cut 1 inch thick

Heat the olive oil in a saucepan. Add the onions, garlic, carrots, and bacon. Sauté 10 minutes. Mix the cornstarch with a little broth, then with all the broth, and add to the vegetables, stirring constantly to the boiling point. Add the wine, tomato paste, and bay leaf. Cover, and cook over very low heat 1 hour. Taste for seasoning. Discard the bay leaf and stir in parsley. Cut each sweetbread in half, to make them thinner. Select the six most perfect pieces for breading, and dice the remaining sweetbreads.

Mix the breadcrumbs with 1 teaspoon salt and ¼ teaspoon pepper. Dip the halved sweetbreads in the mixture. Heat half the butter in a skillet. Brown the sweetbreads in it. Keep warm.

Beat egg yolks in a bowl. Gradually add wine sauce, stirring constantly to prevent curdling. Cook, stirring constantly until thickened, but do not allow to boil. Add diced sweetbreads.

Heat the remaining butter in a skillet. Add the fillets and cook over high heat 3 minutes on each side. Sprinkle with remaining salt and pepper. Arrange the fillets on a heated serving dish and put a sweetbread over each. Pour the sauce over them.

Serves 6.

## Côte de Veau à l'Orange
## VEAL CHOPS WITH ORANGE SAUCE

> 6 veal chops, cut 1 inch thick
> 1½ teaspoons salt
> ½ teaspoon freshly ground black pepper
> ¼ cup flour
> 3 oranges
> 1 lemon
> 2 tablespoons vegetable oil
> 4 tablespoons butter
> ¼ cup dry white wine
> 3 tablespoons sugar
> ¼ cup cider vinegar
> 1 cup chicken broth
> 1 tablespoon arrowroot or cornstarch
> ¼ cup orange liqueur
> 1 tablespoon currant jelly

Rinse the chops, dry and trim any excess fat. Season with the salt and pepper, and dip lightly in the flour. Let stand 15 minutes.

Wash and dry the oranges and lemon, then peel them carefully, being sure you don't have any of the zest (white membrane) adhering to the inner part. Cut the peel into matchlike strips, cover with water, bring to a boil and cook 5 minutes. Drain. Remove all the zest from the oranges and lemon, then slice them over a bowl, so that the juice can run into it. Reserve.

Heat the oil and butter in a skillet. Add the chops, and cook until browned on both sides. Add the wine, cover, and cook over low heat 45 minutes, or until tender, turning them once or twice.

Melt the sugar in a saucepan, stirring with a wooden spoon, until sugar turns light brown. Very carefully (to prevent spattering) add the vinegar, broth, and fruit juice. Bring to a boil, and cook 5 minutes. Mix together the arrowroot and liqueur, and add it to the sauce, stirring steadily until thickened, then add the currant jelly.

Arrange the chops on a heated serving dish, and pour any pan juices into the sauce. Taste for seasoning. Garnish the chops with the sliced fruit and peel, and pour the sauce over all.

Serves 6.

## Blanquette de Veau
### VEAL STEW IN CREAM

This is a slightly different, and I think better, version of the Blanquette usually served. The veal is lightly seared, instead of merely being boiled.

> 2 pounds breast of veal
> 2 pounds leg of veal
> 2 tablespoons vegetable oil
> 10 tablespoons butter
> 1 cup chopped onions
> 2 cloves garlic, minced
> 1 cup grated carrot
> ½ cup sliced celery
> 1 turnip, diced
> 2 leeks or 4 green onions (white part only), sliced
> 2 teaspoons salt
> ½ teaspoon white pepper
> ½ teaspoon thyme
> 1 bay leaf
> 4 sprigs parsley
> 2 teaspoons grated lemon rind
> Boiling water
> 18 small mushroom caps
> 18 small white onions
> 4 tablespoons flour
> ½ teaspoon tarragon
> 4 egg yolks
> 1 cup heavy cream
> 2 tablespoons lemon juice

Have the breast of veal chopped up into 2-inch pieces through the bone. Cut the leg of veal into 2-inch cubes.

Put the oil and 2 tablespoons of the butter into a Dutch oven or heavy skillet. When the butter melts, add the veal, and cook until it begins to change color, but don't let it brown. Turn pieces to sear all sides. Remove the pieces with a slotted spoon. To the fat remaining, add the chopped onions, garlic, grated carrots, celery, turnips, and leeks. Cook over low heat, stirring frequently until vegetables turn limp. Return the meat, and sprinkle with the salt, pepper, and thyme; turn the meat a few times to coat, then add the bay leaf, parsley, lemon rind, and enough boiling water to just cover. Bring to a boil, cover, and cook over low heat 1¼ hours, or until the meat is tender. While it's cooking, sauté the mushrooms and whole onions separately in 2 tablespoons of butter for each vegetable. Put these vegetables in a large casserole, and when the meat is tender, remove the pieces with a slotted spoon and add them to the sautéed vegetables. Keep warm.

Strain the liquid, and skim off the fat. There should be about 4 cups of the liquid—if there is more, cook it until it reduces, if there's a little less, don't worry about it.

Melt the remaining butter in a saucepan, blend in the flour until lightly browned, then gradually add the liquid, stirring constantly, until thickened and smooth. Add the tarragon, and cook over low heat 15 minutes, stirring frequently. Beat the egg yolks and cream in a bowl. Gradually add a little of the hot sauce, stirring steadily to prevent curdling. Return to all the sauce, add the lemon juice, and taste for seasoning. Pour over the veal, mix, and heat, but do not boil.

Serves 8–10.

## Poitrine de Veau Farcie
### STUFFED BREAST OF VEAL

4-pound breast of veal
3½ teaspoons salt
1 teaspoon freshly ground black pepper
1½ teaspoons thyme
¼ pound boneless veal, ground
¼ pound boneless pork, ground
¼ pound chicken livers, minced raw
1 cup fresh bread crumbs
1 egg, beaten
2 tablespoons minced parsley
3 tablespoons peanut oil
1½ cups minced onions
½ cup grated carrots
2 cloves garlic, minced
½ cup dry white wine
Boiling water

Have the butcher cut a large pocket in the breast. Wash and dry the veal. Mix together 2½ teaspoons of the salt, ½ teaspoon of the pepper, and 1 teaspoon thyme, then rub the mixture into the veal.

Mix together the ground veal, pork, livers, bread crumbs, egg, parsley, and remaining salt, pepper, and thyme. Stuff the veal, and sew or skewer the opening. Score the top in a crisscross design, then tie the veal with strings to help hold its shape.

Heat the oil in a pan large enough to hold the veal. Brown the veal in it on both sides. Add the onion, carrots, garlic, and wine. Cover, and cook over low heat 2½ hours, or until the veal is tender. Add boiling water as necessary to keep the veal moist. Transfer to a platter, and cut away the strings and fastenings. Strain the pan juices, skim the fat, and serve in a sauceboat.

Serves 6–8.

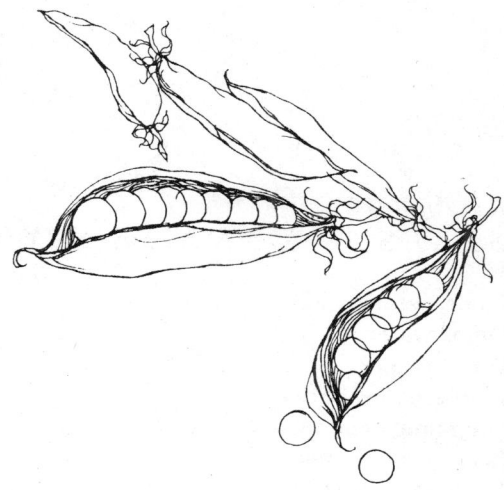

*Rognons Clamart*
## KIDNEYS WITH PEAS

>   6 veal kidneys
>   2 cups water
>   2 tablespoons vinegar
>   ⅓ cup flour
>   1½ teaspoons salt
>   ½ teaspoon freshly ground black pepper
>   2 tablespoons vegetable oil
>   3 tablespoons butter
>   ½ cup finely chopped onions
>   2 tablespoons minced parsley
>   ½ cup dry red wine
>   ⅛ teaspoon thyme
>   2 cups cooked or canned green peas

Wash the kidneys, trim the fat, and remove the membrane and core. Mix together the water and vinegar; soak the kidneys in the mixture 1 hour. Drain, dry, and slice. Toss the pieces in a mixture of the flour, salt, and pepper.

Heat the oil and butter in a skillet; brown the kidneys on both sides over high heat. Mix in the onions; cook 2 minutes. Add the parsley, wine, thyme, and peas. Cook over medium heat 5 minutes.

Serves 6.

## Ris de Veau à l'Oignon
### SWEETBREADS, LYONNAISE STYLE

3 pair sweetbreads
2 cups water
¾ teaspoon salt
6 tablespoons butter
1 cup finely chopped onions
2 cloves garlic, minced
2 carrots, grated
1 bay leaf
¼ teaspoon thyme
½ cup dry white wine
½ cup chicken broth
Onion Purée (see below)
½ cup sliced sautéed mushrooms
Grated Swiss cheese

Wash the sweetbreads and soak in ice water 1 hour. Drain. Put in a pan with the water and salt. Bring to a boil and cook over low heat 10 minutes. Drain and put in cold water for 15 minutes. Drain. Remove membranes and connective tissues and dry on paper towels. Put between two plates with a weight on top and cool.

Melt 4 tablespoons of the butter in a large skillet; add the onion, garlic, carrot, bay leaf, thyme, and sweetbreads. Sauté the sweetbreads 5 minutes on each side. Stir in the wine and broth; cover, and cook over low heat 5 minutes. Remove the sweetbreads and slice them; keep warm. Strain the pan juices into another pan and mix in the onion purée and mushrooms. Taste for seasoning. Arrange the sweetbreads on a heatproof serving dish; cover with the sauce, sprinkle with the cheese, dot with the remaining butter and put in a preheated 425° oven until top browns lightly.

Serves 6.

## Onion Pureé

7 tablespoons butter
4 tablespoons flour
1 cup chicken broth
1 cup light cream
1½ teaspoons salt
½ teaspoon white pepper
3 cups sliced onions
1 tablespoon tomato paste
¼ teaspoon sugar

Melt 4 tablespoons of the butter in a saucepan; blend in the flour, then the broth and cream, stirring steadily to the boiling point. Stir in the salt and pepper and cook over low heat for 5 minutes.

Cover the onions with water, bring to a boil, and cook 2 minutes. Drain, then sauté in the remaining butter until soft, but not brown. Add to the sauce with the tomato paste and sugar; cook over low heat 10 minutes. Purée in an electric blender, or force through a sieve.

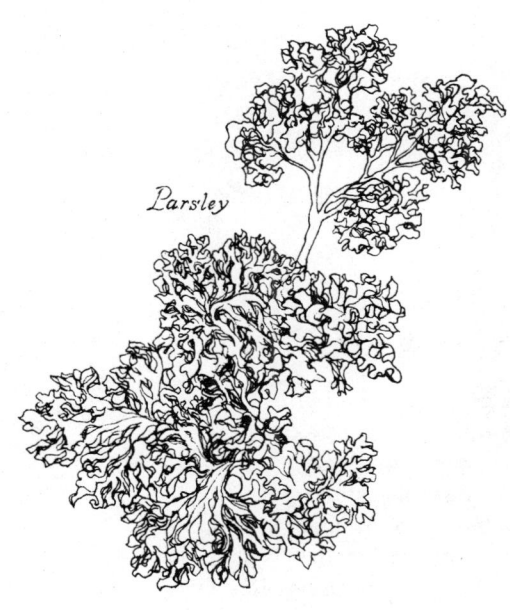

Parsley

## Artichauts à la Provençale
### ARTICHOKES WITH MUSHROOMS AND PEAS

> 2 packages frozen artichoke hearts, thawed
> 6 tablespoons olive oil
> 1 pound mushrooms, sliced
> 2 cloves garlic, minced
> 1 package frozen tiny green peas, thawed
> 1¼ teaspoons salt
> ¼ teaspoon white pepper
> 2 tablespoons minced parsley

Dry the artichokes on paper towels. Heat half the oil in a skillet; sauté the mushrooms 5 minutes; remove and reserve. Heat the remaining oil in the skillet; lightly brown the artichokes in it. Add the garlic, peas, salt, and pepper. Cook over low heat 5 minutes, adding a very little water if necessary to keep from burning. Add the mushrooms, and cook 3 minutes longer. Taste for seasoning, and sprinkle with the parsley.
Serves 8–10.

## Fondue aux Champignons
### MUSHROOM FONDUE

> 2 pounds mushrooms
> 6 tablespoons butter
> 1½ teaspoons salt
> ¼ teaspoon white pepper
> 2 tablespoons flour
> 1 cup light cream
> 1 cup (¼ pound) grated Gruyère or Swiss cheese

Slice the mushrooms very thin. Melt 3 tablespoons of the butter in a skillet; add the mushrooms and cook over high heat 5 minutes. Season with the salt and pepper.

Melt the remaining butter in a saucepan; blend in the flour. Gradually add the cream, stirring steadily to the boiling point. Cook over low heat 5 minutes. Add the mushrooms; cook 5 minutes longer. Stir in the cheese and taste for seasoning. Turn into a shallow buttered baking dish and bake on the upper level of a preheated 450° oven 5 minutes or until delicately browned.

Serves 4–6.

*Purée Saint-Germain*
## GREEN PEA PURÉE

 1½ cups water
 1 teaspoon salt
 ½ teaspoon sugar
 3 pounds green peas, shelled, or 3 packages frozen
 1½ cups shredded lettuce
 2 tablespoons grated onion
 1 tablespoon minced parsley
 4 tablespoons butter
 3 tablespoons heavy cream

Bring the water, salt, and sugar to a boil; add the peas, lettuce, onion, and parsley. Cook over medium heat 12 minutes for fresh peas, or 5 for frozen. Drain well; purée the vegetables in an electric blender or force through a sieve. Beat in the butter and cream; taste for seasoning, reheat and serve.

Serves 6–8.

## *Pommes de Terre Auvergnate*
## FRENCH POTATO PIE

### Pastry

2 cups instantized flour
½ teaspoon salt
½ pound (2 sticks) butter
6 tablespoons sour cream

Sift the flour and salt into a bowl. With the hand, work in the butter, then the sour cream, until the dough holds together. Form into 2 balls, one a little larger than the other. Wrap each ball in foil or waxed paper and chill 4 hours, or overnight.

### Potato Filling

1½ pounds potatoes
2 cups sour cream
1½ teaspoons salt
½ teaspoon freshly ground black pepper

Peel the potatoes, and cut into very thin rounds. Dry on paper towels. Roll out the larger ball of pastry, and fit it into an 11-inch pie plate.

In the lined pie plate, make a neat, even layer of the potatoes, then add some sour cream and sprinkle with salt and pepper. Continue making the layers and finish with sour cream.

Roll out the remaining ball of dough and place over the potato mixture, sealing the edges well. Cut 3 small slits on the top. Bake on the lower level of a preheated 425° oven 20 minutes. Reduce heat to 350° and bake 20 minutes longer. Serve hot, cut into wedges.

Serves 6–8.

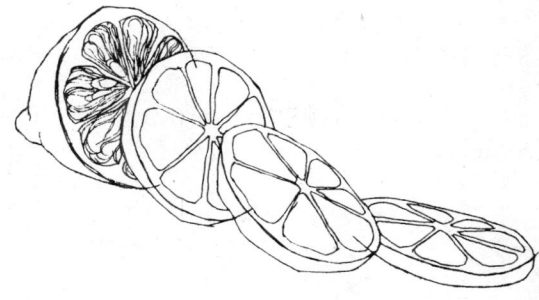

*Tarte aux Fruits*
FRUIT TART

    3 tablespoons cornstarch
    ⅛ teaspoon salt
    1¼ cups sugar
    2 cups light cream, scalded
    3 egg yolks, beaten
    1 teaspoon vanilla extract
    ½ cup heavy cream
    ½ cup water
    1 teaspoon lemon juice
    2 cups pitted black cherries, sliced peaches,
        blueberries, etc.
    Baked 9-inch tart shell

Mix the cornstarch, salt, and ¼ cup sugar in the top of a double boiler. Stir in the light cream until smooth. Cook over low heat, stirring steadily until thickened. Place over hot water and cook 10 minutes, stirring occasionally. Beat the egg yolks in a bowl; add a little hot sauce, stirring steadily to prevent curdling. Return to balance of sauce and cook over hot water 2 minutes, stirring constantly. Stir in the vanilla and cool. Whip the cream and fold it in.

Cook the water, lemon juice, and remaining sugar 5 minutes. Add the selected fruit; cook cherries and peaches 10 minutes, blueberries 5 minutes. Remove with a slotted spoon and cool. Cook the syrup until thick and jelly-like.

Fill the shell with the cream mixture, and arrange the fruit over it in an attractive design. Brush with the syrup and cool.
    Serves 6–8.

## Croquembouche
## PYRAMID CAKE

This is a dramatic dessert, usually served at Christmas or New Years.

>3 cups water
>½ pound (2 sticks) butter
>2 cups sifted flour
>½ teaspoon salt
>8 eggs
>2 cups heavy cream
>4 tablespoons confectioners' sugar
>6 tablespoons orange liqueur
>1⅓ cups granulated sugar
>¼ teaspoon cream of tartar
>2 cups hot water

Bring 2 cups of the water and the butter to a boil in a saucepan. Add the flour and salt all at once. Cook over low heat, stirring with a wooden spoon until the mixture forms a ball and leaves the sides of the pan. Remove the pan from the heat. Add the eggs, one at a time, beating with a wooden spoon after each addition. Then beat until the mixture is thick and shiny. Place the batter in rounded teaspoonfuls 1 inch apart on an ungreased cooky sheet. Bake in a preheated 400° oven 30 minutes or until dry and a light gold. Cool on a wire rack. Make a small hole in the base (flat side) of each puff. Whip the cream until peaks form, sweeten with the confectioners' sugar, and fold in the liqueur. Using a pastry bag with a plain tube, fill the puffs with the whipped cream by inserting the point of the tube into the hole in the base of each, or use a demitasse spoon.

Combine the granulated sugar, cream of tartar, and the remaining cup of water in a small skillet. Bring to a boil, stirring constantly. Lower the heat and cook until a light amber color, stirring occasionally. Keep the syrup warm over very low heat while building the pyramid. Roll a cream puff in the warm syrup and set it, rounded side facing out, around the outer edge of a 9-inch flat, round plate. Continue to form a ring around the edge of the plate. Fill in the center with more puffs. Over the spaces between the puffs in the first row, make a slightly smaller circle of dipped puffs. Fill in the center again. Continue until there is a total of five circles. Top with one cream puff.

Add the 2 cups of hot water to the syrup left in the skillet. Cook slowly, stirring occasionally, to 232° on a candy thermometer. Cool the syrup to room temperature and drizzle it down the sides of the pyramid. Serve the *croquembouche* immediately, starting at the top, or refrigerate until needed.

Serves 10–12.

*Mousse au Chocolat et Orange*
CHOCOLATE-ORANGE MOUSSE

> 4 ounces semi-sweet chocolate
> 2 tablespoons orange juice
> ¼ pound (1 stick) softened sweet butter
> 3 egg yolks
> ½ cup fine sugar
> 3 tablespoons orange liqueur
> 2 tablespoons chopped candied orange peel
> 1 cup heavy cream, whipped

Combine the chocolate and orange juice in a small bowl; place over hot water until melted. Add 2 tablespoons of butter at a time, beating after each addition.

Beat the egg yolks and sugar in the top of a double boiler until very thick. Beat in the liqueur, then place over hot water and beat until mixture is hot. Remove from the heat and beat until cool. Beat in the chocolate mixture, then stir in the orange peel. Fold in the whipped cream. Turn into a 1½-quart soufflé dish or mold and chill until firm. Serve from the dish or mold—this is too delicate to be unmolded.

Serves 8–10.

*Riz à l'Impératrice*
## RICH RICE MOLD

4¼ cups water
1 cup long-grain rice
½ teaspoon salt
1½ cups milk
1 envelope (tablespoon) gelatin
4 egg yolks
⅔ cup sugar
1½ cups light cream
1 cup finely chopped candied fruits
2 tablespoons fruit liqueur
1 cup heavy cream, whipped

Bring 4 cups of the water to a boil; add the rice. Cook over high heat 4 minutes, then drain. Combine the rice in the saucepan with the salt and milk. Cover, and cook over very low heat 25 minutes or until the rice is very soft.

While the rice is cooking, sprinkle the gelatin into the remaining ¼ cup water. Beat the egg yolks in the top of a double boiler. Mix in the sugar, then the light cream. Place over hot water and cook, stirring constantly until mixture thickens and coats the spoon. Stir in the gelatin until dissolved. Mix in the rice, and chill until mixture just begins to set. Mix the fruits with the liqueur and let stand 5 minutes. Fold into the rice mixture with the whipped cream. Turn into an oiled 2-quart mold and chill until set.

Carefully unmold and decorate with whipped cream and candied cherries, if desired.

Serves 8–10.

*Génoise*
## BUTTER SPONGE CAKE

    **6 eggs**
    **1 cup sugar**
    **1 cup sifted flour**
    **¼ pound (1 stick) butter, melted and cooled**
    **1 teaspoon vanilla extract**

Remove the eggs from the refrigerator 2 hours before needed. Grease two 9-inch layer-cake pans and dust lightly with flour, or use a 9-inch tube pan.

Use an electric mixer if you have one, because this batter must be beaten a long time. Beat the eggs in a large warm bowl, then beat in the sugar. Continue beating until almost tripled in volume. Scrape the bowl several times. Gently fold in the flour and butter, a little at a time. Then fold in the vanilla. Use a very light hand, or an electric mixer set at lowest speed, so as not to break the air cells. Turn into the pans or pan. Bake in a preheated 350° oven 25 minutes for the layers, or 35 minutes for the tube pan, or until the top springs back when pressed with the finger. Invert onto a cake rack, remove pans, and let cool.

Variations:
*Chocolate Génoise:*
Use ½ cup sifted unsweetened cocoa and ½ cup sifted flour in place of all the flour. Sift together before adding. Proceed as directed.

*Nut Génoise:*
Add ½ cup ground nuts when adding the flour.

## Crème Brûlée
### CARAMELIZED CUSTARD

6 egg yolks
⅓ cup granulated sugar
2 cups heavy cream, scalded
1 cup milk, scalded
2 teaspoons vanilla extract
½ cup packed brown sugar

In a bowl, beat the egg yolks and granulated sugar until thick, light, and smooth. Gradually beat in the cream and milk, then mix in the vanilla. Strain into a 9-inch ring mold. Place in a shallow pan of hot water.

Bake in a preheated 325° oven 30 minutes or until a knife inserted in the center comes out clean. Cool, then chill.

Just before serving, spread the brown sugar over the custard. Place the dish on a board or in a pan over cracked ice. Put under a hot broiler until sugar melts completely, but watch carefully to prevent burning. (The Crème Brûlée may be chilled again, or served hot.)

Serves 6–8.

## Tarte Tatin
### CARAMELIZED APPLE TART

#### Pastry

1 cup sifted flour
⅛ teaspoon salt
¼ cup sugar
¼ pound (1 stick) butter
3 tablespoons ice water

#### Filling

6 tablespoons butter
¾ cup sugar
4 cups peeled, sliced apples
3 tablespoons brown sugar

Sift the flour, salt, and sugar into a bowl; cut in the butter with a pastry blender or 2 knives. Add the water and toss lightly until a ball of dough is formed. Chill 1 hour. Preheat the oven to 375°.

Use a deep 9-inch pie plate and spread 2 tablespoons of the butter on it. Sprinkle with 4 tablespoons of the sugar. Arrange a layer of apples in an attractive design, dot with a little butter, and sprinkle with some sugar. Continue making similar layers until all the apples are used up. Roll out the pastry and cover the apples with it. Bake 30 minutes. Cool 5 minutes, then carefully invert onto a serving plate, so that the pastry is now underneath and the apples on top. Sprinkle with the brown sugar and place under the broiler until sugar browns. Cool.

Serves 6–8.

# INDEX

*Agnello arrosto* (roast lamb, marinated, Italy), 280-81
*Ajiaco* (potato, corn, and avocado soup, Colombia), 316
*Aji de gallina* (chicken in spicy bread sauce, Bolivia), 326
*Albondigas de pescado* (fried fish croquettes, South America), 309
Almonds:
    baklava (flaky nut pastry, Iran), 178-79
    fish with (*poisson Carcassone*, France), 373
    halva (dessert, Middle East), 176
    jelly with fruit, China, 54
    lamb curry with (*malai korma*, India), 104
    lobster with, China, 21
    rice with currants and (*pilaf Ali Pasha*, Turkey), 168-69
    sauce, shrimp in (*camarónes con salsa de almendras*, Ecuador), 306
    torte (*torta de almendras*, Spain), 347
*Alose à la provençale* (shad Provençale, France), 377
*Anitra farcita e arrostita* (roast stuffed duck, Italy), 273
*Anticuchos* (meat skewers, Peru), 332
Apple:
    strudel (*rétes*, Austria-Hungary), 235
    tart, caramelized (*tarte tatin*, France), 414-15
Arabic bread (*khoubz Araby*), 166-67
*Aragosta piccante* (lobster in piquant sauce, Italy), 254
*Arangini* (rice-meat balls, Italy), 278-79
Artichokes:
    with mushrooms and peas (*artichauts à la provençale*, France), 406
    stuffed (*carciofi Borghese*, Italy), 289
*Ashe reshte* (noodle-meatball soup, Middle East), 134-35
*Aush bhogar* (lamb curry with dumplings, India), 102
*Avgolemono, soupa* (lemon soup, Greece), 132-33
Avocado:
    cream of tomato and, soup (*velouté Aurore*, France), 370

418  INDEX

soup with potato and corn (*ajiaco*, Colombia), 316

*Baba ghannouj* (eggplant spread, Middle East), 128
*Bableves* (bean soup, Hungary), 200
*Bacalao à la Argentina* (codfish, Argentine style), 307
Bacon-tomato sauce, spaghetti with (*spaghetti all'amatrice*, Italy), 262
*Bahmi goreng* (noodles, chicken, and shrimp, Indonesia), 105
*Baklava* (flaky nut pastry, Iran), 178-79
*Balik çorbasi* (fish chowder, Turkey), 133
*Balkanishe chlodnik* (shrimp-beet soup, Austria), 199
Bananas:
    batter fried (*kluay khaek*, Thailand), 116
    omelet (*tortilla de banana*, South America), 304
*Barszczyk* (beet-beef soup, Poland), 196
*Basar tz aloouie* (sweet and sour meat, Israel), 164
Beans:
    beef, braised, with (*estouffat*, Spain), 331
    black, and mixed meats (*feijoada completa*, Brazil), 336-37
    black, sauce: Chinese, shrimp with, 17; spareribs with, 41
    goulash (*ungarishes bohnengulyás*, Austria-Hungary), 226
    lamb and, casserole (*fassolia me arni*, Greece), 155
    lima, and meat (*cholent*, Israel), 159
    soup:
        *bableves*, Hungary, 200
        with macaroni (*pasta e fagioli*, Italy), 265
        minestrone (vegetable-bean, Italy), 266
        *miso-taki*, Japan, 70
        mixed (*sopa de frijoles meturado*, South America), 320
Beef:
    boiled in beer (*rindfleisch in bier*, Austria), 205
    boiled dinner, Argentine (*puchero argentino*), 339
    braised, and beans (*estouffat*, Spain), 331
    broiled marinated (*bul-googi*, Korea), 94
    broth, basic, France, 364
    -corn pudding (*pastel de choclo*, Chile), 345
    curry, Siamese (*kaeng phed*, Thailand), 95
    figs and, casserole (*sikbaj*, Iran), 157
    fillets:
        in pastry (*filet de boeuf en croustade*, France), 394-95
        with pepper sauce (*manzo peperonata*, Italy), 278
        stuffed (*filetto ripieno*, Italy), 275
        with sweetbreads (*filet aux ris de veau*, France), 398
    goulash (*gulyás*, Hungary), 208
        Viennese style (*wienersaft gulyás*, Austria), 208
    ground:
        cabbage rolls, stuffed (*dolma*, Iran), 148; (*töltött káposzta*, Hungary), 222
        curry, Bengal style (*keema korma*), 94-95
        eggplant and (*musaca cu patlagele vinete*, Roumania), 154-55
        eggplant, stuffed (*eierpflanze*, Germany), 223
        grape leaves, stuffed (*yaprak dolmasi*, Turkey), 156
        kohlrabi, stuffed (*töltött kalarábé*, Hungary), 224-25
        peppers, stuffed (*dolmeh felfel sabz*, Iran), 151; (*töltött zoldpaprika*, Hungary), 225
        roll (*coulebiac*, Russia), 152-53
        stew (*spezzatino*, Italy), 280
    ground (meatballs):
        in Korean fire pot, 88
        *kufta* (Middle East), 146
        in noodle soup (*ashe reshte*, Middle East), 134-35
        with rice (*arangini*, Italy), 278-79
    heart, skewers (*anticuchos*, Peru), 332

INDEX 419

in Korean fire pot, 88-89
with olives (*carne en salsa negra,* Spain), 332-33
with parsley sauce (*manzo in salsa di prezzemolo,* Italy), 276-77
with peanut sauce, Indonesia, 85
and peppers, China, 46
*picadillo* (mixed meat hash, South America), 343
pot roast:
   *boeuf à la mode,* France, 396-97; *en gelée,* 397
   *sauerbraten,* Germany, 212-13
   *stufatino alla Romano,* Italy, 276
ribs, short, and noodles (*sztufada,* Poland), 207
roast:
   *boeuf rôti à la bordelaise,* France, 393
   *carne asado,* South America, 335
with sauerkraut (*moskovskaya solyanka,* Russia), 164-65
sauerkraut-meat casserole (*erdélyi rakott kapusta,* Poland), 206
soups:
   beet-beef (*barszczyk,* Poland), 196
   chick-pea (*potaje de garbanzos,* Spain), 319
   goulash (*gulyásleves,* Hungary), 198-99
   *pot-au-feu,* France, 365
steak:
   braised (*Eszterházy rostélyos,* Austria), 210
   breaded (*bistecca parmigiana,* Italy), 274-75
   with chili-cheese sauce (*lomo à la huancaina,* Peru), 334
   in coconut cream (*opar daging,* Indonesia), 91
   with onions (*wiener rostbraten,* Austria), 208-9
   with peanut sauce (*cariucho,* Colombia), 333
   with peppers and tomatoes (*bistecca alla pizzaiola,* Italy), 277
   rolled stuffed (*sobrebarriga,* Colombia), 337
   skewered, Hawaiian style (*tariyaki*), 93
   spiced strips (*dondeng,* Indonesia), 96
   in *sukiyaki,* Japan, 92
   Tuscan style (*bistecca alla fiorentina,* Italy), 274
stew:
   with fruit (*carbonada criolla,* Argentina-Uruguay), 338-39
   *stiffado,* Greece, 149
   sweet and sour (*basar tz aloouie,* Israel), 164
   with vegetables:
      China, 45
      Japan, *chabu-chabu,* 90-91
   in white wine (*manzo al vino bianco,* Italy), 279
Beet soup:
   beef (*barszczyk,* Poland), 196
   shrimp (*balkanishe chlodnik,* Austria), 199
*Bigos myśliwski* (hunter's stew, Poland), 204-5
Bisque de homard (lobster bisque, France), 368
*Bistecca:*
   *alla fiorentina* (steak, Tuscan style, Italy), 274
   *alla pizzaiola* (steak with peppers and tomatoes, Italy), 277
   *parmigiana* (breaded steak, Italy), 274-75
Black bean sauce, Chinese:
   shrimp in, 17
   spareribs in, 41
*Blanquette de veau* (veal stew in cream, France), 400-401
*Boeuf:*
   *à la mode* (marinated pot roast, France), 396-97; *en gelée,* 397
   *rôti à la bordelaise* (marinated roast beef, France), 393
*Bogrács gulyás* (mixed meat goulash, Hungary), 211
Boiled dinner, Argentine (*puchero argentino*), 339
Bolognese sauce (*ragu,* Italy), 261

# 420 INDEX

*Borghul (bulgour)*, crushed wheat, Middle East, 132, 158
*Bouillabaisse:*
   *de chapon* (capon in spicy sauce, France), 385-86
   *marseillaise* (fish soup, Marseille style, France), 382-83
Bread:
   Arabic *(khoubz Araby)*, 166-67
   Chinese, 10-11
   Indian, deep-fried *(poori, chapatis)*, 114-15
*Briani machchi* (marinated fish and rice, India), 76
*Brinjal boortha* (eggplant relish, India), 111
*Brioche à la moëlle* (brioche with marrow and foie gras, France), 356-57
Broccoli with crab sauce, China, 24
Broth:
   Chinese, basic, chicken or pork, 24-25
   French, basic, chicken *(fond blanc)*, 364
Brown sauce:
   for chicken:
      Brazil *(frango ao môlho pardo)*, 325
      China, 30
   for fish: China, 18-19
   espagnole, France, 371
*Buerek* (flaky cheese appetizer pastries, Middle East), 129
*Bul-googi* (broiled marinated beef, Korea), 94
*Bulgour (borghul)*, crushed wheat, Middle East, 132, 158
*Buñuelos* (crullers in brown sugar sauce, South America), 349

Cabbage:
   pickled salted *(kim-chee,* Korea), 112
   pickled vegetable salad *(tourlu guvech,* Middle East), 168
   soup, browned *(káposztaleves,* Hungary), 195
   spiced vegetable salad *(gado-gado,* Indonesia), 113
   stuffed, rolls:
      *dolma,* Iran, 148

      *töltött káposzta,* Hungary, 222
   (*see also* Sauerkraut)
Cakes:
   *gênoise* (butter sponge cake, France), 413
   nut *(nustorte,* Austria), 241
   pyramid *(croquembouche,* France), 410-11
   walnut *(mazourka,* Russia), 174
*Camaroes fritos* (batter fried shrimp, Portugal), 305
*Camarónes con salsa de almendras* (shrimp in almond sauce, Ecuador), 306
*Canard:*
   *aux lentilles* (duck with lentils, France), 386-87
   *aux pêches* (duck with peaches, France), 388-89
*Canja* (thick chicken rice soup, Brazil), 318
Capon:
   and eggplant *(cappone alla siciliana,* Italy), 272
   in spicy sauce *(bouillabaisse de chapon,* France), 385-86
Caramelized apple tart *(tarte tatin,* France), 414-15
Caramelized custard *(crème brûlée,* France), 414
*Carbonada criolla* (beef and fruit stew, Argentina-Uruguay), 338-39
*Carciofi Borghese* (stuffed artichokes, Italy), 289
*Cariucho* (beef steak with peanut sauce, Colombia), 333
*Carne asado* (marinated roast beef, South America), 335
*Carne en salsa negra* (beef with olives, Spain), 332-33
Carrot, cream of, soup *(potage crème à nivernaise,* France), 366
Cauliflower, beef ribs and noodles with *(sztufada,* Poland), 207
Caviar, 120-21
   custard *(caviar au gratin,* France), 357
   Greek *(taramasalata),* 127
*Çerkes tavugu* (Circassian chicken, Turkey), 144

INDEX 421

*Chabu-chabu* (steamed beef with vegetables, Japan), 90-91
*Chapatis* (bread, India), 115
*Chatni* (chutney, India), 114
Cheese:
  breaded steak (*bistecca parmigiana*, Italy), 274-75
  chili-cheese sauce, steak with (*lomo à la huancaina*, Peru), 334
  cream (*see* Cream cheese)
  dessert, rich (*crema di formaggio*, Italy), 292
  in *Lasagne alla Partenope*, Italy, 257
  macaroni casserole (*pastichio*, Greece), 147
  macaroni pie (*pasticcio de maccheroni*, Italy), 259
  pastries:
    *empanadas de queso*, South America, 303
    flaky, appetizer (*buerek*, Middle East), 129
  peas and (*mattar panir*, India), 107
  pudding soufflé (*käsepudding*, Germany), 190-91
  sauce, Greek:
    for chicken pie, 142
    for lamb and eggplant casserole (*moussaka*), 160-61
  spinach pie (*spanakopeta*, Greece), 150
Chestnut dessert, chilled (*gato di castagne*, Italy), 293
Chicken:
  barbecued, China, 32-33
  boiled dinner, Argentine (*puchero argentino*), 339
  broth, basic:
    China, 24-25
    France, 364
  in brown sauce:
    Brazil (*frango ao môlho pardo*), 325
    China, 30
  capon:
    and eggplant (*cappone alla siciliana*, Italy), 272
    in spicy sauce (*bouillabaisse de chapon*, France), 385-86
  and chicken-pea curry (*murghi dal*, India), 84

  in *cholent* (meat and beans, Israel), 159
  Circassian (*çerkes tavugu*, Turkey), 144
  in coconut cream (*por ajam*, Indonesia), 87
  coconut-ginger (*renden santan*, Indonesia), 86
  cutlets (*cotletki pojarski*, Russia), 139
  enveloped, China, 11
  fricassee with wine (*pollo in fricassea*, Italy), 269
  fried:
    garlic (*spezzatino di pollo*, Italy), 268
    Peking, 30-31
    *wiener backhendl*, Austria, 203
  and giblets, soy (*yakitori*, Japan), 68
  hunter's style (*pollo alla cacciatore*, Italy), 270
  lemon, China, 32
  lichee, China, 33
  liver:
    mousse (*terrine de foie de volaille*, France), 356
    with noodle pancakes, China, 49
    pastries (*piroshki*, Russia), 130
    ragout (*hühnerleberragout*, Austria), 119
    *rumaki* (with water chestnut and bacon appetizer, Japan), 66
  noodles and shrimp with (*bahmi goreng*, Indonesia), 105
  orange-flavored pilaf (*shirini polo*, Iran), 140-41
  oregano (*kates riganati*, Greece), 141
  paprikash (*paprikahuhn*, Austria), 201
  pie (*kotopita*, Greece), 142-43
  poached stuffed (*poularde demi-deuil*, France), 384-85
  sautéed, Sicilian style (*polla alla siciliana*, Italy), 271
  on skewers with peanut sauce (*saté ajam*, Indonesia), 84-85
  soups:
    with fluffy dumplings (*sopa de espuma*, Mexico), 318-19
    hot-and-sour, China, 26

lemon (*soupa avgolemono*, Greece), 132-33
murghi shoorva (mulligatunny, India), 72
with rice, thick (*canja*, Brazil), 318
soto ajam (with bean sprouts, Indonesia), 68-69
umani (chicken patty-vegetable, Japan), 71
velvet, China, 28-29
spiced marinated (*murghi tandoori*, India), 83
in spicy bread sauce (*aji de gallina*, Bolivia), 326
*tchakhokhbili* (stew, Russia), 138-39
tortillas stuffed with (*enchiladas de pollo*, Mexico), 324
walnut, China, 29
wings, spiced, China, 13
Chick-peas:
appetizer (*hummus*, Middle East), 128-29
chicken and, curry (*murghi dal*, India), 84
codfish with (*bacalao à la Argentina*), 307
soup:
*potaje de garbanzos*, Spain, 319
Tuscan style (*minestra di ceci alla Tuscana*, Italy), 267
*Chiles rellenos con puerco* (pork-stuffed peppers, Mexico), 344
Chocolate:
-orange mousse (*mousse au chocolat et orange*, France), 411
torte:
*rigo torte*, Hungary, 238-39
*torta de chocolate*, Mexico, 348
*Cholent* (meat and beans, Israel), 159
*Chupe de mariscos* (seafood casserole, Peru-Chile), 310-11
Chutney, fruit (*chatni*, India), 114
Circassian chicken (*çerkes tavugu*, Turkey), 144
Clams:
pork and:
China, 39
*porco con amêjoas à Alentejana*, Portugal, 342

sauce, white, for *spaghettini zingarella*, Italy, 260-61
in seafood casserole (*chupe de mariscos*, Peru-Chile), 310-11
in seafood soup stew (*zarzuela de mariscos*, Spain), 312-13
soup (*zuppa di vongole*, Italy), 250
Coconut:
beef steak in coconut cream (*opar daging*, Indonesia), 91
chicken:
in coconut cream (*por ajam*, Indonesia), 87
coconut-ginger (*renden santan*, Indonesia), 86
cream and milk, Southeast Asia, 63
cream custard pudding, Malaysia, 115
fish croquettes in coconut cream, Polynesia, 81
pastries (*pastelitos de coco*, South America), 346-47
rice, Malaysia, 110
sambal (*seroendeng*, Indonesia), 110-11
sauce, shrimp in spiced, Indonesia, 78
shrimp and, stew (*vatapá*, Brazil), 308-9
Codfish, Argentina style (*bacalao à la Argentina*), 307
Cookies, walnut (*kourambiedes*, Greece), 173
Corn:
meat-corn pudding (*pastel de choclo*, Chile), 345
soup:
Chinese, 25; chicken velvet, 28-29
with potato and avocado (*ajiaco*, Colombia), 316
Cornmeal pie (*polenta pasticciata*, Italy), 262-63
*Cotelettes de porc en papillote* (pork chops in paper, France), 392
*Côtes de veau à l'orange* (veal chops with orange sauce, France), 399
*Côtes de porc grillées* (pork chops, marinated broiled, France), 391
*Cotletki* (veal croquettes, Russia), 165
*pojarski* (chicken cutlets, Russia), 139
*Coulebiac* (beef roll, Russia), 152-53

Crab:
   broccoli with crab sauce, China, 24
   with cucumber (*kani sunomono*, Japan), 67
   soft-shell, fried (*kani agemono*, Japan), 82
   in stuffed peppers, China, 23
Cream cheese:
   dessert (*crema di formaggio*, Italy), 292
   pancakes (*sirniki*, Russia), 171
   pastry (*vatroushki*, Russia), 172
   potato soup with (*kartoffelsuppe mit käse*, Germany), 197
   strudel filling, Austria-Hungary, 236
Cream pie, Viennese (*rahmstrudel*), 240
*Crema di formaggio* (cheese dessert, Italy), 292
*Crème brûlée* (caramelized custard, France), 414
*Crème St. Jacques* (cream of scallop soup, France), 369
*Croquembouche* (pyramid cake, France), 410-11
*Croustade de langouste bonne auberge* (lobster in puff pastry, France), 358-59
*Croûtes aux champignons* (mushrooms on toast, France), 362-63
Crullers:
   in brown sugar sauce (*buñuelos*, South America), 349
   *gozleme*, Iran, 175
*Csipetke* (dumplings, Hungary), 198-99
Cucumbers:
   pickled salted (*kim-chee*, Korea), 112
   soup (*jajik*, Middle East), 135
   and tomatoes in yogurt (*raita*, India), 109
Currants, rice and nuts with (*pilaf Ali Pasha*, Turkey), 168-69
Curry, 61
   beef:
     ground, Bengal style (*keema korma*), 94-95
     Siamese (*kaeng phed*), 95
     chicken and chick-pea (*murghi dal*, India), 84

lamb:
   with almonds (*malai korma*, India), 104
   with dumplings (*aush bhogar*, India), 102
   with lentils (*dhansak*, India), 100
   with rice (*pulao yakhni*, India), 98-99
   *roghan josh*, India, 101
   with spinach (*sagh mhas*, India), 103
   shrimp and rice (*machchi pilau*, India), 80

*Daikon* (radish or turnip pickles, Japan), 112
*Dal* (fried lentils, India), 108-9
*Darne de saumon à la Montpellier* (salmon in green butter, France), 374-75
Date-stuffed fish (*uskumaru dolmasi*, Turkey), 136
Desserts:
   almond *halva*, Middle East, 176
   almond torte (*torta de almendras*, Spain), 347
   *baklava* (flaky nut pastry, Iran), 178-79
   cakes:
     *génoise* (butter sponge cake, France), 413
     nut (*nustorte*, Austria), 241
     pyramid (*croquembouche*, France), 410-11
     walnut (*mazourka*, Russia), 174
   caramelized apple tart (*tarte tatin*, France), 414-15
   caramelized custard (*crème brûlée*, France), 414
   cheese, rich (*crema di formaggio*, Italy), 292
   chestnut, chilled (*gato di castagne*, Italy), 293
   chocolate-orange mousse (*mousse au chocolat-orange*, France), 411
   chocolate torte:
     *rigo torte*, Hungary, 238-39
     *torta de chocolate*, Mexico, 348

coconut cream custard pudding, Malaysia, 115
coconut pastries (*pastelitos de coco*, South America), 346-47
cream cheese pastries (*vatroushki*, Russia), 171
cream pie, Viennese (*rahmstrudel*), 240
crullers:
  in brown sugar sauce (*buñuelos*, South America), 349
  *gozleme*, Iran, 175
eight precious pudding, China, 53
fruit:
  with almond jelly, China, 54
  glazed, China, 55
  tart (*tarte aux fruits*, France), 409
gnocchi alla crema, Italy, 292-93
meringue soufflé (*salzburger nöckerl*, Austria), 230
noodle custard pudding, Israel, 170-71
pancakes:
  cream cheese (*sirniki*, Russia), 171
  in custard sauce (*topfenpalatschinken*, Austria), 232-33
  raisin omelet (*kaiserschmarn*, Austria), 233
  walnut (*oladyi*, Russian), 174-75
  walnut with chocolate cream (*gsusztatott palacsinta*, Hungary), 230-31
poppy seed candy pastries (*lomanci z makom*, Poland), 236-37
rice flour candy (*fereni*, Iran), 177
rice-fruit custard pudding (*shir berenj*, Iran), 176-77
rice mold, rich (*riz à l'impératrice*, France), 412
rice-raisin (*keskul*, Turkey), 178
strudel (*rétes*, Austria-Hungary), 234-36
  apple, 235
  cream cheese, 236
  poppy seed, 234-35
  walnut, 237
vermicelli (*sevian*, India), 117
walnut cookies (*kourambiedes*, Greek), 173

*Dhansak* (lamb curry with lentils, India), 100
*Dolma* (stuffed cabbage rolls, Iran), 148
*Dolmeh felfel sabz* (stuffed peppers, Iran), 151
*Dondeng* (spiced steak strips, Indonesia), 96
Duck:
  braised with olives (*pato con azeitunas*, Spain), 328-29
  fried, China, 34
    spiced, 35
    Szechuan style, 38
  with lentils (*canard aux lentilles*, France), 386-87
  in orange sauce (*pato con môlho de laranja*, Brazil), 327
  with peaches (*canard aux pêches*, France), 388-89
  pressed, China, 36-37
  roast stuffed (*anitra farcita e arrostita*, Italy), 273
  with walnuts (*fesenjan*, Iran), 145
Dumplings:
  *csipetke*, Hungary, 198-99
  egg drop (*spätzle*, Austria), 228
  lamb curry with (*aush bhogar*, India), 102
  liver (*leberknödel*, Germany), 228-29
  potato:
    gnocchi di patate, Italy, 258-59
    *kartoffelklösse*, Germany, 227
  soup with (*sopa de espuma*, Mexico), 318-19
  veal (*gnocchi di vitello*, Italy), 283

Egg drop dumplings (*spätzle*, Austria), 228
Eggplant:
  beef and, layers (*musaca cu patlagele vinete*, Roumanian), 154-55
  capon and (*cappone alla siciliana*, Italy), 272
  lamb and, casserole (*moussaka*, Greece), 160-61
  relish (*brinjal boortha*, India), 111
  spread (*baba ghannouj*, Middle East), 128

INDEX 425

stuffed:
    *eierpflanze*, Germany, 223
    *imam bayeldi*, Middle East, 153
Egg rolls (spring rolls), China, 12-13
Eggs with spicy sauce (*telur masak*, Indonesia), 75
*Eierpflanze* (stuffed eggplant, Germany), 223
Eight precious pudding, China, 53
*Empanadas:*
    *de camarónes* (shrimp pastries, South America), 302
    *de queso* (cheese pastries, South America), 303
*Enchiladas de pollo* (chicken-stuffed fried tortillas, Mexico), 324
Enveloped chicken, China, 11
*Erdélyi rakott káposzta* (sauerkraut-meat casserole, Poland), 206
*Escabeche de camarónes* (marinated shrimp, Mexico), 304-5
Espagnole sauce (brown sauce, France), 371
*Estouffat* (braised beef and beans, Spain), 331
*Eszterházy rostélyos* (braised steak, Austria), 210

*Fassolia me arni* (lamb and bean casserole, Greece), 155
*Fegato con risotto* (calf's liver with rice, Italy), 264
*Feijoada completa* (mixed meats and black beans, Brazil), 336-37
*Fereni* (rice flour candy dessert, Iran), 177
*Fesenjan* (duck with walnuts, Iran), 145
*Fettucine alla papalina* (noodles with egg sauce, Italy), 256
Figs, beef and, casserole (*sikbaj*, Iran), 157
Filberts:
    in chocolate torte (*rigo torte*, Hungary), 238-39
    in nut cake (*nustorte*, Austria), 241
*Filet aux ris de veau* (beef fillet with sweetbreads, France), 398
*Filet de boeuf en croustade* (beef fillet in pastry, France), 394-95

*Filetto ripieno* (stuffed fillet of beef, Italy), 275
Fire pot, Korea (*sin-sullo*), 88-90
Fish:
    baked, in papers (*poisson en papillote*, France), 376-77
    *bouillabaisse marseillaise* (fish soup, Marseille style, France), 382-83
    in brown sauce, China, 18-19
    chowder (*balik çorbasi*, Turkey), 133
    codfish, Argentina style (*bacalao à la Argentina*), 307
    croquettes:
        *albondigas de pescado*, South America, 309
        in coconut cream, Polynesia, 81
    date-stuffed (*uskumru dolmasi*, Turkey), 136
    fillets, stuffed (*huachinango relleno*, Mexico), 311
    fish-ball soup (*uwo dango no shiru*, Japan), 73
    fried spiced (*tali machchi*, India), 77
    mackerel in onion sauce (*maquereaux aux oignons*, France), 375
    marinated:
        and rice (*briani machchi*, India), 76
        *ryby marinovaná*, Czechoslovakia, 192
        *seviche chileño*, Chile, 313
    mousse (*mousseline de poisson*, France), 361
    mousse balls (*quenelles de brochet*, France), 378-79
    in nut sauce (*poisson Carcassone*, France), 373
    paprika (*szegedi pontyhalaszle*, Hungary), 194
    *pochouse bourguignonne* (mixed fish chowder, France), 381
    salmon in green butter (*darne de saumon à la Montpellier*, France), 374-75
    sea bass in tomato sauce (*spigola alla livornese*, Italy), 255
    shad Provençale (*alose à la provençale*, France), 377
    -shrimp chowder, Polynesian, 74

# 426 INDEX

in sour cream (*wiener fischfilets*, Austria), 193
sweet and pungent sliced, China, 19
sweet and sour, baked, Israel, 138
*tempura*, Japan, 78-79
trout, poached stuffed (*truite poêle*, France), 380
vegetables and, casserole (*ghivetch*, Roumania), 137
*Fond blanc, le* (chicken broth, France), 364
*Fondue aux champignons* (mushroom fondue, France), 406-7
*Frango ao môlho pardo* (chicken in brown sauce, Brazil), 325
Fruit:
with almond jelly, China, 54
chutney (*chatni*, India), 114
in crullers (*gozleme*, Iran), 175
glazed, China, 55
meat and, stew (*carbonada criolla*, Argentina-Uruguay), 338-39
rice-fruit custard pudding (*shir berenj*, Iran), 176-77
tart (*tarte aux fruits*, France), 409
*Funghi ripieni* (stuffed mushrooms, Italy), 291

*Gado-gado* (spiced vegetable salad, Indonesia), 113
*Gamberetti*:
*alla crema* (shrimp in tomato-cream sauce, Italy), 253
*alla griglia* (broiled garlic shrimp, Italy), 252
*Fra Diavolo* (shrimp with wine and tomato sauce, Italy), 251
Garlic:
fried chicken (*spezzatino di pollo*, Italy), 268
shrimp (*gamberetti alla griglia*, Italy), 252
spareribs, China, 14-15
*Gato di castagne* (chestnut dessert, chilled, Italy), 293
*Gazpacho andaluz* (cold vegetable soup, Spain), 315
*Gefülte gans* (stuffed goose, Germany), 202-3

*Gênoise* (butter sponge cake, France), 413
*Ghee*, India, 61-62, 64
*Ghivetch* (fish and vegetable casserole, Roumania), 137
Gnocchi:
*alla crema* (sweet, Italy), 292-93
*di patate* (potato dumplings, Italy), 258-59
*di vitello* (veal dumplings, Italy), 283
*Gombaleves* (mushroom soup, Hungary), 194-95
Goose, stuffed (*gefülte gans*, Germany), 202-3
Goulash (*gulyás*, Hungary), 209
bean, dried (*ungarishes bohnengulyás*, Austria-Hungary), 226
mixed meat (*bogrács gulyás*, Hungary), 211
pork and sauerkraut (*székely gulyás*, Hungary), 215
veal (*kalbsgulyás*, Austria), 218
Viennese style (*wienerschaft gulyás*), 208
Goulash soup (*gulyásleves*, Hungary), 198-99
*Gozleme* (fried crullers, Iran), 175
Grape leaves, stuffed (*yaprak dolmasi*, Turkey), 156
*Gratin de crevettes* (shrimp ramekins, France), 360-61
Green butter, salmon in (*darne de saumon à la Montpellier*, France), 374-75
Green rice (*risotto verde*, Italy), 263
*Gsusztatott palacsinta* (walnut pancakes with chocolate cream, Hungary), 230-31
*Gulyás* (*see* Goulash)
*Gulyásleves* (goulash soup, Hungary), 198-99

*Halva* (almond dessert, Middle East), 176
Ham:
in goulash, dried bean (*ungarishes bohnengulyás*, Austria-Hungary), 226

# INDEX 427

peas and (*piselli alla romana*, Italy), 290-91
prosciutto:
  and veal, medallions (*saltimbocca romana*, Italy), 281
  in veal pastries (*pasticceria con vitello*, Italy), 282-83
  roast fresh (*schweinebraten*, Germany), 213
Hollandaise sauce, France, 370-71
Hot-and-sour soup, China, 26
*Huachinango relleno* (stuffed fish fillets, Mexico), 311
*Hühnerleberragout* (chicken liver ragout, Austria), 191
*Hummus* (chick-pea appetizer, Middle East), 128-29
*Hunter's stew* (*bigos myśliwski*, Poland), 204-5

*Imam bayeldi* (stuffed eggplant, Middle East), 153
*Involti di vitello* (veal birds, Italy), 286

*Jajik* (cucumber soup, Middle East), 135

*Kaeng phed* (beef curry, Thailand), 95
*Kaiserschmarn* (raisin omelet pancake, Austria), 233
*Kalbsbraten* (roast veal with mushroom sauce, Germany), 220
*Kalbsgulyás* (veal goulash, Austria), 218
*Kani agemono* (fried soft-shell crabs, Japan), 82
*Kani sunomono* (crab meat and cucumber, Japan), 67
*Káposztaleves* (browned cabbage soup, Hungary), 195
*Kartoffelklösse* (potato dumplings, Germany), 227
*Kartoffelsuppe mit käse* (potato cheese soup, Germany), 197
*Käsepudding* (cheese pudding soufflé, Germany), 190-91
*Kates riganati* (oregano chicken, Greece), 141
*Keema korma* (ground beef curry, Bengal style), 94-95
*Keskul* (rice-raisin dessert, Turkey), 178

*Khoubz Araby* (Arabic bread), 166-67
*Kibbe* (baked lamb and wheat, Middle East), 158
Kidneys, veal, with peas (*rognons Clamart*, France), 403
*Kim-chee* (pickled salted vegetables, Korea), 112
*Kluay khaek* (batter fried bananas, Thailand), 116
Kohlrabi, stuffed (*töltött kalarábé*, Hungary), 224-25
*Korhelyleves* (sauerkraut soup, Hungary), 196-97
*Kotopita* (chicken pie, Greece), 142-43
*Kourambiedes* (walnut cookies, Greece), 173
*Krebspfannkuchen* (shrimp pancakes, Germany), 190
*Kufta* (meatballs, Middle East), 146
*Kukuye sabzi* (vegetable pie, Iran), 169

Lamb:
  beans and, casserole (*fassolia me arni*, Greece), 155
  broiled marinated (*shashlik à la Karsky*, Russia), 162
  in *cholent* (meat and beans, Israel), 159
  cubes, marinated (*saté kambing*, Indonesia), 98
  curry (*roghan josh*, India), 101
    with almonds (*malai korma*), 104
    with dumplings (*aush bhogar*), 102
    with lentils (*dhansak*), 100
    with rice (*pulao yakhni*), 98-99
    with spinach (*sagh mhas*), 103
  ground:
    eggplant and, casserole (*moussaka*, Greece), 160-61
    *samosas* (meat stuffed pastries, India), 65
    and wheat, baked (*kibbe*, Middle East), 158
  leg of:
    marinated (*raan*, India), 97
    roast, marinated (*agnello arrosto*, Italy), 280-81
  stew:
    *navarin de mouton*, France, 389

428  INDEX

Provence style (*ragoût d'agneau à la provençale*, France), 390-91
Langosta criolla (lobster in tomato sauce, South America), 314
Lasagne with sausage (*lasagne alla Partenope*, Italy), 257
Leberknödel (liver dumplings, Germany), 228-29
Lemon:
chicken, China, 32
soup (*soupa avgolemono*, Greece), 132-33
Lentils:
duck with (*canard aux lentilles*, France), 386-87
fried (*dal*, India), 108-9
lamb curry with (*dhansak*, India), 100
soup (*sukke dhal*, India), 69
Lichee chicken, China, 33
*Limba cu masline* (tongue with olives, Roumania), 163
Liver:
calf's, with rice (*fegato con risotto*, Italy), 264
chicken (*see* Chicken, liver)
dumplings (*leberknödel*, Germany), 228-29
Lobster:
and almonds, China, 21
bisque (*bisque de homard*, France), 368
in piquant sauce (*aragosta piccante*, Italy), 254
in puff pastry (*croustade de langouste bonne auberge*, France), 358-59
in seafood casserole (*chupe de mariscos*, Peru-Chile), 310-11
in seafood soup stew (*zarzuela de mariscos*, Spain), 312-13
steamed, China, 20
tails, stuffed, China, 22
in tomato sauce (*langosta criolla*, South America), 314
*Lomanci z makom* (poppy seed candy pastries, Poland), 236-37
*Lomo à la huancaina* (steak with chili-cheese sauce, Peru), 334
*Lomo de puerco en salsa raja* (marinated loin of pork with pepper sauce, Mexico), 341

Macaroni:
and bean soup (*pasta e fagioli*, Italy), 265
casserole (*pastichio*, Greece), 147
pie (*pasticcio de maccheroni*, Italy), 259
*Machchi pilau* (curried shrimp and rice, India), 80
Mackerel in onion sauce (*maquereaux aux oignons*, France), 375
*Malai korma* (lamb and almond curry, India), 104
*Manzo*:
*peperonata* (fillet of beef with pepper sauce, Italy), 278
*con salsa di prezzemolo* (beef with parsley sauce, Italy), 276-77
*al vino bianco* (beef in white wine, Italy), 279
*Maquereaux aux oignons* (mackerel in onion sauce, France), 375
Marinara sauce for spaghetti, Italy, 258
*Marinierte krebse* (marinated shrimp, Germany), 189
*Masa Harina* (corn flour, Mexico), 323
*Mattar panir* (peas and cheese, India), 107
*Mazourka* (walnut cake, Russia), 174
Meat, mixed:
boiled dinner, Argentine (*puchero argentino*), 339
in *feijoada completa*, Brazil, 336-37
goulash (*bogrács gulyás*, Hungary), 211
hunter's stew (*bigos myśliwski*, Poland), 204-5
Korean fire pot (*sin-sullo*), 88-89
*picadillo* (hash, South America), 343
*spezzatino* (ground meat stew, Italy), 280
Meatballs:
in Korean fire pot, 88
*kufta*, Middle East, 146
in noodle soup (*ashe reshte*, Middle East), 134-35
with rice (*arangini*, Italy), 278-79

Meringue soufflé (*salzburger nöckerl*, Austria), 230
Midea yemista (stuffed mussels, Greece), 131
*Minestra:*
  *di ceci alla tuscana* (chick-peas, Tuscan style, Italy), 267
  *di riso e prezzemolo* (rice and parsley soup, Italy), 264-65
*Minestrone* (vegetable-bean soup, Italy), 266
*Miso-taki* (bean soup, Japan), 70
*Mole de guajolote* (turkey with *mole* sauce, Mexico), 329
*Mole Poblano*, Mexico, 328
*Mollejas al jerez* (sweetbreads in sherry, Spain), 346
*Mondongo* (pepper pot, South America), 321
Moo Shoo pork, China, 40-41
*Moskovskaya solyanka* (beef with sauerkraut, Russia), 164-65
*Moules à la crème* (mussels in wine-cream sauce, France), 372
*Moussaka* (lamb and eggplant casserole, Greece), 160-61
*Mousse au chocolat et orange* (chocolate-orange mousse, France), 411
*Mousseline de poisson* (fish mousse, France), 361
*Murghi:*
  *dal* (chicken and chick-pea curry, India), 84
  *shoorva* (chicken mulligatunny, India), 72
  *tandoori* (spiced marinated chicken, India), 83
*Musaca cu patlagele vinete* (meat-eggplant layers, Roumania), 154-55
Mushrooms:
  artichokes and peas with (*artichauts à la provençale*, France), 406
  fondue (*fondue aux champignons*, France), 406-7
  soup (*gombaleves*, Hungary), 194-95
  stuffed (*funghi ripieni*, Italy), 291
  on toast (*croûtes aux champignons*, France), 362-63

Mussels:
  in seafood casserole (*chupa de mariscos*, Peru-Chile), 310-11
  in seafood soup stew (*zarzuela de mariscos*, Spain), 312-13
  stuffed (*midea yemista*, Greek), 131
  in wine-cream sauce (*moules à la crème*, France), 372
Mustard, China, 16

*Nasi goreng* (fried rice, Indonesia), 106
*Navarin de mouton* (lamb stew, France), 389
Noodles:
  beef ribs and (*sztufada*, Poland), 207
  chicken and shrimp with (*bahmi goreng*, Indonesia), 105
  Chinese:
    pancakes, with chicken livers, 49
    rice, 50
    soft, with pork, 48
  custard pudding, Israel, 170-71
  with egg sauce (*fettucine alla papalina*, Italy), 256
  Japanese:
    in *chabu-chabu*, 90-91
    in *sukiyaki*, 92
  soup, meatball (*ashe reshte*, Middle East), 134-35
*Nustorte* (nut cake, Austria), 241
Nuts:
  cake (*nustorte*, Austria, 241
  chocolate torte (*rigo torte*, Hungary), 238-39
  fish with nut sauce (*poisson Carcassonne*, France), 373
  poppy seed candy pastries (*lomanci z makom*, Poland), 236-37
  (*see also* Almonds; Peanuts; Walnuts)

Okra, batter fried (*sabzi bhindi*, India), 108
*Oladyi* (walnut pancakes, Russia), 174-75
Olives:
  beef with (*carne en salsa negra*, Spain), 332-33
  duck, braised, with (*pato con azeitunas*, Spain), 328-29

# 430 INDEX

tongue with (*limba cu masline*, Roumania), 163
Omelets:
    banana (*tortilla de banana*, South America), 304
    raisin, pancakes (*kaiserschmarn*, Austria), 233
Onion:
    pancakes, China, 15
    purée, France, 405
    soup with cheese crusts (*soupe à l'oignon gratinée*, France), 363
*Opar daging* (beef steak in coconut cream, Indonesia), 91
Orange:
    chocolate-orange mousse (*mousse au chocolat et orange*, France), 411
    -flavored chicken pilaf (*shirini polo*, Iran), 140-41
    sauce:
        duck with (*pato com môlho de laranja*, Brazil), 327
        veal chops with (*côte de veau à l'orange*, France), 399
Oregano chicken (*kates riganati*, Greece), 141
*Ossi buchi* (braised veal knuckles, Italy), 287

*Paella* (Spanish national rice dish), 322-23
Pancakes:
    cream cheese (*sirniki*, Russia), 171
    in custard sauce (*topfenpalatschinken*, Austria), 232-33
    noodle, with chicken livers, China, 49
    onion, China, 15
    raisin omelet (*kaiserschmarn*, Austria), 233
    shrimp (*krebspfannkuchen*, Germany), 190
    walnut:
        with chocolate cream (*gsusztatott palacsinta*, Hungary), 230-31
        *oladyi*, Russia, 174-75
Paprika fish (*szegedi pontyhalaszle*, Hungary), 194
*Paprikahuhn* (chicken paprikash, Austria), 201

*Paprika rahmschnitzel* (veal sautéed in paprika sauce, Austria), 217
*Paprikás burgonya* (potatoes in paprika sauce, Austria-Hungary), 226-27
*Pasta e fagioli* (macaroni and bean soup, Italy), 265
*Pastel de choclo* (beef-corn pudding, Chile), 345
*Pastel de mole* (stuffed patty shells, Mexico), 328
*Pastelitos de coco* (coconut pastries, South America), 346-47
*Pasticceria con vitello* (veal pastries, Italy), 282-83
*Pasticcio de maccheroni* (macaroni pie, Italy), 259
*Pastichio* (macaroni casserole, Greece), 147
Pastry:
    almond torte (*torte de almendras*, Spain), 347
    *baklava* (flaky nut pastry, Iran), 178-79
    beef fillet in (*filet de boeuf en croustade*, France), 394-95
    beef roll (*coulebiac*, Russia), 152-53
    caramelized apple tart (*tarte tatin*, France), 414-15
    cheese (*empanadas de queso*, South America), 303
    cheese, flaky, appetizer (*buerek*, Middle East), 129
    chicken liver (*piroshki*, Russia), 130
    chicken pie (*kotopita*, Greece), 142-43
    chocolate torte:
        *rigo torte*, Hungary, 238-39
        *torta de chocolate*, Mexico, 348
    coconut (*pastelitos de coco*, South America), 346-47
    cream cheese (*vatroushki*, Russia), 172
    cream pie (*rahmstrudel*, Austria), 240
    fruit tart (*tarte aux fruits*, France), 409
    lobster in puff (*croustade de langouste bonne auberge*, France), 358-59
    meat stuffed (*samosas*, India), 65
    patty shells, stuffed (*pastel de mole*, Mexico), 328

INDEX 431

poppy seed candy (*lomanci z makom*, Poland), 236-37
potato pie (*pommes de terre auvergnate*, France), 408
shrimp (*empanadas de camarónes*, South America), 302
spinach pie (*spanakopeta*, Greece), 150
strudel (*rétes*, Austria-Hungary), 234-36 (*see also* Strudel)
veal (*pasticceria con vitello*, Italy), 282-83
*Pato con azeitunas* (braised duck with olives, Spain), 328-29
*Pato com môlho de laranja* (duck in orange sauce, Brazil), 327
Peaches, duck with (*canard aux pêches*, France), 388-89
Peanuts:
  pork with, China, 44
  sauce:
    beef steak with (*cariucho*, Colombia), 333
    chicken with, Indonesia, 84-85
Peas:
  artichokes and mushrooms with (*artichauts à la provençale*, France), 406
  and cheese (*mattar panir*, India), 107
  green, purée (*purée Saint-Germain*, France), 407
  and ham (*piselli alla romana*, Italy), 290-91
  kidneys with (*rognons Clamart*, France), 403
  and rice (*risi e bisi*, Italy), 290
Peking chicken, fried, China, 30-31
Pepper pot (*mondongo*, South America), 321
Peppers:
  beef and, China, 46
  stuffed:
    Chinese, 23
    Hungarian (*töltött zoldpaprika*), 225
    Iranian (*dolmeh felfel sabz*), 151
    Mexican, pork-stuffed (*chiles rellenos con puerco*), 344
Pepper sauce, marinated pork loin with (*lomo de puerco en salsa raja*, Mexico), 341
*Peru al jerez* (marinated braised turkey, Spain), 330
*Phyllo* leaves, 129, 142-43, 150, 178-79
*Picadillo* (mixed meat hash, South America), 343
*Piccata di vitello Venezia* (veal scaloppine with zucchini, Italy), 288
Pickled vegetable salad (*tourlu guvech*, Middle East), 168
Pickles:
  radish (*daikon*) or turnip, Japan, 112
  salted vegetables (*kim-chee*, Korea), 112
  Szechuan, China, 52
Pigs' knuckles, jellied (*sülze*, Germany), 221
Pilaf:
  chicken, orange-flavored (*shirini polo*, Iran), 140
  rice with currants and nuts (*pilaf Ali Pasha*, Turkey), 168-69
*Piroshki* (chicken liver pastries, Russia), 130
*Piselli alla romana* (peas and ham, Italy), 290-91
*Pochouse bourguignonne, la* (mixed fish chowder, France), 381
Poisson:
  *Carcassonne* (fish in nut sauce, France), 373
  *en papillote* (baked fish in papers, France), 376-77
*Poitrine de veau farcie* (stuffed breast of veal, France), 402
*Polenta pasticciata* (cornmeal pie, Italy), 262-63
Pollo:
  *alla cacciatora* (chicken, hunter's style, Italy), 270
  *alla siciliana* (sautéed chicken, Sicilian style, Italy), 271
  *in fricassea* (chicken fricassee with wine, Italy), 269
*Pommes de terre auvergnate* (potato pie, France), 408
*Poori* (deep-fried bread, India), 114-15

Poppy seed:
  candy pastries (*lomanci z makom*, Poland), 236-37
  strudel filling, 234-35
*Por ajam* (chicken in coconut cream, Indonesia), 87
*Porco com amêjoas à Alentejana* (pork and clams, Portugal), 342
Pork:
  barbecued, China, 14
  broth, basic, China, 24-25
  in cabbage rolls, stuffed, (*töltött káposzta*, Hungary), 222
  casserole (*rindslendenragout*, Austria), 214
  chops:
    marinated broiled (*côtes de porc grillée*, France), 391
    in paper (*cotelettes de porc en papillote*, France), 392
  and clams:
    China, 39
    *porco com amêjoas à Alentejana*, Portugal, 342
  in fried rice, China, 50-51
  goulash, with sauerkraut (*székely gulyás*, Hungary), 215
  in Korean fire pot, 88-89
  in lobster tails, stuffed, China, 22
  loin, marinated, with pepper sauce (*lomo de puerco en salsa raja*, Mexico), 341
  Moo Shoo, China, 40-41
  with noodles, soft, China, 48
  with peanuts, China, 44
  with peanut sauce, Indonesia, 85
  *picadillo* (mixed meat hash, South America), 343
  pigs' knuckles, jellied (*sülze*, Germany), 221
  rice and (*sopa seca*, South America), 340
  roast fresh ham (*schweinebraten*, Germany), 213
  sauerkraut-meat casserole (*erdélyi rakott kapusta*, Poland), 206
  soup:
    corn, China, 25
    hot-and-sour, China, 26

  spareribs (*see* Spareribs)
  spring rolls (egg rolls), China, 12-13
  -stuffed peppers (*chiles rellenos con puerco*, Mexico), 344
  sweet and pungent, China, 42
  twice-cooked, China, 43
*Potage crème à la nivernaise* (cream of carrot soup, France), 366
*Potaje de garbanzos* (chick-pea soup, Spain), 319
Potato:
  dumplings:
    *gnocchi di patate*, Italy, 258-59
    *kartoffelklösse*, Germany, 227
    in paprika sauce (*paprikás burgonya*, Austria-Hungary), 226-27
  pie (*pommes de terre auvergnate*, France), 408
  soup:
    with corn and avocado (*ajiaco*, Colombia), 316
    with cream cheese (*kartoffelsuppe mit käse*, Germany), 197
*Pot-au-feu* (beef soup, France), 365
*Poularde demi-deuil* (poached stuffed chicken, France), 384-85
Prosciutto:
  veal and, medallions (*saltimbocca romana*, Italy), 281
  in veal pastries (*pasticceria con vitello*, Italy), 282-83
*Puchero argentino* (Argentina boiled dinner), 339
*Pulao yakhni* (lamb and rice curry, India), 98-99
*Purée Saint-Germain* (green pea purée, France), 407
Pyramid cake (*croquembouche*, France), 410-11

*Quenelles de brochet* (fish mousse balls, France), 378-79

*Raan* (marinated leg of lamb, India), 97
*Ragoût d'agneau à la provençale* (lamb stew, Provence style, France), 390-91
*Ragu* (Bolognese sauce, Italy), 261
*Rahmstrudel* (Viennese cream pie, 240

Raisin omelet pancakes (*kaiserschmarn*, Austria), 233
Raisins, rice and, dessert (*keskul*, Turkey), 178
*Raita* (cucumbers and tomatoes in yogurt, India), 109
Relishes:
   chutney, fruit (*chatni*, India), 114
   eggplant (*brinjal boortha*, India), 111
   (*see also* Pickles)
*Renden santan* (coconut-ginger chicken, Indonesia), 86
*Rétes* (*see* Strudel)
Rice:
   calf's liver with (*fegato con risotto*, Italy), 264
   chicken-rice soup, thick (*canja*, Brazil), 318
   coconut, Malaysia, 110
   with currants and nuts (*pilaf Ali Pasha*, Turkey), 168-69
   flour candy dessert (*ferani*, Iran), 177
   fried:
      *nasi goreng*, Indonesia, 106
      Yangchow style, China, 50-51
   -fruit custard pudding (*shir berenj*, Iran), 176-77
   green (*risotto verde*, Italy), 263
   with lamb curry (*pulao yakhni*, India), 98-99
   in meat balls (*arangini*, Italy), 278-79
   mold, rich (*riz à l'impératrice*, France), 412
   noodles, China, 50
   *paella* (Spanish national rice dish), 322-23
   and parsley soup (*minestra di riso e prezzemolo*, Italy), 264-65
   and peas (*risi e bisi*, Italy), 290
   and pork (*sopa seca*, South America), 340
   -raisin dessert (*keskul*, Turkey), 178
*Rigo torte* (chocolate torte, Hungary), 238-39
*Rijstaffel*, Java, 60
*Rindfleisch in bier* (boiled beef in beer, Austria), 205
*Rindslendenragout* (pork casserole, Austria), 214

*Ris de veau à l'oignon* (sweetbreads, Lyonnaise style, France), 404-5
*Risi e bisi* (rice and peas, Italy), 290
*Risotto verde* (green rice, Italy), 263
*Riz à l'impératrice* (rice mold, rich, France), 412
*Roghan josh* (lamb curry, India), 101
*Rognons Clamart* (kidneys with peas, France), 403
*Rumaki* (chicken liver with water chestnuts and bacon appetizer, Japan), 66
*Ryby marinované* (marinated fish, Czechoslovakia), 192

*Sabzi bhindi* (batter fried okra, India), 108
*Sabzi salade* (mixed salad, Iran), 167
*Sagh mhas* (lamb-spinach curry, India), 103
Salads:
   cucumbers and tomatoes in yogurt (*raita*, India), 109
   mixed (*sabzi salade*, Iran), 167
   pickled vegetable (*tourlu guvech*, Middle East), 168
   spiced vegetable (*gado-gado*, Indonesia), 113
   wheat and tomato (*tabbouleh*, Middle East), 132
Salmon in green butter (*darne de saumon à la Montpellier*, France), 374-75
*Saltimbocca romana* (veal and prosciutto medallions, Italy), 281
*Salzburger nöckerl* (meringue soufflé, Austria), 230
*Sambal oedang* (shrimp in spiced coconut sauce, Indonesia), 78
*Samosas* (meat stuffed pastries, India), 65
Sardine antipasto (*sardine alla Veneto*, Italy), 249
*Saté kambing* (marinated lamb cubes, Indonesia), 98
Sauces:
   almond, shrimp in (*camarónes con salsa de almendras*, Ecuador), 306

bacon-tomato, with spaghetti, Italy, 262
black bean, China:
   for shrimp, 17
   for spareribs, 41
Bolognese (*ragu*, Italy), 261
bread, spicy, for chicken (*aji de gallina*, Bolivia), 326
brown, for chicken:
   Brazil (*frango ao môlho pardo*), 325
   China, 30
brown, for fish, China, 18-19
brown (espagnole) France, 371
brown sugar, crullers in (*buñuelos*, South America), 349
chili-cheese, steak with (*lomo à la huancaina*, Peru), 334
clam, white, for *spaghettini zingarella*, Italy, 260-61
coconut, spiced, for shrimp, Indonesia, 78
espagnole, France, 371
hollandaise, France, 370-71
*mole*, turkey with (*mole de guanajote*, Mexico), 329
*Mole Poblano*, Mexico, 328
orange:
   duck with (*pato com môlho de laranja*, Brazil), 327
   veal chops with (*côte de veau à l'orange*, France), 399
peanut:
   beef steak with (*cariucho*, Colombia), 333
   chicken with, Indonesia, 84-85
pepper, marinated pork loin with (*lomo de puerco en salsa raja*, Mexico), 341
sesame (*taratoor*, Middle East), 170
sweet and pungent, for fish, China, 19
*tempura*, Japan, 79, 82
tomato:
   lobster with (*langosta criolla*, South America), 314
   marinara, with spaghetti, Italy, 258
   with shrimp: China, 18; *crevettes à l'américaine*, France, 362
tuna fish:
   with spaghetti, Italy, 260

veal in (*vitello tonnato*, Italy), 284-85
*Sauerbraten* (marinated pot roast, Germany), 212-13
Sauerkraut:
   beef with (*moskovskaya solyanka*, Russia), 164-65
   -meat casserole (*erdélyi rakott kapusta*, Poland), 206
   soup (*korhelyleves*, Hungary), 196-97
   spareribs with (*wieprzowina z kapusta*, Poland) 216
Scallops:
   cream of, soup (*crème St. Jacques*, France), 369
   in seafood soup stew (*zarzuela de mariscos*, Spain), 312-13
   and shrimp, soup (*sopa de pescado*, Peru), 317
Scaloppine, veal, with zucchini (*piccata di vitello Venezia*, Italy), 288
*Schweinebraten* (roast fresh ham, Germany), 213
Sea bass in tomato sauce (*spigola alla livornese*, Italy), 255
Seafood:
   casserole (*chupe de mariscos*, Peru-Chile), 310-11
   *tempura*, Japan, 78-79
   *zarzuela de mariscos* (soup stew, Spain), 312-13
   (*see also* Crab; Fish; Lobster; Mussels; Scallops; Shrimp)
*Seroendeng* (coconut sambal, Indonesia), 110-11
Sesame sauce (*taratoor*, Middle East), 170
*Sevian* (vermicelli dessert, India), 117
Shad Provençale (*alose à la provençale*, France), 377
Shark's fin soup, China, 27
*Shaslik à la Karsky* (broiled marinated lamb, Russia), 162
*Shir berenj* (rice-fruit custard pudding, Iran), 176-77
Shrimp:
   in almond sauce (*camarónes con salsa de almendras*, Ecuador), 306
   balls, fried, China, 16

INDEX 435

batter fried (*camaroes fritos*, Portugal) 305
-beet soup (*balkanishe chlodnik*, Austria), 199
in black bean sauce, China, 17
coconut stew (*vatapá*, Brazil), 308-9
curried, and rice (*machchi pilau*, India), 80
-fish chowder, Polynesia, 74
garlic, broiled (*gamberetti alla griglia*, Italy), 252
marinated:
   *escabeche de camarónes*, Mexico, 304-5
   *marinierte krebse*, Germany, 189
noodles and chicken with (*bahmi goreng*, Indonesia), 105
pancakes (*krebspfannkuchen*, Germany), 190
pastries (*empanadas de camarónes*, South America), 302
ramekins (*gratin de crevettes*, France), 360-61
and scallops, soup (*sopa de pescado*, Peru), 317
in seafood casserole (*chupe de mariscos*, Peru-Chile), 310-11
in seafood soup stew (*zarzuela de mariscos*, Spain), 312-13
in spiced coconut sauce (*sambal oedang*, Indonesia), 78
-spinach soup, China, 28
*tempura*, Japan, 78-79
toast, China, 9
in tomato-cream sauce (*gamberetti alla crema*, Italy), 253
in tomato sauce:
   China, 18
   spicy (*crevettes à l'américaine*, France), 362
with wine and tomatoes (*gamberetti Fra Diavolo*, Italy), 251
Sikbaj (beef and fig casserole, Iran), 157
Sin-sullo (Korean fire pot), 88-90
Sirniki (cream cheese pancakes, Russia), 171
Sobrebarriga (rolled stuffed steak, Colombia), 337

Sopa:
   *de espuma* (soup with fluffy dumplings, Mexico), 318-19
   *de frijoles meturado* (mixed bean soup, South America), 320
   *de pescado* (shrimp and scallop soup, Peru), 317
   *seca* (pork and rice, South America), 340
Soto ajan (chicken and bean sprout soup, Indonesia), 68-69
Soupe:
   *à l'oignon gratinée* (onion soup with cheese crusts, France), 363
   *au Pistou* (vegetable-herb soup, France), 367
Soups:
   bean:
      *miso-taki*, Japan, 70
      mixed (*sopa de frijoles meturado*, South America), 320
   beef (*pot-au-feu*, France), 365
   beet-beef (*barszczyk*, Poland), 196
   *bouillabaisse marseillaise* (fish soup, Marseille syle, France), 382-83
   cabbage, browned (*káposztaleves*, Hungary), 195
   chicken:
      and bean sprouts (*soto ajam*, Indonesian), 68-69
      with dumplings, fluffy (*sopa de espuma*, Mexico), 318-19
      mulligatunny (*murghi shoorva*, India), 72
      patty-vegetable (*umani*, Japan), 71
      -rice, thick (*canja*, Brazil), 318
      velvet, China, 28-29
   chick-pea:
      *potaje de garbanzos*, Spain, 319
      Tuscan style (*minestra di ceci alla tuscana*, Italy), 267
   clam (*zuppa di vongole*, Italy), 250
   corn, China, 25
   cream of carrot (*potage crème à la nivernaise*, France), 366
   cream of scallop (*crème St. Jacques*, France), 369
   cream of tomato and avocado (*velouté Aurore*, France), 370

cucumber (*jajik*, Middle East), 135
fish-ball (*uwo dango no shiru*, Japan), 73
fish chowder (*balik çorbasi*, Turkey), 133
fish-shrimp chowder, Polynesia, 74
goulash (*gulyasleves*, Hungary), 198-99
hot-and-sour, China, 26
lemon (*soupa avgolemono*, Greece), 132-33
lentil (*sukke dhal*, India), 69
lobster bisque (*bisque de homard*, France), 368
macaroni and bean (*pasta e fagioli*, Italy), 265
minestrone (vegetable-bean, Italy), 266
mushroom (*gombaleves*, Hungary), 194-95
noodle-meatball (*ashe reshte*, Middle East), 134-35
onion with cheese crusts (*soupe à l'oignon gratinée*, France), 363
pochouse bourguignonne (mixed fish chowder, France), 381
potato, corn, and avocado (*ajiaco*, Colombia), 316
rice and parsley (*minestra di riso e prezzemolo*, Italy), 264-65
sauerkraut (*korhelyleves*, Hungary), 196-97
shark's fin, China, 27
shrimp-beet (*balkanishe chlodnik*, Austria), 199
shrimp-spinach, China, 28
vegetable, cold (*gazpacho andaluz*, Spain), 315
vegetable-herb (*soupe au Pistou*, France), 367
yogurt (*yogurt çorbasi*, Middle East), 134
Spaghetti:
alla boscaiola (with tuna fish sauce, Italy), 260
all'amatriciana (with bacon-tomato sauce, Italy), 262
marinara (with tomato sauce, Italy), 258

Spaghettini with white clam sauce (*spaghettini zingarella*, Italy), 260-61
Spanakopeta (spinach pie, Greece), 150
Spareribs:
barbecued, China, 10
with black bean sauce, China, 41
garlic, China, 14-15
with sauerkraut and barley (*wieprzowina z kapusta*, Poland), 216
Spätzle (egg drop dumplings, Austria), 228
Spezzatino (ground meat stew, Italy), 280
di pollo (garlic fried chicken, Italy), 268
Spigola alla livornese (sea bass in tomato sauce, Italy), 255
Spinach:
lamb curry with (*sagh mhas*, India), 103
pie (*spanakopeta*, Greece), 150
shrimp-spinach soup, China, 28
vegetable pie (*kukuye sabzi*, Iran), 169
Spring rolls (egg rolls), China, 12-13
Steak (see Beef, steak)
Stiffado (beef stew, Greece), 149
Strudel (*rétes*, Austria-Hungary), 234-36
apple filling, 235
cream cheese filling, 236
poppy seed filling, 234-35
walnut (*diósrétes*), 237
Strudel leaves, 129, 142-43, 150, 178-79
Stufatino (braised breast of veal, Italy), 285
alla Romano (pot roast in red wine, Italy), 276
Sukiyaki, Japan, 92-93
Sülze (jellied pigs' knuckles, Germany), 221
Sweet and pungent:
fish, China, 19
pork, China, 42
Sweet and sour:
fish, baked, Israel, 138
meat (*basar tz aloouie*, Israel), 164
Sweetbreads:
fillet of beef with (*filet aux ris de veau*, France), 398

Lyonnaise style (*ris de veau à l'oignon*, France), 404-5
  in sherry (*mollejas al jerez*, Spain), 346
Sweets (*see* Desserts)
Szechuan pickles, China, 52
*Szegedi pontyhalaszle* (paprika fish, Hungary), 194
*Székely gulyás* (pork and sauerkraut goulash, Hungary), 215
*Sz*ᵗ*ufada* (beef ribs and noodles, Poland), 207

*Tabbouleh* (wheat and tomato appetizer salad, Middle East), 132
*Tali machchi* (fried spiced fish, India), 77
*Taramasalata* (Greek caviar), 127
*Taratoor* (sesame sauce, Middle East), 170
*Tariyaki* (skewered steak, Hawaiian style), 93
*Tarte:*
  *aux fruits* (fruit tart, France), 409
  *tatin* (caramelized apple tart, France), 414-15
*Tchakhokhbili* (chicken stew, Russia), 138-39
*Telur masak* (eggs with spicy sauce, Indonesia), 75
*Tempura* (batter fried seafood and vegetables, Japan), 78-79
  sauce, 79, 82
*Terrine de foie de volaille* (chicken liver mousse, France), 356
*Töltött kalarábé* (stuffed kohlrabi, Hungary), 224-25
*Töltött káposzta* (stuffed cabbage rolls, Hungary, 222
*Töltött zoldpaprika* (stuffed peppers, Hungary), 225
Tomato:
  cream of, and avocado soup (*velouté Aurore*, France), 370
  and cucumbers in yogurt (*raita*, India), 109
  wheat and, appetizer salad (*tabbouleh*, Middle East), 132

Tomato sauce:
  bacon-, with spaghetti, Italy, 262
  lobster with (*langosta criolla*, South America), 314
  *marinara*, with spaghetti, Italy, 258
  shrimp in:
    China, 18
    *crevettes à l'américaine*, France, 362
Tongue with olives (*limba cu masline*, Roumania), 163
*Topfenpalatschinken* (pancakes in custard sauce, Austria), 232-33
*Torta:*
  *de almendras* (almond torte, Spain), 347
  *de chocolate* (chocolate torte, Mexico), 348
Tortillas, Mexico, 300, 323
  *de banana* (banana omelet, South America), 304
  chicken-stuffed fried (*enchiladas de pollo*, Mexico), 324
*Tourlu guvech* (pickled vegetable salad, Middle East), 168
Tripe, pepper pot (*mondongo*, South America), 321
Trout, poached stuffed (*truite poêle*, France), 380
Tuna fish sauce:
  spaghetti with (*spaghetti alla boscaiola*, Italy), 260
  veal in (*vitello tonnato*, Italy), 284-85
Turkey:
  marinated braised (*peru al jerez*, Spain), 330
  with *mole* sauce (*mole de guajolote*, Mexico), 329
Turnips:
  pickled, Japan, 112
  pickled vegetable salad (*tourlu guvech*, Middle East), 168

*Umani* (chicken patty-vegetable soup, Japan), 71
*Ungarishes bohnengulyás* (dried bean goulash, Hungary), 226
*Uskumru dolmasi* (date-stuffed fish, Turkey), 136

# 438 INDEX

*Uwo dango no shiru* (fish-ball soup, Japan), 73

*Vatapá* (shrimp coconut stew, Brazil), 308-9
*Vatroushkis* (cream cheese pastries, Russia), 172
Veal:
  birds (*involti di vitello*, Italy), 286
  braised breast of (*stufatino*, Italy), 285
  chops with orange sauce (*côte de veau à l'orange*, France), 399
  cutlets:
    breaded (*wiener schnitzel*, Austria), 218-19
    sautéed in paprika sauce (*paprika rahmschnitzel*, Austria), 217
  dumplings (*gnocchi di vitello*, Italy), 283
  goulash (*kalbsgulyás*, Austria), 218
  ground:
    in cabbage rolls (*töltött káposzta*, Hungary), 222
    croquettes (*cotletki*, Russia), 165
    in kohlrabi, stuffed (*töltött kalarábé*, Hungary), 224-25
    stew (*spezzatino*, Italy), 280
  kidneys with peas (*rognons Clamart*, France), 403
  knuckles, braised (*ossi buchi*, Italy), 287
  pastries (*pasticceria con vitello*, Italy), 282-83
  and prosciutto medallions (*saltimbocca romana*, Italy), 281
  roast, with mushroom sauce (*kalbsbraten*, Germany), 220
  scaloppine with zucchini (*piccata di vitello Venezia*, Italy), 288
  stew in cream (*blanquette de veau*, France), 400-401
  stuffed breast of (*poitrine de veau farcie*, France), 402
  sweetbreads (*see* Sweetbreads)
  in tuna fish sauce (*vitello tonnato*, Italy), 284-85
Vegetables:
  beef with:
    *chabu-chabu*, Japan, 90-91
    China, 45
  in boiled dinner, Argentina (*puchero argentino*), 339
  fish and, casserole (*ghivetch*, Roumania), 137
  in Korean fire pot, 89
  mixed, salad (*sabzi salade*, Iran), 167
  pickled, salad (*tourlu guvech*, Middle East), 168
  pickled salted (*kim-chee*, Korea), 112
  pie (*kukuye sabzi*, Iran), 169
  soup:
    cold (*gazpacho andaluz*, Spain), 315
    -herb (*soupe au Pistou*, France), 367
    *minestrone*, Italy, 266
  spiced, salad (*gado-gado*, Indonesia), 113
  in spring rolls (egg rolls), China, 12-13
  in *tempura*, Japan, 78-79
  (*see also* names of vegetables)
*Velouté Aurore* (cream of tomato and avocado soup, France), 370
Vermicelli dessert (*sevian*, India), 117
Viennese cream pie (*rahmstrudel*), 240
*Vitello tonnato* (veal in tuna fish sauce, Italy), 284-85

Walnuts:
  *baklava* (flaky nut pastry, Iran), 178-79
  cake:
    *mazourka*, Russia, 174
    *nustorte*, Austria, 241
  chicken with:
    *çerkes tavugu*, Circassian, 144
    Chinese, 29
  cookies (*kourambiedes*, Greece), 173
  duck with (*fesenjan*, Iran), 145
  fish with (*poisson Carcassonne*, France), 373
  pancakes:
    with chocolate cream (*gsusztatott palacsinta*, Hungary), 230-31
    *oladyi*, Russia, 174-75
  strudel (*diósrétes*, Hungary), 237
Wheat:
  and baked lamb (*kibbe*, Middle East), 158

and tomato appetizer salad (*tabbouleh*, Middle East), 132

*Wiener:*
  *backhendl* (fried chicken, Austria), 203
  *fischfilets* (fish in sour cream, Austria), 193
  *rostbraten* (steak with onions, Austria), 208-9
  *schnitzel* (breaded veal cutlets, Austria), 218-19

*Wienersaft gulyás* (goulash, Viennese style), 208

*Wieprzowina z kapusta* (spareribs with sauerkraut and barley, Poland), 216

Wonton, fried, China, 47

*Yakitori* (soy chicken and giblets, Japan), 68

*Yaprak dolmasi* (stuffed grape leaves, Turkey), 156

Yogurt:
  cucumbers and tomatoes in (*raita*, India), 109
  soup:
    cucumber (*jajik*, Middle East), 135
    *yogurt çorbasi*, Middle East, 134

*Zarzuela de mariscos* (seafood soup stew, Spain), 312-13

*Zuppa di vongole* (clam soup, Italy), 250